History of Washington County, Iowa

HISTORY

OF

Washington County Iowa

From the First White Settlements to 1908

By HOWARD A. BURRELL

Also Biographical Sketches of Some Prominent Citizens of the County

ILLUSTRATED

VOL. I.

CHICAGO
THE S. J. CLARKE PUBLISHING COMPANY
1909

DEDICATION

In proof of my appreciation of the Washington County Historical Society, I dedicate this book to that body of men, proud to be admitted to fellowship with those who honor the memory of the Pioneers and those later Old Settlers who made to our hand, out of the Wild and the Raw, the civilization in this county that we all prize and enjoy.

HOWARD A. BURRELL.

PREFACE.

But why a preface? Unless, indeed, to make my acknowledgements.

I have had satisfaction and help from Hon. Nathan Littler's History of this county, and from the county history issued in 1880, and from the Atlas of Washington county, date 1906, and from several papers in the Iowa Annals written years ago by Irving A. Keck, and I have received, with gratitude, much help in preparing data for this first volume, from Colonels D. J. Palmer, W. B. Bell, Charles J. Wilson and S. W. Brookhart; from Captains J. A. Young, D. E. Cocklin, J. S. Gray, D. A. Boyer, J. J. Kellogg; and from J. W. Morton, Porte Lewis, Tom Allen, D. J. Eichelberger, Marion O'Loughlin, and in civil and social life from Hon. C. H. Wilson, Hon. C. J. Wilson, Recorder Hugh Kendall and his deputy Miss Ruth E. Latta, Auditor Chauncey Myers and deputy Miss Anna Dawson, Mesdames Judge Dewey, J. A. Harwood, Ab. Anderson, Dr. Bailey, Cora Bell Wilson, Miss Anna Henderson; and from Wm. A. Cook, O. E. Brown, W. E. Kerr, Charles Hebener, John Yockey, Squire Neiswanger, Wm. Coppock, John Parks, Nate Jones, Marsh W. Bailey, Senator Alberson, John Williams, Henderson Wallace, James Eckles, John Shields et al.

All these I thank, and to them I orient myself and kowtow.

HOWARD A. BURRELL.

Howard A. Burrell.

HISTORY OF WASHINGTON COUNTY, IOWA.

CHAPTER I.

EVOLUTION OF WASHINGTON COUNTY.

Washington county is a part of the vast region once called "Louisiana," which embraced all the territory west of the Mississippi river, except Texas and the areas ceded to the United States by Mexico and Russia. It was called "The Louisiana Purchase," or "The Colony," or "The Province of Louisiana." France claimed it in 1671 by virtue of the voyages of certain zealous, holy, romantic, heroic Frenchmen, whose eyes had absorbed many horizons of that terra incognita. And at the peace of Ryswick in 1697 all Europe recognized the validity of her claim.

It is an easy way to get title to real estate—easier than by conquest, cheaper than by purchase. When the world was new, this western world that was stumbled on by mistake, as it were, in a dark night or in a day of fog, all an European sovereign had to do, to gratify his earth-hunger, was to send out a discoverer, who should go ashore, set up his patron's standard, draw his sword, take a gallant attitude before the wondering natives, and say, "I take possession of this island, this continent, in the name of my sovereigns, Ferdinand and Isabella, or of Louis XIV, or of the king of England." That island or continent was thus transferred to said king, and all that was needed, more, was to give a commission to an artist to paint the scene—C. Columbo and his men standing near their small boats, saluting with drawn swords the imperial banner whose staff was stuck in the sand, a lot of aborigines grouped around unconscious of their physical charms, in very decollete dress, or undress, looking on this strange pantomime. The poor creatures were surprised that they had been discovered. In fact they did not know that they had been lost.

Because two gentlemen from France, Marquette and Joliet, had paddled down the Mississippi from the mouth of the Wisconsin river, as far as the mouth of the Arkansas river, and there learned that the big river did not empty into either the gulf of California or into Virginia, but into the gulf of Mexico, and cast their eyes over their right shoulders and saw leagues on leagues of land to the west, they filed a claim to all that sunset region for France; claiming not only what they saw, but the whole stretch of land above and below the terminals of their voyage. Faith is the substance of things not seen. In 1682 La Salle went down the river and took possession of some more. Spain missed out on this imperial claim. De Soto had marched from Florida to the Mississippi river in 1542, but, wounded by an Indian arrow, he had died and his body was buried in the river at night, before he could take possession, set up a standard, file his claim, and hire a painter.

Balboa, another Spanish gentleman, carried this easy mode of gaining real estate to a ridiculous extent. One day, September 26, 1513, to be exact, he climbed a peak in Darien, and looked all over the isthmus, and instantly annexed it to Spain per formula, and then he exclaimed, "Holy powers, bless me, if that blue dampness out in the offing is not the Pacific ocean." And he hastened down, before any body else could get it, waded in as far as he dared, jabbed the standard into the sand, and with naked sword waving solemnly to the west he took possession of the whole ocean as a Spanish lake. Just as easy! No such snaps now? Yes, as we shall see.

The wild continents and the islands of the sea were in this simple fashion seized by globe-trotters for Portugal, Spain, France, Italy, Great Britain and Holland in the sixteenth and seventeenth centuries in somewhat the same unceremonious way that Africa in our day was partitioned by Germany, England, France, Italy and Belgium, under the unwritten law of ethics, Might makes Right.

Easy come, easy go. In 1763 France tossed that easily won estate to Spain, as carelessly as a steamer passenger throws a biscuit to a gull. In 1800 the shuttle shot back, and Spain ceded Louisiana to France. Our early statesmen fretted under the situation—Spain holding Florida and France, Louisiana. The correspondence of Washington, Jefferson, Hamilton, Pickering, King, Livingston, Madison, Monroe, beginning August 27, 1790, and extending to January 4, 1804, on "who shall own Louisiana?" is published, showing that these great men did not relish the fact that powerful Spain and France were on our flanks and rear. Livingston was sent to Paris to try negotiations with Napoleon for the purchase of Louisiana, but the wary first consul was coy, and skillfully pretended he wished to colonize Louisiana

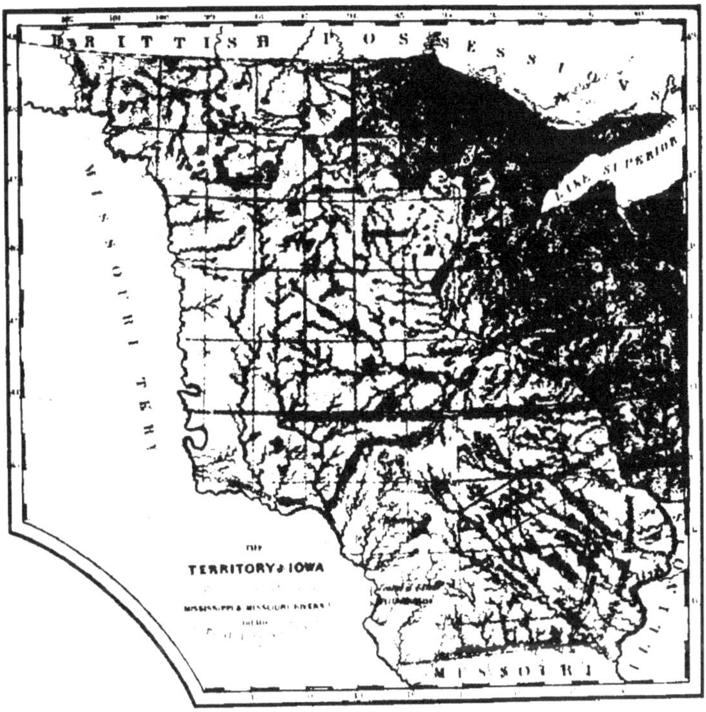

IOWA TERRITORY

a la Egypt. Monroe was sent to help Livingston. Finally, when war between England and France seemed likely, Napoleon, in 1803, knowing the fickle nature of war and foreseeing that the English navy would wrest this region from his grasp, put the vast province on the bargain counter and marked it down to fifteen millions. President Jefferson took it, though he had no authority to buy it. But congress backed him, with here and there a dissenting critic who could see no farther than an owl at noon. Even Daniel Webster, later, had no faith in our great northwest. It would never, could never, be settled, and was practically worthless, in his judgment—not quite infallible. Men, even shrewd men, said Seward was a fool to pay seven millions for Alaska, but it has paid for itself dozens of times over.

Congress on October 31, 1803, authorized the president to take possession and provide a temporary government for Louisiana. If far-off Washington county, and Iowa proper, as parts of one stupendous whole, felt a thrill at the announcement, I know not, but have strong affirmative suspicions. On March 4, 1804, congress divided the territory, and on the following October 1, all the area south of the thirty-third parallel of north latitude was named "Orleans," and the rest "the district of Louisiana," the latter to be under the government of Indiana territory. But this district was on July 4, 1805, made a territory, self-governing, called "Louisiana," and so it continued till 1812. The territory of Orleans was on April 30, 1812, admitted into the union as the state of Louisiana, and the next December the territory of Louisiana was recognized as the territory of Missouri. On March 2, 1819, congress created Arkansas territory, comprising the present limits of the state of that name plus the country to the west of it, and Missouri came in as a state in March, 1821. For the next thirteen years there is no record of an organized territory west of the Mississippi river, north of the Missouri line. Washington county and indeed all Iowa were then in No-man's land. There were but few whites in this region, and they had permits to trade with the Indians and live among them. They needed government no more than do colonies of prairie dogs, owls and rattlesnakes, tenants of the same hole, and they doubtless endorsed the political maxim, "that government is best, that governs least."

A red-hot nebula has to rotate a long while in the frightfully cold interstellar spaces before it radiates its heat and solidifies into a habitable sphere. In 1838 we began to see the crystals shooting into a solid organization. On June 12 of that year congress divided Wisconsin territory and established the territory of Iowa. Before that, the territory had been a sort of protoplasmic "district" which, from 1834 to 1836 was attached to Michigan territory for judicial purposes, and all of the country north of a line drawn west from the lower part of Rock Island was to be Dubuque county, and all south of that west line to the north line of Missouri was to be "Demoine" county, and that county was to constitute a township known as Flint Hills, that is, Burlington. Each of these two counties was to have a court with annual sessions in April and September. The people could elect township officers. That was the first legislative enactment by Michigan. From 1836 to 1838 we were attached as a tail to Wisconsin's territorial kite. Then the umbilicus was cut, and we stood on tottering baby feet under our proper name "Iowa," and the territory reached from the north line of Missouri to the southern boundary of British Columbia. The map appended will be scanned with interest by the reader, a map published in Newhall's Sketches of Iowa, issued in 1841.

At last, we were "Iowa," a word meaning "this is the place," "the beautiful," or "beautiful land," as one chooses to interpret it. Some say the word is a modification of the old name of a tribe of Indians, Ayouas, or from the river Ayoua, which was finally spelled Ioway, Iowa. As late as the expedition of Lewis and Clarke, the Indians here were called Ayouas.

Iowa was for long a pollywog, but its absurd yet nutritive tail was long since absorbed into a frog that can sing and croak for itself.

The first territorial governor of Iowa was Robert Lucas. He served from 1838 to 1841. President Harrison, a Whig, hated Lucas, a Democrat, and removed him. It was the first political scalp raised in this state, but not the last. John Chambers was appointed governor March 25, 1841, and re-appointed by Taylor in 1844, and removed by Polk October 20, 1845. The only thing noteworthy about him was, he wrote his autobiography for his son, but he couldn't spell or punctuate any better than high school pupils do now.

Sixteen of the twenty counties of Iowa took part in the first election, September 10, 1838, for members of the first legislative assembly. Des Moines county cast the largest vote, eight hundred and fifty-four, and Johnson, Linn, Jones, Slaughter (the first name for Washington) plumped from twenty-seven to thirty-five votes each. The total vote was four thousand four hundred and ninety-two. James M. Clark was elected councillor or senator for the Muscatine, Louisa and Slaughter district, and John Trierson, W. L. Toole, Levi Thornton and Clinton Hastings were the representatives, and W. W. Wallace delegate in congress. This legislature held three sessions in Burlington in Old Zion church.

Congress had on January 26, 1835, passed an enabling act for Iowa territory, to form a constitution and state government. The delegates went to Detroit. George W. Jones was chosen delegate to congress, and Major Jerry

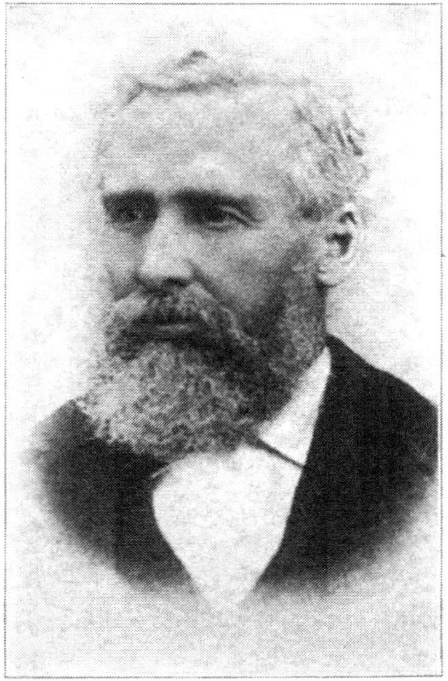

NATHAN LITTLER

Author of Littler's History of Washington

IRVING A. KECK

Author of Keck's History of Washington

Smith, Jr., and Joseph B. Teas were elected members of Michigan territorial legislature, and attended at Green Bay. Henry Dodge, father of Augustus Caesar Dodge, was governor, and he ordered a census, which revealed a population of ten thousand five hundred and thirty-one in Iowa territory. "Demoine" county had six thousand two hundred and fifty-seven, Dubuque county four thousand two hundred and seventy-four, in 1836. He also ordered an election of thirteen senators and twenty-six representatives, Demoine to have seven representatives and three senators, and the winners were Jerry Smith, Jr., Joseph B. Teas and Arthur B. Ingham senators, and representatives Isaac Leffler, Thomas Blair, Warren Jenkins, John Box, George W. Teas, Eli Reynolds, David R. Chance. The Teases were brothers and lawyers. Later, George W. Teas became a Methodist minister, preaching in Washington, and dying here. His son Lucien, who never was a clergyman, is living now in Crawfordsville.

Burlington was the capital of the territory until March 4, 1839. The capitol building cost fourteen thousand dollars, and burned December 13, 1837. Zion church received the body, which deliberated amid the subdued echoes of Amens. The first enactment was the divorce of Mary McArthur from John, and the second was like unto it, and several more couples, loaded with incompatibility, absence of cohering affinity, and inability to stand without hitching, had their bonds unsoldered by the assembly. It seems that way back there the State of Matrimony was a state of insurrection. Parties then were joined, but not mated. They were in theory one, but the trouble was to find which was the one. Two souls with but a single thought, and that thought to get rid of each other, to cleave to some one else, very likely; two hearts that beat not as one, but as two, most decidedly. Marriage was a good deal of a failure and gamble then, as now. In fact, the time of the legislature was so taken up, rectifying Captain Dan Cupid's wretched work, there was not time to attend to matters of state. Hearts were trumps, till the assembly by statute, in sheer desperation, turned these miseries in the chest, over to the courts. Lawyers could afford to deal with them for the fees.

The sixth act set the boundaries of the counties Dubuque, Jackson, Johnson, Jones, Linn, Cedar, Clinton, Clayton, Scott, and authorized the formation of Buchanan, Delaware, Benton, and Fayette. Under an act passed December 7, 1836, "Demoine" county was divided into the counties Lee, Van Buren, Des Moines, Henry, Louisa, "Musquitine," and Slaughter. Our county was first named in honor of Wm. B. Slaughter, a clever territorial secretary, but a merciful and esthetic Providence, perhaps stirred into action by vigorous protests, dropped that ugly name and adopted that of the Father of his Country, and we have been trying ever since to live up to it, and succeeding beautifully, as all know. The date of that change was January 25, 1839. Think of living now, and having others know we are living in the city and county of Slaughter, a word that rhymes with nothing fair but "daughter," and nothing ethical but "ort-er."

Let's get this fact fixed fast in memory. The legislature of Wisconsin, January 18, 1838, named "us" Slaughter. We have never liked Wisconsin since that day, and the grudge has been accumulating down to the climax—La Follette. I find this bit of history in a paper by Frank Harmon Garver in the January, 1909, Iowa Journal of History and Politics, and I quote:

"This act was one redefining the boundary lines of those counties carved by the law of December 7, 1836, from the original county of Demoine. The two laws differed in that the earlier one included a county called Cook, which was omitted from the later act, while the latter included a county called Slaughter not mentioned in the former.

Slaughter county is not to be considered as a continuation of Cook county. None of its territory came from the latter. Most of it, in fact, was received from the original counties of Louisa and Musquitine. Possibly the southwest corner had been within the limits of the original county of Henry. It is certain that the northwest corner was new territory. All except this part had been within the limits of the original county of Demoine at an earlier date.

As first established, Slaughter county included townships 74, 75, and 76 north of ranges 5, 6, 7, and 8, west. The three easternmost townships, those in range 5, are now part of Louisa county. The remaining nine townships are part of Washington county to-day.

The original county of Slaughter was reduced in size by an act of the legislature of the territory of Iowa approved on January 12, 1839. This act, the title of which referred only to Louisa county, redefined the boundaries of that county so as to include within them the three easternmost townships of Slaughter county, although the latter was not mentioned in the act. This loss of territory left Slaughter county only three townships, or eighteen miles square in size—the smallest county ever included within the limits of Iowa. In this reduced form it remained in existence only thirteen days, for on January 25, 1839, there was approved an act of the legislature of the territory of Iowa which changed the name of Slaughter and then enlarged the latter by extending its limits one township farther north and one range farther west. Thus the county gained seven townships and received practically its present territory. Yet one more change had to be made to secure permanence, and this was made by the legislature June 1, 1845, by the terms of which the Iowa river was made the boundary line

WASHINGTON COUNTY COURT HOUSE

between the two counties for six or eight miles. Washington county lost to Johnson that part of township 77 north, range 6 west, which lay east of the Iowa river. Since 1845 the boundaries of Washington county have not been altered.

The territory included within the present limits of Washington county was acquired from the Indians in three separate treaties. All of it was ceded by the Sac and Fox Indians. Nearly half of the county (the southeastern portion) belonged to the Black Hawk Purchase of September 21, 1832. The northeastern corner was part of the Keokuk Reserve ceded to the United States government September 28, 1836. The western and northwestern portions were acquired by treaty of October 21, 1837.

The eastern portion of the county also belonged, for a time, to the original county of Demoine. Certain portions were included a little later within the limits of Cook, Musquitine, Louisa, and Henry counties as established by the act of January 18, 1838."

The state capital was removed in 1839-40 to Iowa City, when the place had but twenty families, and not a grist mill nearer than the Mississippi river, till one was built in '41. All roads led to Rome, but not to Iowa City, and folk got lost on the prairie trying to find it, especially those coming from Dubuque way, and the citizens hired Lyman Dillon to plow a furrow one hundred miles long, from Iowa City to Dubuque. His outfit was five yokes of oxen, a two-horse wagon filled with bedding and provisions, and the cattle lived on grass along the way. It was the longest furrow on record. Later, a road was made alongside the furrow, which served as a sort of balustrade.

This county was a part of Demoine county till January 18, 1838, when its boundaries were defined thus: "Beginning at the north-east corner of Henry county, thence west to the north-west corner of same, thence north to tap a line dividing townships 76 and 77 north, thence east on the same line to the line between ranges 4 and 5 on it, thence south with said line to place of beginning, is hereby set off into a separate county by the name of Slaughter, and the seat of justice of said county is hereby established at the town of Astoria, and all the territory west is hereby attached to the county of Slaughter for judicial purposes."

But our people would tolerate neither Slaughter nor Astoria, so things were not "established." Astoria was located on the south-east quarter, section 25, township 76 north, range 7 west, that is, in what is now Oregon township, near to and south of Ainsworth. It was laid out in 1837 by three Henry county men as proprietors—Lawson B. Hughes, Col. W. W. Wallace and Dr. Jacob Myers, who were, later, members of the territorial legislature.

The town was surveyed, but the records are lost. Simpson Goble helped the trio lay off the town. They built a cabin of hewn logs, with a rear addition, for a court-house. It was not a noble specimen of Renaissance architecture; it lacked a plaster of paris heroic-sized figure of a woman in directoire gown slashed down part of one leg, as an effigy of the Goddess of Justice, with bandaged eyes, like the Amazon perched above the south door to our present court-house, holding scales and a sword, but who was probably, really, hunting a man, as usual. But this primitive court-house, that was, indeed, quite ambitious for a back-woods period, was never used. It and its site were left with Mr. Goble to sell as a common claim. It was the first grave-yard of Great Expectations, the sepulcher of the Last Sixpence, and the scene of "vaulting ambition o'erleaping itself and falling on the other side," and getting a bad sprain.

Many years later, Judge Francis Springer, of Louisa county, said a court was held at Goble's Point near Ainsworth (called Astoria in 1839), and he was prosecuting attorney and Cal. Shelladay foreman of the grand jury. No bills were found, and no one was there to be prosecuted.

This county was Slaughter county but one year, and the records are mostly lost. However, a spectral figure glances across our vision for a moment. One John C. Ellis was sheriff, and his acts were legalized at a special session of the legislature in June, 1838, and he got thirty-four dollars and ninety-eight cents for taking a census and finding our population was two hundred and eighty-three. Why did he not make his bill an even thirty-five dollars? He seems to have been marked down to ninety-eight cents. And then he went off at that price, and no more is known of him than of men who lived five thousand years ago. In the record of the legislature this featureless, almost bodyless man flits like a ghost across the platform, like Hamlet's father's shade, very pale, as the cock-crowing was near and he must be off, and so with that far-off dawn he fades away utterly from men's ken, being of such stuff as dreams are made of.

Another spectral thing, that fairly haunts the historic imagination, is that pale session of court at Astoria, May 7, 1838, David Irwin judge. Thomas Baker was appointed clerk and gave bond in two thousand dollars, with Nelson Ball and David Goble sureties, and he used a seal made from an old style ten-cent piece, and, after doing nothing mightily, they voted themselves a day's pay all round and adjourned till next term. All that is dim and shadowy, yet there are a few gleams of realism shed on the scene by a Goble youth who recalls that the honorable court left the cabin, and sat in its shirt-sleeves, to simulate ermine—if the shirts were clean—under the trees on the north side of the house where the expectoration was safer. And at the fall term, the aforesaid Goble deposeth and saith that he carried water to the elephants, as it were. That is, he toted watermelons to the court, and Francis Springer, then and there present, gave the Goble aforesaid a ten cent piece for his share of the said fruit, and no lawyer interposed an objection on the ground that the said melons were immaterial, incompetent, irrelevant, leading, and not the best evidence.

Astoria, or Castoria, failing to materialize, and wearing itself to a frazzle, as Slaughter barely got beyond birth, christening and baptism, Washington county swam into men's eyes. The first legislature appointed John Gilliland, of Lee county, Thomas Ritchey, of Henry county, and Wm. Chambers, of Muscatine county, commissioners to locate a county-seat for Washington county. Two of them met in the metropolis, Astoria, June 1, 1839, and were paid three dollars a day each. Mr. Chambers was absent. Mr. Gilliland wanted the county-seat to be at the geographical center of the county, one mile north-west of the present city, while Mr. Ritchey would go a mile south-east of the city. Finally, they agreed on the south-west quarter, section 17, township 75 north, range 7 west. The lands chosen were a part of Nathan Baker's claim. He gladly let it go, as it enhanced the value of the rest of his land. The whole board of commissioners met June 13, 1839, and affirmed the selection, and named it Washington.

It should have been noted that when the name of the county was changed, the boundaries were re-stated thus:

"Beginning on the range line between the ranges 5 and 6 west, where the township line divides townships 73 and 74 intersect said line, thence west with the said township line to the line dividing ranges 9 and 10 west, thence north on said line to the line dividing townships 77 and 78 north, thence east with said line between ranges 5 and 6 east, thence south with said line to the place of beginning."

So, after all the travail of our souls, as a part, in turn, of Louisiana, Missouri, Indiana, Michigan, Wisconsin, and Iowa territories, and also a part of the counties Demoine, and Louisa and all of Slaughter, we emerge at last into calm waters, with a clear identity and an individuality all our own. We could then sympathize with James W. Woods, alias "Old Timber," one of the earliest lawyers in Burlington, who rather bragged on his own omnipresence and ubiquity, in a playful mood, that he had had a child born in each of the territories of Michigan, Wisconsin and Iowa, and one in the state of Iowa, and all of them born in the self-same house.

CHAPTER II.

OUR PREDECESSORS.

No history of Washington county proper could be ancient history. There were but few traces of white folk in this region prior to 1835. But if we knew the details of all that went on here before the white men's coming, we might have a history far more ancient than anything written about Egypt, Persia and China.

At the close of the Black Hawk war in 1832, adventurous white men who, as rangers and "landless resolutes," had caught sight of the Canaan west of the Mississippi river, stole across, hoping to make lodgment as squatter sovereigns, but the government ousted the trespassers. The small garrison at Fort Armstrong on Rock Island was kept busier evicting these "sooners" than they had been in protecting the whites east of the river from Indian attacks. In the main, this region was held sacred to the redskins, and their good-will was kept by the honorable purchase of their lands, which they held by the right, not of discovery, but of possession.

In this county "civilization" began in 1835. The life of a man seventy-five years old spans the entire development of the order that supplanted barbarism on this ground. It is a short foreground, and we find no picturesque ruins in it. Therefore, we could not interest our English cousins, if they should visit us. Matthew Arnold could not be pleased even in Virginian and New England towns three centuries old, because they held no ruins of abbeys, coliseums, Roman walls, broken aqueducts, or ancient mosaic pavements. We probably could not show our cousins so many as a half dozen log cabins in this county, dating from the '30s. The best we could do, as hosts showing old things as curios, would be to set before them the remains and memorials of forgotten races of various colors—flint arrow-points, stone axes and hoes, granite mortars and pestles, stone or bone needles, and perhaps a few etchings of animals and birds on teeth or polished stone, and specimens of picture writing on bark and carvings on slate ledges, and rude copper utensils, ruder pottery, vast mounds used as burial places, temples, fortifications, etc. These implements, rude or fine, hark back millenniums ago to the Stone Age, but they were not the work of the Indians we superseded, though they used these tools of necessity to a still more ancient race. Our red men do not know how these were made. Thoreau asked the New England Indians how arrow-heads were chipped, and he bade a friend going to the Rocky Mountains to ask the red men there how it was done. None knew. The darts, spear-points, stone axes and other rude cutlery were flaked and fashioned long ages ago, and the art has faded out of all barbarian tradition.

Our ancestors and the various peoples of the old world are more fortunate. They can trace their histories back of tradition till they are lost in the mists of fable and myth. Britain may wander back B. C., and wonder at her mysterious Stonehenge, and muse on the curios left by Caesar and Hadrian in various parts of the islands. Italy may grope back to the she-wolf that suckled Romulus and Remus. France is so composite in nationalities, she can only guess at the mixture of her bloods, the result of the many fusions of the myriads of fighting men in migrations from the Germanic forests, nay, from the wilds of Asia, race crowding on race till the sea stood them at bay to fight to the death for a foothold and a home, or a grave.

Our records in the Mississippi valley are brief, like

"The short and simple annals of the poor."

We have to push these records back only seventy-five years to touch the edges and fringes of the prehistoric ages. Life, animal and human, had gone on here eons of time. We might as well call it millions of years as thousands. Time is the cheapest thing we have, if we, indeed, have that. In fact there is no such thing as time, or space, either—they are mere forms of thought, terms of convenience that we use, and must use. So we need not skimp in using big figures to denote duration.

Prior to seventy-five years ago there are but very few records of the lands and men west of the Mississippi river that we can dignify by the name of history. Indians wrote no history, for they made none. They needed no government outside narrow tribal range, and they organized none. Having no use for institutions, they created none. They lived, loved, hated, fought, died, and there is small trace of their experiences. If they had been bison, deer and snakes, the record could not be leaner. Voiceless, silent races, as still and mute as the dust they turned into. Why should there be art and literature, speech and music, if eternal races fall into graves from which not even echoes come?

All that precedes white men's coming here, lure and teaze the imagination far more than what has happened since their arrival. Let us state what is actually known and supposed to be known of the procession of ghosts that

GROUP OF INDIANS

for ages prowled over these prairies, their war-whoops, ponies, game, tomahawks, pipes of peace, war bonnets, ochres, headdress and ornaments, bows and arrows, scalping knives, tepees, wampum, all vanished irrecoverable.

The Indians we met here in the '30s were the confederated tribes of Sacs and Foxes, who were two of the many tribes composing the Algonquins. This powerful family roamed all over British America, as far as Hudson's Bay and the Eskimos, covered Canada and New England, the middle west and the south. They once numbered a quarter million, but disease and wars with the Iroquois decimated them to forty thousand. The Sacs and Foxes maintained the race reputation for prowess, and kept Iowa hot and red, fighting the Sioux. The forty mile wide Neutral Territory between them was hardly a barrier or buffer. The Sacs and Foxes had fought their way hither from the northern lakes. Very long ago they settled on the Wisconsin river, and, though detesting agriculture, they made the squaws raise a world of corn—maize, or grass, it was called—but they never learned the combination of corn and hog, of corn and steer. They loved the shrill music of war, and thrived on scrapping. And wherever we find men who love savage fighting in politics and reform, and are eternally rowing, it is proof that they are not near civilized.

The Sacs and Foxes numbered seven thousand when white men came to their villages on the Des Moines river and to Poweshiek's village on the Iowa river. The villages of Keokuk, Wapello and Appanoose were a mile apart on the Des Moines. It was an idyllic life—for the braves, who loafed, dressed gaily, raced ponies, gambled, smoked, and drank whisky when they could get it, flirted with the maidens, hunted and fished, while the squaws did all the work, and their dogs diligently dodged the boiling pot. "The partridge loves peas, but not those that go with her into the pot." The dogs hated the altar of sacrifice as cordially as the pot. For each dog boiled for food, another was lynched by a buckskin thong to a tree, to appease the wrath of the Evil Manitou or Spirit, who, as in our enlightened theology, divides the moral government of the world with the Great Spirit or Good Manitou. Nevertheless, the dogs kicked at the arrangement. A dog never did understand theology, anyhow. When company came, the dogs were troubled, as our chickens are when they see the minister coming. Uncivilized dog and civilized rooster have a common bond of sympathy. It was the old see-saw game—eat, avoid being eaten.

Let us not laugh at the superstitions of our red brethren—we have a few ourselves quite as silly. How many of us will not start on a journey on Friday, or plant in the light of the moon when it should be the dark of the same, according to agricultural sages of that breed? How many shiver in the night if they hear the death-watch bug ticking on the wall? We have a lot of fool notions, too.

Luckily, we have a picture of Indian hospitality in Iowa, and, it is supposed, quite near us, and as this was probably the first dinner ever served by reds to whites in this state, let the reader live it over with Father Marquette and Joliet. On the seventh of June, 1673, they floated down the Wisconsin river in two birch bark canoes, with five attendants, and discovered not only the Mississippi river, but Iowa. For days they did not see a human face on the southern voyage, but on the twenty-fifth they saw, like Robinson Crusoe, men's footprints on the river margin. They must have been near the site of Burlington. They traced the steps to a trail, and the two men took that path into the interior. An Indian village soon appeared, and the whites shouted and the reds leaped to their feet, all eyes fixed on the strangers. Four chiefs advanced toward them, but silent. The whites were wary, yet noticing that the redskins wore cloth that they must have got from the French, it was taken as a good omen. Arrived at the village, they were welcomed by the main chief, stark naked, as a token of respect. As Marquette could speak ten Indian languages or dialects, he learned that the Indians were the Illinois tribe, that he had long burned to preach to. More ceremonial of smoking. Then all hands, men, squaws, papooses, dogs, fleas, set out gaily to another village where the chief of all Illinois received them with rigid etiquet—he stood nude between two aged men in the same striking costume, and they were welcomed again, with more smoking. The naive ceremonial display of anatomy must have been as comical as Carlyle's conceit of a naked House of Lords in Westminster, described in "Sartor Resartus." Two betinselled pipes of peace were carried along, and now and then a co-operative whiff, and a young slave was given them, and a calumet, and a feast was ordered, but more tobacco first. It was a common mode of hospitality for Indians to urge wives upon guests, but the kindness was embarrassing to timid priests. By this time, tobacco had done its perfect work, and all fear fled in its benign aroma. Could tobacco be put to better use than to establish amity? Its use may be an evil habit, though smoking is still a social habit rather than a solitary vice. The two whites had such a good time, they staid all night, some writers say six days, spent in hunting and fishing on the red men's game preserves. Anyway, they spent the night, delighted guests of the most picturesque Indians they had met. Marquette describes the feast. It was a four-course dinner, in this order: 1. A big wooden bowl was brought on, filled with boiled corn meal, downright mush. A male Indian dipped a wooden spoon into the mess he called "tocamity," cooled it by blowing on it, and put it in the mouths of the guests, in turn. 2. Fish, nicely cooked, all bones removed, and fed as before. And yet it was hardly "spoon vittels." 3. Roast dog—politely declined, and instantly removed from sight, the hosts probably wondering what was the matter with the dog —or the guests. 4. Buffalo boil, the juiciest cuts given to the Frenchmen. There is no mention that the tepee was decorated, or any color scheme, or of place or button-hole bouquets, ice cream, angel cake, etc. Being fed, the men needed no china, silver, napkins, finger bowls, and if there was pie, the polite French forgot to say so, nor do they hint of after-dinner coffee in ridiculous thimble cups or cubes of cheese, but tooth-picks would really have been acceptable. It was a neater meal than the dinner given by the Khedive of Egypt to Miss Amelia B. Edwards, the English authoress, and her party, a very swell diplomatic dinner. The greasy meats were in a common central dish, and each guest "jest reached to and helped himself," clawing out one's portion with one's bare hands. Cleopatra may have served the same sort of meal many a time to Antony and Caesar, on the Nile. Amelia needed a napkin, a finger bowl, and a bath. The untutored barbarian was the tidier host.

When the Frenchmen left for their boats, six hundred reds accompanied them, and there was after-dinner oratory, with this characteristic Indian speech:

"I thank the Black Gown Chief (Father M.) and his friend for taking so much pains to come and visit us. Never before has the earth been so beautiful nor the sun so bright as now. Never has the river been so calm or free from rocks which your canoes have removed as they passed down. Never has the tobacco had so fine a flavor, nor our corn appeared so beautiful as to-day. Ask the Great Spirit to give us life and health, and come ye and dwell with us."

On this voyage, the men lay-by at night, anchored out in the deep stream for safety. The trip down to the Arkansas river mouth had one bad effect—Marquette contracted dysentery, that became chronic.

The Indians rather over-did the welcome business, with pipes and speeches. On one occasion a white party were feted, and the old chief washed all the faces in warm water as a mark of respect, and they were placed on a rude cane rostrum and forced, in courtesy and diplomacy, to listen four hours to speeches of welcome in a tongue they could not understand. Are the Indians humorists? We, though boasting of our culture, etc., have not yet shed the silly welcome habit on all sorts of occasions, even at a home farmers' institute. There is always a lot of that sort of palaver at meetings. Better cut the absurdity clean out. Else have it in a foreign tongue without gestures.

The Indians in Iowa, when it was first explored, were the Dakotas in the north and in the south the Illinois, Sauks, Foxes, Chippewas, Pottawattomies et al. The Iowas were first heard of in 1690, migrating from the great lakes, crossing the big river and locating in the lower valley of the Iowa river. Schoolcraft says they migrated fifteen times, which means at least fifteen wars. They long warred with the Sacs and Foxes, and the latter nearly exterminated them in 1824, at Iowaville. Being heathen and wicked and knowing no better, the Iowas were racing ponies and betting, and Providence punished them by giving them into the hands of their treacherous Sac and Fox hosts. It was an outrageous massacre of all ages and both sexes. The Iowas never recovered from the blow. The remnant offered their land in 1825 to the United States for one hundred and fifty-seven thousand dollars, to be kept in trust at five per cent. interest to be paid annually to the tribe, and they dissolved as smoke into Missouri. Many of the younger ones enlisted in the union army in the Civil war and made good soldiers. Black Hawk helped in this massacre, and that fact discounts our pity for him in his downfall in 1832. His village was at Rock river, near Rock Island. He says in his autobiography that it was built in 1831 and had eight thousand population. The houses must have copied the Iroquois "long houses," as they were thirty to one hundred feet long, sixteen to forty wide, roofed with sheathing of elm bark laid on a frame of poles, curtains of buffalo skins at the three by six doors. The house was divided into rooms separated by a lengthwise hall, and holes were cut over the fire pots to let out the smoke. The beds were skins on elevated frames of elastic poles. Here Black Hawk had a watch tower commanding a vast sweep of noble scenery.

In 1804 Jefferson had negotiated for the lands of the Sacs and Foxes. Unknown to Black Hawk, several chiefs were lured to St. Louis, made drunk, and thus they were induced to sign a treaty, granting the government millions of acres east of the Mississippi, extending from East St. Louis to the Wisconsin river, for two thousand two hundred and thirty-four dollars worth of goods and one thousand dollars in cash a year. Black Hawk and the other chiefs repudiated the treaty as an outrageous swindle, because these sots had no authority to cede the tribe's lands, and this led to the villainous Black Hawk war in 1832. When he returned from a hunt west of the river, the whites had surveyed his lands and sold them to settlers, and his cabin had been seized and his wife and children evicted. He drove off the intruders. Governor Reynolds, of Illinois, sent sixteen hundred soldiers to the Sac villages and sent the population across the Mississippi, with orders never to return. It was too late to plant corn, and the Indians had no prospect of food in the fall. In April, 1832, Black Hawk and others did re-cross, to

CHIEF BLACK HAWK

CHIEF KEOKUK

join the Winnebagoes in planting. It was like Napoleon's return from Elba. Black Hawk refused to go back, as his people would be destitute. General Whiteside, with twenty-four hundred militia went against him, and with him were Captain Abraham Lincoln, Lieutenant-Colonel Zachary Taylor, and Lieutenant Jefferson Davis, all destined to be presidents. There were less than five hundred Indians. Major Stillman and two hundred and seventy-five mounted men approached Black Hawk, who sent flags of truce by eight young warriors. They were taken prisoners and three of them shot. Black Hawk had but forty warriors, in ambush, and when the troops came on, the reds gave a war-whoop and fired. The contemptible white cads skedaddled thirty miles before stopping, and fifty rode clear home, to tell of the murderous fire that had killed eleven of them, and to report that there were millions of the braves charging on them. Perhaps the cowards are running yet. It was worse than Bull Run. Black Hawk retreated to the Wisconsin river, where he held the whites in check till his women and children had made bark canoes and crossed, when his men forded the stream. Lieutenant Davis said it was a masterly retreat against great odds. Indians were shot after surrender. It was wretched business, and one is sorry that Lincoln was in such damnable business, a war as mean as hell. The scurvy war cost us two millions and two hundred white and five hundred red lives. Black Hawk was taken to Washington City, and when presented to President Jackson, said, "I am a man, you are another," and added:

"We did not expect to conquer the whites. They had too many men. I took up the hatchet to avenge injuries my people could no longer endure. Had I borne them longer without striking, my people would have said 'Black Hawk is a squaw, he is too old to be our chief, he is no Sac.' These reflections caused me to raise the war-whoop. The result is known to you. I say no more."

When an Indian is done, he quits. He is not brief and sententious because of a famine of thoughts. The fewer ideas a white speaker has, the longer he rants, the louder he roars, and the more convulsive his gestures. How quiet, as with consciousness of reserve power, Indian orators are! Indian speeches were not edited by white men. For they are all alike, have common racial traits and characteristics, have the same pitch, tone and mannerism, because the red men all stood on one plane of culture, or lack of culture. Likewise the best written English journals read alike, have a common quality and style, for scholars, too, are of one plane and type. The Indian says his say, and stops, and it is very impressive. And it is a great virtue. The red man is a child of nature, brother to animals, birds, rivers, clouds, stars, trees, and his similes and images are of natural objects. He does not jump beyond his range. When he wishes to indicate a host of men, he speaks of the leaves that whisper in myriads, as the old Greeks also poetically spoke of "the multitudinous laughter of the sea," meaning the sparkles and smiles on its face. Indian oratory is as close to nature as muscle to bone, and how tense, terse, concentrated, poetic it is. Our red brother was a poet without the jingle, but with the sea-water swing of rhythm, and he had an eye for simple beauty, and to him nature is all symbol. That beautiful speech of Logan, and Black Hawk's thumb-nail cameos, and Keokuk's, are above praise as literary gems. So short, so pithy, like Lincoln's immortal little classic at Gettysburg. These speeches have all the depth of color and light that floats in the heart of an opal or diamond, or in the clear eyes of a child or woman.

We might expect this finished sort of oratory from red men, if we study their splendid faces, especially in profile. Such impassive, inscrutable faces, keen, steady eyes, even if cruel, all the lines indicating poise and supple strength, nature's man every inch of him, a medieval American, savage in frame, bearing, presence, and novelty of personal adornment. His words must keep all that in countenance.

Black Hawk was soon released and went to Fort Armstrong, humiliated because his hated rival, Keokuk, had risen on his downfall. Keokuk was the shrewder politician. He had adopted the peace policy because there were too many whites. His young braves were on fire to join Black Hawk, when Keokuk poured cold water on them in this canny way—could it be improved?

"Warriors: I am your chief. It is my duty to lead you to war if you are determined to go. The United States is a great nation, and unless we conquer them we must perish. I will lead you against the whites on one condition, that we shall first put all our women and children to death, and then resolve that when we cross the Mississippi we will never retreat, but perish among the graves of our fathers rather than yield to the white men."

Thus deftly he rubbed a big chunk of ice down their feverish spines.

At the fort Keokuk was in fine fettle, in gay dress of buckskin, voluminous cloak, bunches of feathers, fringes, scepter, necklaces of bear claws and teeth, wristlets, and tufted electrical hair, posing and strutting as chief of the Sacs and Foxes, as glorious as a drum-major in toggery that make him look like God in the eyes of wondering children. This peacock had supplanted Black Hawk, who drank then and there the cup of humiliation to the dregs. But Black Hawk retired with dignity and pride, with his one faithful wife, two sons and one daughter, to the Des Moines river near Iowaville, the scene of his treachery and cruelty, and he made garden, raised corn, melons and vegetables, and sorrowed as he saw his tribe giving away their lands for a song and sinking the proceeds in saloons. At a celebration in Fort Madison, July 4, 1838, he made this swan-song speech:

"It has pleased the Great Spirit that I am here to-day. I have eaten with my white friends. It is good. A few summers ago I was fighting you. I may have done wrong. But that is past. Let it be forgotten. Rock river valley was a beautiful country. I loved my village, my cornfields, and my people. I fought for them. They are now yours. I was once a great warrior. Now I am an old and poor man. Keokuk has been the cause of my downfall. I have looked upon the Mississippi since I was a child. I love the great river. I have always dwelt upon its banks. I look upon it now and am sad. I shake hands with you. We are now friends. I may not see you again. Farewell."

Can that bit of homespun pathos, coined right out of nature's heart, be surpassed?

He died October 3, 1838, almost seventy-two years old, and was buried on a spot he had selected on the shore of the Des Moines river, near the north-east corner of Davis county, Iowa. A bill is in this legislature to erect a monument above his fiery dust.

His face is striking, but more refined than strong. Some Indian faces are superb and right royal in their lines.

After the surrender of Black Hawk, he was taken to Washington and other eastern cities, and at this time the colonization of the negroes was being agitated. Black Hawk was asked to give his opinion of the best way to solve the race problem. After reflection he said that the question was easy of solution, and that the following would be, in his judgment, the best plan: "Let the free states remove all the male negroes within their limits to the slave states; then let our Great Father buy all the female negroes in the slave states between the ages of twelve and twenty, and sell them to the people of the free states, for a term of years, say those under fifteen until they are twenty-one, and those over fifteen, for five years, and continue to buy all the females in the slave states as soon as they arrive at the age of twelve, and take them to the free states and dispose of them in the same way as the first, and it will not be long before the country is clear of the black-skins, about which I am told they have been talking for a long time, and for which they have expended a large amount of money."

This great man's character is worth studying. Here is another side-light on it:

In Black Hawk's Autobiography is Elijah Kilbourn's story: He was taken prisoner and adopted by Black Hawk himself into the tribe. After a long while he escaped. Years later, as a scout in the wilderness, he drew his gun on a red drinking at a spring, but the hammer failed. The click electrically raised the Indian who approached with leveled guns and took K. captive. It was Black Hawk himself. Kilbourn was left bound, tied to a tree, all day. In the evening Black Hawk came and whispered, "Does the mole thing that Black Hawk forgets?" Black Hawk had instantly recognized his adopted son. Kilbourn expected to be killed. Cutting the thongs, Black Hawk took him an hour through the forest. Expecting death, and death by torture, Judge Kilbourn's surprise when the Chief turned him loose, directing him how to return to the whites, and he made this speech: "I am going to send you back to your chief, though I ought to kill you for running away a long time ago, after I had adopted you as a son—but Black Hawk can forgive as well as fight. When you return to your chief I want you to tell him all my words. Tell him that Black Hawk's eyes have looked upon many suns, but they shall not see many more; and that his back is no longer straight, as in his youth, but is beginning to bend with age. The Great Spirit has whispered among the tree tops in the morning and evening and says that Black Hawk's days are few, and that he is wanted in the spirit land. He is half dead, his arm shakes and is no longer strong, and his feet are slow on the war path. Tell him all this, and tell him, too, that Black Hawk would have been a friend to the whites, but they would not let him and that the hatchet was dug up by themselves and not by the Indians. Tell your chief that Black Hawk meant no harm to the pale faces when he came across the Mississippi, but came peaceably to raise corn for his starving women and children, and that even then he would have gone back, but when he sent his white flag the braves who carried it were treated like squaws and one of them inhumanly shot. Tell him too," he concluded with terrible force, while his eyes fairly flashed fire, "that Black Hawk will have revenge, and that he will never stop until the Great Spirit shall say to him, come away."

The Sacs were called Sauks, or Sau-kies, meaning "a man with a red badge." Red was a favorite color. The Indian name for Foxes was "Musqua-kies," signifying "man with yellow badge." Red and yellow were their color scheme, and they could no more do without colors than classes in schools. Colors and a yell are the basis and arch of the higher education, and red men caught on early. The first "yellow kids" were the Foxes who ceded their lands. On September 21, 1832, General Scott made a treaty with the Sacs and Foxes, in Davenport, by which we acquired six million acres—a tract one hundred and ninety miles long, averaging fifty miles wide at the ends and forty in the middle, measured from the Mississippi river, known as "Black Hawk Purchase." The lines ran from the north line of Missouri to the mouth of the upper Iowa river. We were to pay twenty thousand dollars

INDIAN RELICS
(From Collection of Col. Charles J. Wilson)

for thirty years, and fifty thousand dollars to extinguish debts to traders in Rock Island, plus six thousand bushels of corn, fifty barrels of flour, thirty barrels of pork, thirty-five beeves, twelve bushels of salt, to support the women and children of Indians killed in the war. The land cost us about nine cents an acre. There was a small bit of land at the junction of the Mississippi and Des Moines rivers known as the half breed tract, reserved for families of whites who had married squaws. This treaty was signed by Keokuk and thirty other chiefs and warriors. There were reserved four hundred square miles on the Iowa river, called "Keokuk's Reservation." The tract lay either side the stream, from its mouth to a point near Wapello, quite covering Louisa county. This, however, was bought in September, 1836, by Henry Dodge, governor of Wisconsin territory, three hundred thousand acres at seventy-five cents per acre. The reds were to vacate the first purchase June 1, 1833, and this reservation in '37, going to the Des Moines river, at Agency City. Here Keokuk, Wapello and Appanoose had each a large farm under shiftless cultivation. Three counties bear their names, and Black Hawk has another for a monument.

Another reservation comprised a section in east Davenport for Mrs. Antoine Le Claire, on condition he should build a home on it, and another was the site of Le Claire in Scott county, given to Antoine. Under a former treaty they had given him the site of Moline. They trusted this honest friend, and he was a god to them as a man is to a dog. He was their interpreter, and spoke a dozen Indian tongues, and helped them draw up ten important treaties. His father was a Canadian Frenchman, his mother a daughter of a Pottawattamie chief. That combination put all sorts of red and white corpuscles in Antoine's blood. In 1833 he was post-master and justice of the peace at Davenport, his jurisdiction extending from Dubuque to Burlington. He owned Le Claire, and was joint proprietor of Davenport, a stirring business man, rich, generous. He died at the age of sixty-four. Antoine was as short in stature as Zaccheus, so short that when he had a pain he could not tell right off whether it was headache or corns. Nature seems to delight now and then in making caricatures of men and women. His equator was phenomenal. He carried everything before him, as it were. A hogshead set on two short posts symbolled his anatomy.

The second purchase had included the south-west part of this county, as Dutch Creek, which came into market October 21, 1837, but there was a pocket up Wellman way, that, in the various surveys, had got lost in the shuffle, and our county did not get its present shape and extent until May 1, 1843, when every inch of our county, in its present limits, was forever closed to the Indians.

On October 11, 1842, these tribes ceded all the rest of their lands in Iowa, to the United States, and were to go, May 1, 1843, and for good and all October 11, 1845. Keokuk went to bleeding Kansas to drink instead of bleed. He had four wives and a band of forty to fifty roystering favorites, and all were drunkards. In July, 1848, a tribesman poisoned Keokuk. A few years later, the city of Keokuk so pined for its illustrious founder, it sent a deputation of first citizens to bring back his bones as sacred relics. They disinterred something or other, at a guess, and these lime formations were planted in the park, and a queer pyramid placed over them to hold him down, that his harem might know where he spent his nights. It was fancied that in the gloamings, when the battery of wives were pensive, each one softly sang, "Where is my wandering boy to-night?" It is safe to say that Keokuk was not hob-nobbing with Black Hawk in Shadow-land.

CHAPTER III.

INDIANS AND MOUND-BUILDERS.

Few Indians were known as individuals. The vast mass lived and died as unknown as ants and worms. The fame of not more than a dozen chiefs survives. Here and there a tribal chief's name is known because he was an orator, like Red Jacket, Black Hawk, Logan, Keokuk. Eloquent breath outlasts all else. Dr. Eastman, himself an Indian, says "the chiefs of clans were the real representative men, and the so-called head chiefs were spokesmen at best, that is, talkers. The ablest man led each clan. There was no chief of the tribe as a whole." The tribal chiefs ranked the warrior chiefs. Rarely did an Indian leap into fame. Perhaps the names of a dozen are remembered.

The great man of the Sacs and Foxes was Black Hawk. He had character and high ability. Keokuk was quite as able a lord of men. Our earliest settlers recall him. Mr. James, of Sigourney, heard him speak, and was strongly impressed by his high qualities, his oratorical power, his striking presence.

Keokuk was born in 1780, was loyal to Americans in the war of 1812, and was shrewd enough to join the peace party twenty years later. He crossed the Mississippi in 1828, settling on the Iowa river. Was he handsome, as Mr. James says? Look at his face. Amiable? It is as savage as a meat ax, and would turn milk like a thunder storm. It was said of a superior man in old age, "his cold, aristocratic face looked the sarcophagus of buried passions." But Keokuk's face is alive—those lines suggest forked tongues; the face suggests a nest of just hatched rattlesnakes; suggests an Egyptian pitcher of eels, twisting to escape. It would be hard in an artist to paint, in the small compass of an average face, intenser malignity than gleamed diabolic on that human, or inhuman, clock-dial. It is hardly curious that the Indians accused such a looking man of grafting the tribe's money—the first graft in Iowa history. But, then, he was a heathen. His name means "the watchful fox."

Poweshiek was a power after Keokuk, a wise, honest man, living on the Iowa river near Iowa city. A rich county serves as his headstone. But he was inferior in rank to Keokuk, and endowed with less ability.

Wapello lived, later in life, on the Des Moines river. The place is now Ottumwa, and the county bears his name.

The flower of the chiefs was Kisk-ke-kosh. He lived in Jasper county, on the Skunk river, and became a progressive reformer. He said women should not do all the work, but only their fair share, and men should help them, for work is not degrading, he said. But the standpatters were too much for him. His wife was beautiful, they say, and when he could make no headway with his reform, he aided her, washing the dishes, boiling the dogs, skinning the game, etc.

Chief Appanoose was an Apollo. His portrait is like that of a lovely, pretty woman. By diligent attention to the arts of love he accumulated a quartet of wives, and it was naively said "he lived a very quiet life." The horse marines believe it not.

Mahaska lived near the present town of Eldon. He must have had winning ways, for he rounded up a harem of seven alleged beauties, having the best matrimonial record of our chiefs. His favorite was, indeed, a beauty, all say. The other six wives were not jealous of her, so she must have been tactful and good, as well as pretty. Our Indian women, like the black women of Africa, welcome polygamy for economic reasons—the more wives, the greater the division of labor. Mahaska, who had a county named for him, took his little brown jug of a wife to Washington city, where she was universally admired, and an artist painted her portrait. She fell from her horse, soon after getting home, and died, well mourned.

Taimaeh was the last local chief of note. He lived in Burlington in 1820, and was at the head of a secret society of Indians famed for courage and lofty character. No, it was not a lodge of Masons, for women were also eligible to membership. Could it be the Woodmen?

What about Indian beauty? Was there ever a real pretty Indian woman? There is, of course, no universal standard of female beauty. Tastes differ. Some fancy fat women, others lean, still others, just plump and round.

Probably male Indians think the red sex are quite as uniformly good-looking as the whites esteem our women folk. But I confess that, though I have seen a great many Indians, I never saw but one girl that really was pretty.

"If she be not fair to me,
What care I how fair she be?"

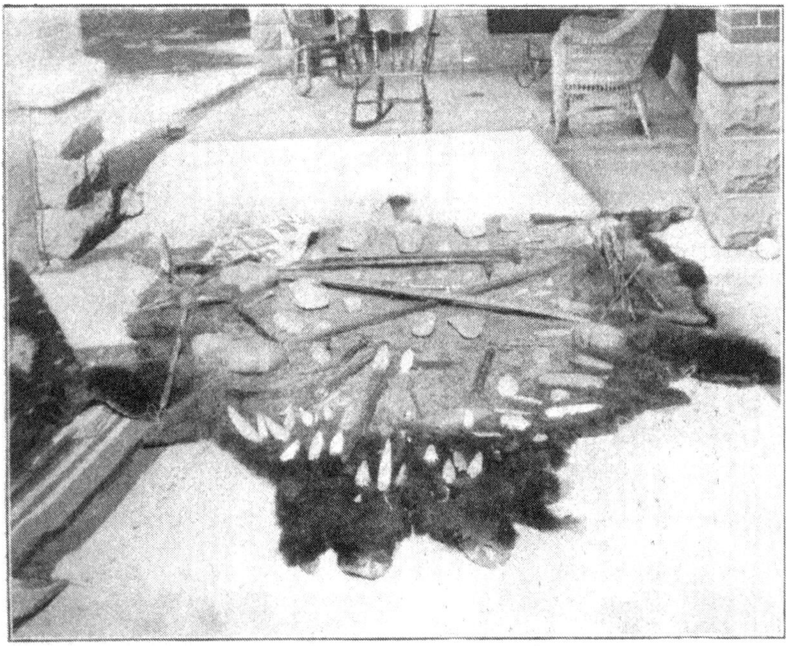

BUFFALO ROBE AND INDIAN WEAPONS
(From Collection of Col. Charles J. Wilson)

She was in a crowd of basket-sellers at a train halting in Albuquerque. Perhaps she was eighteen to twenty years old; she had been at Carlisle school for Indian youth, and she was neatly dressed, evidently knew the virtue of a daily bath, and was certainly charming. I bought a trifle of her just to encourage her to keep on being pretty, to cheer some other tourist on his dusty way.

Perhaps the red girls in their early teens have a fresh, pretty look and lithe, graceful motions, but the bloom passes from them as quickly as from an apple tree. At thirty an Indian woman is a hag.

Far more often the red men are genuinely handsome. For one thing, they are not over-worked, as the women are. They are lithe athletes. And they get all the aids from nice dress. Is there anything more beautiful than feathers? Really look at a peacock feather, and report. It is the Creator's master-piece. Well, the bucks are fond of feathers, their colors and grace of form. And millinery of all sorts appeals mightily to them, and they paint as skilfully as an actor and make up splendidly. A tall, graceful Indian in full dress is a lordly creature, finer than a peacock or bird of paradise, because in beaded, braided, picturesque moccasins he manages his feet better. A peacock would be perfectly glorious if he would take voice culture and shoe his feet with a preparation of concealment. Never look at a pretty woman's feet.

The buck Indian is on the right track—on the track with animals and birds all through creation where the male is beautiful, and ought to be the beautiful one in the family—not near so much matter about the female. The male Indian is bound to be handsome, and all his ambition and art run to self-beautification. Men in Europe, in England and America did the same over a century ago. Beau Brummells were quite common phenomena. George Washington was a great dandy, and so were all the Continentals. Their costume was beautiful—would that it could come again—powdered hair, lace at throats and wrists, knee breeches, white silk stockings, shoes with silver or gold buckles, cocked hat, cane, snuff-box and all—weren't they fine? Napoleon was a master dresser, and was as handsome as a god. The Indian bucks had the same instinct. But just look at a gentleman now in solemn black evening dress—he is a sorry looking mortal, and all pity him.

Appanoose, Wapello and other chiefs went to Washington and Boston in 1837. Wapello "allowed" that "Boston is a ni-she-shing" of a place, and that Governor Edward Everett was a "great brave," and "a great medicine man," and had a "big wick-e-up on the hill (state house), and on the prairie below (the common) had all his warriors out with their big guns." "He would like to have the great Boston brave at his wick-e-up beyond the great

Sepo" (Mississippi). Appanoose was still vainer, a very handsome and chesty brave indeed, who did much mileage on his shape. He had lately fallen "sick" at a celebration in Fort Madison, and when rallied about the attack, by the jesters, he owned that he had got a little "squipee." But at Boston, Appanoose was as proper as the W. C. T. U., and was much set up by Governor Everett's reception in the capitol. Fancy the scene: the polished orator, the profound scholar, the elegant man of the world, only lately an Unitarian minister who, the wags said, "put up the most eloquent prayers ever addressed to a Boston audience," this cosmopolitan gentleman doing the Indians honor. That fired Appanoose, that lit his fuse, and he started across the stage, fizzing and radiating glory, bound to patronize the governor, and extending his hand and swelling up to his full lung capacity, he said oratorically, in hearing of all the crowd,

"Where I live by the Mississippi I am respected by all people, and they consider me the tallest man among them. I am happy that two great men have met to shake hands with each other."

Another reporter gave this version:

"It is a great day that the sun shines upon, when two such great chiefs take each other by the hand."

Powesheik and Wapello lived in this county a few years. There were two Indian villages, each containing several hundred population. One was located near the old Stewart farm on the Brighton road a mile or more southwest from this city, ruled by Powesheik; the other at Sandy Hook, a mile or two north of Brighton, in control of Wapello. As a rule, the reds were friendly to the few whites; only once were they ugly—when the head men were in Washington city, and an annuity had not been promptly paid. The hostile upstart in temporary charge drove off the Moores to Henry county. There were enough braves in this county to have massacred all our people, and very likely these would have felt the tomahawk if we had not fairly bought their lands and honestly abided by the terms of the treaty. Every white race that has dealt with red races testifies that honesty is the best policy, by a large majority, for it is the safest. Truth, justice, kindness shown to Indians have made the wisest investment.

Wapello died in Keokuk county, in March, 1844, before his tribe had moved to Kansas. He was fond of the southern part of our county. He was on Skunk river, opposite the mouth of Crooked creek when he learned that his son was slain. Dashing across the creek to a saloon or trading booth, he gave his best pony for a barrel of whisky, and set it up to the company, and they drowned their sorrow in the usual bowl. While hunting in Keokuk county, he sickened and died. The body was taken to Agency city, and Keokuk, Appanoose and other chiefs came to the funeral. Burials varied. They might lay a body in a grave, or put it in a sitting posture against a tree or rock, or place it in a box, basket, or skin-case, or lash it in a tree or on a high platform. The lamentations were loud. The dishevelled widows carried his clothes to the grave and addressed their co-operative grief to a pair of empty breeches instead of a vacant chair. Occasionally, a sort of obituary or epitaph was painted on boards in red ochre. But they lied as hard then as now. The Indians were kind to the sick, and as long as there was hope, they nursed them, and the big medicine man powwowed over them. But when dog bouillon and herb teas, and the hair of a yellow dog slain in the dark of the moon, and magic and incantations and the soothing music of a very dull-thuddy drum failed, they dressed the patient gaily in his best clothes, feathers, ornaments, trinkets, badges, etc., laid him on a platform to die, surrounded by his gun, dogs, bow and arrows, axes and knives, to show respect to the Great Spirit that was coming to take his soul to the happy hunting grounds, and wanted no show of resistance made.

Our Indians were religious, according to their lights, worshiping Kitche Muleto. So many of their religious ceremonies were like those prescribed by Moses, that many scholars thought the North American Indians are remnants of the lost tribes of Israel, who, somehow, were never advertised for, with suitable reward offered. The red men persistently said, "Injun not lost--wigwam lost."

These two Indian villages were quite imposing, also decidedly smelly. There were trails for paved streets, with here and there picturesque dumps of ashes, fish-heads, bones, fins, and more personal bric-a-brac, dogs doing stunts at those heaps of offal and awful. Mamas, human and canine, were playing with papooses and puppies, but not a cat in sight. A good deal of statuary was visible among the children, and many a maid and squaw wore more slashed directoire and decollete gowns than the New York four hundred. The huts were made of poles stuck in the ground, the spaces between plaited with bark of the "water elm," thatched with slough grass and weeds. The chief had the longest house, forty to sixty feet long, ten to twelve wide, bunks on either side, and equi-distant from the sides, trenches two feet wide and eight to ten inches deep, where meals were cooked under holes cut in the roof to let out the smoke. and the sort o' royal fellow had a court in front, where he held dalliance, was shampooed with a fine-toothed comb, and had his scant beard tweezered, while another servant now and then relieved his majesty of an over-obstreperous grayback, and houris fanned his highness when he took a siesta. He lived in considerable state.

Indians were sensible as to house-keeping. They did not want a costly house—it was dead capital. Rather than clean house twice a year, they burned the village, cremating bedbugs and all the fleas that were really not necessary to give the dogs all the exercise they needed. It was cheaper to move out and burn the hut and rebuild than to clean the old one, slay the vermin, and scratch. No reasonable person could expect a lordly brave to be scratching all the time, and personally answering the door bell every time a bedbug, flea or grayback pressed the electric button, so to speak. The wise Indians reduced house-keeping to its lowest terms and led a simple life. A hut, bedding and furniture that a poor family could afford to burn and renew each year—could anything be more ideal? And as they owned all the land, they could shift the village site when it became intolerable. That simplified things, obviated all sanitation, sewerage, etc., and the Indian never lived who cared a straw about germs and malaria. And they never levied a tax, or took up a collection, or made an assessment. If they wanted anything and hadn't got it, and couldn't beg it or steal it, they did without it, and that is moral philosophy with the bark on. No officer was paid; they had no disputed questions, so needed no lawyers and judges; they were real socialists, yea, communists, holding all things in common, no one rich, none poorer than another, since all might have plenty in August and all be poor and hungry in February. They were heathen, sure, and polygamists, socialists, communists, but they had many ideas that were not half bad, as—a congested population is unwholesome, like gross fat on the person; plenty of room, fresh air and sunlight; and marriage in the clan forbidden—no lovers within the fourth degree of cousinship; a minimum of clothing was a good notion—let air and the solar ray caress the skin; and no stuffiness in houses. So in the old days before reservations and tight houses and store clothes, they were the most athletic race on the continent, the most perfectly developed human animals, their children not having our children's common diseases at all, not even bothered with teething. When the red men were cooped up on reservations, in houses, in our clothing, forbidden to roam and hunt, their physiques gave way at once.

When white company came to these villages, the dogs had a bad quarter of an hour. Several would be killed, and squaws stretched them on stakes above the ground and singed the hair with dried grass fired, and cut them up to boil in pots with corn. After the feast, guests were entertained with green corn dances, medicine dances and scalp dances. Indians are merry people, fond of jokes and stories ripe to the degree of putrescence.

But when not playing the role of hosts, they were trained to be silent and affect to be stoical. It is odd, but Indians were drilled in the art of silence.

SCENE ON THE SKUNK RIVER

SCENE ON MAIN CREEK

Goethe, in "Wilhelm Meister," inculcated silence in education. Be silent. Listen. Think much. Speak little. This accounts for the wonderful sententiousness and compactness of all Indian speech. It is a model of utterance. A woman who was six years old when the reds would come in, still, into her father's cabin here, on moccasined feet, said they startled her by softly saying "How?" That was short for "How-de-do?" They were saving their extra breath to die with, and so abridged the common salutation. Why waste words any more than money? "How" was plenty. An Indian, old or young, would stand or sit in a bright blanket by the hour and watch you afar off, silent and motionless as if they had grown there. And they would not allow themselves to seem surprised at anything, say, a steam boat, machine, or anything else, but the shrill steam whistle on a boat would make them forget their role, and they'd scamper and shriek, with fingers in their ears. Such a screech as that broke down all their stoical reserve, and they always ran, as if fancying it was Mon-i-ton-ke-suth, devil, seeking them for a final accounting. This reserve kept breaking down. The reds would quite often hang out a painted stick, which meant, "come to dog meat feast." In Keokuk, in the dull winters, whites and reds raced ponies and bet on them, and whites and half breeds danced to the tune of Guilmah, or stump-tailed dog.

But the Indian's alleged stoicism is a good deal of a sham. Fenimore Cooper's novels are largely responsible for our impression and estimate of the Indian character. He idealized red folks ridiculously, and he sits high up in the literary Ananias club and is a nature faker. They say red babies do not cry, but they do. If Indians make a show of heroism, fortitude, endurance of pain, etc., it is because they are under observation. It is a big bluff. They break down when alone, and scream with tooth-ache, ear-ache, rheumatism, and whatnot. A friend who had lived fourteen years among the Apaches in Arizona, the fiercest of our Indians, said they are cowards, whimperers, whiners, and can't or don't stand pain. It is only when the odds are much in their favor that they are brave, and then they are incredibly cruel.

Of course, we should not expect too much of Indians. They are nature's men and women. They live in the basement, perhaps the sub-basement, of the mind. They speak in terms of nature, as is natural. When they speak, it is as if beavers, bison, muskrats, deer, foxes, woodchucks, snakes spoke. It is not exact to say that what they say is "common sense," but it is "the common sense," that intelligence that is a more fundamental faculty, without any stimulus or embroidery from culture, precisely common to natural men and to animals. The schools have had no part in the making of Indians. An Indian knows wood-craft, weather, and all natural phenomena exactly as bird and animal are weather-wise and otherwise. They all went to the same school, and it is the only school they ever did attend.

These folk in our county had summer villas and outings. The summer houses were tents made by squaws when hunts were on, out of circular rows of willows planted in the ground, tying their tops together. While planting corn and beans, and harvesting, they all staid at home, then took a brief hunt, and left the villages in winter, hunting by families or in small parties—a nomadic life. They hugged the wooded streams for wind-breaks and fuel. On one such trip Chief Kisk-ke-kosh and party invited themselves to stay the night in a white man's small cabin, and in the morning that exquisite kept his eye on the woman cooking the breakfast. He noticed that she did not wash hands or face, or comb her hair, and he left, fasting, in disgust at her untidyness, a result she perhaps counted on. All the party declined breakfast, and told of it as a personal merit.

Way back there the red temperance league had to deal with drunkenness, and their mode was to tie the horrid example by the neck and heels, and roll him like a hoop till the coma of congestion cleared up. The victim had no resentment when he came-to, for that was the natural order of the universe.

Mrs. Rachel Buck told this true incident. Five slaves ran off from Missouri and took refuge among our Indians, who had never seen black men, and puzzled over them, and concluded they were a new kind of bear. They led the slaves by thongs around their necks, to the whites, hoping to swap them for fire-water, and they did. The negroes worked well around here for a year or two, till their master heard of them and carried them back.

Disdaining agriculture, as a squaw's side issue, hunting became the resource as well as amusement of the bucks. They were not vegetarians. They chased elk, deer, buffalo, shot wild turkeys, prairie chickens and pheasants, caught fish, trapped muskrats for both food and pelts. That rat had a wild, musky odor and a nutty flavor like creosote. They lived on a heavy proteid diet, but an active life in the air and sun prevented auto-intoxication in their colons. No one ever heard of a case of liver complaint in an Indian, who rode a pony, chased game, and struck the trail with pigeon-toed feet. Did bare-back riding and clasping the barrel of the horse make them pigeon-toed? Did the trail incline the toes inward? In the snow, the trail was narrow, as red men swung each foot around and planted it straight ahead of its mate. A white man's path in snow is double the width of a red man's trek, as the white toes out and does not track. Besides, the white man's foot strikes heel first, while the Indian's grips the ground with the front of the foot; the toes bite the grit sharper when the toes turn in.

The Indians were true sports. Their work was play. Happy the man who can earn his living in fun! White men earn their bread in the sweat of their faces, because some one sinned, they say. Thoreau said they must sweat easier than he did, if that was necessary, but the Indian gets and eats his meat and saves his perspiration.

Indians never exterminated game. They did not kill in wantonness, but just for food and hides and for glee. Buffalo would have lasted a million years on these prairies if Indians had been the sole human tenants. It is just as well that both departed. They cumbered the ground. Look at a buffalo: a jack rabbit beats it for steaks, and bison is no good at all for milk, cream, butter, cheese. High in shoulders like camelopard, head like a boulder, it slopes down like a roof to the little end of nothing, such a ridiculous rump! It ate much grass, that would have fared better in the four stomachs of cow or steer. The only way a red or white camper can eat buffalo flesh is to "jerk" it. It took exercise, oxygen, ozone to digest the tough stuff. Such food would have disrupted the alimentary canal of a sedentary white man. Let the bull-headed creature go extinct. Were it not for the zest of the chase of bison, the Indians would better have bred dogs for food.

The Indians were made true sports by the necessity of preserving the game they lived upon. The squaws might have worked, in worsted, in place of the motto, "God bless our home," this adornment of the wick-i-up, "Arise, Peter, slay and eat," if they had had also this motto,

"He who slays and runs away,
May live to hunt another day."

It required Americans and the English to exterminate the buffalo, not for any sound economic reason, but to gratify a lust for murder. But neither barbarians nor even savages are butchers like these modern gunners, who kill in sheer wantonness, and are far more brutal than Indians, Bushmen, Hotentots and African pigmies. For the latter killed, for food and skins, superfluous males, and did not molest female mammals and juveniles.

Our Indians are to be considered children, in process of evolution, rather than cases of arrested development or samples of degeneracy. They had outgrown savagery and taken a step upward to barbarism. They were far beyond the men of the Stone Age; nomads and hunters still, but capable of several notable things. They were up to the level of Prometheus respecting the offices of fire; they domesticated the horse and dog, and tamed and made pets of many wild animals; they tattooed artistically; and as beginners in agriculture, they raised corn, beans, squashes, tobacco, plantain, cassava, and were as fond of berries and honey as bears. The supreme virtues of wheat, barley and other cereals than maize, they had not learned. As manufacturers, they made canoes of bark or tree trunks hollowed out with rude tools and fire; lodges of bark and skins, clothes of skins, basket work, did rude weaving, sewed cloths and skins, carved weapons, pipes, images. The birch bark canoe is a work of art, as perfect and charming a thing as a flaked arrow-head of flint or quartzite.

But were they the aborigines? They themselves held that they were comparatively recent comers. Both the Algonquins and the Iroquois had traditions that they migrated eastward, and the Athabascans speak of migrating across the Pacific.

It has been held by many that there was a much older race than our Indians here, called mound builders, and that the Stone Age creatures antedated them. The redskins have a tradition that their progenitors came from the north-west and drove the mould builders south and south-west. Where did these Indians, migrating in reverse direction, come from? Usually, crowded races go west, with the sun and "empire." Did these savage men come across Behring strait? Were they Malays? It is all silence and vacuum; there is not even an echo, for there is no history. But this traditional avalanche was powerful enough to sweep away a race apparently much superior except in physical strength. Their works and accomplishments are superior, but they were short and small in physique, and their skulls are far more gorilla-like than those of our Indians, many of whom are splendid specimens of manhood, topped with superb heads. It seems to be the accepted scientific opinion now that the mound builders are a hypothetical people, not antedating our Indians in any other sense than that they preceded them in time as ancestors and representatives must—that that is precisely what the mound builders were, Indians, the ancestors of ours, and not another race at all. The custom of building mounds for mortuary and sacrificial purposes, and also for homes, was wide-spread; most primitive peoples did it either habitually or at some stage in their development; the main contents of the mounds are skeletons and ceremonial and other objects buried with the bodies, and the structures are wholly of earth; in some, home-like structures within are the nucleus of the mound. It is a fair supposition that in a long period of comparative quiet and freedom from formidable attack, they had developed a considerable civilization, as in these mounds are found copper as well as stone implements, pottery, cloth, etc. These earthworks are specially plentiful in the Mississippi and Ohio valleys, and they appear in every state and territory in the United States, and of all sizes up to two hundred feet high; from three to four yards to a half mile in diameter; from one hundred square feet to several acres; tens and hundreds of thousands of them, most of them tumuli or burial places, and they extend all over our arid south-west and to Mexico,

PUBLIC SQUARE IN 1909

Yucatan, Honduras, and some South American countries. Many were used for temples of worship and ceremonial purposes. In Minnesota, Wisconsin and Iowa some mounds are shaped in animal forms—mammals, birds and reptiles, suggesting that they stand for the totems of tribes and clans. Iowa is full of mounds, especially the counties of Dubuque, Jackson, Clinton, Scott and Louisa. Some are plainly sacrificial, designed for temples of worship, some for sepulchers, astronomical uses like the Egyptian pyramids, and still others for domestic uses. They are full of skeletons, vessels of ceremony, pipes nicely carved, the eyes of birds and animals on them set with copper points and pearls. Samples of cloth are found within. In one central cell in a mound near Dubuque were eight skeletons sitting in a row, a large sea shell for a drinking bowl before them, as if it had been a caucus of antedeluvian democrats, populists or republicans, stricken in the midst of their conviviality. A group of ten mounds near Davenport revealed bones, copper axes and hemispheres, sea shells, stone knives, pottery, eleven copper awls and twenty copper pipes, but the tobacco was out. It pains one to realize that these poor heathen smoked the vile weed perhaps fifty thousand years ago just around us. If they had not smoked, they might be living yet. There were also stone altars and tablets of hieroglyphics. In a Muscatine mound was a pipe carved in the form of an elephant, and another traced the shape of the mastodon. The artist must have seen those animals in this neighborhood. Great game, and Roosevelt need not have gone to far Africa. There is a string of mounds in Louisa county, on the Iowa river, many of them showing engineering skill. These folk were not nomads—they cleared forests, made roads, wove cloth, worked metals clumsily, but the aborigines never succeeded in thoroughly smelting ores. They began on the art, and if they had not been molested, they might have achieved it. Anyway, they showed varied skills. The evil day came—they were over-borne, pushed out of their defenses, killed, hustled off, and those who survived and breathed the last sigh of the Moor retreated to the gorges in the arid regions in the southwest to be later called the Pueblo cliff-dwellers, and farther south. For many writers think they originally came north from Mexico, Central America, or, perhaps, from Peru where their forebears became scientific enough to trephine skulls. We have the evidence of that feat, in their tombs. But who knows? It is as deep a mystery as how the first grass blade sprang, or the primordial protoplasmic slime fashioned itself into the first amoeba, and starting all animal life in that way. Anyhow, we have had right here all sorts of folks and faiths and customs and habits—heathen, savages, semi-civilized, barbarian, polygamists, communists, and who would not like to know all about them, their origins and careers here? For one, I would rather look at a string of films showing those peoples in continuous motion and endless procession, than to know all about the white pioneers from the fabled Argonauts sailing to get the golden fleece, to the last special car-load of land-seekers going to the Gulf coast or to the wheat belt in Canada. For they were so different from us. They give a zest like the contents of a zoo collected by a Hornaday or a Hagenbeck.

There is an interesting speculation as to the origin of these mounds. It is believed that their type was the shell-mound on all our coasts, in British Columbia, Alaska, Greenland, California, Florida, Oregon, Louisiana and New England. Probably the midden came first, as along the shores of European lakes—villages built on piles over water, for protection or ease of defense, and the shells of fish consumed were dumped beneath till a mound arose around the piling, just like filling in a wooden railway bridge. These shell mounds or middens are of great size, and their foundations are food debris, in which all sorts of instruments were lost and are now found when the structures are opened. Shells, bones, refuse, offal, curios are unearthed in great abundance. When the old fish-eaters and clam-bakers moved inland they would, under the well known power of habit and use and wont, make habitations like the old lake dwellings, and the mound, whether for tomb, or altar, or fort, or house, would hark back to the shell mound. Men are such monkeys and sheep. Hold out a rod at a gate-way, and if the first sheep jumps over it, all the rest of the flock will vault at that point, even after the stick is taken away. Just so with fashions—we all follow suit, do as others do—it is the easiest way out of it.

As to the above mentioned Indian village and farm ruled by Chief Poweshiek, the Stewart farm—Michael Wilson said it extended from Crooked creek to John Parks' present residence on South Iowa avenue, or the Mount Pleasant road. That long strip was by the squaws planted in corn and beans, for succotash. The Reds were very fond of legumes, and they seem to have had an infallible sense of wholesome diet. Food scientists now say there is no food of more excellence than the cereals and legumes—corn and beans. They made a living of it without sow-belly. While the lordly bucks were loafing and enjoying siestas, the industrious squaws were cultivating beans out in the open where the plants could absorb all the wind that was going full tilt across the upland. It is curious that Indians knew as if by intuition how hearty are beans and corn. However, they were nature's children, and were guided by an instinct like that which keeps cattle and other live stock from eating poisons in plants, and which guides sick dogs to eat the particular grass blades that hold the antidotes they need. The average dog, when sick, is a first-class hand at diagnosis.

CHAPTER IV.

STILL FARTHER BACK.

When Washington Irving set out to write the Knickerbocker History of New York, he began with the creation of Adam, thus securing a vast foreground in which to take a long hop, skip and jump. It was whimsical logic, for if Adam had not been yonder, the Dutch could not have taken Holland in Manhattan. Inasmuch as Iowa, and particularly Washington county, are a far better country than New York, I need to go much farther back, in order to show that the pioneers would not have come here in the '30s and '40s if nature or the Secular Providence had not prepared our matchless soil, carved the water courses, laid the coal, planted the borders of the streams with timber, in a latitude and longitude that yield the four wholesome, agreeable seasons. Can we get some sort of a picture of the way this splendid furniture was supplied to our hands?

Things, persons, events come in their natural order, and must so come; impossible to come otherwise. The universe is in the swim, and things happen, as we say, in logical order. Only there's no "happen" about it. It is the old, old necessity—lock-step we go, as in a prison procession, until we drop out in death. Folks sometimes say, "Oh, if I could have lived in the golden Greek days of Pericles," or any other period they may chance to fancy, but they could not. Pericles came in his turn, could not arrive earlier, or postpone a bit; he was a speck of protoplasm floating on the bright stream of existence, and at precisely the point where he had to pop into visibility—pushed by all the forces from behind and pulled by all those in front—and grow, and rule in glory, and create, he did pop, and no power could have hindered him or stopped him. Abraham had to come in his appointed hour, and King David in his, and Cæsar later, and Jesus when his divine clock struck twelve, and Napoleon much later, and you, and you, and you when you severally did, just like the fishes, reptiles, worms, insects, birds and animals. We are all in the same boat of necessity. "O, but that is fatalism!" Yes, but Calvinism is fatalism, and so is heredity, and logic, and environment, and much else, all else. How could our old settlers have come here before this wonderful country had been fashioned and provisioned for them? They could not, and they did not.

It seems that a little matter of billions of years ago, the swift-rolling sun dislodged a vast mass of fiery matter from its envelope, and slung this red-hot cinder of a nebula into our earth's present orbit, to wheel round its central source, in the cold spaces, and radiate its heat, solidify from the cooling crust downwards till it had a solid surface on which rains fell and oceans gathered; there was three times as much water as land, and that ratio has been maintained ever since. If the yielding crust sank or subsided here and uplifted on the other side of the sphere, the waters would cover this part of the globe, while yonder part would be dry land, and these long alternations caused by subsidence and elevation continued for ages too long to bother about. When the waters were on here, sediment was precipitated to the ocean bed, and strata of rock, clay, shale, sandstone, limestone, whatnot, were deposited, and the weight of the superincumbent ocean compacted them into the dense masses we know. Stratum after stratum was thus laid on the sea's bottom, tier on tier. After thousands of years this part of the globe rose like a whale to blow, shaking brine from its shoulders and flanks, and on the dry land the sunlight and heat grew rank vegetation that fell and turned into coal measures during another long submergence. No one knows how many times the ocean covered this region.

The borers of our artesian well penetrated the earth's crust eighteen hundred feet, passing through successive formations, each slab solidified by the tremendous weight of the water world above. All that had to be before Stone Age man, Mound Builder, Indian could find footing here, before Adam Ritchey and the Gobles and the Moores could take up claims. Of the two, I would rather have seen how all that preparation was made, than to have greeted those pioneers. Really, it is astonishing, to think that all those colossal, cosmic things had to happen just to let Ritchey, Goble, Moore et al., get in here on the ground floor at one dollar and a quarter per acre. It seems as incongruous as for the mountain to labor and bring forth a mouse. But that was exactly the logical order.

And when these gigantic slabs were laid, and all finished, and the ocean drained off to cover a depression in the rim of the earth elsewhere, we cannot tell what that ancient landscape looked like. No doubt, a very uneven surface; hills, mountains, gorges, valleys, lakes, rivers; a landscape totally unlike the present. The poets from David down, speak of "the everlasting hills," but they are not eternal, by a long shot; they, indeed, run, and skip, and clap their hands, for they are as fugitive as playful animals and children, as shifting as mists, fog and dew. Nor do the brooks go on forever. Nature

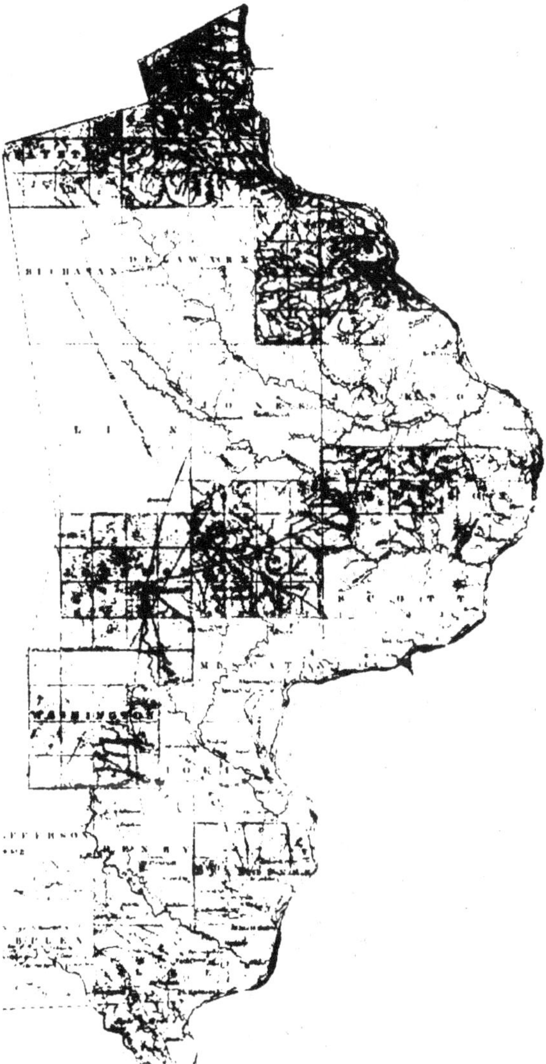

NEWHALL'S MAP OF IOWA, 1841

is fluid; nothing stays put; all things are in ebb and flow; rain, frost, snow, ice, gravity, scale down the mountains, pulverize their granites into soil, and some day Rocky mountains, Andes, Cordilleras, Himalayas will be ground down into farms and garden patches. The ranches, gardens and vineyards in Colorado, Utah, Nevada, California, Montana, Oregon, Washington are mere pulverized mountain, melted and diffused by rivers like sugar in a cup of tea. And not only that, but the offices of glacial ice had to be invoked to grind and mix into paste and smear over the landscape a dump of soil. Five or six times an ice sheet from five hundred to one thousand feet thick came creeping down from the pole, smashing everything before and under it, grinding ledges of rock into fine meal, mixing the elements thoroughly, and spreading this drift, as it was called, over all this area, filling chasms even full, grinding forests into wood pulp, grading all the region. No one knows what started these long cold spells—perhaps an inclination of the earth's axis to the sun, that robbed the north of solar heat and light, shortening the summers, lengthening the winters. The scientists are not agreed as to the cause, but whatever it was, science sees now the beginning of a recurrence of another glacial age. The ice sheet in Greenland is thickening and advancing southward again, and in many, many thousands of years, our descendants may be ousted from here and driven southward precisely as men and animals and plants were forced to retreat ages ago. Anthropologists, geologists and the other "ists" agree that man was present at the last glacial period, that they reckon anywhere from one hundred to one hundred and seventy thousand years gone by. When our posterity are evicted, as was primitive man, not a shred of our civilization, our cities, parks, railways, monuments, buildings will survive the passage of that ice plow and harrow.

There was such a chill in the air in glacial eras that only arctic flora and fauna could exist here, as, in alternating hot epochs, when the tilt of the globe's axis gave the extreme north an excess of heat and light, tropical plants and animals saluted the north pole. Palms grew in Greenland, coal was laid there in the fierce summers, brilliant plumaged birds flew and mated and nested in the balmy air, and conditions were so genial that the missionary hymn, "From Greenland's icy mountains" was absurdly mal-apropos. In those eras Greenland was as beautiful as Eden, and there was not a seal, a walrus, a white bear, a furred Eskimo within ten thousand miles of the pole.

There have been surprising things in Iowa, in Washington county. In what geologists call the tertiary period the flora was tropical; the gayest flowers bloomed and the tenderest trees blossomed and bore fruit from northernmost Greenland to Medicine Hat and the Mississippi valley, and such trees as magnolia, cinnamon, fig, cypress, and palms flourished. And the fauna was tropical. Birds, gilded beetles, sun-painted butterflies, as brilliant as bouquets and as flashing jewelry, flew in the air, and Polly wanted a cracker in all woods. In the swamps huge reptiles crawled, unconscious of their ugliness, their ponderous jaws paved with horror and bad intentions, and tremendous turtles, snakes and lizards made the slime and ooze hideous. Animals quite like the rhinoceros walked abroad, and tapirs, and a species of horse with three hoofs on each foot, and three toes on each hoof, and panthers, tigers, monkeys of quite Asiatic type.

What a dangerous place it was to raise children in! Mothers dared not leave them out of sight and care, lest a plesiosaurus, mylodon, or pterodactyl should come upon them, even as the automobiles and motor-cycles run over us now. These frightful things scared people like aeroplanes, and in the gloaming bats of enormous spread of pinion flitted about on leather wings big enough to make a buggy top.

This warm wallow and riot of prodigality lasted for ages, and then the climate began to change, gradually grew colder. Folk, if there were any, talked about it; editors, such as were, filled columns with evidences that the winters were changing and growing colder and longer. All their correspondents, signing "Oldest Inhabitant," "Vindex," "Observer," "Old Bore," said ditto. Springs came later; gardeners could not plant potatoes on Good Friday, either in the light or the dark of the moon; summers and autumns were shorter-waisted. The flora gradually changed; trees ceased bearing and flowers blooming in Greenland, and the poet began to write that missionary song about her "icy mountains." The fauna retreated southward; monkeys scolded about the climate and clustered in knots for warmth, and birds invented migration; parrots could not say enough about the change for the worse, and the animals, bored by their chatter, chided them and bade them ring off. The hides on the rhino and elephant thickened and toughened; the elephant and mastodon grew an enveloping whisker of wool, and the good sprinters among animals moved south, while others, like bears, several species of squirrels, and snakes, frogs and reptiles in general adopted the cunning expedient of hibernation, and as the autumn came on cold, they gave the drowse free rein and went to sleep to save domestic expenses. Food, fuel, hunting game—all abolished by the strange coma of suspended animation. The earth, year by year, froze to deeper depths; people could hear it crack, thump and jump in the night, like ice-bound ponds. The stronger animals pre-empted the deep gorges and wooded ravines, out of the blasts, yet had a sad, sour time of it even there. Most animals as well as plants winter-killed, as the snow drifted higher, not melting in the brief summers. The drifts became hills and mountains of snow, and the rains penetrated it, soaked it, and frost compacted it into ice; it became a toboggan by sheer gravity, and started slowly down the grade of the country. That is, it was a glacier, growing ever thicker, and this ice-sheet reached to the latitude of St. Louis before it melted. No vegetation but arctic could live amid its terminal moraines, and arctic plants held on by pure grit—those that were not run over by the planers of ice; and it is the bark, cones and bits of woods from these mangled forests that we bring up in our well-borings. The imagination staggers at thought of computing the millions on millions of cubic miles of rock pomace this gigantic ice sledge brought down from the north to scatter as soil deeply over British America and the northern part of the United States, filling the gorges and valleys with drift.

Professor Samuel Calvin, of the Iowa State University, and state geologist, tells how the soils of Iowa were produced by the action of ice:

"Glaciers and glacial action have contributed in a very large degree to the making of our magnificent state. What Iowa would have been had it never suffered from the effects of the ponderous ice sheets that successively overflowed its surface, is illustrated, but not perfectly, in the driftless area. Here we have an area that was not invaded by glaciers. Allamakee, parts of Jackson, Dubuque, Clayton, Fayette and Winneshiek counties belong to the driftless area. During the last two decades numerous deep wells have been bored through the loose surface deposit, and down into the underlying rocks. The record of these wells shows that the rock surface is very uneven. Before the glacial drift which now mantles nearly the whole of Iowa was deposited, the surface had been carved into an intricate system of hills and valleys. There were narrow gorges hundreds of feet in depth, and there were rugged, rocky cliffs and isolated buttes corresponding in height with the depth of the valleys.

"To a person passing from the drift-covered to the driftless part of the state, the topography presents a series of surprises. The principal drainage streams flow in valleys that measure from the summits of the divides, six hundred feet or more in depth. The upper Iowa river, in Allamakee county, for example, flows between picturesque cliffs that rise almost vertically from three to four hundred feet, while from the summit of the cliffs the land rises gradually to the crest of the divide, three, four, or five miles back from the stream. Tributary streams cut the lateral slopes and canyon walls at intervals. These again have tributaries of the second order. In such a region a quarter section of level land would be a curiosity. This is a fair sample of what Iowa would have been had it not been planed down by the leveling effects of the glaciers. Soils of uniform excellence would have been impossible in a non-glacial Iowa. The soils of Iowa have a value equal to all of the silver and gold mines of the world combined.

"And for this rich heritage of soils we are indebted to great rivers of ice that overflowed Iowa from the north and northwest. The glaciers in their long journey ground up the rocks over which they moved and mingled the fresh rock flour from granites of British America and northern Minnesota with pulverized limestones and shales of more southern regions, and used these rich materials in covering up the bald rocks and leveling the surfaces of pre-glacial Iowa. The materials are in places hundreds of feet in depth. They are not oxidized or leached, but retain the carbonates and other soluble constituents that contribute so largely to the growth of plants. The physical condition of the materials is ideal, rendering the soil porous, facilitating the distribution of moisture, and offering unmatched opportunities for the employment of improved machinery in all the processes connected with cultivation. Even the driftless area received great benefit from the action of glaciers, for, although the area was not invaded by ice, it was yet to a large extent covered by a peculiar deposit called loess, which is generally connected with one of the later sheets of drift. The loess is a porous clay, rich in carbonate of lime. Throughout the driftless area it has covered up many spots that would otherwise have been bare rocks. It covered the stiff intractable clays that would otherwise have been the only soils of the region. It in itself constitutes a soil of great fertility. Every part of Iowa is debtor in some way to the great ice sheets of the glacial period.

* * * * *

"Soils are everywhere the product of rock disintegration, and so the quality of the soils in a given locality must necessarily be determined in large measure by the kind of rock from which they were derived.

"From this point of view, therefore, the history of Iowa's superb soils begins with first steps in rock making. The very oldest rocks of the Mississippi valley have contributed something to making our soils what they are, and every later formation laid down over the surface of Iowa, or regions north of it, has furnished its quota of materials to the same end. The history of Iowa's soils, therefore, embraces the whole sweep of geologic times.

"The chief agents concerned in modifying the surface throughout most of Iowa since the disappearance of the latest glaciers have been organic, although the physical and chemical influences of air and water have not been without marked effect. The growth and decay of a long series of generations of plants have contributed certain organic constituents to the soil. Earth worms bring up fine material from considerable depths and place it in posi-

TIMOTHY BROWN MONUMENT IN ELM GROVE CEMETERY

A Revolutionary Soldier

tion to be spread out upon the surface. They drag leaves and any managable portion of plants into their burrows, and much of the material so taken down into the ground enriches the ground to a depth of several inches. The pocket gopher has done much to furnish a surface layer of loose, mellow, easily cultivated and highly productive soil. Like the earth worm, the gopher for century after century has been bringing up to the surface fine material, to the amount of several tons annually to the acre, avoiding necessarily the pebbles, cobbles and coarser constituents. The burrows collapse, the undermined bowlders and large fragments sink downwards, rains and winds spread out the gopher hills and worm castings, and the next year, and the next, the process is repeated; and so it has been for all the years making up the centuries since the close of the glacial epoch. Organic agents in the form of plants and burrowing animals have worked unremittingly through many centuries, and accomplished a work of incalculable value in pulverizing, mellowing and enriching the superficial stratum, and bringing it to the ideal condition in which it was found by the explorers and pioneers from whose advent dates the historical period of our matchless Iowa."

Did Adam Ritchey, Simpson Goble, Billy Moore and the rest stop to think of all this preliminary work of the infinite Providence, to get Washington county ready for them? Probably not. If they had realized that truth, it would either have made them humble and devout, or so stuck up over their implied or assumed personal importance, they would have burst with conceit.

And now, having conquered Washington county from the chaos of "Louisiana," and got rid of the Indians, and paid our respects to the Indians' predecessors, the Mound Builders, and to the still more ancient, and probably the real, aborigines, the race of the Stone Age, who fashioned all these delightful stone implements and ornaments, and who had the grit to stick out here the glacial period by sharing caves with shaggy bears and saying boldly to them, "Come out of those furs and skins, I want 'em as clothes for myself and my family, and while I'm about it, I'll put your fat carcass in my pantry, where it will come handy in my business;" and having cast a long backward glance at the process by which nature provided a tempting soil for our waiting settlers, not nomads, for farmers instead of hunters, let us ring up the curtain and show a modern scene.

Exeunt, Reds; enter, Whites.

CHAPTER V.

INVENTORY OF THE PIONEER PERIOD.

The Indians gone from a part of the county, their lands surveyed and put on the market, white settlers began to come in, in 1835. It will be convenient to group them by years in the order of their coming.

1835.—Adam Ritchey and John Black—no more, unless it be Tommy Tucker. They were Pennsylvanians, but had moved to Illinois, to be ready to cross into Canaan when the treaties were ripe. Both returned to Illinois in the fall. The Crooked creek region looked good to them. Before the forties no settlements were risked on the "prairie," which is French for "meadow." All stuck to the brush with the unerring instinct of a squirrel and 'coon for available trees. Fuel, cabin, fence and furniture material and shelter were on the wooded streams.

Ritchey put in the winter bragging about the country, its assets of soil, climate, water courses, timber, grasses, and his hot air inflated his brothers Matthew and Thomas, Mr. Humphrey and a few others.

1836.—They came with him in February, crossing the Mississippi river on the ice, staked out claims on Crooked creek, but all save Adam went back. Black moved to Henry county. Adam built a cabin near the spot where the road running south from Crawfordsville crosses the creek. He fell sick. Friendly Indians ministered to him several weeks. At last he returned to Illinois, and came back with his boy Matthew, aged fifteen, and his daughter Sarah, thirteen years old. The lad drove the team, the lass kept house, and Adam made fence, and when a bit of corn was planted, he went home to fetch the rest of the family. By October they were settled. Little Sarah in due time became Mrs. S. McCulley.

Ritchey was our first man. How happy that his name was Adam, for this county was Eden number two. What a pity we have no picture of him. R. T. McCall says he was a quite robust man, thick-set, roundish, plump body, full of energy. But we cannot see him from those few strokes. What the color of his eyes and hair? the timbre of his voice? what his habits and tastes? We ache to apply a sort of ancestor-worship to this man, and he is so vague. Yet he looms on the imagination as a large, imposing figure, as Abraham in the dim fore-world stands as a massive column. Sentiment requires that our forebear, Adam Ritchey, should be a giant.

John Black makes no such appeal, but he shrinks into a Mormon and drifted to Utah. How many wives he amassed history saith not, but really "this is too much," as Artemus Ward murmured when Brigham Young's widows fell on his neck and wept. Adam, too, soon left us, selling his claim to the Matthew Moorehead folk, one of the notably fine families of the olden time, and in all their years shedding sweet influences like the Pleiades. Mr. Moorehead was long a justice of the peace, and kept a sort of sub-tavern. He and Robert Glasgow were elected members of the eighth general assembly.

Ritchey went down the river, built a mill in 1839, and died in 1848. He and his brother were killed, hauling barrels from Brighton. But before he goes, let it be stated that he was the first justice of the peace appointed by the territorial governor, for this county, and in the summer of 1837 he married John Hulock and Nancy Goble, the first wedding in the county, and he farther distinguished himself by coming up on the blind side of the stork—his daughter Isabelle Ritchey was the first baby born in the county. Glory enough!

Reader, would you not like to know all about that wedding? How John was dressed, perhaps in "conventional black," and Nancy in linsey-woolsey, with prairie flowers in her belt and delicious wild thorn blossoms in her hair. Was there a feast, a dance, a tour, a charivari, a serenade, a reception? Had Nancy been caught out in many preliminary "showers?" Was there a gold ring on the third finger of her left hand? How did John propose? on his knees, think? Did Nancy say "yes" so softly and still that the recording angel had to say, "Ahem! Louder, please!" How can I be expected to write an authentic history when Clio, Muse of History, denies me all the essential raw material?

Editor John H. Pearson says the bridal parties were Harrison Goble and Lydia Osborn.

Well, what is history, anyhow? Napoleon said it was a fable that had been agreed upon. Let both records stand. Two couples could have more bliss than one pair. Perhaps Adam married both. If so, I hope he kissed both brides, enjoyed it, and counted it a good day's work.

In the spring, another columnar figure moved across our spaces—Richard Moore, of Indiana. He made a claim in what is Washington township. His sons Amos and Thaddeus, and son-in-law John C. Maulsby took claims also, and all went back in the fall and brought their families—Richard's wife

Pioneer Transportation

Log cabin in which first court was held

Old "Elm" Schoolhouse

Old Bunker Mills
Built in 1842; photo taken 1881

PIONEER SCENES AND EVENTS

Rebecca and sons Amos, Thaddeus, William, Jesse, Dick, jr., and girls Rebecca and Averila. Mrs. Maulsby came, George Baxter, Wm. Hunter, John Mosteller and wife, though the latter died on the way, in September. A coffin was made of puncheons, split from sections of a log, rudely fitted together, and in that she sleeps till the trump shall sound.

Amos' claim became the James Looney farm, Thaddeus' the John C. Malin place, and Maulsby's the Michael Wilson farm. Mosteller and Wm. Moore settled in Marion.

These folk were well-to-do in the east, and brought household goods, horses, young cattle, sheep, hogs, four yoke of oxen, chickens, apple and garden seeds. They had force enough to build cabins and make prairie hay. Richard's log cabin was double and very swell, floored with puncheons, roofed with clap-boards laid on logs and weighted with poles, and it took the shine off from all the other architecture. It belonged to the order of Renaissance Americano Romanesque.

At Christmas a blizzard stampeded the cattle, and most of them perished. Indians at the village a mile from this city, in the absence of their chief, and mad because their annuity had not been paid in March, and so dissatisfied with the survey and the treaty boundary line that they tore up the stakes, sent a protesting delegation to Washington, D. C., and, getting no redress, vented their spleen on the Moores and especially on Thomas Baker who had settled near where Washington now stands, and he was persona non grata. The reds conceded that the Moores were well within their legal rights. The village was red-hot. Baker stuck till May 31, in spite of the advice of the whites. The Indians burned him out, and he went to Ritchey's, made a claim and worked it till the second purchase. Later, he was given exemplary damages and full remuneration from the Indians, through the general government assessing them. Thaddeus and Wm. Moore were warned by the unreasonable redskins, who went to the boys where they were plowing, and tried to scare the oxen by waving blankets in front of them, and clawing sod back into the furrow. And a temporary upstart chief with a gang armed with war-clubs and new guns threatened with infinite chatter and clamor. Some reds, camped on Crooked creek near Ritchey's, got into a heated confab, struck pugilistic attitudes, when a Ritchey knocked one brave down. That tickled the other Indians, and they guyed the bored warrior and laughed—it was such a good joke. The Moores thought it prudent to go to New London, where they stayed till 1839, and, returning, found cabins, fences, etc., intact, and the Indians gone. Amos and William Moore held their claims longest, and were our oldest settlers at their deaths.

Another Cleopatra Needle in our landscape was David Goble, in Oregon township, with his sons David, George, Simpson and daughter Nancy, and young Oliver Sweet, who came from Kentucky August 1, crossing the river on a flat boat at Flint Hills, now Burlington. They drove forked posts in the ground, put clapboards a-top and hung quilts on sides and rear for tapestries, and lived cosily till after haying when they built a cabin of hewn logs, sixteen by eighteen, and made another so near that a door connected both. It was the first house in that township. David was a Daniel Boone sort of man, hunter, trapper, and lover of solitude and plenty of room. Daniel, when he heard of a man within a hundred miles of him, felt crowded and stifled. Goble's boon companion was Reuben B. Davis, who settled on a creek in Iowa township, that took his name. They made money on furs. Goble was a prominent man in county affairs, but sold out, went to Kansas, and died in 1855.

Milo Holcomb and John B. Bullock, of Illinois, settled at Hoosier Bend, on the site of what was later the Van Doren mill, had a post, and traded with Indians. In 1839, Holcomb married, in Monmouth, Rachel Jackson, sister to the first Mrs. Joseph Keck and Mrs. Martha Jackson Burrell, and he brought her home with the June roses, but the Indians, who gave her an unique reception, were more picturesque in scarlet blankets, red petticoats, feathers, buckskin raiment and other brilliant toggery, than the prairie flowers. They turned out en masse, four or five hundred of them, and it was a wonderful scenic festival.

Those white men built a saw mill on Crooked creek, and sawed the first lumber in the county, late in 1836. In 1839, John Jackson, father to Mrs. Holcomb, came to her home and got out lumber for the first two-story house in Washington or the county. That place was a knot of first things. Holcomb was the first sheriff, he ran the first store, ground the first grist in '39. At the mill was a post-office called "Marcellus." That two-story house stood on the site of the Joseph Keck brick, now a sanitarium. After the Jacksons, Mr. Keck lived in it, and when he built the brick, it was moved to Jefferson street, and still serves, owned and occupied by S. P. Kiefer. John Jackson was one of the earliest surveyors, and was deputy sheriff when his boat went over Skunk river dam and he was drowned, as was also his son John, years later, when he was post-master in Washington.

Godfrey Augustine came to Dutch creek and sort o' settled, though the Indians still owned the land, but they were kind to him. War parties met nearby, once, and had a skirmish, and a bullet made one "good " Indian. Augustine worked two winters in Wisconsin woods, then at packing in Burlington, but when the land was surveyed and title clear under the new treaty, he bought two hundred acres at one dollar and twenty-five cents per acre.

1837.—Few came this year, on account of the grouchy Indians. But Silas Washburn and Morgan Hart reached Brighton. Washburn's claim included the mill site, and he made a cabin on the national bank lot. They slept in their clothes, on prairie hay, in a shanty, that winter, and did not have carpet, lace curtains, piano, silverware, napkins and finger bowls, but they had health plus. Hart became a prominent man, serving with superb common sense on the board of commissioners.

Josiah Smart kept a trading post on the north side of Crooked creek, and traded with the Indians, and left when they did. For several years a large section of tree bark, bearing Indian picture writing on its inner surface, lay on his store roof, and finally rotted. If only some one of archeological tastes had preserved it, varnished it, given it to the county historical society, it would now be worth its weight in bank notes, if not in gold. It is said that Smart's wife was a full-blooded squaw. She did not organize the first W. C. T. U. in this county, and rarely wore a blue or white ribbon. She advertised in her own proper, or improper, person her husband's goods. The choicest he kept locked in a valise, but she is charged with burglarizing that, and then proceeded to publish the glad tidings of great joy to the bucks and squaws, and they raised more hades than maize. If all is true they say about her, she was the first "horrid example" in our history. When she was jagged with this sort of locomotor ataxia she could walk seven Indian trails at once, whether they ran parallel or at right angles, and give the war-whoop in solo or chorus. I shall always regret that editor Heacock never met this ornament of her sex.

J. W. Neal came to Crawford township and built a cabin south of the bridge across the branch south of Crawfordsville. There was a block house or fort that he shared the first night, and seven families had gathered there, but six of them moved out. Neal kept guard all night, but the Indians swarming all around made no attack. Other comers were Isaac Pence and family and his son Samuel and family, with the Gobles, and settled in Crawford on a claim sold by John Drake for two hundred dollars, improvements thrown in; and Thomas and John Caldwell, Henry Osborne, Wm. Huston, James McElroy, Wm. Wooley, Wm. Kinnear, Wm. Kinsley, David Sykes, Nathan Griffith. Mr. Kinsley started a nursery in '37 or '38, and many an orchard was its offspring.

Wm. L. Harvey located on what was later better known as the Stewart farm on the Brighton road a mile from Washington.

The scene shifts to English river, where there was more brush. Joseph Edelstein, a Swiss, made a cabin, but it burned before the family came from Ohio, and they holed up in a cave awhile. He was farmer and wagon-maker, and, being a Catholic, he attracted settlers of that faith.

In the fall James, Thomas and Samuel Watters and Joseph, Hiram, Benjamin and Robert Wasson went hunting on English river in Lime creek township, and in camp noted a promising mill site, made a claim and cabin and left Hiram Wasson in it to hold the fort. A few weeks later, N. W. and Daniel McFarland came, staked claims, including the mill site and land to the east, built a cabin and took squatter sovereignty. But the first set of men won out, and built a mill the next year on the north side of the river. It burned in '48, was rebuilt, and used as a saw mill till '56. The present mill was erected in '50, and does a good business.

The records are conflicting as to arrivals in

1838-39.—The Lime Creek comers were Marcus Hull, Benj. Parker, W. A. Davisson, Josiah Morrow, John Wasson, W. G. Griffith, Wm. Bevans, W. L. Hewett, H. H. Willson, George Pinkerton, John R. King, Merlin Carpenter, Messrs. Perrington, Smith, Gilliam, Roberts and the Rickeys. Wassonville was laid out in 1840.

Wm. Bussey located near Colonel Palmer's farm, and on October 25 Ann was born to him, the first child the stork brought into "Widow" Washington.

Wm. Myers settled on what is now the county farm, and Captain Moreland, who had quit steamboating, bought a farm on the Brighton road, four miles from this city, and began to give his neighbors specimens of the raciest, most vivid and picturesque English heard up to date.

The year 1838 is credited with John and James Neal, Daniel Powers, the Crills, Conrad Temple, John Lewis, George Farrier, Robert Risk, Seneca Beach, Francis Thorn, Parks, John Grimsby, Thomas Wilson. Most of this invoice went towards Brighton.

This good bunch came in 1839: Thomas Ritchey, the Gordons, the Longs, John Hobbs, James Dawson, one of the biggest brained men among all the emigrants; Wm. Ayres, David Bunker, a large personality; the Moons, Abe Custer, Gideon Bear, the unique; John ("Paddy") Connelly, the first Irishman in the county; Jonathan Wilson, T. Neal, Joseph Bealman, Joseph B. Davis, Nathan Baker, Edward Clemons, and their families, for nearly all the men were married.

John Adams arrived from Ohio in Washington, October 17, '39, bought two lots on the southeast side of the square and built a log cabin fourteen by sixteen, and a smithy sixteen by sixteen, the first "improvements" here.

WILLIAM H. JENKINS MARGARET REISTER JENKINS

PIONEER PRIVATE BANKER AND WIFE

JOSEPH SOMMER ELIZABETH SOMMER

PIONEERS IN MARION TOWNSHIP

This Adams is sometimes called Joseph, and generally "Quincy" Adams. It seems he came the last week in 1839, with Jesse Ashby and Jonathan and Michael Wilson, yet the last three are credited as October arrivals. Never mind. Adams bought lots 3 and 4, block 22, on the corner of Iowa and Jefferson streets. His furniture was scanty, bunks for beds, floors of puncheons, while most settlers had dirt floors, but Quincy was not stuck up. That winter of '39-40 was very cold; snow drifted thro' his roof and lay ten inches deep on his bed, equal to arctic down.

He was proud, however, September 22, 1840, when his Margaret was born, the first birth in this city. She is still living, as Mrs. John Farra. As if this was not glory enough, Quincy wanted the credit of the creation of the first boy in town, and Henry arrived, date not given so far as I can learn—no matter. The jesters called the house "No 7" for some reason I know not what, but "Stork's Nest" would be more appropriate.

John Diehl, a German Lutheran, reached English river, saw Elizabeth Spaner, and his fate was sealed.

Dr. Simeon Teeples and Dr. Stone were the earliest pillists in the county. Teeples went to the territorial legislature, and did not feel disgraced by it. The first election, held in 1840, took place in this house.

Ab. Owens, A. H. and Charles Haskell also came, and the Haskells built a mill, but the March freshet took it out, and in trying to save the timbers, in a boat, Charles was drowned. Two years later a dog, tugging at a bone buried in the sand, revealed his skeleton. A mill was not built till 1841. It was sold to N. McClure.

Other home builders on that river were Wm. Duvall, C. D. Gillam, Nixon Scott, Ab. Tansey, and Reuben Davis erected the first frame house, sixteen by thirty-six, weather-boarded with shaved clapboards, split puncheon floors, shingled, a stone chimney in the center, and two fireplaces. It was meant for a tavern on the military road.

That "Haskell mill site claim" on the English, was the first transfer of real estate in the county, and the conveyance was acknowledged in December, 1839.

Cyrus Cox came from Michigan, Stephen and Jonathan Bunker and George and John O'Loughlin from Indiana, S. B. Cooper from New York, B. Criswell from Illinois, Wm. Shaw from Ohio, John and Joel Tyler. It is said that two men claimed the whole township, George O'Loughlin all south of the river, Jonathan Bunker all north of it—in vain.

Clay township was lively about this time. Martin Bedwell and John Pennington came from Indiana. C. L. Morgan is of the fifth generation still living on his place.

Moses Hoskins, Ellis Walton, Richard Disberry, John McClintic, Robert McCarty, and Robert Pringle came. Walton liked not only the country, but Elizabeth J. Edwards, and 'Squire Orson Kinsman married them July 1, '40. With great firmness of spirit, they did not wait till the Fourth. The stork brought Disberry a son William, September 25, '40. McClintic is the progenitor of all the Macs in Clay and Brighton. Walton was a mighty hunter and a warm friend of Chief Wapello.

Mr. Roberty, a bee man, dates from this period. All the Pringles in that region sprang from Robert.

It is worth noting that Clay township, that has always been a canny, thrifty New England or Yankee settlement, furnishes the first case of consumption cured by deep breathing of pure air. When Julius Wolcott came of age, the doctors gave him the cheerful information that he could not live three years. Julius "guessed" not. Every day he went out doors and made a business and religion of breathing deeply twenty minutes. In six months his chest had expanded three inches, the lungs were healed, and he lived to be over seventy, and died from other causes. The doctors never forgave him for proving they were bad guessers.

John Brier settled on the Indian burial ground at Sandy Hook, with reds all around, both quick and dead. His father John came also, and loaned Mr. Pickerell money to build the first mill there, but it burned.

The old settlers were always talking, at the celebrations, about the early hard times, the privations, distress, etc., but Dan Cupid jollied them right along. In that year Brighton had its first wedding—Orson Kinsman and Hannah Dinsmore—and Philo Dray was born, and the Fourth of July celebrated, Horace Carley reading the Declaration, and Mr. Calkins orating.

1840.—English river was re-inforced by John R. Hawthorn, John Holland, a Thompsonian doctor, and R. McReynolds, a farmer and preacher, who married the first pair of lovers up that way. Frank Forbes, Elizabeth Holland and H. S. Guy also came.

Toward Richmond, George O'Loughlin and Elvira Smith were the first to wed, and their baby was the first fruits of the stork aforesaid. Its death a year later was the first tragedy.

Other comers were Henry Rogers, Lewis Vanbuskirk, W. S. Britton, Eli and Ephraim Adams, Levi Randall, and Mr. Ramsey who gave his name to the stream he settled on, where he built a small grinding mill, the first in the township.

Jonathan Bunker and Mary Randall were married by 'Squire Gillam in '40, and Mr. Gilchrist and Cynthia Tyler. Cyrus Cox gained a daughter and Daniel Bunker lost one. All these incidents were township "firsts."

MR. AND MRS. ALEXANDER YOUNG

MR. AND MRS. MICHAEL HAYES

MR. AND MRS. SIMPSON GOBLE

Mr. Clark was the first settler in Highland. It was slow work there. The next settler was Ahira D. Liming, in '41, and the third was John Forbes in '42.

In the spring, Alexander Young came from Rush county, Indiana, built a hewn log cabin twenty-six by twenty, in Cedar township, which is still standing, and is pictured elsewhere. The Youngs say there was not a house in Washington, and only five houses between Washington and the head of Crooked creek then, but, surely, Mr. Adams' cabin and smith shop in this city were up.

John Ingham, from whom all the Inghams and Hortons in Clay descended bought two hundred and forty acres, but he sold out and went to Peoria, but got home-sick, came back, bought one hundred and sixty acres, and died in '60.

Daniel Powers built the second house in Washington in '40, a double log, one and a half story, four rooms, very swell indeed, style of architecture Greco-Romano Renaissance, to be exact. It stood on the Yellow Brick corner, and had an elevator plying between the first and second floors, a rung ladder. Women were rather disinclined to use it when folks were around. The house was the first tavern, Bloomer Thompson succeeding Powers. When General A. C. Dodge and Alfred Rich stumped for congress, they lodged there one night, and for supper had tea and onions. There was nothing else in the house, Bloomer being off to mill in Des Moines county, but he got back in the night, and the great men had a good breakfast. If an Indian had run that house, they would have got boiled white dog, sure. They raised white dogs for the table.

The authorities conflict as to the Yellow Brick building. One says Powers built it, another credits it to A. Lee, who came here to build a jail in '41; he could find no house for the family, and put up that log house, hauling brick for chimneys and fireplaces from below Crawfordsville, and also made a one-story addition on the west for dining and sitting room. There was lots of custom—men seeking homes and staying the night, and members of the legislature, from south and west, going to and from Iowa city were guests. February and March, '42, were very cold, and the five fireplaces burned thirty cords of wood.

The next comer was John Dougherty, en route to Missouri with merchandise; he was so struck with the place, he rented the lower room in the tavern just below the elevator, and set up groceries and notions, in 1840, but he soon had a rival in Almon Moore from Wapello, who built a one-story frame next door west of tavern, and he so mixed up his family with the stock that patrons hardly knew which to take, a wife or a bolt of muslin, a mother or a gingham dress, a kid or a bushel of potatoes.

Then, to remove the reproach of this being a dry town, Amos Embree put up a one and a half story log cabin on the south side, with a shed attached to hold the booze. To deflogisticate the liquor, he hitched the casks and barrels to the water-wagon and enfeebled the stuff with aqua pura to such a degree that it would freeze o' nights. An early morning customer was tickled to see the good Amos kick a long icicle off the spigot. That ice wore high colors, too, like a red-purple over-ripe nose. Patrons grew censorious because the liquor was so affected by chronic fatigue, he lost his business and went to Richmond. But Amos was a much more honorable retailer than later dealers who used to drain into their casks rain-water from barrels at the house corner, and soaks complained of wigglers, the larvae of mosquitoes, that tickled their throats and nested in the holes of their teeth. Besides, these dealers slipped into the barrels of whisky, enfeebled by water, such compensatory condiments as plug tobacco, rusty nails, red and green peppers, pints of red and black ants, etc., to give tang, bite and qui vive to the juice, and by the time a man got four or five fingers of that hot lava in his system he fancied he was a company of Wide Awakes marching gloriously in a torchlight procession. By morning the enthusiast was cured of his delusion, though his head was as big as the dome on a building full of clanging bells. Amos had an honest wife, who made for sale delicious pies, cakes, etc.

1840-41.—Our first doctor, George H. Stone, came in one of those years, the record being uncertain. His brother Hiram was sheriff.

In '41 a one-story sixteen by thirty-two frame was built by Emily Carmichael, the Malin corner site of the present Columbia pharmacy. An addition to the south took in Dr. M. C. Parker, and Dr. Wm. H. Rousseau above both. For years this was a fine fire-trap and rat and cockroach retreat.

John Cameron had a grocery and whisky joint in the south room of the tavern here, and it was said that his whisky was water-wetter than the load of elm that Dr. Rousseau got from a Sockum Ridge debtor, who had shaken his teeth out in ague fits. Meeting him a few months later, the doctor gravely asked him if he had any more of that same sort of wood and could spare another load. "Yes." "Well, bring it, just one load, for that would put hell out." Folks got down on Cameron, a temperance society was formed, and he moved his joint out.

I have thus traced, as closely as the records bear witness, the families that came to this county from 1835 to 1840 inclusive. In 1840, the population was one thousand five hundred and ninety-four. That is a good many, con-

MARGARET MORRISON YOUNG

MARGARET MUNCE PALMER

SAMUEL ROBERT PALMER

sidering the problem of transportation. There were no railroads, or canals, or stage coaches. Aside from the rivers, there was "the long blue wagon" hauled by oxen, and many came horseback or afoot. Ten years later we scored four thousand nine hundred and fifty-seven. The Rock Island road came in '58, and in that decade we jumped to fourteen thousand two hundred and thirty-six. It is curious about emigration—as a rule, folk go on in the plane they start in, like a bicycle. Most of our immigrants came from our latitude in the east. Northern Europeans strike north of us, while Italians and Spaniards prefer the south, California and Mexico. We got men from Illinois, Indiana, Ohio, Pennsylvania, some from New York, but not many from the extreme north or south. At that time the river could be crossed only at Dubuque, Davenport, Muscatine, Burlington and Keokuk, and land-seekers, once across, usually made a bee-line west from the ferry. When, later, they could cross at New Boston, settlers followed the Iowa river, instead of the Des Moinės, as formerly.

I may be wrong, but the real pioneer period runs from '35 to '41. Many important men came soon after, but they were rather settlers than pioneers. Our civic condition was nebulous until the early forties; there was no politics in the thirties; we did not bother about such things. But in '41 a web of civil, if not of political, relations began to form, as crystals shoot into ice at the right temperature. Iowa was in a formative state from, say, 1841 to 1846 when she was admitted into the union. Constitution had been adopted, counties, townships and school districts established, popular education provided for, churches organized. We could not amount to much until we had numbers. In 1838 we had but two hundred and eighty-three folks, and they were trying to make a live of it. They would not have succeeded, at first, if the Lord had not provided them their meat in due season, secured by their own dogs and guns. If they had been conscientious vegetarians, they would have starved. And this brings me to the caption of this chapter. What did we have in this county as assets, we pioneers, from '35 to '41?

Any approximate inventory of blessings would have included these items:

Soil.—Most excellent, unrivalled for depth, richness, fertility, ease of cultivation. Outside the timber belt, no stumps, or roots, or stones disturbed the breaking plow. On the alluvial bottoms the soil was twenty-four to forty-eight inches deep, eighteen to twenty-four on the undulating prairie, and the lime in it makes it stick closer than a brother. The vegetable mould that had accumulated for centuries could not be exhausted in a hundred years by the most reckless farming. The land stands drought well. There is a bed of bluish clay down twenty to thirty feet, that makes a perfect well-pocket. The sole criticism on the soil is, it is so good it defies the making of good roads. We have worked at roads for seventy-five years, and the more the traffic, the worse they got, in wet seasons. It is always a poor country that has ideal roads.

This soil grew any and everything but cotton, bananas and citrus fruits. All the cereals and legumes, vegetables, grasses, trees, fruits of the temperate zone, grew by magic. Wheat easily produced thirty to fifty bushels per acre, oats seventy-five, corn fifty-nine to ninety. Till weevil and chintz bug took the wheat, thirty to forty years after the pioneer period, no one imported flour. Even now, many a farmer raises enough wheat to bread his family, and to spare. But from the first corn was king. It was not aborigine, however, though it is mis-called "Indian." The redskins raised "maize," a thing that nature started as a grass, "zea mays." She changed her mind and promoted it from a fodder to a human food. Her second thought was best, as our after-thoughts are apt to be. Indians in North and South America would learn the merit of the sweet cobbed ear as soon as woodpecker and robin caught the excellence of cherries reddening on a tree, or a squirrel the worth of a nut.

The first thing the Pilgrims stumbled on, on Cape Cod, was an Indian cache of corn. They took it, but paid for it. Before Boston "knew beans" it gnawed corn off the cob, and parched the kernels. Parched corn was the Indian ration on the war-path—it was more portable than their birch bark canoes—far more portable than prisoners that, on a pinch, they ate.

Every September, as the shocks of corn are set up in wigwam form on our boundless Iowa lands, we are reminded, by these pleasing forms, that corn, our staple crop, is an Indian memorial. Few races have been so happy in the relics they have left us, as the Indians. The stone axes, the flint and quartz arrow-heads—what imperishable and beautiful things are these survivals of the American Stone Age! Architecture has no such staying qualities. Cities pulverize, cities rise on the debris of former cities, tier on tier of cities; columns fall and go to wreck and crumble; pompous tombs disappear; but our plows keep turning up darts and axes, and they are as sound and clean as they were ten, twenty, or who knows how many thousands of years ago. And this annual that the squaws planted, and tended to the roasting-ear and succotash stage is a still more lasting memorial. The seed keeps it a perennial, as deathless as the Norse tree Ygdrasil, the Ash Tree of Existence.

What a happy-go-lucky thought it was in the white man to shock corn in the shape of a wigwam! It is an annual tribute to the memory of the Indians. There is nothing in our autumnal landscapes more charming than these mimic wickiups, broad-based, tied at the top with a pumpkin vine. As

W. W. KENDALL

A. H. GUZEMAN

SAMUEL CONNER

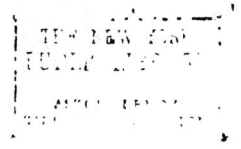

you drive by the fields filled with these rude imitation tents, musing sympathetically on the vanished red race, glad that this compliment is paid unconsciously to it, your fancy sees a subtile smoke rising from the center of the sheaf of tassels, and you are persuaded that if you pawed away the butts, papooses would be seen rolling in the dirt around the fire-pots. The illusion is all the stronger when snow is on the ground. Glance over a whited field—the wigwams suggest an Indian village.

The red men left us no books, no score of music, no sculpture, or paintings that were more permanent than picture-writing on skins, bark or rocks; they left no monuments; but they did hand down this classic corn. It is tender to frost and heat, but it persists like that transient fugitive breath called language. You cannot kill a wise spoken or written word. "It comes down generation after generation, as if God brought it in his hand."

The institutions, literature, laws, art, that other nations have left, have not a tithe of the commercial value of this Indian legacy. It has sugar, starch, fatty matter, flesh-forming materials that are transmuted into beef, pork and mutton, not to mention whisky.

No other grain, except rice, is eaten by more people than corn. Think of the corn-bread, johnny-cake, hoe-cake, tortilla, mush, puddings, roasting-ears, etc.—infinite in amount.

Corn had many uses, but not as many as the palm, which was said to have three hundred and sixty uses. We use corn for food, fodder, fuel, make from it alcohol, pipes, oil to burn, mattresses, mats, etc., and what fiddles boys make of it!

Don't you like to see a man gnawing corn off a cob? After buttering and salting it, he seizes either end with an energetic hand, and you'd think he is playing a mouth organ.

Even more amusing is the sight of a cow mouthing a big ear. She turns her head from side to side, rolls up her eyes in ecstasy, wraps her rough tongue around the slippery member, and her gums slide over it, and it sounds much like the playing on a corn-stalk-fiddle.

What a fool a hog, a steer is, to gorge itself, day after day, month after month, with corn, to fatten itself—for death.

Bless the Indians for our corn. How could Mrs. Mary Lease advise the Oklahomans to "raise less corn and more hell?"

Good Drinking Water.—In the early time springs gushed on almost every farm, at the foot of a hill. Most of them have ceased, and it is a pity. A spring bubbling under the roots of a tree, and stealing down a run-way, leaving an intense ribbon of green, was a symbol of life. Wells were made at convenient depths. The water in creeks and rivers at first was wholesome.

Streams had not been contaminated with farm drainage, factory refuse and city sewage. It was the age of innocence.

Timber.—Plenty to furnish raw material for all the log cabins, fences, fire-places, furniture, coffins, etc. There were fourteen to sixteen varieties of oaks, white and black walnut, hickory, sycamore, hard and soft maple, locust, dogwood, mulberry, linn, hackberry, and the like. And the settlers soon found that a dense woodland could be grown anywhere in a few years, and the groves as wind-breaks changed the expression of the entire face of the country, so that the prairie disappeared, and "lone tree" lost its significance as a land-mark.

Climate.—We have four seasons. The Pacific coast and most of our south have but two seasons: we are twice as rich, and perhaps a country that might boast eight seasons would rank all others. Three of these four seasons are free enough from frost to ripen all the products of the soil. The elevation of the county ranges from six hundred and sixty feet to seven hundred and fifty feet above sea-level. The winters are exhilarating, and never too severe save for invalids; the cold cuts all the cobwebs of malaria out of the crystal air. People who patronize the air and breathe it properly do not have consumption, but cure their lungs, if weak. Winters should have such an edge as to quicken foot-steps. Young people and all under middle age do not mind snow and cold—they sleigh-ride, sitting in straw on the bottom of the box, feet and legs stuck straight out, under quilts, blankets, buffalo robes, and keep warm by those pleasing arm and labial exercises that all remember—yes, you do, I don't care how old, demure and grouchy you may have become. Pshaw! what's cold? A mere meteor that you forget as soon as you step inside. Sleigh rides are a proper meter of winter climate—anything that "spoons" can stand, goes.

Winter weather records have been kept by Mr. Wm. A. Cook, government observer, since 1882. The average January temperature since then was from four to twenty above at seven a. m. The first snow never came earlier than October 20, and later than March 31. From December 14 to February 23, the below zero temperature ranged from 8 to 32.

The springs have a touch of languor at first, that some call "fever," but they are delicious. A spring on an Iowa prairie is Paradise. Flowers, birds, bees, odors come in mobs, and fairly riot. Everybody outside asylums writes poetry then—just can't help it.

Summer is rich and decidedly warm, but how else can we grow corn? Mr. Cook's record of highest temperature since 1883 gives two June days of ninety-six and ninety-nine degrees; eighteen July days from eighty-one to one hundred and eight, and eight August days from ninety-two to ninety-

HUGH SMITH

JONATHAN H. WILSON

MICHAEL W. WILSON

eight and five-tenths. Usually, the heat is mitigated by an all-day breeze. Perhaps there may be two or three muggy nights when sleep is banished, unless one stalks out into the dim and stilly watches of the night, on the north side of the hydrant, with hose attached, and lets 'er go!

The autumns are delightful; crops ripen and are safely gathered, and every one can play in the corn field bowling alley, sending pumpkins with a vim at Thanksgiving day. The Indian summers are glorious. They are the very choicest things the red folk left us—thanks! Since 1886, according to Mr. Cook, frost has pinched not earlier than September 1. White frosts through that month and October. The last frosts in Cook's period ranged from April 16 to June 2, though only twice in June.

In the first five years not a single case of consumption originated here, but weak and diseased lungs, imported, were cured in hundreds of cases by folk being in the air and sunlight. Fireplaces ventilated log cabins. No stoves were seen by Mr. McCall in Crawford township before '46, and Job McClelland first sold stoves here, on the north side, in 1848, Mr. Samuel Conner thinks. Later comers brought stoves with them from the east.

Breaking up the sod let loose miasm, and folks shook with chills and fever or bone-break, and many became "bilious," as they called it, and had "yaller janders," in the vernacular of that day. Norman Everson made himself an angel of light as a volunteer nurse when so many were ailing. Dr. Rousseau said he was the best nurse he ever knew. Cabins in the woods got dark, dank and noisome, and dwellers on low lands shook like peat beds, and marshes were sore neighbors. Pioneers should have been healthy, but there was a lot of malarial sickness, and there always is in breaking up the rich virgin soil. After the deadly gases from fermenting vegetation had exhaled, the country was salubrious indeed.

Rainfall.—Since 1876, Mr. Cook makes an average of thirty and two one-hundredths inches. The highest notch was forty-nine and eighty-six one-hundredths in 1902. The greatest single fall was four and ninety-one one-hundredths. Plentiful precipitation may be depended on, and ordinarily rains are well timed.

Lay of the Land.—The county is undulating, and drains well, to the south and south-east. From the north line to the southern, the slope or grade is some ninety feet.

Streams.—The county is well watered. Of rivers, the Iowa, English, Skunk; creeks, Crooked, Long, Davis, Goose. There was another creek, but it got lost, and should have been advertised for, with suitable reward for return of the same. John B. Newhall, in his "Sketches of Iowa," issued in 1841, has this amusing paragraph:

"Washington is the seat of justice of Washington county. It contains about one hundred inhabitants, is handsomely situated near one of the tributaries of Crooked creek, is twenty-nine miles from Iowa city, and promises to become a thriving and important town."

Local geographers like Colonel Charles J. Wilson believes this "tributary" was the run that cuts through Colonel Scofield's grounds and scoots down below Jugenheimer's extinct brewery. Maybe, it dried up when said brewery did.

In pioneer days those water courses were clear as New England and Colorado brooks, because the whole county was in grass, that prevented soil-wash, and the infinite maze and mesh of rootlets held back the streams, and freshets were not destructive. As a consequence, and because dams did not obstruct, there were myriads of fishes, good ones, too, ready to rise to the hook whenever sputum was ejaculated on the bait. The pioneers caught speckled trout—what would you think of that? and white perch, black and rock bass, pike, catfish, shad, red and white horse-sucker, muscalonge, sturgeon, eels, etc. Sports were not put off with shiners, minnies, bull-heads and "crawfish."

Game.—There was everything but buffalo; Indians had chased them seventy-five to one hundred miles west of us, but plenty of elk, deer, some bear, squirrels, 'possum, 'coon and ground-hog remained, and vast flocks of wild turkeys, prairie chickens, passenger pigeons, quail and wild aquatic fowl. Men driving from this town, on the Crawfordsville road, shot mallard ducks in a pond about opposite our opera house. There were no panthers or bob cats, and but few gray wolves, but the smaller prairie wolves were native and plentiful. Otters and even beaver still survived, and muskrats and rabbits galore; venison was a very commonplace dish, and buckskin was worn by most men.

Fruits, Berries, Etc.—A world of these wild things, berries black and straw, and sweeter far than our cultivated kinds. Not everything improves by fussing with it. "Doubtless God could make a better berry than the strawberry, but doubtless God never did," was said by the Spaniard, not about our modern big sour strawberries, but of the small sweet bits that reddened the ground everywhere. Blackberries stood like grinning pickaninnies in all fields and on the margins of all woods, and a great deal of sparking was done, picking 'em. Girls picked their aprons and sun-bonnets full in a few minutes, and strung raspberries on blue-stem grass stalks six to ten feet tall, such pretty rosaries—the maids could count their prayers by eating off the string a red or black berry, and stain their lips a still more bewitching color. A world, too, of crab-apples, plums, grapes, persimmons, all wild, but suddenly tamed into glory by the house-wives. Waste no sympathy on those women for lacking preserves, jams and things. And the wild honey, nectar from hollow trees, flavored with prairie flowers! Why are wild things, whether animals or plants or fruits, so delicious, making all their tame cousins insipid? There was never a more gorgeous display of blooms on the globe than on our prairies, right here in pioneer days. They say bees and hollow trees were invented specially for Tommy Tucker. He gathered in one day one hundred and fifty gallons of honey, thirty pounds from one tree, and one hundred and twenty pounds of beeswax, and sold the honey at fifty cents per gallon and the wax at twenty-five cents a pound. "Can these things be, and overcome us like a summer cloud, without our special wonder?" Perhaps we think of the Scot, stumped by a whopper, who said, "Aiblins, they may be leears." Did an Ananias club flourish here from '35 to '41?

Rock, Clay.—Building rock, rich in fossil crinoids, and good brick clay abounded along Crooked creek, Skunk and English rivers.

On the natural side, the sole discount was lack of coal, but the settlers did not know it. As a rule, they had not burned it in the east. If coal once underlay this county, as is likely, it went many ages ago into the air, dipped out, thanks to the disintegration of the over-lying shales and the erosion of the drift by water, frost, gravity. Coal is found in the next county west, and abundantly in the county west of that. A few pockets of coal were found here and there in this county, and geologists claim that the color of our soil is due to the presence of ancient coal. The sand pits we find are the remains of the sandstones and shales that roofed the old coal beds, and they were pulverized eons ago.

I shall not be foolish enough to deny that the pioneers in the thirties and early forties had many discomforts and privations. Folks have them now, right here. But the hardships have been exaggerated, like the reports of Mark Twain's death. Uncle Billy Moore every year, at the anniversary meetings, used to bewail the old hard times, the suffering. Norman Everson denied and laughed at his hard-luck stories, and said that on the whole, the early settlers had a bully and corker of a time, as Roosevelt would express it. We must remember that folk do not miss things they were never used to. It would be tough for a rich family to drop into poverty. But does anyone suppose that Adam Ritchey, David Goble and the Moores and others were put out by the absence of bath tubs, closets, furnaces, cooking ranges, operas, Chautauquas, public libraries? Not a bit—they had never been in a tub, closet, opera house, or a course of lectures and amusements in their lives. To find none of those things here in the brush would be no deprivation or cause of unhappiness. Would they miss steam heat or electric light?

Absurd! They had been used to fire-places, iron cranes, hooks and pots and kettles, fire-dogs and Dutch ovens, and tallow candles or just wicks soaked in grease in saucers. To get warm at fire-places and cook by them would be familiar sensations. Probably, the main inconvenience in the thirties—and it was a serious and vexatious one—was the lack of grist mills, saw mills, roads, bridges. The first mills used no bolts, and there were no fanning mills; bread was as black as a Derby hat, and gritty, more like a baked black sand heap than the staff of life. But it was not an unwholesome diet. It astonished and acted on the alimentary canal like a King drag on bad roads, that's all.

What with their varieties of flesh, fruits, corn mushes, pones and johnny cake, pies, puddings, cobblers, etc., if any one tells me they did not live well, and feed their tape-worms abundantly, and wisely worship the belly-gods, I am from Missouri.

In the main, the "old settlers" were young settlers, robust, lusty, hearty, accustomed to out-door life and hard work. They were not dyspeptics, much less cadavers. Their blood ran rapidly, and was full of red and white corpuscles. They did not feel cold as we do when we step out of our hot houses. Their cabins rarely exceeded sixteen by sixteen feet, and half a dozen people in such a room would take the chill off from it by the mere radiation of their body heat. They did not often take cold, and their noses were presentable. Handkerchiefs were not the main things in the laundry. They made snuffers of thumb and fore-finger and blew their noses as they snipped the snuff off the wick on a tallow dip. If there are any colds, grippe, influenza going, we degenerates are sure to take them, for that red-hot, oxygen-consuming iron dragon in the cellar has made us effeminate. As fire kept all night in those big fire-places, it was not martyrdom to dress in cold mornings. The brick or stone jambs and hearths exhaled heat all night, and the breaths of the family in the small room that such huge-throated chimneys ventilated, raised the temperature of the room. Of all modern discomforts, since we have quit taking exercise to keep warm, a sense of cold leads. In a frigid room, to shed gown or pajamas and pull on a union suit that is as cold as a horse's frosty bridle bits, is the Ultima Thule of discomfort, unless it be the scud in bare feet over oil-cloth carpet, to a refrigerated bed room. We suffer lots more from cold in our houses than the old settlers did in their small log cabins, where dogs and cats also shed caloric into the general fund. A log house is warmer than our frame houses, made of woods so far from a seasoned state that in a year or two window sash and doors gape and let in cold like a sieve. On the whole, the old settlers did not ask for sympathy. Healthy people dislike to be pitied. What folks, especially in hard lines,

MARY W. ASHBY
First Teacher

need, is the stimulus of good cheer. The old settlers had a good time—all the evidence points that way, as the hearty amusements they enjoyed with mighty relish, the singing and spelling schools, the husking bees plus the red ear, the kissing parties, the gossipy quiltings, the "settings up," the house and barn raisings, the love affairs, and the hilarious country weddings, the hops, the traipsing far to church, to throw sheep's eyes at each other and let the poky preacher go braugh. They had a deal of hard work to do, but no matter how much drudgery there may be in constant work, it does not eat as the rust and acids of the ennui of modern, well-to-do life corrodes the leisure class.

Besides, the old settlers did not know they were uncomfortable. A Kansan truly says that when he was a boy he walked nearly two miles every day in winter to school, across a wind-swept prairie, wore no overcoat and protected his hands only by keeping them in his pockets. Frequently he froze his ears, and occasionally his fingers and toes, but nobody ever sympathized with him, or seemed to think his experiences unusual. "My youngest sister is a sophomore in high school and is equipped with all the appurtenances for fighting the weather. But if it happens to be misting when she starts to school in the morning, the family worries all day for fear she will catch her death of cold."

Speaking of eels, they were delicious food, and to catch one was good fortune. A woman had a husband who was "no 'count," though a fisherman. He disappeared, and for days it was not known whether he had deserted or was drowned. A corpse was dragged ashore, and while the woman was identifying the swollen body, a lot of eels ran out of the mouth of her deceased. She walked calmly away, and when asked what should be done with the body, she said: "Set him again—he is good to catch eels, and for nothing else—set him again in the river."

CHAPTER VI.

GETTING ON—LAND.

The Indian titles extinguished and the Indians gone, or going, the transfer of ownership and the plantation of Washington county were made in the thirties, and, as said above, the real pioneer period, the picturesque, interesting part of the pioneer era was, in this county, from 1835 to 1841. Emigrants kept coming in the forties, and the fifties, and even in the sixties, but the real old settlers, the genuine stuff that would be recognized by the Pure Food law, and none genuine unless their names were blown in the bottle, were the men, women and children who can read their titles clear to a place in the Pioneer Book, bearing the imprint of the thirties and the first two years of the forties. It was fitting that picturesque whites should follow picturesque reds. Let us now take leave of the Indians. They were in the child stage of development, their villages pure democracies. Like the whites, they were full of human nature, and were good and bad, believers in miracles and magic, and scoffers, cowards and braves, no more the idyllic creatures that Cooper paints in his novels than are we the superior beings the actors depict in melodrama. Hornady knew the redskins well, and says, "If an Indian is not picturesque, why is he? Ethnologically, he is a squeezed lemon, and is welcome to a long rest. Indian guides are handicaps, and not dependable—leave you in the lurch, desert you." But they were artists in dress and poets in naming people. Think of Chief Mahaska, lord of seven wives, calling his beautiful favorite "Raut-che-wai-me," female flying pigeon—Jane, for short.

The best thing I know about an Indian is told of Seconodoah, an Oneida chief, who planted apple trees and tended them so well that from 1791 they bore fruit, and were still in good bearing condition, one hundred and twenty years old.

The pioneers came here ostensibly for land, and they came before surveys were made and land offered for sale, and did not wait for surveyors and auctioneers, and staked out claims and improved them, built cabins and fences, broke prairie, felled woods, and, for mutual protection, in making and holding claims, formed "claim associations," "land clubs," etc., their constitutions and by-laws and resolutions being for pioneers the law of the land. Our pioneers were orderly, and, though they did form such organizations, it was to keep cut-throats from jumping their claims before the public land sales.

A Few Convenient Dates.—Let us see what was going on in this county before any white owned land. Paste this table of events in your hat.

First Indian treaty for land, September 1, 1832.

Second treaty for land, October 21, 1837.

Third treaty for land, October 11, 1842.

First settler, Adam Ritchey, 1835-6.

Birth first white child, Isabelle Ritchey, June 12, 1837.

First marriage, Hulock-Goble, Sunday morning, early in 1837.

County named and boundaries set, January 25, 1839.

Washington located as county-seat, June, 1839.

County formally organized, 1839.

First land entered by Matthew Moorhead, September 11, 1839.

First land transfer, C. D. Haskell to Abe Owens, Dec. 31, 1839.

First mortgage, David Bunker-M. Moorhead, Oct. 3, 1839.

First chattel mortgage, Dan Powers-Allen Philips, December 14, 1839.

First saw and grist mills, Holcomb-Bullock, 1837, 1839.

First mail to Washington, March 10, 1839.

First land sale in Burlington for this county, March, 1840.

First school house, on Tom Baker's claim, 1840, teacher Mattie J. Crawford; followed by Mattie Junkin, children before that going across line to Henry county, to a Miss Smith from New England.

Court house built, July, 1841.

First newspaper, The Argus, 1854.

Celebration of completion of Rock Island road to Washington, September 1, '58.

What were people doing between Ritchey's coming in 1836 and the first land sale in 1840?

In truth, those organizations and clubs tell the story in a whisper. The settlers took claims, went to work on them, made cabins and fences, broke prairie, slashed the timber, planted and gathered crops, lived, laughed, loved, married, just as if they had bought the land. Now and then a trespasser did jump a claim, but the settler, rousing his neighbors who were fellow-members of those protective associations, made it hot for the intruder. Bloody noses and broken heads were incidents not unknown. Those clubs served just such a purpose as our anti-horse-thief associations in later years.

WASHINGTON WOOLEN MILL

The first land sales for Washington and other counties were held in March, October and December, 1840, in Burlington. Big crowds, but little money, and but few pieces were entered in this county, in March, and they by such forehanded men as Holcomb. J. L. L. Terry, accredited to Oregon township, bid them in. In October and December, some of the choicest lands in the south-east and central parts of this county were bought. As it is a good way to learn who was here and who was who, in 1840, the list of buyers is entered here. Some of the men, like John Graham, bought several tracts.

CRAWFORD TOWNSHIP.

John and Wm. Marsden, M. G. Maize, John Hendree, Daniel Hervey, Richard Hudson, Anthony Smith, W. B. Sexton, John and Robert Neal, John Lyen, W. C. Kinnear, Robert Jamison, Wm. Huston, Wm. and James Wooley, W. R. Wallace, James G. P. McElroy, Margaret Denholm, James Woodworth, David Haines, Jesse Botkin, James McCulley, John Crawford, James Colwell, George, Rebecca P., Mary and Catherine Gearhart, Wm. B. Sexton, Matthew Moorhead, James T. Playmate, Solomon and Wm. McCulley, W. H. Knott, Samuel Pence, Isaac Waldriss.

OREGON TOWNSHIP.

John Hendee, John Hendel, R. W. Burton, Isaac Mills, Wm. Stronoch, A. and John Hulick, Samuel Stephens, M. G. Mize, David Goble, J. D. Welch, Anthony Smith, Hiram Peabody, Wm. Marsden, Geo. W. Ferguson.

MARION.

Thomas Evans, Benj. Tucker, Baalam Anderson, Sam Hanby, Michael Senff, Mr. Lambreth, J. H. Randolph, James Dawson, J. S. Dill, Adam Ritchey, Henry Williams, John Graham, John Armstrong, Geo. Dill, I. M. Whitsol, Alvin Saunders, Robert Clemens, Wm. and Richard Hudson, Jos. Buffington, Thaddeus Moore, Noah Parrish, Allen Philips, Ezekiel Cooper, Jacob Westfall, Aaron Conger, Wm. L. Essley, Lyman Whitcomb, Claudius Hendrix, Nesley Rumble, Cyrus McMillen, M. Holcomb, Lee O. Plunkett, Wm. I. Springston, Milton Benson.

WASHINGTON TOWNSHIP.

Jos. B. Rodgers, Michael Hayes, Jas. Dawson, Jesse Botkin, John Hendee, Simon Teeple and Richard Moore, commissioners of Washington county, Jas.

W. Isett, Wm. Conner, Wm. Basey, Nathan and Thos. Baker, Jonathan Wilson, Jas. DeLong, Jesse Ashby, Wm. B. Thompson, John Graham, Jas. McCulley, Amos Moore, Baalam Anderson.

This first real estate record is still extant, a half quire of foolscap stitched and covered with brown wrapping paper, the first record in it dated October 1, 1839, the last April 11, 1840, so that all the real estate transactions in the county for the first six months occupied less than six sheets. J. B. Davis was the first recorder. The first real estate transfer was the English river mill site, December 31, 1839, C. D. Haskell to Abe Owens, one hundred dollars for a third interest. The last entry in that book is in 1840, Thomas and Nathan Baker, conveying eighty-five and seventy-two one-hundredths acres, their claims which were a part of the site of Washington, for four hundred dollars. Acknowledgment before John J. Jackson, J. P., April 11, 1840.

Surveying took a lot of time. The township lines 74 and 75 north, were run before May, 1837, and the details were several years filling in.

Land hunger is supposed to be a keen appetite in the Anglo-Saxon race. But millions do not seem to have that hunger at all, do not own homes, or even lots in the cemetery. Mechanics, teachers, doctors, lawyers, ministers did not care to stake out claims and buy them in, in the sales in Burlington, Iowa city and Fairfield. They did not realize that this vast country could ever be settled, or that the land would appreciate, get scarce, become a thing to conjure with and speculate in. How could folk get here? Boat transportation was inadequate; they were just beginning to build railroads, but people could not conceive that this continent would be belted by steam roads. Foreign immigration had not set in; horses and oxen could not haul in enough emigrants to fill this great west. The government price of land, one dollar and twenty-five cents per acre, was held quite high enough. Had the settlers been told by credible authority that farms here would in that century sell at one hundred dollars to one hundred and fifty dollars per acre, they would have dropped dead of apoplexy in squads, in sheer surprise and shock. So, many were indifferent, and neglected to buy. Why, just see—do half the folk in this city now own their homes, or a lot in the bone-yard, not to mention farms? Probably not, and it is so everywhere now just as it was then, though we know well enough that real estate has not near reached its height, and will double and treble during this century. However, a good share of the comers did want land, and it may be well to tell at once how it was acquired.

In the new states and territories, the lands owned by the federal government are surveyed and sold under one general system. Meridian lines are first established, running north from the mouth of some noted river, and these are intersected by base lines. The Iowa surveys were made from the same meridian and base lines as the Arkansas and Missouri surveys. The fifth principal meridian is a line running due north from the mouth of the Arkansas river, crossing Missouri state and river, running over a part of Illinois and entering Iowa in township 77 north, and, passing through Iowa, intersects the Mississippi river again in township 91 north, where it ends. The base lines from which all townships in Arkansas, Missouri and Iowa are numbered, run west from the mouth of the St. Francis river in Arkansas, cutting the fifth principal meridian at right angles, and from this base line townships are numbered northwardly and southwardly, and all surveyed townships in Iowa number north of the base line. The principal meridian and its corresponding base lines having been formed for a district of country, the surveyor divides it into townships six miles square; townships are subdivided into square miles or tracts of six hundred and forty acres each, or sections. Sections are divided into halves by a north and south line, and into quarters by a transverse line. Quarters are sold in equal divisions of eighty and subdivisions of forty acres each. So any settler could for one hundred dollars buy an eighty and get title from the government. Sections or square miles are numbered, beginning at the northeast corner of the township and run west to the range line, then back east to range line, alternately, ending at the southeast corner of township, from 1 to 36. By this nice system, all divisions are in mathematical forms. When surveyed, government lands are offered at one dollar and twenty-five cents per acre, cash. All lands so bought are exempt from taxes for five years. The sixteenth section in each township is reserved for school uses.

An old settler saw a desirable tract and took steps to get it; he broke five acres, which held the claim six months, or built a cabin eight logs high, with a roof, which was equivalent to the plowing, and that held it for six months more; he stakes out a half section as a full claim, part timber and part prairie —his home is secure from trespass, as the claim cannot be safely jumped. He can sell the claim, transferring all his rights to the buyer. Each township had its societies for dealing with jumpers.

In 1838, congress put Iowa and Wisconsin in one survey district; G. W. Jones made all the surveys and proclaimed land sales in Burlington November 19, A. C. Dodge register; twenty-five townships were offered; in Muscatine three, Louisa one, Des Moines and Jefferson three each, Van Buren six—total, two hundred and ninety-five thousand dollars worth. This, with later public sale entries, private sales and pre-emptions, up to June, 1840, amounted to a million. In eighteen months government sold two and a quarter millions. Only gold, silver, and Missouri bank notes in denomination twenty dollars, United States treasury notes, and military land scrip were received in payment. All the claim-owners in the several townships attended en masse, with some one agreed upon to bid off in their own names the land marked and registered to each man. Men camped out and made a time of it. Speculators were there to loan settlers money at fifty per cent. That is, the capitalist would enter the land in his own name and file a bond for a deed. At the end of two years the settler got the land by paying double its original cost. Two men thus loaned one hundred thousand dollars each. There must have been a lot of poor devils.

The land rushes then were just like those made in our time. For weeks and months prior to May 1, 1843, when the last of the redskins were to evacuate the country hereabouts, the border was thick with settlers and their flocks and herds, eager to break for claims, and they and their families made a rush; from midnight till sun-up, on May Day, the whole country was dotted with claimants, every man singing, "For I'm to be queen o' the May, call me early, mother dear." As early as 1836-7 the roads in Indiana and Illinois were crowded with "long blue wagons" of emigrants, ten, twenty, thirty wagons in a string, hogs, cows, horses, dogs, women, kids trailing behind. Westward the star of empire takes its way; it never has gone east, always west.

A Land Sale.—Let's look in on a sale: The set day comes; settlers from all directions are in, crowding the taverns, sleeping on settles, in wagons, on the floor, in the bar-room, stable, anywhere, sleeping in their clothes. There were no hotels in those days; public houses were just taverns. Men now eighty and ninety years old habitually say "tavern" yet. The differences between a tavern and, say, Hotel Coronado or Astor or Palmer House are these: The landlord of a tavern is a jolly Boniface in dirty shirt sleeves, a shrewd fellow, a good judge of a horse, and a keen trader, not over-scrupulous, smelling of the barn, a straw for a toothpick in his mouth. His manner is free, and he sings out, "Hello, Brown, h're ye, old hoss," as he whacks Brown on the back. He takes a drink, at Brown's expense, and a cigar at Smith's expense, in his own bar room. The dining room is a free-for-all—all the stuff is put on the table at once, and guests are told to "jest fall-to and help yerself." Food is not served in courses at taverns, and there is no napkin or finger bowl. The waitress is busy keeping the flies off you, by waving a bush she broke off a fruit tree in the yard. A cat or two rubs against your leg, looks in your face and remarks Meough! and a melancholy long-eared dog watches the guests shoveling in stuff with case knives shoved to the hilt. In the evening the landlord, who is clerk and all, sees you to bed in a stuffy room, carrying a guttering candle eclipsed with snuff, or a saucer-like dish holding melted grease, and a wick hanging out of it, lolling over the edge like a leather latch string from a log cabin door, or the tongue of a hot dog or ox.

CALEB S. CLEAVES

JESSE ASHBY

R. W. McELROY
Charter Member Masonic Lodge

SAMUEL BIGGER
County Judge

There's no style about a tavern—it is a pure democracy, simplicity gone to seed.

But a public that has hotel in front and house after its name is swell. You will know the clerk by the loud diamond flaming on his shirt front, or by his air of hauteur and his indifference or scorn. I have never got over being scared by the manners of these superior beings.

Then, too, at a tavern everything is fried except the coffee and slough water. The skillet is what knocks at taverns. The landlord might hang it up in the office over the placard, "in hog signo." The meats, eggs, toast, potatoes, are fried, and reek with grease. The hired girl takes pains to put a few of her hairs in the butter.

However, the settler is up early, washes hands and face in a tin dish outdoors, and fortifies himself with ham and eggs for the stress of the day. His claim is cried off to him, and if he has saved up the price he opens the old saddle-bags and counts two hundred dollars or four hundred dollars, takes a certificate from the government, and is set up by the consciousness that a bit of this globe is his very own. At one such sale, which lasted three weeks, the land office took in about half a million dollars. Up to September 30, 1851, the land sales in Iowa—thirty-two million three hundred eighty-five thousand six hundred acres—yielded Uncle Sam four million five hundred and seventy-four thousand six hundred and thirty-six dollars and nineteen cents. Subtracting the total expenses of Iowa territory, five hundred and eighty-five thousand eight hundred and sixty-seven dollars and forty cents, and deducting Iowa's pro rata share of the Louisiana Purchase, five hundred and seventy-nine thousand three hundred ninety-eight dollars and ninety-six cents, left a balance of three million four hundred and sixty-nine thousand three hundred eighty-nine dollars and eighty-three cents, contributed by Iowa to the general government.

Congress, on May 20, 1785, provided for surveys of all public lands, dividing the land into townships six miles square, the ranges of the same to be numbered from Pennsylvania boundaries west, and the townships themselves to be numbered north from a point on the Ohio river due north of western termination of the southern boundary of Pennsylvania. The townships were divided into thirty-six sections, each a mile square. This was the origin of our good system of surveying, dividing and describing public lands. The system is now substantially as then. After surveys were made and recorded, the lands in certain limits were offered for sale at not less than one dollar and twenty-five cents per acre. In one year a million acres were acquired by treaty from Indians of various tribes. Within a year after the northwest territory was organized under the ordinance of 1787, twenty thousand people had settled in that region forever devoted to freedom, viz., Ohio, Indiana, Illinois, Michigan and Wisconsin.

Our 'Squire J. L. L. Terry helped survey in 1837 two tiers of townships, 74 and 75, to the boundary of the Black Hawk Purchase. His party were bothered by drunken Indians at Wapello. They visited the Indian village at what was later the W. G. Stewart farm, a mile from this city, whose chief Poweshiek was off with Keokuk and Wapello to Washington, D. C., and White Fish, who was left in charge, was very mean and arbitrary, saying to this one and that, "Puck-a-she, che-mo-ke-mon," get out of my wickiup, white man. All that Terry's party wanted was a few kinds words—and a chance to rasp the scales and fins off from the said White Fish.

The survey of township 74, range 6, was finished September 10, 1837, of township 74, range 7, September 25, '37, of township 75, range 6, October 21, '37, of township 76, range 6, November 14, '37. Probably, all the land in this county was surveyed before the winter of 1837, except township 77, range 9, up Wellman way, which the government did not acquire by treaty until 1842.

By common consent a few parcels were entered in 1839, to-wit, by Matthew Moorhead and David Goble, and by Simon Teeple and Richard Moore, commissioners of the county. Meanwhile, what were the settlers doing? Organizing, getting together, starting the civic machine. They had to organize to get roads, bridges, and manage local affairs. Steps at organizing began in 1838, but they were not ended. We were chaotic till January 25, 1839. The county was not named and its boundaries defined, as recorded in a preceding chapter, till three years after the coming of the first settler. In 1838 the territory of Iowa was divided from the territory of Wisconsin, and the next week this county was named Washington instead of Slaughter, and a commission was appointed to locate a county-seat, as heretofore stated. The land for a county-seat had to be entered, surveyed and platted, and a sale of lots ordered. The old board of commissioners, Joseph Neil and J. B. Davis, met at Richard Moore's, May 5, '39, to do this, and also divide the county into election precincts, as follows:

1. East Fork, townships 74 and 75, range 6, election at J. W. Neil's.

2. Crooked creek, township 74, range 7, at Holcomb's.

3. Skunk river, all country south of that river, election at Orson Kinsman's.

4. Walnut creek, country between Skunk river and center of prairie between said river and west fork Crooked creek, election at Robert Risk's.

5. Washington county between center of prairie between Skunk river and west fork of Crooked creek, and center of prairie between west fork

CITIZENS SAVINGS BANK
AND WEST SIDE OF PUBLIC SQUARE

MASONIC TEMPLE AND
NORTH SIDE OF PUBLIC SQUARE

aforesaid and English river, elections at Washington.

6. English river, elections at S. P. Teeple's.

These precincts are tell-tale of the settlements in the bush, on the water courses. Every body was on the water wagon, as it were.

The regular time to hold territorial and county elections was the first Monday in August, and the first officers to serve under the new organization were to be elected in August, 1840. The twenty-five judges of election got one dollar a day, each. Nathan Baker was chosen probate judge, D. Goble treasurer, Reuben Hiatt commissioner, J. B. Davis surveyor; commissioners, Richard Moore, S. P. Teeples, Morgan Hart.

The board ordered the town site to be entered at the land office, and it was done October 15, '39, and a sale of lots was advertised for August 19 and 24, to raise the financial wind, and twenty-four lots were sold at an average of thirty-eight dollars and fifteen cents, amounting to nine hundred and fifteen dollars and fifty cents. The yellow brick corner, fifty-four dollars; Hotel Colenso corner, seventy-two dollars; Temple corner, sixty-nine dollars; Klein corner, sixty-eight dollars; First U. P. church lot, thirty-one dollars. This meeting, unless it be the ordering of the election of the board, was the first movement of the cranks, pulleys and horse or other power of the civic machine.

City Credit Low.—When the county-seat was located, the board could hold the site only by pre-emption under United States law, and for title give a bond for a deed. They had to borrow money on their own personal liabilities. Capitalists had so bad an opinion of the poor town, they would not loan it money, though only two hundred dollars was needed to get title from the government. The board borrowed at twenty per cent, and had to go outside, at that, and as the law allowed but ten per cent, the other ten had to be made up by private subscription, and the members of the board paid the most of it. It ordered a second sale of lots June 16, 1840, one-fourth cash, the rest in three installments of six, twelve and eighteen months. Twenty-eight lots were sold for eight hundred and sixty-one dollars, the highest, fifty-four dollars, for the present Crail corner, and the average price was thirty dollars and seventy-five cents. Later buyers obligated themselves to build a good frame house not less than sixteen feet square on each lot, by June 16, 1841.

Court House.—On September 7, 1839, the board ordered the erection of a temporary court house, and James Neal contracted to build it for seven hundred and fifty-nine dollars, on Chilcote's corner, now Cook & Sherman. It was to be eighteen by twenty-eight, two stories, the lower one nine feet, the upper seven, joint shingles, weather-boarded with black walnut floors oak or walnut planks, one panel door below, and two batten doors above, one twenty-four-light window, four fifteen-light windows, and four twelve-light, the upper story to be partitioned in the middle for offices. All to be plastered. It was finished late in July, '41, and he was docked one hundred dollars. First court held there in November of that year. It was a very eclectic building. All church folk met there, turn about, and schools "took up" in it; it was town hall, tailor shop, offices of clerk, recorder and surveyor, and it was used several years by all peripatetic preachers, lecturers, showmen, freaks, fakirs and phrenologists fumbling heads at so much per skull. There was an outside stairs on the east. It lasted till 1848, when it was moved to the north of town and humiliated into a stable.

Quincy Adams said the first session of court was held in his house, but was he here then? It is also said that court No. 3 was held here June 17, 1839, no bills found, no cases for trial, no jury. In '40, grand and petit juries are reported, and most of the bills found were for liquor irregularities

Road Districts.—On April 7, 1840, the board divided the county into road districts, each surveyed township to be a district, and there were only seven in the county. At the July meeting, the board re-districted the county into voting districts, viz.:

1. Crawfordsville, the township of Crawford; 2. Long Creek, or Oregon; 3. Washington, the township; 4. Crooked Creek, present township of Marion; 5. Brighton, a small part of present Brighton and all of Clay; 6. Richland, what is now Richland in Keokuk county; 7. Walnut Creek; 8. Dutch Creek, same as township; 9. English River; 10. Iowa, the present township, plus Highland and part of Fremont township in Johnson county; 11. All west of English River; 12. Lime Creek, the present township and most of Cedar and Seventy-six. In April, '41, English River precinct was somewhat changed.

Ferries.—As there were no bridges, the board licensed, for two dollars, ferries to ply in high water at these fixed tolls: Footman, six and one-fourth cents; horse or mare, twelve and one-half cents; single horse and wagon, twenty-five cents; double, thirty-seven and one-half cents; each additional horse, twelve and one-half cents; live stock, any kind, six and one-fourth cents per head, drivers included; yoke oxen and wagon, thirty-seven and one-half cents; additional yoke, twelve and one-half cents; but this vexatious thing did not last long. Wm. Pickerel, T. J. Gordon and Thompson Dray ran ferries.

Jail.—Sin entered in, and we had to punish. Bids for a jail were opened in June, '41, and contract let to Alex. Lee, J. B. Davis and Thomas Baker. This bastile was to be a hewn log affair, two stories, sixteen by eighteen, lower story of double strength, and as solid as possible, the space between the walls six to eight inches, to be filled solid with broken stone the size of macadam; ceiling of hewn logs lying close together: the upper story a single wall thickness of logs; to cost one thousand and eighty dollars. Town orders should pay nine hundred and eighty-four dollars, and two town lots to count as thirty-six dollars. The lower room lined on the sides, ends and bottom with two-inch solid white, black or burr oak plank, spiked on with double ten-penny nails, four to the square foot in floor, and intermediate spaces in floor filled with six-penny nails, one to every square inch. The sides and ends to be spiked on with double-pennies, three tiers spiked to sides from bottom to top, viz., ends and middle of sides and ends, thirty-three spikes each. Floor to rest on tiers of hewn logs put together as overhead. Stairs on the north side, on outside reaching to a platform on a level with the upper floor, the only door to the building. In the middle of the upper floor a hatchway was cut, big enough to let a man go down on a ladder to the ground floor, and then the elevator was pulled up, and the poor devil left to his reflections, and to chew remorse if he had no tobacco or gum. Narrow grates could be opened for a feeble circulation of air, but the dungeon was dark, and the inmates could not see the landscape, and had no company but the ghosts and hobgoblins their imaginations created. "Leave hope behind, all ye who enter here," wrote Dante on the lintel to the door to hell. "Leave air behind, ye who go chuck into this black limbo where there is weeping and wailing and gnashing of teeth," seemed to be engraved on the wall of this piece of architecture, only one could hardly read it in the gloom. The board was not malicious or cruel aforethought, but they were shy on ideas of hygiene. A prisoner would exhaust the vital air in ten minutes, and suffer in that bath of carbonic acid gas like a mouse in an air-pump. The fact of that beastly black hole is a stain on our history. It must have smelled as loud as a menagerie and Noah's ark. Neither was Noah up in ventilation. The report that this was our second jail is no doubt false. C. J. Wilson has the big key to this bastile.

The sale of town lots paid for both jail and court house, without the levy of a cent of tax. This jail stood on lot 3 block 8, east of Sanford's livery stable, north of the square, and faced north. Bad crooks lodged below, trivial offenders above, and there was an occasional jail-delivery. Court once ordered a lot of rowdies into the upper room; toward morning they got out, but they waited for the jailer to come, when they impressed him into a bear dance with them, and so they discharged the contempt of court with a dose of impudence. After twenty years this bastile was declared a nuisance, and court ordered it removed. Everson tore it down.

Public Square.—The board, in October, 1841, contracted with Albert Sturges, for seventy dollars, to enclose the commons with a board fence, posts of white oak, six feet apart, four feet above ground and two feet in the ground, and one entrance gate in the middle of the south side. Not finished by April 1; his time was extended till July 1, but the job was never done, but why? will never be known. It remains one of the secrets lost.

The Trail of the Serpent.—The board, though composed of men who, later, became strong prohibitionists, granted liquor licenses to W. B. Thompson and John Cameron here, and others, at twenty-five dollars per quarter.

Mill and Fishery.—In 1840, Matthew D. Ritchey, Sr., built a saw mill on Crooked creek, on the site of the McFarland mill, three and a half miles south-east of this city. Most of the oak and walnut lumber for houses here was got out there. Later, he added machinery for carding wool, the first concern in the county, and it was kept busy. The dam arrested fish coming up to spawn, and it was a favorite resort for men and boys, using spears and clubs, and torches by night, and doubtless the first Ananias club was formed there—lying about the size and weight of the catch, especially of the big fish that got away. Imps would kick fishes into the moonlight, and the violet rays corrupted them. A fish simmering in moonshine is not a moonlight sonata. You know what the bait was. It had to be corked, but not to float, nor did it look a bit like a section of the prohibitory constitutional amendment. When there was a run of hoop-mouthed mullet or suckers, boys played shinny with 'em on the riffles, and the dull-thud blows sounded like the falls of Roosevelt's big stick.

Post Offices.—Probably the first one in the county was "Marcellus," at Holcomb's mill, in '38 or '39. At an early date there was an office at Amboy, a mail by stage from Muscatine to Oskaloosa. Albert Allen was the first post-master at Clay, and later the Meachams and Morgans kept the office some sixty years. The first office in Crawford was kept by Mr. Prather, and but one letter came in the first delivery, addressed to Mrs. Caldwell Neal. She seemed to have the price, twenty-five cents postage. An office was opened near Washington in the fall of '38 or spring of '39, Thomas Baker, postmaster. Mail came from Wapello every fortnight, carried on foot by J. H. Higbee, in his pockets, hat and a meal sack. It was providentially arranged that as almost no one had the price, few letters came. Thus, in the first delivery, there were but three letters. One was for Jonathan Wilson, and as it was not from his girl, it was not worth twenty-five cents. Otherwise with John S. Reeves—he got one of the three from his sweetheart way back east, wishing to follow the star of empire, but, alas! he had no silver, so he worked for a farmer all one day and walked eight miles to redeem the precious missive, and he covered it with kisses, the silly old thing! Still, it was worth all the stress, John said, and he was an expert. Wm. Basey

COURTHOUSE IN PUBLIC SQUARE, WASHINGTON

Erected in 1847. Vacated and torn down in 1868

claimed to be the first post-master in Washington, and John J. Jackson was his deputy, in '39. The first mail came March 10 of that year. In the early forties, Norman Everson was post-master, and carried the mail around in his capacious hat, and delivered it casually as he met people on the street. No one was in a hurry in those days; they had all the time there is. That humorist had a deal of fun tantalizing folk about love letters. Franklin did not get an office till about 1858, at Alonzo Waterman's house. Highland had an office in 1848, on section 5, C. G. Maynard, post-master. In '59 an office on section 28, by Robert Prettyman, and her last office was White Ash, section 1, by Montgomery Clark, grandson of the first settler in the township. It was discontinued when rural delivery came in. Yatton had an office in '41, N. P. Cooper, master. Before that, people in that region went to Iowa city or to Washington. The records are silent as to any more offices.

Second Court House.—The board contracted with Alex. Lee for a brick court house in the public square, in February, '45, and it was finished in July, '47. Agreement and specifications are lost. He was docked fifty dollars on the cupola and one hundred and ten dollars on the rest.

Rare Extravagance.—The board must have had some trouble, for they employed an attorney at an annual salary of twenty-five dollars a year.

Man on Horseback.—The old board of commissioners was superseded in 1851 by a county judge, Enoch Ross, incumbent. The system was true one-man power, centralization with a vengeance, but it was not a bit abused by that honest, candid man. This officer's say was final in settlement of claims against the county; he located roads, levied taxes, built bridges, erected court house and jails. The system worked well, and the trust was not betrayed, in more than one case in the whole state. Those old settlers were honest. Judge Ross' administration had been so good, clean and sensible, that when the system gave way to the board of supervisors of fifteen members, one man from each township, on January 1, 1861, the judge was promoted to the chairmanship of the board. The other elected members were B. H. Wilder, Clay; D. W. Cauffman, Brighton; Evan Park, Marion; M. Moorhead, Crawford; James Stewart, Oregon; D. W. White, Franklin; W. S. Hamilton, Seventy-six; Marshall Goodspeed, Cedar; Alex. Gibson, Jackson; Geo. Means, Highland; Thos. M. Moore, Iowa; Robt. M. Calister, English River; S. A. Waters, Lime Creek; John Rheinart, Dutch Creek. They met January 7, 1861. The board was too cumbrous—too much talk—two or three men really did all the work, and the rest—visited. It was a Gabfest. It was wise, many years later, to reduce the number to three men.

After they got pretty well organized, what did the old settlers do? Built another saw mill. Went to grist mill—and waited. Went hunting bee trees and wild honey that is always tame. Went hunting game worth while. Or, rather, did not have to "go." Game came up to smell the muzzle of their guns. Quincy Adams said it was not uncommon to see forty to fifty deer within a radius of a mile from Washington. He would kill three or four every time he left his shop. When snow was on the ground, he would hitch a slain deer to his horse's tail, and scoot, and keep on adding deer to his string, deer tied to deer, tandem, and he would snake them into town! What a president of an Ananias club, that gifted man!

Michael Wilson, himself a great hunter, said Jesse Ashby was the most skilful Nimrod he ever knew. Jesse had killed more deer hereabout than could be packed into the public square, and bears no end. Whatever he fired at was his mutton. And Morgan Hart said he saw Jesse walk straight up to a wild deer, wrapped in a white coat, his head drawn down to his shoulders, and walk so evenly that the deer took him for a stump, and, I suppose, let Ashby present his visiting card. O, ring off, before I lose my natural faith in my fellow men. David Goble hunted and trapped weeks and months at a time, even going up the Iowa river for beaver.

And, then, the amusements. The old settlers had more fun than we have now. And several men were phenomenal as reapers of fun. I have never been able to decide which one of the old settlers whom I chanced to know, had the most fun every day, whether Jonathan Wilson, or Caleb Cleaves, Captain Moreland, Clark Conger, Lyman Whitcomb, Reeves, or Everson. On the whole, it is safe to give the cap and bells to Jonathan. When he lounged in Chilcote's store, slipped down in a chair and sat on his fifth vertebra, his heels up high on the stove, a vast cube of plug in his mouth, and dropped into Indian stories and patois, and laughed in convulsions, and, with a face broader than long, exclaimed in his peculiarly soft, caressing voice, "Puckachee, che-mo-ke-mon, fetch back them wap-a-col-ons," (water melons), and landed a thirteen-inch shell of nicotine far away, I thought no man on the planet could have such another tickle aboard his anatomy.

Yes, I shall give the belt to Jonathan. When the simple hearted good old man was on his death bed, and he knew he was doomed and accepted it kindly, the minister, Dr. Chilcote and a relative called in the sick chamber. Of course, the clergyman had to talk shop a bit, and asked Jonathan if he were prepared and resigned, and all that, and the patient said, "yes, that is all right, I have no fears," etc., then turning to the doctor, with a broad grin he said, "Doc, I have had a lot of fun, haven't I?" It was so natural and characteristic, they were inwardly convulsed, but to save appearances they had to wait till they were out doors before daring let the tickle explode.

A somewhat similar speech was made to me, many years ago, by John Rheinart. His life had been full of bonhomie. He had been reciting the good and gay times he had had in Europe and in America, the barricade fighting he as a conscript had been obliged much against his will to do in terrible fright, in the streets of Paris, the plays he had seen, the music he had heard there, and all that round of art, beauty, and jollity and revelry, and, drawing a sigh out of his cigar, he said, "when I am dead, and folks come up to my coffin to take a last look, I want no man to stand there and muse and say, 'poor devil, he never had any fun.' " I do not think any one who knew them well, would make a denial in the case of either Jonathan or John.

ANSON MOORE
Settled at Brighton in 1841

GEORGE W. FORMAN
Settled in Brighton in 1841

L. B. FLEAK
Came to Brighton in 1854

ISRAEL H. FRIEND
Came to Brighton in 1840

REUBEN ISRAEL
Settled at Brighton in 1847

WILLIAM G. ISRAEL
Settled at Brighton in 1846

CHAPTER VII.

TOWNSHIPS IN DETAIL.

In a dream, the pioneers appeared in a cloud full of cherubs, to protest against compressing their period between the years 1836 and 1841, and to give good reasons for extending it to 1846 when Iowa became a state. They looked so like angels and "clouds of witnesses," that I accepted their amendment, only qualifying it by saying that the years from 1841 to '46 were distinctively the formative period, when constitutions were adopted, churches organized, school houses built, etc. Many men of the greatest importance in the development of the county and city came from 1840 on. .

At the meeting of the board of commissioners January 3, 1844, the county was first sub-divided into these civil townships, that perfected their organizations later, Brighton, township 74, range 8; Cedar, 75, range 8; Clay, 74, range 9; Crawford, 74-5, range 6; Dutch Creek, 75, range 9; English River, 77, range 7; Iowa, 76-7, range 6; Lime Creek, 77, range 8-9; township 76, range 8: Marion, 74, range 7; Washington, 75, range 7.

On the first Monday in April, '45, Brighton, Cedar, Dutch Creek, English River, Lime Creek were duly organized by the election of township officers, and in October, '45, the boundaries of Dutch Creek were changed to extend from Skunk river to the center of what is now Seventy-six township.

BRIGHTON.

Brighton was among the first townships to be settled, and at first that settlement bid fair to head the procession in the county, for it had timber, building stone, and water power for mills—great advantages as the pioneers estimated things. If they had had a herald's college, their armorial bearings would have included a tree, a catfish and a bullfrog rampant. From the first, Pickerell's mill was a Mecca to pilgrims from all about, and it attracted settlers and retail trade to the hamlet on the hill. In 1839, John Brier hauled a stock of goods from Burlington to the first store, owned by John Lewis, sixteen by twenty, and Jeff. Gordon had a very wet grocery that the Indians patronized.

Up to 1840, there were four settlements in the county, Crawfordsville, Brighton, several claims on English river, and a dozen families in Dutch Creek. In that year, the northern settlement doubled in population, and the county then had one thousand five hundred and seventy-one. By '44, there were three thousand one hundred and twenty, and in '46, three thousand four hundred and eighty-three.

Early in the forties came to Brighton, Wm. Spencer, J. W. Stone, J. S. Erwin, L. J. Washburn, Ed Deeds, R. C. Risk, S. O. Kirkpatrick, W. D. Hoagland, W. B. Lewis, I. H. Friend, and the following men came stringing along soon after: S. G. Rhodes, R. S. Mills, Jacob Dillon, J. R. Shields, James Frederick, John H. Prizer and Dr. Prizer, Daniel Elliot, J. P. and Alex. Hamilton, David Robertson, Ol. Sweet, Jos. Earl, and T. E. Purrington who went insane.

Early Campaigning.—Wm. B. Lewis, father to Sam, Porte and James, rode a horse from Kentucky to Brighton, four hundred and fifty miles, in ten days, in 1840, and he came again, and for good, in '44. In 1860, he was sent to the state senate. On November 25, '78, he and his wife celebrated their golden wedding, with the help of one hundred and fifty guests. He was a very merry, vivacious man, and he enjoyed the campaign he made in '60, calling on Democrats and all, though he was a Whig. He did not expect to get 'em all, nor did he. He and a friend alighted one hot summer day at the house of a noted Democrat, Batterson, and saw the fat man sitting under a tree, fanning and fighting flies. As Mr. Lewis approached, he sang out in his high treble voice, "I'm running for the senate and want your vote"— "Not by a dam site," came the rebuff, and the visiting statesman laughed and drove on, hunting more promising fields of alfalfa.

It is a puzzle how Captain Moreland, in 1839, settled on the prairie four miles south of Washington. He had sailed the Mississippi river many years, knew General Sam Houston and Colonel David Crockett. The latter was noted for holding a dialogue with a coon up a tree. David had called to Zaccheus, and the coon said, "Don't shoot, Colonel, I'll come right down." The jolly man did not freeze outside the pale of the brush, but kept himself warm, laughing. At that time, and for a year later, there were but twelve families in Washington—Jos. Adams, Henry McCullough, Dr. G. H. and H. A. Stone, Dan Powers, Bloomer Thompson, John Dougherty, Almon Moore, Amos Embree, J. J. Jackson, John Hendel, Samuel Joy.

John Prizer came to Brighton in '45, took the gold fever in '50, spent two years in California, scraped up quite a bit of gold and returned. In '79 he was sent to the state senate, and was a level-headed, merry, wise man, and delightful company.

THE YOUNG CABIN IN CEDAR TOWNSHIP
Built about 1841

PIONEER SOD HOUSE

Navigation of Skunk.—I. H. Friend was the most original man that ever lived in Brighton. A giant in stature, he was bold in business. He came in '41, to retrieve his fortunes failing in the east, sold goods, packed pork, handled grain. He was in the hog packing business five years, handling five thousand to six thousand head a year, paying one dollar and twenty-five cents to two dollars per hundredweight, net, and in winter he sledded them to Burlington and shipped the cargo to St. Louis and New Orleans. He bought and sold yearly fifteen thousand bushels of grain, grinding some and shipping flour down Skunk river in flatboats, thence to St. Louis. It was risky boating on the Skunk, for there were ugly snags, and seven dams to shoot. In '43, Gilbert Levell's boat had struck the dam at Wilson's mill, and the cargo of beef and pork was a total loss, but the next year Wm. Compton's load of corn and potatoes got through all right, and he made a good spec. In '45 Friend and Heaton loaded two boats with one thousand six hundred bushels of wheat and four hundred and fifty barrels of flour, jumped the seven mill dams and ever so many other damns, and made a profitable three weeks' trip. In prudence, they tied up at night. The last boating was by George Fisher and G. W. McCullough, but the boat smashed on Merrimac dam, and two thousand dollars' worth of corn, potatoes, wheat, oats, brooms, etc., went to Davy Jones' locker.

Mrs. John Brier was weaving cloth in '38, on a rude loom made by hubby with a broad ax.

Seneca Beach, for whom Sen. Dewey was named, was J. P. in '39. His handsome son and his wife re-visited the old haunt in 1908, drawn by the magnet of home sentiment.

Orson Kinsman and Hannah Dinsmore were the first pair to wed; in '38, Virtue A. Milton was born, and in '40 Thompson Dray's boy came to town, the first fruits of the stork.

David Powers in 1851 unearthed a part of the very earliest settler, in the river bottom where it had mired down ages ago—a portion of the foreleg of a mastodon, three and a half feet long, fourteen inches wide, weight eighty-three pounds. The huge molar teeth of these monsters have been turned up many times. Ancient politics made strange bed-fellows here.

Another old relic: On section 5 a coal bank was operated several years, but the coal was scanty and of very poor quality.

The original town of Brighton was laid out in '40 by Kinsman and Dray, on section 31, township 74, range 8, and additions were made by G. W. Tuel, I. H. Friend, Charles Dunham et al.

The church organizations are classified elsewhere.

Brighton had a scourge of cholera in the fifties. The Elijah Smith family was decimated. Their son, and a man named Smith, and a hired man were freighting from Burlington to Richland, and stopped at a house where the baby of an in-coming family had the disease. Three or four of the exposed parties died. Obediah Morgan cared for the living and buried the dead in what is now Rubio cemetery. The disease spread. At last, Elijah and wife were so dejected they sold out and started for Oregon, but he died on the way, and his wife and her son and his wife got through, on foot, worn out, their team of an ox and a cow hardly able to pull the wagon with the few contents. Smith had deeded an acre, where his sons were buried, to the trustees of Clay, as a grave-yard.

When Wm. N. Hyde came to Brighton, August 6, 1842, there was only the store of Friend, J. N. Lewis' tavern, Frank Thorn's blacksmith shop and a dozen cabins. An Indian trail, worn a foot deep by their ponies going single file, ran across his father's claim. Hundreds of redskins were prowling around, their kids using bows and arrows. Their burial places were numerous—their main industry seemed to have been dying. Here and there were well-kept graves, one being that of an aged squaw who loved the whites and wished to be buried in a coffin as they were. Her wish was gratified, and here's a bunch of pansies to lay upon her green mound. At Hesseltine's hill were the granaries or caches of Indian corn, places where the drainage was good, and they covered the grain to protect it from the weather and mammals. Caches in the woods were covered with fallen trees or brush. Mr. Hyde saw, as late as 1870, flocks of wild turkeys numbering seventy-five to one hundred.

The list of notable, strong and original men in Brighton is no where near complete if 'Squire Anson Moore, Dr. Prizer, L. B. Fleak, the Tracys and Downs are not included.

CEDAR.

Her history is like "the short and simple annals of the poor," because it developed late, as settlers were afraid to go where there was not brush, water and frogs. In 1875, however, it had gained eight hundred and eighty-three population. Calvin Craven was the first man to go in there, in 1839, but he went away, having the timber belt superstition. Returning the next year, Mr. Duke had taken the "sort o' claim" Craven had made, and was cultivating three acres. Mr. Craven bought the claim, one hundred and sixty acres of timber somewhere and "all the prairie he wanted" for four hundred dollars. He says he could have had then all the prairie around Washington for nothing, as timber was scarce. He went farther and bought a timber

THE CLAY CONGREGATIONAL CHURCH
Organized in 1842

THE OLD CLAY SCHOOLHOUSE

claim for four hundred dollars. The other settlers were Wm. Myers, Wm. Dusenbury, Lenox Dayton, Wm. Hinkston. The latter's child was the first baby born in Cedar, and the first death was that of his wife Elizabeth, buried in the Patterson grave-yard. The first wedding—Newton Smith and Nancy Young.

In '44, Calvin and Wm. Craven, John A. Young, Jas. N. Young, A. Young jointly built a school house on section 28. Schools and churches are classified in another place.

The hamlet of Lexington was laid out by M. D. Story in April, '65, on section 8.

Crooked creek made a bad flight of stairs of the edges of Cedar, Franklin and Washington townships.

Cedar is unique in one respect, having had as members of the legislature four men, Hons. Marshall Goodspeed, B. F. Brown, Sam C. Gardner and B. F. Tipton, and its ex-resident John Alex. Young as state senator for Washington and Henry counties. He also had served as county auditor. Among its other noted men and large land-owners were Adam Wombacher, Jesse Phillips, Enoch Winter, the Youngs, John Knupp, the Pattersons et al.

A Stock Deal.—Calvin and James Craven and Nicholas Dayton drove one hundred fat cattle to Chicago via Burlington, consuming nineteen days, butchered them there and sold at two and a half to three and a half cents a pound. The total expense of the round trip was ninety dollars, and they made money on the deal. In that day, stock dealers went round contracting for stock, giving their notes, and settled after marketing hogs and cattle—if they could; if not then, then when they had cut a juicy melon.

It may be stated in general terms that up to '41, folk did not raise enough products for home consumption, and had to haul in supplies from Burlington with oxen, and spoil a week in the trip. There were few horses in the county. In '40, in English river township there were but two teams of horses, owned by J. R. Hawthorne and Wm. A. Seymour. It took two days to go to Skunk river mill, and water might be too high to grind. Most people used hand mills and even coffee mills to grind corn, and coffee mills and graters for buckwheat. Up to 1846, the trading points for this county were Burlington, Keokuk and Muscatine.

CLAY.

She is the baby township in the county, that is, the smallest, and sweetest. In '75 it numbered six hundred and ninety people. Among the '39-er settlers were Ellis Waters, Moses Hoskins, Sr. and Jr., Richard Disney, Robert McCartey, H. T. Pringle.

Here is where Ralph Dewey came to light, as the first teacher, and he advanced from glory to glory, to clerk of the courts and first mayor of this incorporated town.

Many of these people were New Englanders, and of course Congregationalists. Several very notable families came there, the Meachams, Wolcotts, Millses, Watermans and Waterhouses, Plumbs, Harts, Bosworths, Woodfords, Pringles, Robinsons, Brintons, Griffiths, Hutchinsons, Stephens, Savages, Townsends, Morgans et al. Indeed, Clay has always passed as "Yankee," for thrift and shrewdness. Her people were frugal, tidy, snug in business, and they were well off, well-heeled, so to speak. They believed in churches and schools, and took a lively interest in politics and were not hunkers. They knew their own minds to a man, to a woman, and stood by their convictions political and religious. One could hardly name another community so full of character and individuality.

As late as '78-9 a lot of Indians camped on Honey creek, and braves insulted and scared lone women. Reds came every winter to hunt, fish and beg. Once they brought an old consumptive, and stayed all winter to benefit his health, but as he didn't die fast enough, it is said they helped him to the happy hunting grounds. He wished to be buried among his kin at Sandy Hook. The party charged children at the Farrier school a dime to see a papoose. A half-breed Johnny came every winter, on a fresh honey-moon—having added a fresh bride to his harem, and he was happy.

George Gallup's career had a gait like his name. He had a family, traveled much, and it was reported he married a fair Virginian, sold his place in Clay, deserted his family. Years after word came that he was hung in California, and on the gallows said he had buried five thousand dollars at the foot of a red oak tree in the northwest corner of section 16 in Iowa, but, though it was hunted for, the treasure trove was never found. His wife here went to live with a married daughter in Nebraska, whose husband drove both out into a blizzard; they walked several miles to shelter, and the silent mother died of a broken heart and from exposure. Does the reader taste the bitter dregs in that cup?

On top of Pisgah on Honey creek is an Indian mound, pierced by a big tree, scarred with names cut seventy years ago.

One of the characters was Jacob Dillon who came first in '39 and permanently in '44. He lived to be eighty-six years old, and every fiber of his mind was racy. He hated bull thistles as the devil hates holy water, and he would walk miles to swipe a Canuck thistle, and he had a fad for ponds and German carp. He was the best company ever, and his daughter, Mrs. J. R. McKain is just like him.

THE CLAY CHEESE FACTORY

The Griffiths, Robert, Elias and others, had the most striking and amusing English vocabulary extant. They were artists in its use. Shrewd business men, too, and, Midas-like, everything they touched turned to gold, except food, drink, raiment and the like. Though, when Edward Brinton met these Greeks, and used language, then came the tug of war. Some men have a genius for using words that have a sort of ripping sound as they issue, like the violent tearing of muslin. There is a vast deal of theology in some artists' expletives and explosives. The Griffiths were capital neighbors, warm-hearted, kindly, just tip-top citizens, with that comical foible.

Another peculiar man was Henry Morgan, a Quaker. His retort to Henry Clay Dean made him, perhaps, the most famous man in the county, unless it was Captain Sam Russell. Dean was orating on our public square, some years after he was chaplain in the United States senate, and he yelled a challenge to any one to say when the Democratic party had ever squandered money. Little Henry was huddled up in a group in front, and didn't look bigger than a pint of cider half drunk up, and he squeaked out, "I can tell." "Well," gruffly said Dean, "when was it?" "When they gave you eight dollars a day to pray in the senate," Dean growled out a lot of ineffective abuse; but that arrow stuck and quivered in his equator while the crowd went into gales of laughter. Many years later, Dean said here that he was never worse gravelled than by that sharp squib of Morgan's. Henry carried mail eleven years from Brighton to Ioka in Keokuk county.

Clay produced ninety-five teachers, nine ministers and nine doctors, but we forgive them for that; she also sent seventy-five soldiers to the war, and nine never came back.

Clay was red-hot abolition ground, and had a station on the underground railroad, the engineers and conductors being Henry Morgan, Alfred Meacham and Manning Wells. Many a slave they sent to Washington in care of John L. and Mart C. Kilgore.

Water mills were in the habit of freezing up. R. S. Mills once took a grist to Iowa city, in vain; then back to Wassonville and waited three days to get a bushel of grain ground. McMartin built the first mill in Clay. They used to pound corn, use coffee mills and graters, make hominy, and scrape along. There were no cook stoves. Baby cradles were fashioned out of hollow trees, and the kids never knew the difference. In summer half grown boys darted around in a sole garment of muslin called "factory."

In the winter of '64, R. S. Mills, elected to the legislature, went to Oskaloosa and, with twenty-one men, hired a four-horse sled and went skipping over fences to Des Moines, the snow was so deep and packed. In bad winters, wild creatures became tame by hunger, and would come near houses and beg for food like human tramps, but rarely got a hand-out. Many of the wolves, deer, turkeys perished. Winters have surely changed.

Diocletian Fitch, once a rich Marylander, sympathizing with the Confederacy, went utterly broke.

CRAWFORD.

Here is where things started in '36. Josiah Smart was the first trader in the county, near this point. Matthew Moorhead kept the first "sort o' tavern," that is, a stopping place for man and beast. It was on the military road, one of the leading territorial roads. The population in '75 was one thousand two hundred and forty-one. Crawfordsville was laid out very early, and it has had more dreams of railways and got fewer of them than any village in the county. Hope deferred many years, made its heart sick. The earliest settlers were Adam Ritchey, Isaac Pence, M. Moorhead, Thomas and John Caldwell, Henry Osburne, John Black, Thos. Baker, J. W., Joseph, Robert and Walker Neal. It was nicknamed "Nealtown," but the place was named for Isaac Crawford, the Neal's brother-in-law, and that bribe fetched him there in '41. Who was David Crawford? It is said that he and his came by boat to Burlington, and had so much freight that one box was over-looked and went on to Dubuque, but came back, and he was watching for it. It contained two feather beds, and in them four thousand dollars in cash—that's all.

Dan Ritchey broke the first prairie with oxen on the Moorhead farm; the first house was the Rankin; Abe Prather kept the first drug store and post-office. and George Spears set up the first smithy in '43. A lot-of folk came early in that southeast region,—David Sikes, Berry Fancher, John Grimsley, John Stout, Joel Long, Wm. Disney, Jos. Griffith, Timothy Gaskell, James Heath, Elisha Campbell, R. C. Caldwell; the latter died and was buried in '38 on his claim, the Snider farm, followed that winter by a Mr. Geerheart.

In '49, thirteen men made the six months' trip to California—James Blue, James Boyd, James Crawford, James Spears, Wm. Braden, Wm. Moffit, Wm. B. and W. D. Crawford, Robert Jemison, Peter Mills, Caldwell and Alex. Neal, Charles Barko.

Crawfordsville was a nest of abolitionists, the Rankin house a station on the slave subway; seven blacks landing there at once were put in the attic, and at night scooted to Columbus city. Slave-holders used to be thick as blackberries on Crooked creek, hunting blackberries, too, and swearing, and punishing the weed and bourbon, and "kunneling" and "judging" everybody, sah, and talking negro patois.

When Kansas was "bleeding" in 1855, a wagon and team were raised by subscription and sent with money for the "cause," by Thompson Crawford,

Benjamin Meacham

Jehiel Meacham

Seymour Meacham

Marcellus Meacham

Alfred Meacham

Allen Meacham

JEHIEL MEACHAM AND HIS FIVE SONS

James Allen, Thomas Smith, Wm. Morrow. The first named was with John Brown, and would have been with him at Harper's Ferry if he had not been down with pneumonia. He enlisted and was in rebel prisons twenty-three months. A lot more went to the war, members of the second, eighth, eleventh, thirteenth and twenty-fifth Iowa infantry, one hundred and sixty-three of them.

The most noted men were, perhaps, Drs. J. B. Miles and H. C. Hull, R. T. McCall, John W. Crawford, Moorhead, Samuel E. Rankin, J. H. Stewart, J. B. Crooks, and, above all, the wit and humorist Captain Sam. A. Russell. Take him all in all, he was probably the most distinctive genius in the county. Folk will not for fifty years yet get done quoting him and telling odd stories of him.

Professional men turned out in this township numbered—doctors thirty-three, preachers twenty-three, druggists sixteen, editors fourteen, lawyers eight, statesmen ten.

DUTCH CREEK.

This township's boundaries were changed more than those of any other, at one time including half of Seventy-six, then losing it. In 1875 it had one thousand one hundred and eighty-five population.

In 1836, Michael Augustine and his son Godfrey came among the friendly Indians, but not till 1838 did the former build the first house, as the land still belonged to the redskins. Soon after the Augustines reported, Conrad Temple, Mr. Junkins, David Sikes came. Mr. Place built the first saw mill and McMartin the first grist mill run by water. Going to mill in those early days was a laborious pilgrimage. David and Al. Augustine and Sikes started with oxen, hauling a wagon of corn and wheat to Fox river in Missouri, but water was too high to grind, and they put for Burlington, and got the grain ground in an ox mill, but they were gone four weeks. They saw a good deal of scenery.

Dutch creek flows through the middle of the township, and there are so many minor creeks and runs that it is a prime live stock country. The Singmasters got as rich as Jersey cream on that line. But the people, like those of Crawford, prayed many years for railroads, but only the Milwaukee answered, and that, too, not till the twentieth century.

Wm. W. Wells, the richest man in the county, at his death in 1908, lived in this township. He came early with less than ten dollars in his purse, and got his start, feeding and supplying folk passing through to California.

Wm. Said represented Dutch Creek in the legislature, and was the sole statesman it boasted.

The township raised George L. Reed, a noted teacher, later a racy editor, laying the egg that hatched the Keota Eagle; and in his son William he gave the Wellman region a still more canny publisher and versatile genius.

John Rheinart, an Alsatian, educated in Paris and serving as soldier in the street barricade fights, ran a saw mill here, later moved to Washington and practiced law, and proved a shrewd financier. He set his stakes at fifty thousand dollars, saying he would quit when that notch was cut, and he did. There was never a better talker in the county, a more genial, wider read, wiser man of the world. He moved to Milwaukee and became the champion whist-player in the country, then to Los Angeles, where this Scribe, but not Pharisee bade him and his wife goodbye in 1892. He died soon after.

Another noted character in Dutch Creek was 'Squire B. Varain, learned, polite, punctilious, a gentleman of the old school, and a continental school at that.

Still another prominent man was George Groendycke, once county treasurer. He was eccentric, in some ways "impossible," but scholarly and capable, a prime teacher and a justice of the peace as clear as most lawyers. His sudden death was regretted by all. His father, too, was much in folks' mouths many years agone.

A Mr. Shuman was once and for years publisher of the Chicago Journal. Mr. Robert McCaleb was for many years the dictator of the Democratic party there, and influential in the counsels of the party in the county.

I had supposed the hamlet "Paris," was in name a suggestion of Rheinart's, but Eleazer Kinkade laid it out in '48. Valley is the post-office. At Dublin is another post-office. Grace Hill across the line in Franklin also handed out mail.

A very interesting family was that of the elder Robertson; the wife and mother was the keenest, merriest old lady in the county.

Seth D. Carris is one of the best heads and hearts in the township. He served two terms as county supervisor, and was a wise, just, honest official.

The Griffiths, Brinnings, Luers, Augustines, Crawfords, Luithlys, Blattners, Hollingsworths rank high as desirable citizens.

ENGLISH RIVER.

It was settled early, there was plenty of brush and water, and folk eagerly sought the region, and settled before the land was surveyed, and there was a great deal of violence resulting from jumping claims. Cyrus Cox, Stephen and Jonathan Bunker came in '39, and by 1840 George O'Loughlin, Addison Williams, David Bunker, S. B. Cooper, B. Creswell, Paddy Connolly, Gideon

THOMAS B. DAWSON

Platted town of Richmond, 1840. Lived to be over one hundred years of age

DAVID BUNKER

Member of Constitutional Convention of 1857

Bear, Wm. Shaw, Daniel Bunker, John and Joel Tyler and Joshua Williams, Eli H. Adams, Pressley Figgins. Between 1840 and '46 there was a heavy consignment of settlers—Wm. Gwinn and his sisters, Mesdames Mary Bear, Martha Snyder, Elizabeth Adams, Absalom Bush, J. F. Hamilton, Ephraim Adams, John S. Mapel, Peter Sharp, the Bailey family, Wm. Britton, Michael Ween, John Schillig of Alsace, Brantley Bray and Austin, Madison Lauder, W. B. Kerr, J. P., one of the shrewdest men in the county history, a modest, quiet man with a keen sense of humor, full of dry fun and possessed of the liveliest appreciation of the odd people around. It may be truly said that in that first decade, every body had a distinct flavor of individuality; no two persons suggested each other; each was distinct, going it on his own judgment, not leaning on any one, or imitating any body. Good specimens of what I mean were Gideon Bear, Peter Sharp, and especially C. C. Hasty. He came when he was nineteen years young, one of ten children, breezy, vivacious, humorous, original. By the bye, his claim is still in the family, the only one in English River township, of which that may be said.

The civil township is larger than the congressional. There were territorial local officers before the civil ones had been elected in April, 1840. So many came, and came so fast, organization was a necessity. In 1853 there were cast one hundred and forty-three votes, and in 1878 the population was one thousand four hundred and thirty-one. The township had outstripped Crawford and Brighton, and stood second to Washington.

Jonathan Bunker and Mary Randall were the first wedded pair, 'Squire Gillam tying the knot in '42, and the next candidates for bliss were Mr. Gilcrist and Cynthia Tyler. Rebecca Cox was born in '40 and Abe Bunker in '41.

As early as '40, Richmond was laid out by Thomas B. Dawson, and in '56 he made an addition, and John Bull a second.

Kalona stands on land owned by John G. Myers, and was laid out August 6, 1879. Nine days later S. E. Parker had up a stone building. There was a world of strife between Richmond and Kalona to secure the Muscatine Western railway. Kalona won, and the road ran through it in 1879.

Myers was a leading fine stock raiser, who loved a model steer as that English king loved the tall red deer. He loved to go out in the meadow of a Sunday, lie down on the grass and watch the fat cattle grazing around him, and inhale their fragrant clover breaths. He thought it beat any drug store.

Mr. Ramsey built the first grist mill, a small concern on a stream he controlled; that was in '40, when Lewis Vanbuskirk, W. S. Britton, Eli and Ephraim Adams, Levi Randall came, and in '42 Jeremiah Snider, I. S. Edmondson and son L. E., and A. J. Rogers. The year before, the Bailey family came, and that most vivacious, delightful man, C. C. Hasty. No one like him—the Creator broke the mold when he was fashioned.

David Bunker, as miller and legislator, was a notable man. Nathan Littler and Captain Frank Critz were leading merchants in Richmond, and much in the public eye. Littler was an enthusiast on pioneer life, and for years served as secretary of the old settlers association, and nothing pleased him more on the anniversaries than to dress up in primitive style, half Indian, half pioneer, and kite around the grounds, living over the glorious days. Captain Critz served four years as county treasurer, and won the esteem of all.

Of the farmers, Sam Manatt was a very level-headed, candid, sensible man, a shrewd but fair trader, and he made a good estate. When he and Charley Hasty met, there was a talkfest like a Gatling gun in action.

Kalona is a lively stock shipping point, crowding West Chester closely. The country all around it is unsurpassed. In the season farmers gather in to the enormous barn and buy and sell stock. Market day is as lively as any thing in that line in a big city in Ireland. The town is incorporated, and in every respect it is up to date. A big fire, that at the time seemed calamity pure and simple, turned out to be a blessing in disguise. It is now well built, beautifully built, and an enormous volume of business is done there.

In the old days the stock amusement was chasing wolves on horseback, the men using Roosevelt big sticks. It was more exciting than pony polo.

In the southern belt the settlers are largely Bohemians, who have a passion for land, and are hard workers and saving, and all are getting rich. In the northern part is a large settlement of Ahmish or Mennonites, excellent people and admirable farmers. They are peculiar in dress, plain as Quakers, indeed being Quakers modified by habitat. The young women are frequently very pretty in their demure costume. In time, these fine people will slough that uniform and pass just as Americans, and no better anywhere.

FRANKLIN.

It was originally included in Cedar township, but in '54 Cedar was shoved farther north, and out of that part south of township lines 75 and 76 was organized a township called Franklin. Because it was prairie it was not settled till 1852-56. From '50 to '56 came Joe P., John and William McAnulty, Alex. and Cornelius Houck, George Statler, Andrew Cochran, Bill Clarke, David Anderson, D. P. McConnaughy, Amos Miksch and Mike Schilling.

The Sigourney road ran through this township, and it was beaded with taverns or stopping places, to accommodate people trailing to California.

JOHN THOMPSON ANDERSON

SARAH BAXTER ANDERSON

Cochran kept one, Wells another, and they probably coined more gold than the gold-seekers themselves.

Grace Hill was laid out many years ago, but lacked yeast and did not rise. It has a Moravian church, the only one in Iowa.

West Chester got on the map in December, '72, located on the Knoxville branch of railway, and from it an enormous amount of live stock is shipped by such active men as Dave Munro and Dick Fisher. They for many years have made it an exceedingly lively burg. The passing of the Milwaukee road created a hamlet, Titus, in a corn field. Uncle Jimmy Stevenson would be astonished to see a small metropolis on his farm, and would suspect black art and magic.

For many years A. G. Leet and sons have run a prosperous creamery and cheese factory at Chester.

Among the solid farmers in this township are A. and John and Wm. Libe, W. A. Anderson, Wm. Sutherland, George Hayes, John W. Ingham, late county auditor, John E. Griffith, H. F. Miller. The Enoch Winter estate is large in this township as in Cedar. Here used to live that incorrigible humorist Uncle Billy Dodds. Fun has carried him way into the nineties, that and tobacco.

For several years John G. Stewart kept a short-horn breeding farm here, and did excellent missionary work along those lines. He moved to this city, and served well four years as county treasurer.

HIGHLAND.

It was organized and known as a part of Iowa township, in October, '40, and kept on that lay till '54 when it was really organized. The first settlement was made in '40 by John Clark, with his three sons and three daughters. He died in '65 at the age of eighty years. The next comer was Ahira D. Liming, in '50. John Forbes, Isaac McGruder, Wm. Wallace, Moses Lane, John A. and Amos Bower, Sol. Albaugh, came before '45. The first marriage was that of John Parks and Elizabeth Wallace—why so many Elizabeths in the county? as if Queen Bess were still alive and popular. The next wedding, Eli Wallace and Margaret McGruder, in '45, Rev. John Hayden getting the fee, amount not stated, and we'd like to know prices way back there.

The first settlers here cuddled as near timber as possible; the prairie was held by non-residents till 1850, unsettled.

Johnie Tompkins was the first birth.

Harrisburg was laid out by John Burris in '55, on section 14. He bought lots of land thereabouts, sold lots, built one hundred houses, some of them quite ambitious, then he failed and all collapsed. There are several of these aborted towns.

The solid men are Sidney Coon, Samuel Anderson, once county supervisor, Wilbur Gardner, Sam Miller, W. R. Jeffrey, the Wallaces, Captain and Sherd Wilson, Harry White, J. G. Fordyce, the Havels, Benns, J. R. McCreedy, Horace Steele, C. W. Busby, and so many Bohemians have come in that the political complexion of the township has been changed.

IOWA.

There were few settlements on English river before '40. In that year the first civil officers were elected, C. D. Gillam and L. W. Bay, justices of the peace; John Traft and A. W. Davis, constables; A. H. Haskell, territorial J. P.

Yatton was a post-office in '41, N. P. Cooper the Nasby, mail being brought once a week on horseback. In '42 Mrs. Catherine Marling was weaving carpet, jeans and linen. In '44 Nathaniel McClure got a divorce. Things were doing. In '56 Yatton was quite a place. J. F. VanDyke had laid it out in July, and N. McClure had a flouring mill humming, and it was a stirring trading point, but it began to climb the stairs when the Muscatine Western railway passed through Riverside in 1879. Riverside was laid out that year. The stub road to Iowa city hurts her trade—shoppers will climb aboard and spend their money with the Montgomery Wards and Sears & Roebucks in the university town.

The year 1851 was an exceptional one, so wet, and visited by myriads of passenger pigeons. The flocks darkened the sun and their wings roared like a gale in woods. Boys would catch them in corn cribs before the mob could fly out. The Dautremonts came that year, and the sights made a vivid impression on them. They brought a novelty there, a cooking stove. Log and brick fireplaces were the rule, and these were built on the outside of the houses. Cranes with hooks and pots were used by the women in cooking, and also Dutch ovens, a sort of skillet with a cover, and it was set in live coals and coals were heaped upon its lid of a head for more than biblical effect. The incessant rain so raised the streams that mills could not grind, and folks lived on hominy till it became as tedious as quail on toast every day for weeks on end. But they also had game a-plenty, pork, fish, but no bread or vegetables. Deer would come in herds close to cabins. Rattlesnakes were plentiful on the wonderfully flower-decked prairie. It may be said that flowers were so omnipresent out in the open, that women did not cultivate them in their houses or grounds. Nature was the gardener.

JESSE BOYD
Pioneer Miller near Yatton

Why not here describe the breaking plows in use? The beam was ten to twelve feet long, hauled by four to six yoke of oxen. It took two men to handle the big thing and the teams. The plow was held level by trucks near the forward end with a small wheel on the land side, and the depth of the furrow could be regulated by a lever. A squad could turn one-half to two and a half acres a day, and the price was three dollars per acre or six dollars a day for the outfit. I never heard of more than one man, handling oxen, in all the county, who did not swear like a pirate. Oxen are more provocative of profanity than mules. They are cunning brutes, lolling out a foot of very red tongue as if melting, just to play on one's sympathies in order to stop. The mournful eye the hypocrites would throw on the driver was like the eyes of a love-sick girl, writing po'try to her lover. And it was next to impossible to find the wretches in the morning—they would wander, or hide in bushes, and the one that wore a bell would sneak and lie still and watch the movements of the searchers like an Indian in ambush. If within a mile of water, the oxen would smell it and make a break for it, and snake in plow and all, and drink, or pretend to drink, from June to eternity. I assert flatly, and defy successful contradiction, that no man or youth can drive oxen half a day and not break all the commandments, and would break 'em all if there were fifty more than there are. No ox-driver can lead a consistent Christian life—I know—I have been there. It was a sheer impossibility for me to join the Congregationalists and walk in and out before the congregation in an humble manner, and not be a stumbling block, till we had got rid of the oxen. They caused more wickedness than all other things on the farm. The men folk in any family that kept oxen gave the recording angel a swifter chase for his wages than any other and all other "critters" on the farm, not excepting hogs you are trying to drive, and that run in every direction, to all the points of the compass, except the one way you want them to go. A bas, oxen! The only work on a farm that can begin to compete with oxen as a stimulus to profanity is, to teach a calf to drink milk. One generally loses four or five finger nails in that tuition, and gets his feet split by hooves, and has milk spurted all over him, and not even patient Moses and Job could stand all that without using language, I guess not.

The fall and spring job was splitting rails for stake and rider fences. And rail pens were made as granaries of wheat, corn and oats. Small grain was cut with cradles, and bound by hand, threshed by cylinder machines, or worked out by oxen or horses treading the straw on the ground. There were no fanning mills or straw carriers—grain, straw and chaff were dumped into pens to be cleaned somewhat later by flinging it into the air, and giving the idle wind something to do besides loafing. It was handy.

Everybody but republicans loves Iowa township—she does roll up the biggest sockdolager of a democratic vote—the fellow fetching in the returns always moves like a healthy avalanche in Colorado. The main crop up that way seems to be democrats.

The costliest church in the county is there, a forty-five thousand dollar affair, and a real piece of architecture, and Father Jacobsmeir, a splendid American, has a ten thousand dollar parsonage that takes the gilding and solar shine off from any like concern in this part of the state.

JACKSON.

It was one of the last townships to be settled, though its land is the best, unless Seventy-six be declared the successful rival. The reason, of course, was the superstition about timber. Here was no brush, or fish, or frogs. There were but few settlers before '52. Mr. Lemon came in '43, locating on Goose creek. The "pioneers" there were Wm. Rownd, H. Berdo, Henry Rathmell, W. J. Steadman, George Zeck, David Donaldson, Jos. and Samuel Meek, Samuel Mathers, S. Erwin, M. S. Curtis, the Glasgows, Gallaghers, Wrights, Helwicks, Van Sickles, Gibsons, Caniers, Pearsons, Lytles and others.

The township is well watered; Goose creek drains east, Long creek south, Davis creek southeast, Camp creek northeast; the soil is deep, rich, grows everything; clover and blue grass thrive; few trees to begin with, but groves of maple, ash, walnut, pine, and orchards grow while you wait—just a little while.

A good many of the folk are tinctured with Scotch blood, and the thrifty, industrious Bohemians make the whole countryside a garden. And yet a large number of families left that Paradise to come to town. I can think of but a few—three Babcock families, Beamers, Rownds, Benns, Reynolds, Van Sickles. Smeltzers, Gibsons, Caniers, Glasgows, Lytles, and Hon. A. Pearson sold out at a big figure, but very soon got scared and repentant, homesick, restless and despondent, and bought back his wonderful farm. In 1896, 'Squire Rownd, being sick and without help, sold his farm at forty-five dollars an acre, only to realize how ridiculous he was, and when the late John Smeltzer sold his place for seventy dollars an acre, everybody went straight up in the air looking at the dizzy height of real estate, but that same farm would now sell for, probably one hundred and fifty dollars an acre. So many came in here from Jackson that they were called "The Jackson Colony," and they met as a club and had oysters and oratory and high jinks.

William Moore

Amos Moore Simpson Goble

THREE OF OLDEST SETTLERS OF COUNTY

Robert Glasgow and Abram Pearson sat in the legislature for this township, J. A. Cunningham was clerk of the courts three terms, and John M. Lytle served as auditor and then as post-master in this city. Honors are easy. Possibly the best posted man in economics and politics in the county is Hon. A. Pearson. When he goes on the stump and talks tariff and what not, he is no dude, he hitches up his pants like a sailor, but look out for that speaker. With his facts, arguments and logic, he is as dangerous as the cars at cross-roads.

This beautiful region was ravaged by a cyclone in June, 1873, destroying the houses of Gilcrist, Caldwell, Tom Waters, Alex. Gibson, Pleasant Plain school house, Henry Waters, David Canier, J. P. Babcock, J. M. Davidson, killing Davidson, L. Housel, Mary Rathmell, Rebecca Gardner, Mrs. Thomas Waters, and injuring many. The financial loss was put at seventy-five thousand dollars.

LIME CREEK.

It is the biggest township in the county, containing one and a half congressional townships, and is six miles north and south and nine miles east and west. The first settlers are named in previous chapters. Mills have abounded since 1840. Musquaqua Indians camped at the mill every year, to get corn ground. Under the treaty, they had no right to be there. At one time soldiers from Iowa city ordered the band away. The chief said they would go as soon as their grist was ready. The chesty Lieutenant insisted that they stand not on the order of their going, but go at once. Then D. W. McFarland grabbed a red blanket from a squaw, put it on, rushed at the soldier, giving the Indian war-whoop, and the way those valiant troopers put spurs to their horses was amusing. At the third annual camp a funny incident occurred. Word got abroad that the Indians had a white girl as prisoner. Philanthropists worked themselves into a lather of sentiment, and Washington sent a company there to investigate, and liberate the maiden if detained against her will. Indeed, they ordered the chief to loose her. He said she might go with them if she preferred. Then these patriots got the lass into a tent and traversed a catechism with her. She used good language, thanked the whites for their interest in her, but she would stay with the reds, they had been kind to her! Chivalry instantly oozed and leaked, and humiliation set in—the bare idea that she would stay with red men when she could have her pick of the whites! It was like the courtier Carlyle tells about at a time when their costumes were breeches enormously inflated at the seat with bran—as a swell fellow at presentation to majesty stumbled, fell into a chair that had a nail in it, well, the bran ran out and the courtier collapsed. In such plight were the Washington braves, repulsed by a girl.

Wassonville has a considerable history. She was very prosperous from '49 to '60. Gold-seekers passed that way and left money for supplies. In '56 Jim Lane and company spent a Sunday there, en route to Kansas, and John Brown, before his soul began to march on, halted there three weeks to rest a lame mule, and left two boxes of clothing with a friend, to be called for later, but it was never redeemed. The town was laid out in '40 by Wasson and Waters, Dayton in '54 by Jesse Longwell, and Wellman in '79. Dayton eclipsed Wassonville when the railroad passed that way.

The first marriage was in '41, Philip Hines and Elizabeth McDowell (still another Elizabeth); the first birth, Elijah McDowell. The population of the township in '75 was one thousand three hundred and eighty-three.

Wassonville was another station on the underground railroad, George D. Woodin superintendent in '56. Its people were in earnest about making Kansas a free state, the local aid company being Isaac Farley, Myron Fisher and Dr. N. G. Fields. A great many slaves passed that way.

H. H. Willson and his grandson of the same name, and Daniel W. McFarland and Marcus Hull have represented the township in the legislature, J. S. Mapel served as surveyor, James Waters and S. A. Waters as coroners, Wm. Allen, Joel Farley, V. W. Carris, Jesse Longwell as supervisors, Tom J. Allen as county recorder, Eardley Bell as county-attorney, and Ellery F. Foster as clerk of the courts.

Among the strong men, besides those named, have been E. W. H. Ashby, Henry Foster, Harry Moore, Charles F. Shaffer, M. C. Struble, J. H. Ihrig, F. E. Rickey, J. R. King, A. L. White, A. K. Stoutner, John Desing, S. Gingerich, R. G. Cherry, the Romines, Shavers, Downings, Palmers, Bulls, Deukers, Yoders, Whetstines, Bradfords, Joneses.

The war record was good. Philip Haynes served in the Mexican war and one hundred and thirty-eight in the civil war, serving three years in twenty-two regiments.

MARION.

This was one of the earliest settlements, dating from '37. Holcomb's saw mill started that year and his grist mill in '39. He died in '42, and the mill finally became the Van Doren mill. Holcomb was the first sheriff. In '39 Jos. Griffith came, and in '47 he and E. R. Barton made beef and pork barrels for Friend, the Brighton packer. In '50, they, with E. R. Johnston, built and operated for several years a steam saw mill. Wm. J. Williams

COPPOCK MILL

BRIGHTON MILL

THESE MILLS WERE HOT BEDS OF PIONEER POLITICS

bought the machinery and added wool carding, and ran it in Washington as a woolen factory in Tom McClean's present machine shop, and finally John Graham took it, and tried to run it, but, though he was about a half brother to a sheep, he found it awkward business.

Isaac Edwards came in '38, and 'Squire Moore annexed him to Miss Annie Custer at John Epley's house, the first wedding, date not given.

The first murder in the county was committed here in '48, and detailed in chapter on crimes and accidents. And in '45 there had been a kidnapping case—see same chapter.

The population in '75 was one thousand and eighty-two.

Eureka was laid out in April, '57, by Jacob Z. Bowman, and was once a rather lively trading place. Another hamlet is Noble, in the southeast corner, named for E. C. Noble who once owned a farm of seven hundred and twenty-five acres. A creamery was successfully operated here several years.

This is the only township in the county that owns a township house for elections, and meetings of all sorts.

The longest, steepest hills in the county are here; splendid coasting in winter. They belie the name "prairie."

This was the nucleus of the Mennonites—see chapter on religion, churches, etc.

The prominent families were the Essleys, Cochlins, Kepharts, Leepers, Grays, Bighams, Beenblossoms, Cliftons, Kauffmans, Hessletines, Carmichaels, Eichers, Millers, Davisons, Putnams, Hebels, Conrads, Sommers et al.

The Cliftons, a very important family, came in '39. The two-room log house after the surveys stood partly in Marion, Washington county, and partly in Jefferson township, Henry county. The front door and part of the front room were in Henry, while the kitchen and part of the rear room were in Washington county, and they slept in both counties, and consequently had more air than most folks. They used to go to Augusta to mill; it took a week or two with ox motors; had to go to mill twice a year, and when meal and flour gave out, graters and coffee mills were used, grating and worrying corn into meal, sifting through bobinet and turning it into corn bread. It was tedious, tiresome work to grate so much meal, and as a sort of tobacco filler they used stewed pumpkin. It helped out lots, and was not half bad. But it wasn't fair to cheat themselves so. They served buckwheat the same way, and the cakes were prime. It was impossible to buy a sieve or a wash tub or board. Miss Jane Clifton's wash tub was a trough hewed out of a log, and her washboard was made of a piece of board cut in ridges with a jack knife. And yet people were contented and happy, and believed they lived in a land of plenty.

OREGON.

This was first called Long Creek precinct, and in January, '44, the precinct became a part of Crawford township, but in '47 it was detached and organized and called Oregon. One version is, J. L. L. Terry was talking much about going to Oregon, as Iowa was not near "west." The two other trustees asked him for a name, and as Oregon was eternally running in his head, he said "Oregon," as automatically as if he were a phonograph. But W. R. Jeffrey says it happened thus, as his father Asahel told it: Long Creek precinct petitioned the judge for another voting place, and two of the three trustees suggested "Oregon," but Terry, the third one, demurred, when they said "you have long been talking about going to Oregon, a long way off, and it will cost a lot; you can save all expense and bother by staying here and still be living in Oregon." That rather tickled his funny bone, and so the name stuck. Mr. Terry came to Ainsworth in '44. He was justice of the peace, and he got the claim that the dream city of Astoria was on, a city fashioned out of the imagination, though it was laid out in '37.

Wm. and John Marsden came in '41, also A. Jeffrey, W. H. Jenkins, Thos. and Woodford Marr, Isaac Whitsol. Thomas Tucker came earlier, though no date is given so far as I can find. He had a small mill on Crooked creek, that he sold to Whitsol. Ralph Stafford did not come till 1846.

Ainsworth was laid out in '58 by D. H. Ainsworth, who owned land near the present station, and had a pull with the Rock Island men.

Dr. B. Parkinson once represented the county in the legislature, while living there.

As late as '56 there was hardly a tree, few fences and no hedges and but a trace of fruit trees in that township, just clean prairie spotted with the brilliant fires of flowers, lying under the sun and moon and stars. All the farmers raised wheat and corn, and hauled grists to Coppock or Riverside.

Some of the notable men were John M. Stone, father of more railroad and postal boys than any man since Adam, Colthurst, Pearson, Jesse, John and Cal., J. M. Stewart, the Marrs, Gobles, Swifts, McConnells, Jeffreys, Sands, Woodburns, Hardings, Rowans, Beards, Wickhams, Utterbacks, Porters.

One of John Stone's sons, Warren Sanford Stone, is Grand Chief of the Order of Locomotive Engineers.

SEVENTY-SIX.

The civil township got its name from the congressional, of which it forms a part. As there was no timber, there were no improvements before '50,

MR. AND MRS. WILLIAM MOORE

MR. AND MRS. JOHN MATHER
Came to county about 1840

though a few claims had been made earlier under circumstances very likely peculiar. Thus Charles Patterson of Maryland had made a claim on section 23, in '39, and Mr. Vine on section 24 in '40. James Bartlenson and W. S. Hamilton, a few years later, took out the first prairie claims.

The township was organized in '56, trustees David M. Brooks, John S. Melvin and Samuel Mathers; James H. Sargent, clerk; James Gardner, assessor; W. S. Hamilton, justice of the peace.

The first wedding was that of Wm. Thompson and Jane Patterson in '51, John Eyestone, justice of the peace, tying the knot; first birth, Charles Stewart, in '48; first death, a son of John Batterson; burial in James Batterson's orchard, in '60.

The township has one peculiarity—no town or village in it, no store, no post-office—just pure country, where every prospect pleases and not even man is vile. The inhabitants in '75 numbered nine hundred and fourteen.

The shipping points are West Chester, Keota, Nira, Wellman. Really, it is the best purely agricultural country in the county, unless Jackson contests the claim.

Robert Fisher became county treasurer. The noted men, besides those named already, are David R. Munro, Richard Fisher, the Romines, Statlers, Tallmans, Daytons, Gregories, Singmasters, Ralstons, Stoutners, Hitchcocks, Greens, Flemings, Gardners, Mayers.

WASHINGTON.

The civil township is mainly composed of the congressional township number 75, range 7. On the south it includes part of 74, range 7, on the west part of 75, range 8, and on the southwest a bit of 75, range 7 is attached to Franklin and a bit to Marion, Crooked creek making a sierra of the boundary.

Washington township's boundaries were defined in January, '44, but Washington precinct had been fixed in May, '39, both of said boundaries being given elsewhere. The township is now much smaller than the original precinct and some larger than the township made in '44. The northeast half of the township is a level prairie, the soil rich, hardly a bit of waste land, and no other thirty thousand acres in the world can raise more corn and grass. But the early settlers shied, as there was not a whisker of forest, only a slight down or fuzz of hazel bushes, thick as hair on a dog. The settler thought that one hundred and sixty acre farms were "impossible" without an eighty of timber.

But when the county seat was located at Washington in '39, settlers sat up and took notice, and in a short time all the lands within five miles of the city were taken up.

The city includes the first town plot, plus eleven additions, a cluster of grapes. The county commissioner work dates April 11, '44; October 27, '55, division of out-lot by S. C. Corbin; November 6, '55, by James Dawson: March 20, '56, by J. H. Wilson, Wm. Sinsabaugh, A. P. Becker, Peter Boyle; March 22, '56, by Joseph Keck; April 5, '56, division of out-lot 6 and part of 7, by Wm. Barnes; April 19, '56, by A. N. Miller; April 25, '56, by George W. Thompson, Sr.; May 14, '56, by J. H. Wilson, A. N. Miller, R. B. McMillan; June 10, '56, by A. L. Burris; July 10, '56, division out-lots 9 and 10 of Dawson's addition by David Crandall; October 13, '56, division of out-lot 9 by Dr. Rousseau; November 10, '56, by A. T. Burris; March 7, '57, division east half out-lot 11 of Davidson's addition, by Wm. McGaughey; April 4, '57, by J. C. Conger; May 6, '57, by John Jackson and Wm. A. Stiles; October 19, '57, division of west half out-lot 11 of Dawson's addition, by S. M. Cox; August 23, '59, by N. Everson.

From 1857 to '60 something was doing; the city grew fast. The Rock Island railroad or the M. and M., came in, in '58; this was the trading and shipping point for people fifty to sixty miles south and west; the receipts of stock and grains, etc., were enormous, to be shipped east; each wagon that came in, loaded to the guards, took back groceries, dry goods, hardware, boots and shoes; business houses multiplied; stores were thronged nearly all night, after the men had unloaded. This kept up till the railroad pushed on west and southwest; and we were fools enough to raise money to extend it, thus killing the goose that had for so long laid golden eggs in our pockets. We largely lost that infinite retail trade o' nights, and stock and grain went right on east and did not halt here long enough for our merchants and millers to take toll of them. Washington lost her boom and bulge. The foolish virgins sold both their oil and their lamps.

The town was built around a central square or park—an old, immemorially old, English municipal plan, an enclosed commons being the lungs of the place. In that inclosure the curious student can read more than a thousand years of history.

The story of our incorporation is queer. The first heat was made in '52. An election in the court house, May 29, authorized incorporation, and D. L. Parker, W. H. Jenkins and Samuel Miller were chosen to draw up a charter, and they filed it with the county judge. It was adopted in the election of July 10, but for some cause, not stated, it was revoked, and we were in the old hole. The next trial was in '55, when these officers were chosen: Mayor, A.

THE FIRST TWO-STORY FRAME HOUSE IN WASHINGTON, IOWA

Built by John Jackson, an early surveyor and sheriff

LOG CABIN BUILT IN THE '40S BY JOHN ROWAN

Still standing near Ainsworth

J. Disney; recorder, J. M. Ferguson; marshall, John H. Bacon; aldermen, first ward, Jos. Keck and Nort Chipman; second ward, Hiram Wallingford and W. Perry Organ. The first ward was all west of the square, and the second all east of it. In 1856 there were about one thousand two hundred people here. The building in '55 and '56 was astonishing; the brick blocks were nearly all erected in that golden age. Folks fairly tumbled in here. In '57 the legislature passed a law incorporating Washington, and the law had to be published in an Iowa city paper. A copy got in here on a Sunday, the day before an election must adopt or reject it, and the Press, always wicked, got out an extra, that cracked the holy day into pieces, for the information of voters. It was carried, one hundred and twenty-seven for, two against. Only two knockers was a hopeful average. The officers elected were:

Mayor, S. P. Young; recorder, A. R. Wickersham; treasurer, S. M. Cox; assessor, J. H. Wilson; marshal, J. R. Easton; aldermen—first ward, Andrew Kendall, E. Ross, M. C. Kilgore; second ward, R. H. Marsh, Geo. C. Anderson, W. P. Organ. But—botheration! the district court held that the election notice was insufficient and illegal, hence the charter was null and void.

The third heat for incorporation set in September 17, '58, the limits to be one and a half miles square from the center of the original plot. It, too, failed, and the final spurt came in the winter of '63-4, a petition signed by one hundred and ninety-three voters asking for it. It was heard April 4, '64, and on September 29, these officers were duly elected, and the agony was over: Mayor, Ralph Dewey; recorder, L. F. Sherman; trustees, James Dawson, Dr. A. W. Chilcote, V. W. Andrus, Jos. R. Lewis, W. Wilson, Sr. This stood the test.

Prior to '79, the city was detached, and Washington township has ever since been known as "the Widow." Beautiful in her weeds.

On May 20, '57, the Press said we have a population of near two thousand, five churches and two more under way, four taverns, nine dry goods stores, two of clothing, two hardware, four blacksmith shops, three stove and tinware stores, two drug and one book stores, seven groceries, a bakery, millinery, sash and door shop, two boot and shoe, three furniture, three cabinet shops, boiler factory with foundry and machine shop, flouring mill, carding and fulling, two tailors, eight to ten ministers (rather indefinite), six or seven lawyers, eight doctors. Invested in dry goods, seventy-five thousand dollars, and sales just double; twenty thousand dollars in groceries, sales double, and so on. But what did those fellows tell the assessor? some fairy tale? The Methodists had put up a brick church, the Associate Reforms a nicer one and had Washington College building up to second story, there was a two-story brick for a school, and the Methodists dedicated their church June 28, and raised two thousand dollars backsheesh in payment of it.

To recur to the personnel of the town: One of the early comers was Baalam Anderson, of Virginia, a tanner, in 1840, and in '41, several noted men came, as Wm. Corbin, of Kentucky, a soldier in the Black Hawk war; Norman Everson, a teacher and law student fresh from Kentucky, resumed teaching here; 'Squire B. P. Baldwin, James Lemon, R. B. McMillan, Wm. Benson, S. B. Coulter, Andrew Spillard. In '42, Moses Curry, who helped lay the foundation of the first church here; Daniel Yockey, a red-hot abolitionist and conductor on the underground, who soon went to Brighton and carried on the lumber business. In '43, Joseph Keck, the first cabinet maker, drifting into banking later, the several Chilcote families, Henry Parr, John and Thomas Vincent, Wm. Robertson, and Robert Allen who set up in the old cemetery the first tombstone, to the memory of R. R. Walker, merchant. In '44, Basel Williams, deputy sheriff in the time of murderer McCaully, the first Cain in the county; Samuel Conner, who, happily, is still with us, past eighty years of age, a carpenter whose handiwork is on many an old building —he worked on the Seceder church, on coming here, and in 1860 worked on the old elevator that stood till a few years ago on the site of Whiting's elevator, both of them going aloft in chariots of fire—James Dawson built the original one at a cost of eight thousand dollars. The Seceder church was built by Samuel H. Joy. In '45, Robert McConnell came, and Clark Alexander, and his widow married James McKee, and John L. Kilgore, a famous conductor on the subway.

The community had a picnic feeling for every new family or single man that arrived; the people wanted co-operation and numbers, and as each reinforcement came along, all looked upon the stranger, made warmly welcome, with as much interest, and quite the same sort of interest, that a church in a revival looks upon a sinner who comes forward to accept a new leader. It was the era of good feeling, all were hospitable, helpful, charitable; it was the reign of pure democracy; one as good as another, no one stuck up and putting on a haughty manner; there was no selfish passion to divide the colony; there was no desire for office until after 1846, for there was no pay in office-holding, and no special honor, and for a fact until after that year there was not a single "politic" in the county.

By 1846 Iowa had become a sovereign state, and in that decade, 1836-1846, the population grew to about three thousand five hundred. And churches had been organized, school houses built, mills erected, a railroad and a telegraph realized, some manufacturing being possible, and Washington was a good market for settlers still farther west.

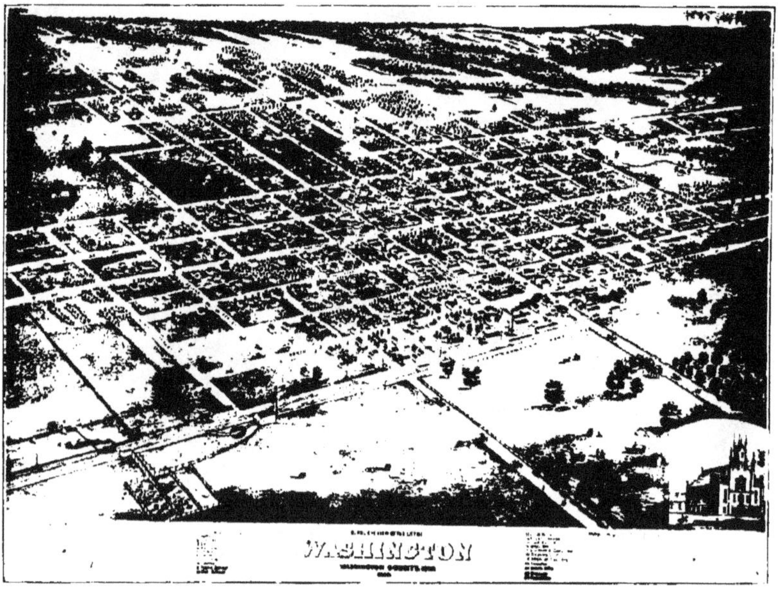
WASHINGTON

CHAPTER VIII.

COUNTY OFFICES AND FINANCES.

As stated, the first election was held in August, '39, and it was not a bit tinctured with politics. It merely recognized the necessity of organization.

Hitherto, the pioneers keenly felt the need of co-operation, hence their democratic spirit and the habit of hospitality; one as good as another, none better than another; no caste, no personal distinction. But by degrees, not very pronounced at first, because, for one thing, office-holding was not then remunerative, men began to wish to be "set apart," detached, marked as officers. Human nature is a queer, vain, weak thing; we are "pore critters;" we "feel our oats" when office-bearing, whether there is a cent of pay in it, or a pot of gold. It "differentiates" a person to be "elect." So this tape-worm of office-holding got into many a pioneer brain, and set up toxins in the blood. The distinction of whig, democrat, or whatnot, lively in the old eastern or southern home, woke up in men's breasts out here just as snakes come out of hibernation when spring suns get hot. However, the worm did not gnaw seriously until 1846. Nor was its appetite for office lusty, since the pay was so small. The officer had to eke out a living by farming or mechanical work. As a sample of salaries, the tax-collector in '40, '41, '42, got for three years but one hundred and fifty-one dollars and sixty cents, and in '43-4 the treasurer's annual salary was one hundred dollars. Nevertheless, by '46 party lines began to be drawn closely. The county was usually non-democratic, that is, whig or republican. Naturally so, too. When Missouri and Iowa were settled, slavery was a vital question. Men of slave-holding proclivities or sympathies would naturally drift into Missouri, while Iowa got a preponderance of freedom-loving settlers.

County Officers.—The record of elections for the first ten years is hopelessly lost. In '40, James Dawson and David Bunker were chosen commissioners and S. P. Teeple representative. Before that, Louisa and Washington counties had been a representative district, and as Louisa was the more populous, she dominated. They also composed a senatorial district, and Judge Francis Springer held the office ten years, and was succeeded by Norman

Everson for one term. He then declined office, publishing in the Press a card, refusing to be a candidate for mayor, tho' in after years he was mayor several times.

The county official directory should appear in this history.

1851.

County judge, Enoch Ross; recorder, W. H. Jenkins; sheriff, W. Perry Organ; coroner, R. H. Marsh; surveyor, Marcus Hull.

1852.

Representatives, H. H. Willson and David Bunker; clerk, Robert Kinkade; prosecuting attorney, David L. Parker.

1853.

Sheriff, W. P. Organ; recorder and treasurer, W. H. Jenkins; coroner, W. B. Bolding; surveyor, Daniel Coryell.

1854.

Representative, Samuel A. Russell; clerk, Albert Allen; prosecuting attorney, A. H. Patterson.

1855.

County judge, John T. Burris; recorder and treasurer, Samuel M. Cox; sheriff, W. P. Organ; surveyor, D. Coryell; coroner, A. J. Disney.

1856.

Representative, W. B. Lewis; clerk, Albert Allen; prosecuting attorney, Joseph R. Lewis.

1857.

Treasurer and recorder, S. M. Cox; county judge, S. P. Young; sheriff, Hiram Wallingford; coroner, R. H. Marsh; surveyor, D. Coryell.

1858.

Clerk, Ralph Dewey; for stock and tax, April railroad election, one thousand four hundred and seventy-one; against, eight hundred and eighty-three.

1859.

Representatives, Matthew Moorhead, Robert Glasgow; judge, S. P. Young; treasurer and recorder, S. G. Owen; sheriff, James R. Easton; superintendent of schools, James McKee.

1860.

Clerk, R. Dewey; Lincoln electors, one thousand seven hundred and twenty-six; Douglas ditto, one thousand and fifty-seven; Breckenridge ditto, twenty; Bell, fifty-seven.

1861.

Representatives, T. H. Stanton, John W. Quinn; judge, S. P. Young; recorder and treasurer, S. G. Owen; sheriff, J. R. Easton; superintendent of schools, James McKee.

1862.

Clerk, R. Dewey.

1863.

Judge, J. F. Brown; recorder and treasurer, S. G. Owen; sheriff, Samuel E. Hawthorn.

1864.

Clerk, C. T. Jones; recorder, W. R. Jeffrey; Lincoln electors, one thousand six hundred and sixty-three; McClellan, nine hundred and thirty-seven.

1865.

Representatives, G. G. Bennett, H. M. Holden; judge, Samuel Bigger; treasurer, R. Glasgow; sheriff, S. E. Hawthorn; superintendent of schools, Charles L. Thompson.

1866.

Clerk, C. T. Jones; recorder, W. R. Jeffrey.

1867.

Representatives, J. D. Miles, M. Goodspeed; judge, S. Bigger; treasurer, R. Glasgow; sheriff, A. Bunker; superintendent of schools, Isaiah G. Moore.

1868.

Clerk, C. T. Jones; recorder, Thomas S. Rowan; Grant electors, two thousand three hundred and fourteen; Seymour, one thousand three hundred and twenty-three.

1869.

Representatives, A. Conner, J. D. Miles; auditor, Ralph Dewey; treasurer, R. Glasgow; sheriff, A. Bunker; superintendent, I. G. Moore.

1870.

Clerk, C. T. Jones; recorder, Tom Rowan; superintendent, E. R. Eldridge; supervisors, John A. Henderson, J. M. Glasgow, Geo. L. Reed; for poor farm, one thousand and eighty-seven; against, one thousand one hundred and fifty.

1871.

Representatives, M. Goodspeed, Charles H. Wilson; auditor, John A. Young; treasurer, R. Glasgow; sheriff, A. Bunker; superintendent, E. R. Eldridge; supervisor, John M. Stone.

1872.

Clerk, C. T. Jones; recorder, T. S. Rowan; supervisor, John A. Henderson; Grant electors, two thousand one hundred and forty; Greeley, one thousand two hundred and twenty; O'Connor, fourteen.

1873.

Representatives, B. F. Brown, E. F. Brockway; treasurer, John W. Anderson; auditor, A. S. Bailey; sheriff, A. M. Bosworth; supervisor, Walter

McKinnie; superintendent, Clara Harris; for poor house and farm, two thousand two hundred and seventy-eight; against, three hundred and twenty-nine.

1874.

Clerk, James A. Cunningham; recorder, T. S. Rowan; superintendent, M. Goodspeed.

1875.

Representatives, George T. Auld, Wm. Said; auditor, David J. Palmer; treasurer, Robert Fisher; sheriff, A. Bunker; superintendent, Mary M. Jerman; supervisor, J. A. Henderson.

1876.

Clerk, J. A. Cunningham; recorder, B. F. Warfel; supervisor, W. O. Wallace; Hayes electors, two thousand four hundred and sixty-four; Tilden, one thousand five hundred and eleven; Cooper, two hundred and thirty.

1877.

Representative, B. Parkinson; auditor, D. J. Palmer; treasurer, R. Fisher; sheriff, Tom E. Johnson; supervisor, S. E. Woodford; superintendent, N. J. Springer.

1878.

Clerk, J. A. Cunningham; recorder, B. F. Warfel; supervisor, Robert T. McCall.

1879.

Representative, Abram Pearson; auditor, W. J. Eyestone; treasurer, John A. Henderson; sheriff, T. E. Johnson; supervisor, David G. Letts; superintendent, N. J. Springer.

1880.

Clerk, S. A. White; recorder, Andrew Kendall; supervisor, Cyrus Bush.

1881.

Representative, A. Pearson; auditor, W. J. Eyestone; treasurer, J. A. Henderson; sheriff, Marion O'Loughlin; superintendent, Nette Rousseau; surveyor, W. J. Livingston; coroner, Dr. H. Cushman; supervisor, Nathan Littler.

1882.

Clerk, S. A. White; recorder, A. Kendall; supervisor, D. G. Letts; surveyor, D. C. Kyle; coroner, Dr. J. D. Miles. Prohibitory constitutional amendment, Yes, two thousand two hundred and one; No, one thousand six hundred and seventy-nine.

1883.

Representative, John P. Huskins; treasurer, George M. Groendycke; auditor, D. J. Eichelberger; sheriff, M. O'Loughlin; superintendent, Belle Kil-

INFIRMARY ON COUNTY POOR FARM

gore; surveyor, Joseph Dudley; coroner, J. C. Boice; supervisor, John Hicks.

1884.

Circuit judge, W. R. Lewis; clerk, Ellery N. Foster; recorder, John W. Morton; supervisor, W. J. Eyestone; supervisor to fill vacancy, Cyrus Bush; court house and tax, Yes, two thousand three hundred and nineteen; No, one thousand three hundred and fifty-three; for jail and tax, two thousand three hundred and seventy-two; against, one thousand two hundred and ninety-two.

1885.

Representative, B. F. Tipton; auditor, D. J. Eichelberger; treasurer, Frank Critz; sheriff, M. H. Sweet; superintendent, Belle Kilgore; supervisor, D. W Ott; coroner, Dr. J. C. Boice; surveyor, D. M. Shearer.

1886.

Clerk, E. N. Foster; recorder, J. W. Morton; supervisor, Uriah Smith; county attorney, C. J. Wilson.

1887.

Representative, B. F. Tipton; auditor, John M. Lytle; treasurer, F. Critz; sheriff, M. H. Sweet; superintendent, Mary A. Tate; supervisor, G. Gregory; coroner, Dr. T. G. Roberts; surveyor, D. M. Shearer; court house tax, No.

1888.

County attorney, C. J. Wilson; clerk, S. W. Neal; recorder, W. P. Moothart; supervisor, D. W. Ott.

1889.

Representative, Samuel C. Gardner; auditor, J. M. Lytle; treasurer, A. J. Dawson; sheriff, John W. Teeter; superintendent, M. A. Tate; supervisor, Joseph M. Huston; supervisor to fill vacancy, Wm. Rownd; coroner, Dr. Roberts; surveyor, Wm. Ott, Jr.

1890.

Clerk, S. W. Neal; recorder, W. P. Moothart; attorney, C. J. Wilson; supervisor, G. Gregory.

1891.

Representative, S. C. Gardner; treasurer, A. J. Dawson; sheriff, J. W Teeter; superintendent, Lucy Swisher; supervisor, W. Rownd; coroner, Dr W. P. Gardner; surveyor, D. M. Shearer.

1892.

Clerk, D. A. Boyer; auditor, W. L. McConnell; recorder, Thomas J. Allen; attorney, C. J. Wilson; supervisor, J. M. Huston.

1893.

Representative, Wm. B. Bell; treasurer, John G. Stewart; sheriff, J. W. Teeter; superintendent, Lucy Swisher; supervisor, G. T. Mathews; coroner, Dr. Gardner; surveyor, D. C. Kyle.

1894.

Clerk, D. A. Boyer; auditor, J. A. Y. Ashby; recorder, T. J. Allen; attorney, S. W. Brookhart; supervisor, H. T. Reynolds, and to fill vacancy, B. F. Warfel.

1895.

Representative, W. B. Bell; treasurer, J. G. Stewart; sheriff, J. W. Teeter; superintendent, Cornelia Klass; supervisor, S. D. Carris; surveyor, D. G. Kyle; coroner, Dr. Charles W. Stewart.

1896.

Clerk, J. B. Young; auditor, J. A. Y. Ashby; recorder, S. E. Parker; attorney, S. W. Brookhart; supervisor, G. T. Mathews.

1897.

Representative, Amos N. Alberson; treasurer, Aaron Hise; sheriff, J. W. Teeter; superintendent, Cornelia Klass; supervisor, H. T. Reynolds; coroner, C. W. Stewart; surveyor, D. C. Kyle.

1898.

Judges, A. R. Dewey, John T. Scott, W. G. Clements; senator to fill vacancy, A. N. Alberson; auditor, John W. Ingham; clerk, J. B. Young; recorder, S. E. Parker; attorney, S. W. Brookhart for full term to fill vacancy; supervisor, S. D. Carris; amendment for biennial elections, No.

1899.

Representative, Charles J. Wilson; treasurer, A. Hise; sheriff, J. W. Teeter; coroner, C. W. Stewart; superintendent, Mary M. Hughes; surveyor, C. S. Coe.

1900.

Railroad commissioner, D. J. Palmer; clerk, John T. Matthews; auditor, J. W. Ingham; recorder, S. J. Cochlin; attorney, Marsh W. Bailey; supervisor, H. T. Reynolds; shall there be a convention to revise constitution, Yes, one hundred and forty-six majority; shall there be an amendment to constitution providing for biennial elections? Yes, five hundred majority.

1901.

Senator, John Alex. Young; representative, C. J. Wilson; treasurer, James S. Shearer; sheriff, J. W. Teeter; coroner, Dr. E. T. Wickham; superintendent, M. M. Hughes; surveyor, Wm. Ott; supervisor, Jesse Longwell.

1902.

Judges, J. T. Scott, Byron Preston, W. G. Clements; attorney, M. W. Bailey; clerk, J. T. Matthews; auditor, F. E. Neal; recorder, S. J. Cochlin; supervisor, Samuel Anderson.

1903.

Railroad commissioner, D. J. Palmer; representative, H. H. Willson;

treasurer, J. S. Shearer; sheriff, J. W. Teeter; superintendent, Cora E. Porter; supervisor, S. M. McCleery; surveyor, W. D. Ott; coroner, Dr. Wickham.

1904.

Elector first district, W. B. Bell; clerk, M. E. Logan; auditor, F. E. Neal; recorder, John S. Wilson; attorney, Eardley Bell, Jr.; supervisor, Jesse Longwell; amendment to constitution to limit senate to fifty members and house to one hundred and eight, Yes, two thousand three hundred and sixty, No, one thousand five hundred and thirty-one; amendment to constitution providing biennial elections, Yes, one thousand eight hundred and sixty-seven, No, one thousand four hundred and seventy-three.

1905.

Officers whose terms should have expired held over this year.

1906.

Senator, W. B. Seeley, Mt. Pleasant; representative, Warren Stewart; auditor, Chauncey E. Myers; treasurer, J. S. Shearer; clerk, M. E. Logan; sheriff, Wm. M. Black; recorder, J. S. Wilson; attorney, E. Bell, Jr.; superintendent, Cora E. Porter; surveyor, W. D. Ott; coroner, Dr. G. W. Hay; supervisor, Wm. H. Cress two year term, and O. H. Dunlap three year term.

1907.

No election on account of biennial rule.

1908.

Primary in June for U. S. senator, W. B. Allison, one thousand two hundred and seventy-six; A. B. Cummins, seven hundred and fifty-six.

Representative, S. M. McCleery; auditor, C. E. Myers; treasurer, J. A. McCoy; clerk, G. S. Eckerman; sheriff, W. M. Black: recorder, Hugh L. Kendall; attorney, Charles A. Dewey; superintendent, Flora M. Purvis; surveyor, D. C. Kyle; coroner, Dr. Hay; supervisor, W. H. Cress, term beginning January, 1909, and W. A. Gibson, term beginning January, 1910; purchase of more land for county farm, Yes, two thousand three hundred and fifty-eight, No, one thousand five hundred and fourteen.

Salaries of County Officers and Deputies.—Early salaries are stated elsewhere; it was the day of small things. By contrast, here is a statement of salaries in this year of grace, 1909. All the county officers now, excepting the attorney and superintendent of schools, have deputies who, each, get six hundred dollars a year, paid by the county. The officers fare better, viz.: Treasurer, one thousand five hundred dollars; clerk and auditor, each one thousand four hundred dollars; superintendent of schools, one thousand two hundred and fifty dollars; recorder and sheriff, each, one thousand two hundred dollars; attorney, one thousand dollars; supervisors get four dollars a day for meetings, three dollars for committee work, two dollars and fifty cents a day and ten cents mileage one way when on outside work. The treasurer charges cities three-fourths of one per cent for their collections, but turns same into the treasury.

The deputies for the several officers in 1909 are: Clerk, Captain J. B. Teller, who has served there since 1871; auditor, Miss Anna Dawson; treasurer, Miss Mame Shearer; recorder, Miss Ruth E. Latta; sheriff, R. H. McCarty.

Holes in Pockets.—This county, as a rule, elected honest, capable men and women. The weak point in our local officialdom was the treasury. Not that the incumbents were dishonest, but, perhaps, not strict, accurate business men. There are so many chances to make mistakes there if one is not clear-headed, alert and prompt in dealing with the many details and many funds. A sleazy, slip-shod man in that office is as dangerous to himself and to the public as a swift locomotive on a surface street crossing in a city. One of the first treasurers was Liston A. Houston, who was one thousand five hundred dollars short, according to the report of October 8, 1845, made by J. H. Wilson, who had succeeded Houston. The board told him to collect the shortage from the sureties, and they were given till April, 1846, to make good. One of the most delightful sensations is forking over surety money. It is genuine exhilaration of spirits, and stimulates the use of language as highly as driving oxen.

Samuel Cox was treasurer and recorder from '57 to '59, and his delinquencies footed eight hundred and twenty-one dollars and forty-eight cents, with interest. Joseph R. Lewis was his attorney. The board also found Cox short eighty-one dollars and ninety-seven cents on the '56 taxes collected and unaccounted for, and seventy-five dollars and fifty-seven cents on the road tax of '57, but he got the first liability cancelled and the second reduced to thirty-four dollars and eighty-four cents by producing receipts, one hundred and twenty-two dollars and seventy-eight cents, for the year '57. Incompetent book-keeping seems to have been the trouble. In later years three as honest men as ever lived were found short, and had to sacrifice or mutilate their estates to make up apparent losses that careless book-keeping was responsible for. In reality, the county had not been depleted a cent, but the officer could not account for the discrepancies. No one believes them dishonest; everybody believes them victims of imperfect clerical work.

County Expenses for Six Months.—Here is a little window through which we can see the money that made the county mare go from July 2, '60, to December 31:

Township clerks and trustees	$ 150.80
District court	956.66

THE IOWA HOUSE
Washington's famous hostelry in war times

COURTHOUSE AND PUBLIC SQUARE OF WASHINGTON IN THE '60S

Elections	290.48
Roads	31.00
Sundries	70.55
Stationery, blanks, books	495.85
Paupers	385.27
Criminal prosecutions to J. P.'s	64.00
County judge's salary	475.00
Treasurer's salary	475.00
Clerk's salary	475.00
Sheriff's salary	90.00
Deputies' pay	115.58
Keeping prisoners	319.79
Wolf scalps	16.00
District attorney	147.50
Attorneys in railroad suits	172.25
Per cent paid to Greene & Stone	100.00
Abstract in land entries	150.00
Interest on county orders	7.89
Balance vs. treasury	96.85
Total	$5,085.48

The total county expense in '41 was two thousand nine hundred and fifty-three dollars and thirty-four and one-half cents; in about twenty years it had not quite doubled, while the population had grown from about one thousand six hundred in '41 to over fourteen thousand in '60; besides, the entire taxable personal property of the county in '39 was but twenty-eight thousand and twenty-five dollars, and it amounted in '60 to nine hundred and thirty-five thousand nine hundred and fifteen dollars.

First tax list, 1839. As a curio, this list is given:

Names.	Val.	Tax.	Names.	Val.	Tax.
Augustine, Michael	$240	$1.20	Black, John	53	.26½
Ayers, Wm.	298	1.49	Blair, Joel P.	16	.08
Bagley, M.	50	.25	Blair, Samuel	120	.60
Ball, Nelson	62	.31	Brier, John	795	3.97½
Ball, Wm.	20	.10½	Bristow, Wm.	365	1.82½
Baker, Nathan	80	.40	Buckhanon, John	15	.07½
Baker, Thos.	70	.35	Banes, James	60	.30
Basey, Wm.	175	.67½	Buel, Elias	280	1.40
Beach, Senaca	145	.72½	Bunker, David	90	.45
Bedwell, Martin	433	2.16½	Butter, John	10	.05

Names.	Val.	Tax.	Names.	Val.	Tax.
Crill, John, Sr.	107	.53½	Gilbannates, T. A.	50	.25
Crill, John, Jr.	10	.05	Galbraith, Robt.	65	.32½
Calwell, Thos.	308	.54	Haskell, C. D.	110	.55
Colens, M.	160	.80	Hulock, John	218	1.09
Camel, James	70	.35	Hulock, Tunis	75	.37½
Cooke, Cyrus	290	1.45	Hiatt, Elihu H.	88	.44
Cajteel, Caliwa	25	.12½	Hiatt, Jesse	510	2.50
Crill, David	20	.10	Hudson, Richard	80	.40
Conner, Wm.	60	.30	Henderson, John	159	.78½
Clemens, E.	405	2.02½	Hiatt, Reuben	145	.72½
Camel, John	439	2.19½	Hoskins	165	.62½
Cooper, S. B.	130	.65	Hulock, Abraham	255	1.27½
Crippen, Samuel	606	3.06	Holcomb, Milo	220	1.10
Duke, John	220	1.20	Hiatt, Stephen	180	.90
Duke, Elizabeth	65	.34½	Hudson, Wm. V.	80	.40
Davis, Philips	60	.30	Harrison, H.	12	.06
Davis, Philips	80	.40	Henderson, Allen	72	.36
Dayton, Lenox	188	.95	Harvey, Wm. L.	348	1.74
Devall, Wm.	30	.15	Janes, David	305	1.57½
Eadstine, Jos.	00	.00	Junkin, James	260	1.30
Edwards, Mary	350	1.75	Jamison, Robt.	285	1.42½
Enos, Jas.	185	.92½	Jourden, Isaac	270	1.35
Earl, Jos.	485	2.42½	Jackson, John	321	1.60½
Fancher, Wm. M.	14	.07	Higginbottom, Jas.	195	.97½
Freta, Jerry D.	80	.40	Haskell, A. H.	20	.10
Farrier, George	128	.64	Hoskins, Wm.	20	.10
Franklin, John	80	.40	Houston, John	220	1.10
Franklin, John	310	1.55	Kendall, Jery	230	1.15
Gill, Mitchell	200	1.00	Kinsman, O. O.	78	.39
Goble, David, Sr.	185	.92½	Lewis, Charles	15	.07½
Gearhart, Samuel	360	1.80	Long, Wiley	354	1.77
Grimsley, John	210	1.05	Livermore, Wilson	100	.50
Griswold, Alfred	10	.05	Lion, John	534	2.57
Goble, Harrison	110	.55	Long, Joel	220	1.10
Galbraith, Wm.	65	.32½	Long, John	515	2.57½
Goble, David, Jr.	266	1.33	Lawcy, Wm.	300	1.50
Gordon, Thos.	195	.87½	McVey, John	20	.10
Gordon, Jerry	130	.65	Maley, Washington	306	1.53
Grimsby, Wm.	94	.47	Mason, Wm.	470	2.35

Names.	Val.	Tax.	Names.	Val.	Tax.
Moore, Jas.	107	.83½	Powers, Daniel	708	3.54
Myers, David	446	2.23	Risk, Robt.	257	1.33½
Miller, Aaron	407	2.03½	Ray, Samuel	20	.10
Moore, Amos	10	.05	Reed, Jas.	262	1.31
Mount, John G.	370	1.85	Ritchey, Thos.	357	1.78
Moloney, Jas.	5	.02½	Ruble, Theo.	20	.10
Miller, John D.	8	.04	Russell, Wm.	575	2.87½
Moreland, Lefever	114	.57	Smith, Hugh	208	1.04
Moorhead, Matthew	190	.95	Smith, Jas	90	.45
Maley, John	140	.70	Shelton, John	220	1.10
Manson, Adolphus	65	.32½	Stone, H. A.	255	1.27½
Moreland, Lefever	215	1.07½	Stout, John	115	.57½
Miller, John A.	100	.50	Sims, John P.	50	.25
Moore, Richard	189	.94½	Sweet, C. E.	20	.10
Maulsby, J. C.	55	.27½	Temple, Conrad	211	1.05½
Mowrey, John	103	.51½	Teal, David	155	.77½
Miller, Jas.	25	.12½	Thorne, Francis	40	.20
Mire, David	45	.22½	Teeple, S. P.	159	.79½
Neil, John	89	.44½	Thornton, W. B.	155	.77½
Neel, John W.	105	.51½	Wilson, Thos.	172	.86
Neil, Jos.	142	.71	Webster, Asa	319	1.59½
Neil, Robt.	105	.51½	Waldridge, Isaac	60	.30
Ormsby, Abraham	250	1.25	Wasson, John	70	.35
Osburn, David	76	.38	Wood, John D.	189	.94½
Osburn, C. W.	117	.58½	Wasson, Jacob	446	2.23
Osburn, Naomi	255	1.27½	Washburn, Silas	25	.12½
Pence, Isaac	239	1.19½	Wells, White	150	.75
Parks, Geo.	238	1.19	Total val.	$28,029	
Pennington, John	75	.37½			
Pence, Samuel	394	1.97	Total tax		$140.14½

There were one hundred and fifty-six tax-payers. But fifty-nine were stuck for so much as one dollar. Fourteen coughed up two dollars, or over; and only three had to pay three dollars or over. John Brier was the Midas; he had seven hundred and ninety-five dollars of property, and was assessed three dollars and ninety-two and one-half cents, the highest paid. How did they make change? There were silver five and ten-cent pieces, but nickels did not come into vogue till our Centennial. Yes, there used to be old-fashioned cent pieces, as big as the dial on your watch, that used to exude verdigris, and it is a wonder people were not poisoned, especially children, by holding those nasty coins in the mouth. It seems to be conclusive that kids way back there never used their mouths as savings banks. They had no money, children didn't, nor even Indian wampum. Alas! the penniless kids. Alas, too, for the old kids—their pockets did not bulge much. Dan Powers was the next Croesus, Sam Crippen the next Vanderbilt. Curious enough, but twenty-five charges on this list were paid—less than ten per cent. The rest was delinquent. Money was scarce. That year, too, a poll tax of six bits was levied, amounting to one hundred and forty-one dollars. The whole revenue of the county the first year after its organization, arising from taxation, was two hundred and eighty-one dollars and fourteen and one-half cents, provided all was paid. To show subsequent increase, in '41 there was a tax collection of three hundred and eighty-eight dollars and sixty-five cents. In '70 the total valuation of all property in the county was four million eight hundred and eighty-five thousand nine hundred and eighty-nine dollars, the total tax levy was one hundred and eighty-eight thousand eight hundred and twenty-one dollars and ninety-one cents, and of this tax levy ninety-seven thousand five hundred and forty-four dollars and eighteen cents was to pay railroad bonds. In '75, the valuation was five million four hundred and fifty-five thousand eight hundred and nineteen dollars, and the levy one hundred and twenty-five thousand three hundred and sixty-five dollars and eighty-one cents, a reduction of sixty-three thousand dollars, because the levy for railroad bonds was but for forty-three thousand seven hundred and thirty-three dollars and seventy cents. In '78, valuation five million five hundred and five thousand nine hundred and twenty-two dollars, levy one hundred and thirty-five thousand one hundred and thirty-one dollars and twenty cents, an increase of some ten thousand dollars, while the levy for R. R. bonds was but thirty-four thousand nine hundred and thirty-one dollars and twenty cents. In '79, the panic depression after "the great crime of 1873," affected both valuation and levy thus: Valuation, five million three hundred and five thousand five hundred and three dollars, levy one hundred and twenty thousand three hundred and sixty-seven dollars and thirty-nine cents, of which twenty-nine thousand seven hundred and eighty dollars and sixty-two cents was levied as aid to railroads. The rate of levy in '78 was eleven mills, and next year eleven and a half.

First Bills Allowed.—On July 1, '39, John Crill got twenty-four dollars for assessing tax. July 17, '39, Colwell Neil got four dollars and fifty cents for three days' work as chain bearer in laying out Washington. For like service, T. M. Neil got two dollars and twenty-five cents, Wm. Basey and Nathan Baker, two dollars and fifty cents each, and on August 15, J. B. Davis was paid nine dollars for laying off the town. On October 7, '39, one hundred and sixty dollars' worth of claims were paid to commissioners, clerks, surveyors, etc.,

OLD EVERSON OPERA HOUSE
Now the Temple Building

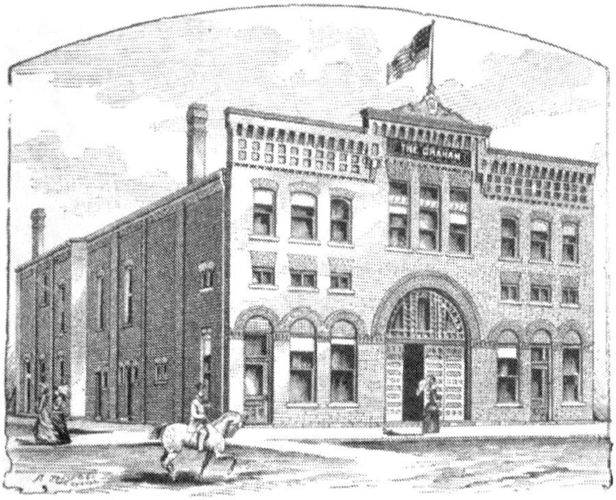

GRAHAM OPERA HOUSE, WASHINGTON

out of town fund, and seventy-nine dollars and twelve cents from county fund. The town fund was created from sale of lots, and the county fund from taxes, licenses, fees, fines, etc. Both town and county orders were at a discount, but town orders rated worth more than the other.

County order No. 1, October 7, '39, went to A. H. Haskell.

The sale of lots made nine hundred and fifteen dollars and fifty cents, and the '39 tax list made two hundred and eighty-one dollars; licenses probably added five hundred dollars to the 1839 county fund. Grocers had to pay twenty-five dollars and clock-peddlers one hundred dollars. What ailed the clock men? That punishment was as bad almost as liquor mulct in 1909.

In the first two years, '39 and '40, one hundred and sixty orders were issued on the county fund, or eight hundred and seventy-one dollars and seventy-nine cents. The clerk, Thomas Baker, got two hundred dollars salary, which was more than all the other salaries combined. The "county rat" didn't have in those lean days near as long a tail as now, and it was not prehensile, either. The commissioners got three dollars a day; the assessor in '39 got all of twenty-four dollars for traveling the whole county, but he kicked, and the next year his pay was shoved up to the sublime notch of thirty-six dollars. D. Goble, the first treasurer, staggered off under the weight of his first year's salary, viz., twenty dollars, but it is not stated what he did with it—all.

But, then, taxes were low. Oh, the good old days of the Golden Age, that will return—"Nevermore," quoth the raven!

Golden Words.—When the reader contrasts the tax levy of 1839 with that of 1908, he will have an impulse to exclaim with ancient Methuselah,

"Blessed be Nothing. Poverty is bereaved of its fabled terrors. A crust and a cobwebbed garret look pretty good to many rich 'poor devils' nowadays. And the tax-ferret was unknown in the Golden Age of Auld Lang Syne."

Valuation, Levy and Tax from 1880 to 1909.—Auditor Chauncey E. Myers kindly furnishes this History the important figures for the period stated:

Year.	Valuation.	Amount of Tax.	Consolidated.
1880	$5,475,171.00	$ 85,915.35	
1881	5,668,768.00	111,892.48	
1882	5,859,507.00	106,319.28	
1883	6,172,555.00	145,438.35	
1884	6,144,928.00	123,090.96	
1885	6,484,124.00	144,400.65	
1886	6,429,372.00	135,605.98	
1887	6,512,993.00	132,005.56	
1888	6,670,058.00	137,778.25	

Year.	Valuation.	Amount of Tax.	Consolidated.
1889	6,730,356.00	135,814.87	
1890	6,783,451.00	132,743.06	
1891	6,976,711.00	131,707.43	
1892	6,998,781.00	136,697.52	
1893	7,180,020.00	146,174.62	
1894	7,078,200.00	160,927.48	12
1895	7,131,733.00	155,413.53	11
1896	7,143,607.00	162,814.50	11.5
1897	7,104,096.00	162,396.84	11
1898	6,460,927.00	158,817.68	12
1899	6,066,856.00	159,920.35	12
1900	6,305,898.00	159,186.68	11.3
1901	6,392,895.00	183,902.72	13.1
1902	6,575,561.00	199,049.29	14.2
1903	6,827,156.00	246,599.54	14.2
1904	7,039,573.00	243,360.76	16
1905	7,083,001.00	265,677.69	16
1906	7,109,559.00	243,989.75	13.5
1907	7,173,907.00	252,726.71	15.2
1908	7,276,337.00	259,497.94	15.5

The delinquent tax list used to be voluminous and formidable to all but the printer who got over five hundred dollars for publishing it, thirty to forty years ago, and several citizens became rich buying tax titles for a song and letting the angels carry the land to one hundred dollars an acre. But in late years that delinquent list is small, hardly amounting to two thousand five hundred dollars or three thousand dollars. The poll tax evaporates, as many move away before the treasurer can get the scalp. The ability to pay taxes promptly, the last dozen years, is an index to the unexampled prosperity that has torn the mortgage roof off from so many farms and city homes.

CHAPTER IX.

ROADS—TERRITORIAL, COUNTY, AND RAILROADS.

It is as hard to think of this county roadless and bridgeless as of a time when the earth was without form and void. But for a respectable number of millions of years there were no roads here, even after the primeval and recurring oceans had rolled away as scrolls. And then for a good many ages, probably, there were aborigines' trails, but roads are nearly as recent as the last dew that did not "fall" in 1908.

For the first three years our settlers were worse off for highways than the Indians. Before 1839-40, there was not even one road in the county. People rode horseback and drove at their sweet will every whither, and forded, waded, ferried streams and sloughs. Indeed, but few roads and temporary bridges were made before 1846. They began to come with statehood in that year and kept on till 1860. Yet one of the first acts of the board of commissioners was to divide the county into road districts and appoint road supervisors. And the earliest territorial legislatures authorized the location and survey of roads, and some work was done on them. In '39, our folk were asking legislation, and two letters are extant, written to our John Jackson, surveyor, by Daniel Brewer, representative for Louisa and Washington counties, concerning roads. Bills were framed for roads from Washington to Mt. Pleasant, Fairfield, Iowa City, Wapello, etc.

The first recorded road was one projected from Iowa City to Burlington, entering this county west of south-east corner of section 35, township 78, range 6 west, following the Iowa river, passing through Crawfordsville and leaving the county at the south-east corner. No. 2 recorded and platted road led from Washington to Crawfordsville, intersecting there a road from Iowa City. Commissioners Ritchey and Kurtz located it, and Wm. Wooley surveyed it. It began at south-west corner of square in Washington, went east a quarter mile, and south-east nine miles, and when within a quarter of a mile of Crawfordsville ran due east. All trace of it is gone, but it was substantially followed by the old narrow gauge, now Burlington, road. No. 3 road five and a half miles long, from Richmond north-east. Though running diagonally across section lines, it has not yet been abandoned, as most of such roads were. Other territorial roads located and surveyed were these: From fifteen mile stake to Washington on military road; from Washington to north line of Missouri; from Richmond to Columbus City; from Brighton to Oskaloosa; from Richmond to Wasson's mill; county road from south-east corner of square in Washington to Holcomb's mill, dated December, 1858. The Sigourney road June, 1846; old military road from Johnson county through Iowa, Highland, Oregon and Crawford townships, January 18, 1859. Road from north line section 4, Iowa township, via Washington and Brighton, to Missouri line dated December, 1858. Wasson's mill to Iowa river, north side of English river, December 23, '58; road from north line Iowa township to cut military road at Crawfordsville, July 15, '59; from Washington to Burlington and Walding's Landing, January 12, '59; Wassonville to Richmond, January 4, '59; Washington to Richmond, November, '58; from south line of county to Indian boundary and from Holcomb's mill to same boundary and from Crippen's mill to Deeds' mill, January 28, '59. Many of these roads have been abandoned.

Thoreau said of the Old Marlboro' road in Massachusetts, that if one followed it well, it ran round the world. All main-travelled roads do, or at least they run to the shores of the oceans. A winding country road, especially if framed with trees, wild flowers, ferns and vines, is charming in its suggestiveness of bewitching possibilities; one does not know what may happen or appear at any turn of it, but for a more exquisite beauty, drive on almost any east and west road on our eastern or western coast—at last the dry road runs away into an offing of roadless, tossing, ridgey, furrowed intense blue. It becomes a submerged road, a sprinkled road, the dust all laid by the spray of seas.

In the spring, rains make our roads not only long, but deep, quite as deep as long. That is the penalty or tax we pay for having a rich soil. Surface water prefers to defy gravity to get a chance to stay on such a fat soil as ours. It does not so much run off as run down. Roads become well nigh bottomless. Until the area around the public square in this city was brick-paved in 1904, four horses would stall, trying to haul an empty wagon round the park. Wags stuck danger flags in the worst mud-holes, pools and maelstroms. In wet seasons people abandon vehicles and bestride and even forsake horses, to walk across lots and on railway tracks. In the open February of 1867, when Ralph Waldo Emerson lectured here, he said, "You seem to be the prisoners of your sidewalks," which was characteristically Emersonian for defining mud. But after the rainy season, our roads are metallic. Hoof-beats and iron tires sound on them like hammer-strokes on anvils. The delightful

MAIN STREET, WASHINGTON, LOOKING EAST FROM PUBLIC SQUARE

sounds are heard afar, for miles. The roads are as hard and glass-smooth as the muscles of a trained pugilist. Polished ivory is not smoother, harder. Our roads have no enemy but water. Crowning them and running ditches along their flanks do not drain them quick enough. The use of the King drag is said to be a remedy, but most Iowans are from Missouri on that proposition. Automobiles are expensive luxuries, as they may be used but half the year.

It always surprises one to see how rapidly the roads mend when the rowdy, roaring winds of March, that "the daffodils take with beauty," descend on the quagmires like enormous brooms, mops, sponges and besoms. A few blustering days put a dry color like alkali here and there, and dry ridges appear as did the slopes of Ararat when Noah's ark beached on the terraces of that mountain.

In a worthless country, on a scanty, lean soil like New England's and Colorado's, roads are superb, a macadam made of pulverized granite mountains. But who would exchange soil for highways? As the champagne-drinkers say, "the camel can go twenty-seven days without a drink, but who wants to be a camel?"

Several years ago, blue grass all at once stole in, no one knows just when and how, on the flanks of our country roads, though every weed vigorously protested against the invasion of their realm. These long, flowing, green tresses look like the wave-combed hair of mer-maids. So say those who have seen the sea-maids.

At first blush, it seems remarkable that a highway like the Sigourney road was not etablished until 1846, when the territory of Iowa was admitted into the Union, and that so many roads were not located till '58, '59, '60 and so on. It shows that enough people had not conquered their superstitions about the prairie to discard the streams and woods and take to the open. When a string of farms had been opened from Washington to Dutch creek, the Sigourney road had to streak the map.

Of course, bridges were as slow coaches as roads, but their character has been improved faster than that of roads. Wooden affairs at first and for many years, mere culverts more or less extended, they have become steel concerns, pierced, trestled, braced, safe, endurable. The load always pulls easily on a bridge, as on paving, but heavily, wearily, on roads soft down to the first stratum of shale or limestone. In comparison with many counties in Iowa, we have lost but few bridges in freshets, a fact that speaks loudly for the sound judgment of our boards of supervisors, used in building them. And there have been but few accidents on them. Carefully inspected, and condemned in time, and repaired, teams and riders rarely went down in a bridge wreck.

No Book of Bridges, as of Roads, was kept: therefore, it is impossible to tell when this bridge and that was built, unless one searched through the minutes of the supervisors, and that blind man's buff game is not worth the candle.

Making all due deductions for soaked roads, on the average we can get about with ease and dispatch and convenience on our highways and bridges, and to do better than now, we shall have to use air-ships. Aeroplanes are coming sure, as automobiles came into liberal use long before we could have expected; and within a quarter century many a Washington farmer and townsman will be flying over our heads, and who then so poor as to do reverence to bottomless roads? And will the inevitable horse, that has been "going" so long, really "go" then? For nearly a generation we have been trying to "relegate" him, predicting that the trolley, the motor truck and car, the automobile, the steam plow, the storage battery would supersede him, but up to date the price of him has been and is climbing because his service is indispensable and he is a favorite and pet, and his neck is still clothed with thunder, praise be! We must not decrease the number of things we can bet on. True, there are prize-fighters, elections—we can gamble on them, but it would be a saddened world to many if they could not bet on the time of a trotter, pacer or canterer, and on the amount of a draft horse's pull.

That many of the ancient roads would be abandoned, it was natural to expect, since so many dream towns aborted. The list of these extinct craters is surprising. There was Astoria, the county-seat—was it the first "city?" No, there was a Marysville on that site, the villa of Mary—who? Named no doubt, for some sweet, dear Mary, whose daguerreotype escapes us. A mere soap-bubble of a burg—where does the beautiful thing go to when it bursts? To the same place the candle light goes to when it is blown out, and the gas and electric glim when the juice is turned off—to limbo. Up to date it is not known where Moses was when the lights went out, and no more do we know, unless we search the Plat Book, where are the towns in this county that were once called Amboy, Winchester, Sandy Hook, Sheffield, Harrisburg, Yatton, Wassonville; Eureka, Lexington, Pilotburg, Dayton, Paris, Dublin are much smaller and less important in this year of grace 1909, than one could wish. There is not much use in keeping up roads to run to them.

However, what was the origin of these dream towns?

Winchester was platted March 25, 1841, by Jacob E. Gale. No one now seems to know where it was. Dig into almost any mound of debris, maybe its foundations would come to light.

May 5, '41, Sandy Hook aspired to civic greatness and swelled up like dried apples in a water-soaked stomach, with municipal ideals. It had been an Indian village, and wished to try the whites awhile. Jesse Hiatt and

Thomas J. Gordon set the yeast in that wee bit sponge. The future city was placed on a sandy ridge two miles north-east from Brighton. The founders admired President Martin Van Buren, and would honor him by perpetuating through all future time the name of his residence, "Kinderhook," but as they could not think of the name, remembering only that there was a "hook" to it, they rallied on the sand heap and let 'er go as Sandy Hook. Give these hero-worshippers a leather medal.

Sheffield was projected in a dream by Nathaniel McClure, August 16, '45. Busted! He probably awoke before the dream was fairly under way. However, he, with John F. Van Dyke, got in his work at Yatton in July, '56. That was a lively milling place till '79, when the railway sapped it to build up Riverside.

Harrisburg was, perhaps, the most iridescent dream of them all. Nathan W. Burris laid it out June 29, '55. It was to cover 160 acres with beauty and glory. He built a stone seminary up to the second story, projected one hundred houses and a steam grist mill, when misfortune overtook him, and the dream exhaled. The stone was used by others, as the Roman Coliseum was plundered by mediæval nobles for their palaces.

Jacob Z. Bowman gave himself a severe wrench in laying out Eureka, April 20, '57, the panic year, though at one time, and for a considerable time, it had quite a smart spurt of trade.

Then there was Pottsville, a villa of pots. It was on David Goble, Sr.'s land in Oregon township. It seems that John B. Potts located it; it was a post-office, with a swift weekly mail. For the first six months a hat, or was it a pot? held all the mail.

As to the other extinct towns, not even tradition remains; such as Glendora, Genoa, Mount Jackson, Middleburg, Rochester, Western City, Walhaven, Xenia, West Liberty. All these were platted around a public square, an English fashion centuries old.

Nor were roads needed to reach several sequestered places, whose names were strokes of rustic humor, such as certain ridges, hollows, runs, acres and the like. English river had Snake hollow. Mr. O. E. Brown remembers a law-suit here, in which most of the witnesses were from the hollow. McJunkin would ask one after another, "Where do you reside?" "Snake Holler." That was many years ago, and the primitive type has no doubt expired by limitation. But can't you conjure up these queer figures—unshaven, hair shorn around the edge of a crock set on the head, a coon-skin cap, traces of egg in the chin-whiskers. The type was once very distinct.

Lime Creek had a cuticle ridge, and Marion boasted sockem ridge. Marion really had more than her share of odd places, and most of her early citizens must have been ingrained humorists. Thus, before the New Lights built Shiloh church, that locality was called "Poverty Elbow." And there was also "Hell's Half Acre" and "Rabbit Gulch."

Highland claimed "Whiskey Run," and the name truly originated thus: Before the settlers broke the ground, the county was heavily sodded, and soil did not wash into streams as it does when our pliable soil is cultivated. But at the foot of the slopes, the drainage became impassioned at times, and swirled and dug deep pits that a horse might be buried in. In an early day before total depravity had gone out of fashion, Indians stole a barrel of whiskey from a trader and hid it in such a pit, and its discovery suggested the name "Whiskey Run."

Until our population became dense and uniformly distributed over the county, there was not special need of roads. The country was not fenced, as now. The timber on the streams could not supply the fencing needed. There was no barbed wire, settlers could not have afforded to buy fencing boards, even if they had been in market; it was many years before rafts of logs floated down the Mississippi river to possible mills at Muscatine and Burlington, and there was no railroad to bring it from Chicago till 1858. Settlers were experimenting with hedges of osage orange, hawthorn, willow, honey locust, and ditches for fences. So, people travelling were not shut in then as now. Doctors took straight cuts on horseback, and so did teamsters. There was more horseback riding than wagoning, and walking was far more common than now. Fellows would streak it across lots to rural hops, and girls, as smartly dressed as possible, walked, barefoot, to the same places, carrying their shoes and stockings in their hands till they approached the rendezvous, washed in a run or swabbed their dusty pink and white feet in dew, dressed their understandings, and after making a night of it by dancing, were seen home, barefoot, by beaux. In England, where the roads are admirable, they are not much used. Fox-hunters take the fences and fields, and pedestrians the lanes and paths through hedges, and the mileage is largely across country, riding or walking. The folk in this county had all the roads they needed up to 1860, at least.

Besides, there were not many here to need roads. The census of '44 gave this county only three thousand one hundred and twenty, and of land-owners many were non-residents, here as all over the state. In '59, there were of the thirty-three million acres in the state only four million acres improved; twenty-four million acres not touched by plows; sixteen million acres owned by non-residents, and speculative absentees never work lands. The assessed value of land then averaged two dollars and seventy-five cents an acre. And there was not much inducement to cultivate, for the average price of wheat was forty

BRYSON HOUSE, IN 1870

HENRY B. ANDERSON'S HOUSE, WASHINGTON TOWNSHIP

Built in 1851 and still occupied

cents a bushel, of corn twelve, oats fifteen, potatoes twenty-five, hay a dollar and a half per ton. They burned corn for fuel way back in pioneer days; it seems wicked, but it was sensible. And they twisted wild hay into tight ropes, and burned that, too.

How could there be much transportation? For years they could not sell anything. The federal census in '40 gives some eye-opener figures: Iowa raised one million four hundred and six thousand two hundred and forty-one bushels of corn, one hundred fifty-four thousand six hundred and ninety-three of wheat, two hundred sixteen thousand three hundred and eighty-five of oats, six thousand two hundred and twelve of buckwheat, three thousand seven hundred and ninety-two of rye, seven hundred and twenty-eight of barley, two hundred thirty-four thousand and sixty-three of potatoes, and about the same yields in '42, when good cows sold at ten dollars, pork at a dollar a hundred, wheat twenty cents, corn and oats ten cents—who needed roads to haul stuff to market forty to fifty miles away to sell at such pitiful prices? They did not need roads any more than birds and angels that have wings. Money was scarce, and they could get little or none at such rates. Interest was twenty-five to forty per cent, banks had suspended specie payment; the Miners' bank in Dubuque was the only one in Iowa; the currency was of doubtful value; there was no business, debts could not be collected; folks were reduced to barter, and burned corn in fireplaces as in their bodies, corn bread being the main food aside from game. That winter was severe, snow from three to four feet deep and lasting long from November on; cattle perished, cabins were cold, food was low. For twenty years prairie grass was the only hay. On the prairie the houses were sod, and water for domestic and stock use was dipped from springs or creeks before wells were dug. Clothing was linsey-woolsey dyed with butternut or hickory bark juice, and skins were worked up into moccasins, boots, shoes and harness. What could they have done for several years, if the muskrat skin crop had not held out? That rat's hide was the sole thing that fetched a bit of coin.

So, take it all in all, roads came quite as soon as they were needed, or could be used, considering their bad quality for full half of the year.

Railroads.—The first railroad projected through this county was the "Ramshorn," which was to connect all the county seats in Iowa and fetch up at Robin Hood's barn. It was only one of many pipe dreams.

The next was the Iowa Western from Muscatine through the northern part of this county. Date, 1857. Just hot air.

Then the Philadelphia, Fort Wayne and Platte Valley Air Line road. It was an "air line"—hot air. It so exhausted the corporation to write the whole name, no energy or breath was left to build the road. This air plant, resembling mistletoe and Spanish moss, had a name as long as foreign princes, shirt-tail names that have to be carried by pages and flunkeys like trails of queens' gowns. A sucker was born every minute back there, as now, and the county issued five thousand dollars in bonds to aid the road, and some grading may still be seen east of Crawfordsville. It is the grave of the last sixpence. The line was to run through Muscatine, Washington and Keokuk counties to Council Bluffs. A big convention was held in Oskaloosa in January, 1868, a corporation was formed by sixty-six men, and they drew up fourteen articles, adding one article to escape the number thirteen and skidoo. A committee of ten named fifteen directors, and they selected the usual officers, one who is not named being from this county. All came back, enthused, to void their dope on their county constituents— spoutings, speeches, felicitations, subscription books, gush, brass bands—sheer crazy to get a railroad. But it evaporated and left not even a smell behind.

About the same time the Mississippi & Missouri Railroad Company was organized and a road really got to Washington in 1858. Infinite blowing, oratory, subscribing, frenzy preliminary. On October 17, 1853, County Judge E. Ross proclaimed an election for November 21, '53, agreeable to a resolution adopted at a mass meeting on October 8, on a proposition for the county to subscribe one hundred thousand dollars in stock to that long named road, in the shape of bonds, payable in twenty years at not more than six per cent interest, and five mills, if needed, to pay said interest, to be increased to ten per cent after fifteen years, and to continue from year to year until principal and interest were paid.

The vote stood thus:

Township	For Bonds.	Against Bonds.
Washington	201	0
Marion	58	0
Crawford	104	4
Oregon	45	4
Iowa	6	63
Lime Creek	7	59
Cedar	55	4
Dutch Creek	39	6
Clay	2	64
Brighton	55	95
English River	37	106
Total	609	405

On June 30, 1854, the judge proclaimed, on petition, a proposition to rescind fifty thousand dollars of the stock bought in November, 1853, in the Hot Air line, and subscribe it to the M. & M., and ordering an election August 7, '54. The bonds to bear ten per cent interest, the company to receive them at par value in payment of stock, and only as fast as the work progressed towards completion within the county limits. The vote stood thus:

Townships.	For	Against
Washington	208	7
Oregon	57	0
Highland	8	0
Iowa	11	63
English River	39	89
Lime Creek	12	76
Jackson	22	14
Cedar	47	0
Dutch Creek	74	0
Clay	18	55
Franklin	54	0
Brighton	32	96
Marion	75	0
Crawford	33	0
Total	690	400

In 1856 voters petitioned to take fifty thousand dollars more stock in the road that should build first into Washington, and Judge J. T. Burris on July 2, '56, proclaimed an election for August 4, the bonds to bear eight per cent and be issued when the road is finished and the rolling stock furnished at a point not over three-quarters of a mile from the court-house—the bonds to be taken at par and the road to be finished by December 1, '57. The vote was hostile, thus:

Townships.	For	Against
Washington	308	33
Clay	8	116
Brighton	23	196
Marion	41	30
Crawford	2	180
Oregon	34	45
Franklin	63	10
Dutch Creek	107	14
Seventy-six	12	14

Township	For	Against
Cedar	55	33
Jackson	23	39
Highland	19	24
Iowa	3	106
English River	18	159
Lime Creek	10	122
Total	726	1121

In '56, also, hundreds of voters petitioned for the submission of a proposition to subscribe one hundred thousand dollars of the capital stock of the M. & M. road to build a road from Muscatine to Oskaloosa via Washington, and the judge, on November 10, ordered an election December 11, '56, bonds to bear eight per cent interest for twenty years, to be used on completion of the road from Muscatine to Washington by December 1, '57. The vote stood thus:

Townships.	For	Against
Clay	24	47
Brighton	28	123
Marion	29	8
Crawford	16	130
Oregon	65	4
Washington	448	8
Franklin	83	1
Dutch Creek	117	1
Seventy-six	16	13
Cedar	76	11
Jackson	34	7
Highland	19	20
Iowa	1	81
English River	36	109
Lime Creek	21	105
Total	1,013	668

In '58, more sucker voters petitioned the judge for a chance to take one hundred thousand dollars more M. & M. stock, and on March 1, '58, an election was called for April 5, '58, bonds at ten per cent, twenty years' run, not to be used until the company gave security that the road would be finished into Washington by September 1, '58, and a depot established not over one-half mile from the court house. The vote was:

Township	For	Against
Washington	550	7
Clay	42	84
Brighton	52	128
Marion	66	20
Crawford	44	146
Oregon	116	16
Franklin	82	4
Dutch Creek	189	8
Seventy-six	26	12
Cedar	102	23
Jackson	81	7
Highland	20	36
Iowa	1	140
English River	62	144
Lime Creek	38	108
Total	1,471	883

July 26, '58, a M. & M. agent demanded these bonds, and they were issued on that date, payable at the Corn Exchange Bank of New York in sums of one thousand dollars with thirty-six coupons of fifty dollars each, attached. The company's bond is recorded here in Book "D," page four hundred and thirty-eight. General John A. Dix of "If any man attempts to haul down the flag, shoot him on the spot" fame, was president of the M. & M. road. On June 7, '58, he demanded fifty thousand dollars of the bonds voted August 7, '54, and Judge S. P. Young issued them. They were for five hundred dollars each and twenty-five-dollar coupons. The bonds dated June 19, '58.

Then the worm began to squirm—it was fun to vote bonds to get roads; it is delightful to dance while the fiddler is scraping; but if he stops until paid, what then? In 1860 N. McClure, Michael Hayes, John Mather, W. R. Nugent, Dr. O. H. Prizer et al. got an injunction restraining the board from levying further taxes and the county treasurer from collecting them. Two levies had been made and the first tax was paid and the second tax partially. The two fiddlers, the M. & M. and the Hot Air Line, brought suits to recover the amounts due on the coupons attached to their bonds, in the federal court. In June, '64, the board of supervisors named John Rheinart, Enoch Ross and H. M. Holden, a committee to compromise with the companies in the settlement of any and all suits between the county and the railroads.

Nevertheless, joy! The road was completed in here according to contract, and there was a jamboree celebration. Mr. Ronde, an artist of Dutch

Creek, illustrated the spectacle for Leslie's. Arrangements were made August 14, '58, in the court house, and they rashly appointed a committee of thirteen to run it, viz.: N. Chipman, James Dawson, Dr. Chilcote, Jonathan H. Wilson, J. J. Higgins, Chas. Foster, J. R. Lewis, A. T. Burris, E. H. Ludington, Thos. Blanchard, John Bryson, W. B. Carruthers, J. S. Beaty. They decided to give a public dinner September 1st, '58, in the square, and one thousand invitations were issued to neighboring towns. Mesdames Higgins, Parker, Rose, Phelps and Miss Dawson were to choose twenty-five other women to engineer the meal. Dr. McKee, Ozro Phelps and S. P. Young were to shade the grounds with bowers of boughs and so forth. Wickersham, Ludington and Foster were to plan toasts and responses. Some three thousand feet of tables were set for three thousand guests from Oskaloosa, Sigourney, Muscatine, Davenport, Iowa City, Columbus City, etc. Before the weather man was born, Phoebus sent a fine day, and by ten a. m., five thousand people were here—nothing draws like a free lunch. G. W. Teas was marshal, and his son "Lush" was doubtless around somewhere with several stone-bruised heels and sore toes. At 12:13 p. m. a train of thirteen cars came in. Why would they have thirteen or twenty-three? It was dangerous. Captain Sam A. Russell welcomed the crowd at the depot and A. O. Patterson of Muscatine said "thank you," and all marched to the square, bands playing, military evoluting to the delight of universal womanhood, flags flying, Captain Garner in fine fettle at the head of his Columbus City Guards.

The toasts with quail roosting on them ranged from railroads to ladies, including Atlantic telegraph, Chicago and ten other towns, newspapers, laborers, etc., and Hiram Price, J. B. Grinnell, Governor Bross of Chicago Press and Tribune, J. Thorington, J. Scott Richman, J. R. Needham, R. S. Leak, Editor Saunders of the Davenport Gazette, Judge F. Springer, General Fitz Henry Warren, Dr. J. Bowen, Nixer, Judge Thayer, responded for their respective towns, and gushed the usual amount of taffy, white lies and insincerities at this Ananias club. Any reader who ever attended a banquet knows just what sloppy stuff is served up in pert, smart-Alec speeches—hates and detests it.

This food turned sour and bitter in our stomachs right off, for we soon learned that those two fiddlers must be paid, no compromise or repudiation possible. State and federal courts collided, supervisors got "sassy" and the district judge ordered their arrest. While the sheriff had them as his mutton, the federal marshal tried to get his clutches on them. The marshal won, took them to federal court, where they were scolded and sent home to levy a tax to pay their debts to the fiddlers aforesaid. They swore under their breaths, but levied a tax and began to pay. Our folly cost us over half a

The most important event in the history of Washington, the opening of the first railroad in the county, now the Southwestern Division of the Rock Island.—From Frank Leslie's illustrated newspaper, Nov. 13, 1858.

million. This silly attempt at repudiation is the one stain on our county record. There is a meaner blot on our city history, that I will come to, not now, but soon.

Despite the vast cost to us of our railroad, it paid big, although the county's stock in the road was rendered almost worthless by the way the C. R. I. & P. R. R. got possession of the M. & M. road. For Washington was for at least a dozen years the terminus of the road, the entrepot for goods consigned to merchants west and south and north of us and the shipping point for live stock and grain in an area of country whose diameter extended beyond Oskaloosa, sixty miles away. Such a distributing point!

James Dawson built in 1860 the big elevator, long years later known as the Dwight Norton, the Ed. Blair and the Whiting elevator, at a cost of seven thousand dollars, and it was a business whale. Stock and grain arrived here by dusk and the owners did shopping until midnight or after, and started back home by dawn. The stores were choked with customers. It was like getting out a morning paper—sleep day times, and rake in coin at night. It was in this era that the two and three-story buildings around the square were built with the profits of this extraordinary trade. All got rich, not alone the shop men but farmers who got prices for their products twice and thrice higher than those that ruled before the railroad came. I saw four years of this tremendous strenuosity by kerosene lamp light. We were as nocturnal in habits as owls, and then we got idiotic, fell down, killed the goose that laid the golden eggs. Washington was so ineffably green as to promote the railroad scheme of extending the road to Kansas City by either or both of two talked-up routes—one via Fairfield and the other through Dutch creek to Ottumwa. This was late in 1869. Jefferson county raised their one hundred and twenty-five thousand dollars subsidy, Brighton raised thirty thousand dollars, and right of way through their township, and Washington—jackass with ears a fathom long and a bray like the laughter of a pond filled with loons and of an idiotic asylum, raised forty thousand dollars and right of way to the Brighton township line, which cost four thousand eight hundred eleven dollars and fifty-eight cents. Judge Aller of the company spouted at the meeting here February 23, '70, and cinched the fatal contract. By September of that year the road was built to Fairfield.

"Insatiate monster! would not one suffice?" The C., R. I. & P. in the fall of '70 proposed to extend from Washington to Sigourney, Oskaloosa and Knoxville, and trains reached Sigourney April 9, '72.

Muscatine, disgruntled at their poor investment in the M. & M. road, induced the Cedar Rapids and Northern Railroad Company to build from

Muscatine to Riverside in this county, and it was done in '73, and a five per cent tax voted in Iowa, English River and Lime Creek townships, carried the Muscatine Western railroad through the northern tier of our townships.

In the late '60s, we made another botch in railroading, crazy to get a north and south road from Cedar Rapids and Iowa City to Keokuk, a point below the rapids, supposed to be vital to get river competition with the railroads. Burlington men urged us to go in with them into the Burlington, Cedar Rapids and Northern railroad, and Washington could have been on that prosperous line stretching now from St. Louis to St. Paul, but no, we stuck to the old I. N. C., and sunk a lot of money. That "hoss" would never "go." Its eyes were "sot." It had poll-evil, blind staggers, heaves, "stove-up" shoulders, botts, burrs in fore-top and tail, the sorriest old crow-bait that ever took dust.

Finally, we got the Burlington and North Western, a narrow gauge, in the winter of '79-'80, and a lot of us went to a jollification banquet in Burlington, and heard effervescent oratory galore. In 1901 it was broad-gauged in one Sunday, badly cracked. At Winfield the line forked, one leg going through Coppock and Brighton to Oskaloosa. The Iowa Central also threads the southern tier of our county's townships.

The Milwaukee road built an air line through Washington from Rock Island to Ottumwa in 1900-01, giving Dutch creek, at last, its fond desire, a railroad, and adding to the map Haskins, Titus and Rubio.

There are about one hundred and thirty miles of railroad in the county, thus—omitting fractions:

Chicago, Milwaukee & St. Paul, twenty-six miles, valuation for taxation, twenty-six thousand eight hundred and twelve dollars per mile.

B., C. R. & N., Muscatine division, four miles, valuation, sixteen thousand eight hundred dollars; same road, Iowa City division, twenty-one miles, valuation, twelve thousand dollars.

C., B. & Q., Burlington and Western division, thirteen miles, valuation, sixteen thousand four hundred and eighty dollars; same road, Burlington & Western division, thirteen miles, valuation, sixteen thousand four hundred dollars.

C., R. I. & P., southwestern division, twenty-four miles, valuation, thirty-six thousand dollars; same road, Oskaloosa division, fourteen miles, valuation, sixteen thousand eight hundred and sixty-four dollars.

Iowa Central, eleven miles, valuation fifteen thousand two hundred dollars.

As a curio, the shipments from here from September 6, to December 31, '58, after the M. & M. road, now the C., R. I. & P., opened, were—hogs, twelve thousand four hundred and twenty; cattle, seven hundred and forty-eight: merchandise, three hundred twenty-nine thousand and twenty-two pounds; total pounds, four million two hundred nineteen thousand and twenty-two.

Shipments into town, in the same time—salt, one thousand eight hundred and ten pounds; lumber, one million eighty-six thousand feet; coal, seven hundred eight thousand pounds; merchandise, one million six hundred seven thousand seven hundred and eighty-six pounds; total pounds, nine millions four hundred twenty-two thousand seven hundred and eighty-four.

Washington station's Rock Island receipts average ten thousand dollars a month, and the Burlington and Milwaukee roads do a good business. The exports of cattle, hogs and horses are heavy. West Chester makes an enormous showing of live stock shipments, and Ainsworth, Wellman, Kalona, Riverside, Brighton make remarkable reports. Our farmers do not ship so much grain; they have not for over thirty years raised enough wheat to bread our population: almost everybody buys flour, and stock-raisers aim to export all the corn into the inwards of their steers and hogs. The horse history is astonishing. A few years ago his extinction was freely predicted, and he did, indeed, become so cheapened that he could hardly be given away. He was disdained as a wedding present, and by thieves. But all that dull time his neck was still clothed with thunder, though the noise was muffled under his mane. He rallied, he cantered down the country lanes, the price went soaring, and hundreds and thousands of him were sent east and south. The country seemed to be made of horses. Throw a few shovels-full of dust into the air, the particles assembled in the shape of a horse, and one could plainly read on his flanks the bright characters, "one hundred and fifty dollars," "two hundred dollars," and even "two hundred and fifty dollars."

The railways have made this county, but it is impossible to gather a jury that will do the roads simple justice, so intense and irrational is the popular prejudice. But—courage! patience! In a thousand years or so this may all come right.

To make the celebration of the advent of the first railroad complete, let me add that Muscatine gave a return party that fall, and a great crowd went from Washington, filling all the passenger coaches and box cars that could be scraped together. The scramble for entrance and for seats was like the assault of ants on a chicken bone. Clothing was torn, skin abraded, and the loss of buttons, sweat, cuticle, women's squeals and men's cuss words was great. Witnesses have never quit laughing at the remembered comical aspect of one very stout woman who despaired of getting in via the platform. A squad of her male friends picked her up and tried to chute her in head first thro' an open window. She sprained the window, and stuck at the hips. No amount of pushing from the outside and pulling of arms, neck and waist from within, could budge her voluminous and redundant corporosity. Men tugged and pulled to the tune of "he' O, he'," as at a house-raising—in vain. She kicked, squealed, screamed, but it was no go. And to yank the wedged-in creature out was quite as serious a proposition. The men feared they would pull out her legs, as they had served grasshoppers, in boyhood. But she was not needed to fill the train. Half the crowd stood up all the way, packing the aisles and dangerous old-style platforms. The train did not stop at Ainsworth, for not another soul could be taken aboard. The crowd there were so mad at the slight, they soaped the track on the stiff grade just west of the station, and the train, returning in the evening, stuck as effectually as that fat woman. The engine spilled all its sand, and more was shoveled on the slick rails, and the big wheels spun around furiously, and the train crew did not talk Sunday school language, while the Ainsworth avengers laughed, guyed, joshed, and made exasperating suggestions. At last, the wheels gripped, and soon tired humanity was dumped at the great metropolis.

A belated report may be inserted here, showing the average Rock Island shipments out and in per month, a monthly business of ten thousand dollars:

Forwarded		Received	
Corn	64 cars	Coal	405 cars
Oats	67 cars	Lumber	56 cars
Horses	38 cars	Salt	12 cars
Cattle	163 cars	Building Material	110 cars
Hogs	132 cars	Vegetables—Fruit	9 cars
Sheep	14 cars	Flour	68 cars
Hay	17 cars	Live Stock	84 cars
Miscellaneous	252 cars	Implements	23 cars
		Miscellaneous	92 cars

CHAPTER X.

CHURCHES—RELIGION.

Norman Everson used to recite with droll animation a lingo that Henry Clay Dean would get off at pioneer meetings:

"No sooner had the hardy pioneer crossed the Mississippi river with his ox team and family and few possessions, close on the heels of the retreating Indians, and made a claim in this beautiful wilderness, built a log cabin, planted a garden and perhaps an orchard, and a field with corn, far removed from his eastern home and all he held dear, than the Methodist circuit rider came along on his old white mare, sitting on saddle-bags containing a Bible and a hymn book, and singing cheerily,

"How happy are they
Who their Saviour obey."

That is, man is an animal re-inforced by an intellect, a heart and a soul. He is a spiritual being. Religious institutions grow out of him like buds, and he puts forth, as leaves, churches, Sunday schools, prayer meetings, camp-meetings, revivals. The new men and women in these new places in the county organized themselves on several lines at once—creating local government, churches, schools. Crystals of organization were shooting in every direction, and at the earliest times the settlers were fashioned into a civilized society, developing and protecting itself by agencies and influences secular and spiritual. In nearly every settlement there was hearty co-operation to provide religious service and education. Of course, there was a difference in communities. In some nooks there was a rough, tough element; the names given to their localities, and which still adhere as tightly as chimney-swallow mud nests, indicate that they were heedless as to religion and education. In all strong migrations such an element was a sort of jail-delivery back east. Here and there, mingled with good people, were "undesirable citizens," rowdies, men with criminal tendencies, lawless, given to drink and violence, men and women who had broken all the commandments, and found it convenient to get out of the scene of broken laws into backwoods localities where their former exploits were unknown. This county was no exception. There are bad streaks in all counties, people who had been or easily might be thieves, adulterers, drunkards, ne'er-do-wells in the old homes. It was a very important matter—the character of the first-comers for they shaped the history of their localities. Birds of a feather flocked together. Good people attracted their like and repelled their opposites, and vice versa. As a rule, it was good, self-respecting, enterprising stuff that came to this county as raw material to be worked up into a thrifty, intelligent, moral body-politic. And it was quite as natural for them to bud out in schools and churches as for a plant in spring to unfold buds and blossoms and bear fruit. Our people had the church-going habit. It is a very good habit. Habit it is. Most people who go, go automatically—it is inheritance or habit, and folk act under this habit as under any other habit. All sorts of things enter into this Sunday-go-to-meeting habit as warp and woof, as custom, requirement, ennui, etc. There is the social instinct. People like to see each other once a week at least, touch palms, touch antennæ like bugs, and there is a subtler strand—the eye-beams that lovers exchange at church are stronger than steel cables and draw from far. Then the enjoyment of music, the gratification to self-respect that comes with the Sunday bath and donning clean clothes, one's best suits; the Sunday shave, and shoe-shine, all these furnishings up of the person are sort o' religious. Then there is the pleasure of hearing new things, new truths, or old truths pleasingly re-stated. Altogether, church-going amounts to a kind of mild inspiration; there is an up-lift both agreeable and helpful. It is a good habit, I repeat. So thought our pioneers, and they went with zest to religious service in log cabins, in school houses, at camp-meetings in the woods, and they seemed to delight more in funerals than in any other form of religious diversion. That is true of all pioneer neighborhoods. It was so on the Western Reserve in Ohio, to my personal knowledge. Funerals appealed to everybody. If a funeral occurred on a week day, still they all dressed in their best and went. The mourners felt it as quite an alleviation to grief, if the string of buggies, wagons and other vehicles was as long as any that had been carefully counted in those parts lately. Every woman had brought from the east some bit of finery, perhaps a black silk dress, that was reserved especially for parties, church and funerals. And the men had brought a best coat and a beaver and perhaps a silk hat of more or less ancient vintage. It had seen so much of such holy service, having been dedicated to religion, that usually the nap was worn off in spots, and the edges of the brim and band were greased as if with spiritual unction. Many a dent had it received, as if in a crowd it had been squeezed or sat upon. Costumes in this county in the '30s and '40s did not change with the present day kaleidoscopic velocity. A pioneer could wear a plug hat fifty years without any real

ONE OF THE GROUP OF ELMS IN WEST WASHINGTON
Under which First Communion was held in Washington County

need of upholstering. Children remembered the different hats in a congregation for a generation. You would no more get confused as to Smith's tile, Brown's cady, and Robinson's plug, than as to the identities of their good wives. Everybody knew everybody else's hat, coat, calf-skin boots as infallibly as each farmer's ox or horse team and vehicle of whatever sort it was.

My vividest memory of the days in the '40s in Ohio was of these venerable plug hats—heirlooms that had been in families for generations. Such a tile was an unique, forgotten and, except in this survival, extinct fashion, like the cold craters of volcanoes—narrow, straight brims, greasy edges, perfect cylinders of uniform bore, the "hair" mostly worn off it; the nap had disappeared in spots, leaving a glazed surface like a horse's flank where the tug has worn off the fell; it looked like a spoon with the nickel or silver wash destroyed. The owner of this fossil curio always wore it on state occasions, to market, to political meetings, elections, church, and especially to funerals. In no other form could he show equal respect to "the remains." It was instinctively felt as an insult to "the corpse," to leave that immemorial plug hat at home. So every funeral was a museum of all the antiquated plugs, brought out in profound respect for "the diseased," as they called the cadaver. In heat, in cold, in rain, in snow or shine, they religiously wore those plugs to the graveyard.

No religious service drew like funerals. All went, even babes at the breast, to see "how hard they took it." The main industry of some people, especially women, was going to funerals, to get thrills, and a chance to weep. The patriarchs tottered to the house of mourning, their dark-veined hands trembling so with palsy they could with difficulty hold their sticks. We see a general outline of the ancient manners yet. The house is reserved for women and children; the men sit outside, whittle, masticate tobacco, gossip, talk crops, expectorate with deadly aim, laugh and tell stories. "The remains" don't know it, and would not care if it did, for that is hoary custom and inviolate. Every body seemed to enjoy funerals, and perhaps folks nowadays get more solid satisfaction out of some people's funerals than in any other sort of matinee.

So with the traditions, customs and habits of the old home places, our pioneers did not long go without means of grace. In nearly every settlement in this county it is known who preached the first sermon in the township, at whose log cabin, on what date—it was a red-letter day, and was set down in the local annals. The minister that day was so very great a man—board measurement—the earth's surface sank quite a bit as he passed along. Some woman is still alive who can tell you just how much that distinguished man ate that day, and she'll count off on her fingers the dishes, wild turkey, squirrel, 'possum, quail, prairie chicken, all the vegetables, butters, preserves, jams, jels, seventeen kinds of pies and puddings, and that holy man—why, to hold all the stuff, he had to be a holy man, full of holes and cavities, and fill 'em all up chuck, or the hostess would be hopping mad. Let's take a few samples of first preachments, leaving out the restaurant details:

At Brighton, at Seneca Beach's home, in 1839, by Rev. Mr. Crill, M. E., just across the line in Clay.

In this city, Rev. Geo. G. Vincent did it on Sunday, February 7, 1841, in Captain Wm. Stone's house. He was sheriff. A sixteen-foot room held the audience, four women and two men, members and all the rest. That was pretty early, and dew was on all things.

In Clay, in 1841, Rev. Mr. Burnham, M. E., followed Mr. Crill who also preached early in Marion.

The first quarterly meeting in the county was held at Matthew Moorhead's cabin in Crawford, in the winter of 1837-8, Rev. Jos. Kirkpatrick, pastor; Rev. Henry Somers, P. E.

In Iowa township Rev. R. McReynolds preached the first sermon in R. B. Davis' house in June, 1840. In '42 a M. E. held forth at Samuel Marlin's home.

In Seventy-six township the first sermon was by Rev. Mr. James, a tanner, in Charles Patterson's cabin, in '46.

In Cedar, Rev. H. Johnson, Baptist, was not "too much Johnson" at Mr. Ayers' house.

In Highland the first service was held in John Forbes' cabin in the winter of '43-4, by Rev. F. R. S. Byrd of the United Brethren church.

As early as '42, Rev. Jos. Hamilton preached at Wm. Wright's cabin in Snake Hollow, English River, and also in the school house, but the first service in English River was by the Methodist, Micajah Reeder, at Jerry Barton's, about 1840. Brother Hamilton practiced as well as preached. He started in a Methodist, but died a Spiritualist.

Nor was Lime Creek destitute of the heavenly manna. The first spiritual downfall was at Jos. Wasson's cabin, Rev. Mr. Nichols, Presbyterian, distributing the provisions.

The first service in Marion was at "Dickey" Moore's log cabin, and people came to it from six to seven miles around, on foot, on horseback, hauled by oxen. At first only six to eight attended regularly, but the congregation grew to twenty. Mother Moore made all stay to dinner, and this mixed material and moral diet seemed to agree with all. Probably angel cake and food were mixed up on the table.

Brother Crill, M. E., organized a church in Clay in '39 or '40, and a Congregational church was founded there July 3, 1842, barely escaping fire-crackers, roman candles and squibs. Rev. Mr. Burnham held a first service, or almost first one, in Hickenbottom's grove, now owned by John Robinson.

Edward Brinton's father was a soldier in the war of 1812, turned Quaker, and burned his wicked uniform, a religious sacrifice or auto-de-fe incident well worth preserving. A religious hallucination may also be noted: At a first service in what is now Rubio in the Fairview neighborhood, at Elijah Smith's house, Wilton Alter, a Friend, preparing for the ministry in Ohio, persuaded himself that he was commanded by the Lord to build a Friend church at Rubio, and a Rev. Mr. Maloy was commanded to bring a tent and help the Lord build it. The sequel is all unknown to this subscriber.

I may say that these were not elaborate services. Probably no flowers, surely no pipe organ, or horn, or trained choir with solos, and no "preludes," "postludes," and "offertories," and other high-sounding things. Probably it was not till much later that there was anything but the baldest congregational singing; perhaps a chorister stood up, bit and gnawed a tuning-fork and tentatively quavered ho, he, hi, ho, hum, then jumped in and swam for dear life in the waves of melody. The minister lined out a psalm or hymn, two lines at a clip, meanwhile the singers getting their second wind—it acted like courses at dinner.

There was more demonstration then, more display of emotion, more fervor, and, perhaps, too much denominationalism or partisanship, or stress laid on doctrines. It was so in Ohio, and probably in Iowa. In hamlets, usually at cross-roads, two churches stood either side of the road, and had a belligerent aspect, as if they were roosters, and their chief function that of game cocks, and each was seeking an opening for a fight. They seemed to have heads lowered, necks extended, both wary, and if they had suddenly jumped into the air off their foundations, struck with wings and spurs, thus bloodily defending the faith, that is, the special doctrines each church stood sponsor and challenger for, you would not have been surprised, as that seemed to be what they were there for—to scrap for a dogma.

There was an amen corner, and it had vigor and vociferation. Churches, as they have become elegant and aristocratic, have gone dumb, lost picturesqueness and what was called "the power." In the time of which I am writing, folks would shout when "happy," and perhaps take a lively run over the tops of benches, leap down, grab a saint or sinner around the neck and tow him toward the mercy-seat, but all that has lapsed; we have left the simple life far in the rear, and "hollering" and blowing noses quite loudly are no longer good form in religion. This is not sneering—it is trying to paint a picture of what once was, but now is lost.

A good many churches were organized in the first ten years, till Iowa became a state in '46, just as immediately after that date a mania set in in this county to build school houses of the better sort, and congregations left log cabins and log school houses, and changed from one church building to a still more ambitious one, a series of transformations from grub to butterfly. Brighton had a Congregational church by July, '41, and went into a one thousand five hundred dollar frame in '56. Rev. Charles Burnham was pastor and the charter members were John, Sarah, Harvey, Bradford Ingham, Seneca and Edna Beach, Eldridge and Jonah Reed, Elizabeth Washburn, Margaret Lyon.

The incorporation books in the recorder's office show that Brighton has so churchy a history, it is in the odor of sanctity. In October, 1848, William, Elizabeth, Reuben, Maria, Elizabeth A., Eleanor and Wm. G. Israel, Nathan Horner, Jane P. Gooderich, Nancy Tracy, Mary McCullough, Joseph Frederick, Phoebe Garrett launched the Church of Christ; Arthur Miller, pastor; James H. Auld, superintendent of Sunday school. A one thousand three hundred dollar church was built in '50.

February 9, '50, Elder Gunn dedicated a Baptist church. In '63 a one thousand four hundred dollar brick church was built. The charter members were Abijah, Sarah, Lewis, Anna, Hannah and Gilbert Fisher, Isaac Arnold, Wm. and Mrs. Mount, Elizabeth Parshall, James and Mary Warren. The elders have been Wm. Elliott, Mitchell, J. C. Burkholder, David Morse, H. H. Parks, J. G. Johnson, N. H. Daily, and these more remote ones will bring the cloth down into the range of current memories.

On January 8, '69, the Seventh Day Adventist church materialized, a Methodist church August 19, '93, and the Presbyterian July 17, '04. At least these dates are of official record, whether of organization, incorporation or re-incorporation, I do not say.

Clay, too, was truly good. The Millses, Meachams, Coopers, Woodfords and more organized a Congregational church in July, '42. It gave two young men to the ministry, Harlow Mills and Wm. Woodmansee, and Clay turned out seven other preachers, Belle Plumb, Ralph Shatto, Jane Smith, Jehu and Oliver Embree, Edward Brinton, Eugene Robinson, Thomas Hyde. There was an M. E. church very early at Black Hawk, the Disberrys, Dillons and others prominent in it, and Mr. Ricker was its first pastor. A six hundred-dollar frame church was built in '63. Other ministers were Koch, Haines, Kirkpatrick, McDowell.

SECOND UNITED PRESBYTERIAN CHURCH

Can I read aright that the Congregationalists worshipped in a log school house till a four thousand-dollar church was built in 1902?

Marion did not hide her lights under a bushel. The M. E's. at Eureka organized in September, '49, and by '58 had an eight hundred and fifty-dollar church. The Baptists were on the map in April, '56, and by '70 had a one thousand seven hundred-dollar house. In '56 the sect called Mennonites began to appear, and in '68 worshipped in a six hundred-dollar church near Noble, but in 1895 it was replaced by the present church. Joseph Goldsmith was the first pastor, but from near the first Rev. Benj. Eicher was a commanding personality in the church not only, but in the community, in the affairs and politics of the county. While a man of perfect suavity, he was full of original force. He died suddenly on December 7, '93, and his memory is a sweet savor there still.

This novel ecclesiastical society merits a sketch, if but brief. Service is held in German and English on alternate Sundays. The ritual and dress persist from long-ago days. Mennonite families came dropping in, from Switzerland, Alsace-Lorraine, Pennsylvania, Ohio. Martin Eicher in '51, Daniel Conrad in '52, Jos. Sommer in '53, Christian Tchauntz in '56. The church grew, and another congregation was formed in Wayland, Pastor Musselman serving it and other churches. The sect is traced back to the twelfth century, to the Waldenses who protested against the abuses of the established church. Before Luther, they held the right of individuals to read and heed the Bible for themselves. The name is applied to Menno Simon, a Catholic monk in Holland. They were Quakers as to non-resistance, disdained office, took no oaths before magistrates, believed in freedom of conscience, adult baptism, consubstantiation, and in the simple life, and take Jesus and his teaching as the guides of life. They are industrious and honest, excellent people.

The Christian church was founded at Shiloh August 18, '76, about which time a man shot a 'possum near there, and ever since there has been an active rivalry to hold the name of the locality, whether 'Possum Hollow or Shiloh. So far, the rodent is ahead, and President Taft's partiality for the animal may nail the prehensile creature to the spot for aye.

Pleasant Hill church is a two thousand-dollar specimen of architecture. The Methodists, the Darbyshires, Grays, Beenblossoms et al, raised their Ebenezer at said place.

A Union Christian conference was created February 7, 1905.

United Brethren got into Ainsworth in '60, the Stones, Hazens and more being of that persuasion, and the United Presbyterians said "present" April 25, '64, their church being made from overflows from Crawfordsville and

Washington. A church was dedicated by Rev. Dr. J. R. Doig in '66, a one thousand two hundred-dollar frame, but it was sold in '73, and a three thousand five hundred-dollar church built and was dedicated by Rev. N. H. Brown. In '64, too, the M. E.'s got in on June 27.

Crawfordsville was a stronghold of United Presbyterians and a fortified home of abolitionists and other groups of humanitarians. The U. P.'s organized in '46, or some of their spiritual progenitors did and the Crawfords, Maxwells, McCalls, Woolleys, Fergusons and others were prominent. In '50 the Presbyterians reinforced Zion, the Youngs, Prathers and more being worthy representatives, and in '54 they had a one thousand eight hundred-dollar church.

But as early as '42, Rev. Charles Burnham and the Neals and others figured as Congregationalists, and in '53 a frame church was dedicated. At Xenia there was an M. E. chapel, January 17, '61.

In Dutch Creek, Pleasant Valley U. P. church was organized in '48 by the Robbs, Jeffries, Junkins, Harrises, and in '56 they spent on a church, two thousand one hundred and sixty-eight dollars. Rev. J. F. Tate was pastor from '54 to '70, and again after Rev. John Lackey had served from '71 to '74.

In Iowa township the M. E.'s had services as early as '42. In '73 they built a three thousand five hundred-dollar church, and the next year Rev. and Professor N. W. Fellows of the state university dedicated it. The Baptists and United Brethren were vigorous, but the Catholics were the strongest of all denominations. St. Vincent's church dates from '44, a frame was built in '48, an addition made in '58, a new two thousand seven hundred-dollar church in '77, and St. Mary's, costing four thousand five hundred dollars, appeared in '76. The costliest, most beautiful church in the county, costing forty-five thousand dollars, crowns the hill and is seen for miles every way, a big school on one flank, and on the other a ten thousand-dollar parsonage of brick, entirely modern throughout. Riverside leads the county in church architecture. Father Jacobsmaier is a remarkable organizer, a public-spirited citizen, a gentleman of the finest type—in all ways a model man. He has done a lot of good in this county.

The Catholics are strong in English River, too. In Richmond, Holy Trinity was built in '55, and a twenty thousand-dollar brick church succeeded it in '68, and twenty-five years ago a parochial school, and St. Vincent's on the hill had a school.

The United Brotherhood got in December 26, '64, and Nathan Littler, Gideon Bear and others organized Missionary Baptist church July 14, '66. In Kalona the M. E.'s incorporated November 26, '88, and renewed October 27, 1908.

Rev. T. H. Holmes
Congregational Church

Rev. John O'Laughlin
Christian Church

Rev. C. J. Greenwood
Baptist Church

Rev. Benjamin Eicher
Emanuel Mennonite Church

PIONEER PASTORS

September 12, '91, the Regular Missionary Baptist church was organized.

In English River and Lime Creek were many Amish, lapping over into Johnson and Iowa counties are Mennonites. Their population is one thousand two hundred, and five hundred communicants. Plain in dress, simple in habits, non-resistants, clergy unsalaried, taking no oaths, thrifty, frugal, God-fearing people. They settled in that region in '46, and Daniel P. Guenerich, Wm. Wertz, Peter Miller, Jacob Schwartzendruber were leaders. Their spiritual kin first settled in West Point in Lee county, but finding land titles faulty, they followed Rev. Joseph Goldsmith in '47 to Marion township. Bishop Sebastian Gerig, of Wayland, is now shepherd of the flock. These people try to keep unspotted from the world, inter-marry, that is, will not take affinities outside their church members, and divorce is utterly forbidden.

There was a Christian church in Richmond, the Bushes being influential members. And the Baptists, the Bears, Kerrs and others built a church, but later the Bohemians bought it for a dance hall, and its dedication got a "crick in its back" and lapsed.

The M. E.'s also had a church in Richmond, and a Bunker Hill church near Bunker Mill, established February 27, '63.

Lime Creek had the usual force of spiritual batteries. The first gun got the range at Wassonville. It was a Presbyterian six-pounder fired from Wasson's house. The Methodists and Seventh Day Adventists limbered up and went off at Pilotburg. One of the most notable of the county clergy, Rev. Dr. Hiram W. Thomas, of later Chicago fame, began his career there, coming to the Washington M. E. church afterwards He was as skinny as an eel, as thin as a lath, and bay-haired, but he advanced from glory to glory. His first wife was the making of him. She was ambitious for him, fenced off bores and cranks, had a world of fun with him, being an irrepressible humorist and wit. She could herself write a spanking sermon, that would make the hair of sinners curl. Probably, she was as delightful and brilliant a woman as ever sparkled in this county. She kept him up to his tasks, and stimulated him with all sorts of ginger, red and green peppers and tobasco sauce, horse-radish and other bitey things, and in revivals she could corral sinners in a barbed-wire inclosure of convictions, and make them feel that "getting religion" was as fine as getting a shave from a lovely girl barber. The M. E.'s captured Daytonville, and a Christian church flourished not far away. In later years Methodists, Baptists and United Brethren took root in Wellman and U. B.'s in Nira.

Wassonville had in 1856 something quite as good as churches, so far as the humanities are concerned. It was a station on the underground railroad, and in the strenuous "free" Kansas times was a point on the highway traveled by abolition emigrants carrying Beecher's twin weapons, bibles and rifles. The late great Sigourney lawyer, George D. Woodin, was an active organizer of the forces that made Kansas a free state. Jim Lane and his band spent a Sunday at Wassonville, and John Brown stayed three weeks nearby, nursing a lame mule, leaving two boxes of clothing with a friend, to be called for later, but he never sent for them. Hero-worshippers would call Wassonville holy ground, slough their shoes at the sacred spot and go barefoot on the places where trod a queer composite—a fanatic, a holy prophet, a crazy man, and a conscience incarnate, all these diverse elements constituting the mightiest moral hero of the nineteenth century, John Brown, whose soul still goes marching on.

Washington township has had the Pleasant Hill church of the Disciples of Christ since November 5, '66.

Franklin Congregational church arose February 20, '63. The Methodists organized in West Chester, February 22, '73, and dedicated a church next year, the U. P.'s August 7, '76, the Baptists some later.

Because of the rarity of a Moravian church, the hamlet of Grace Hill is distinguished as the habitat of the one sole church of that faith in Iowa. There was another one in Newton, but it died. In 1854, Amos Miksch and bride came from Ohio. He entered two hundred and twenty acres of land at Grace Hill, got aid from the Provincial Elders' conference at Bethlehem, Pa., borrowed all the money he could and with it entered three hundred acres adjoining his farm, and turned it over to the church, and it is now a permanent fund for the church's support. A bishop came from Bethlehem, and held a service at Mr. Miksch's house, and a church was organized with eighteen members, and it was incorporated February 28, '74. The leading spirits were said Miksch, C. S. Strohm, E. E. Rehmel, John Buxbaum and others. The numbers increased to forty, the Newton church to half that. The ministers get small salaries on principle as well as necessity, but the superanuates and their widows are pensioned. All members are taxed sixty cents a head. The Moravians claim to be the first Protestant church to send a missionary to the West Indies. When the islands forbade missionaries on account of slavery George Smith sold himself into slavery that he might preach the gospel to the blacks. That started the habit of college professors disguising themselves as tramps, to write books on hobos.

Franklin also had the sect called Dunkards. Stephen Yoder began to preach in his house in '66, and got some fifty adherents, and he also preached in Keokuk and Johnson counties. When he could not find a tallow dip and matches in a school house, he said he would preach by moonshine. These good people never had a church in this county.

MORAVIAN CHURCH AT GRACE HILL

Seventy-six was one of the latest townships to organize, but the United Brethren had services at Martin Cochran's house in '62, and in '73 built a one thousand eight hundred-dollar frame church that President Kephart of Western College dedicated. The first Sunday school in the township was held at Cochran's home.

The Fishers, Weekses, McLaughlins, Robbs and Hamels organized Westminster U. P. church in February, '67, and next year built a two thousand four hundred-dollar frame church. The pastors were Messrs. Tate, Lackey and others.

Zion Center dates from December 3, '93.

Though Highland is a late township, it was threaded with religious organizations. Davis Creek Baptist church started July 11, '68, East Prairie M. E. church in '70, but in May, '76, they bought the East Prairie school house on section 8, for three hundred and fifty dollars, and worshipped in it. Bethel Presbyterian church bears date January 11, '82, the U. B. church August 26, '87, and Haskins First Presbyterian church October 25, 1902.

Jackson, too, waxed with spiritual fatness, thanks to the U. P.'s, M. E.'s and Baptists. The Glasgows, Lytles and more organized Grand Prairie U. P. church August 22, '59, and in '67 built a three thousand-dollar frame church, in which Rev. Dr. J. R. Doig and Rev. H. P. Ferguson preached.

Living Lake U. P. church was founded in '68, and the Meekses and Martins were active in it. Grand Prairie church finally lapsed into a barn, a sad fate, and decided anti-climax.

The Methodists built in Pleasant Plains a two thousand three hundred-dollar church, and the late Rev. F. A. Shearer organized a Presbyterian church April 11, '64. All these bodies had good church buildings running above two thousand two hundred dollars.

It is a shining fact, how much a single man may stand for in a church and county. Take a man like James Dawson, Calvin Craven, Nathan Littler, Martin Cochran, as types, each one a tremendous force. Craven was a power in Cedar, let loose in a seven hundred dollar church in February, '68. Its pastors were John Coffman, J. H. Miller, E. D. Porter, T. H. Jones. Hardly less powerful forces in the Lexington M. E. church were the Youngs, Gardners, Storeys, Bishops, in '63, and the Browns, Melvins and Dicks in the M. E. church that Rev. Mr. Kendig dedicated in September, '73. It cost two thousand two hundred and fifty dollars.

The First United Presbyterian church in Washington was, before its spiritual migration, the Associate Presbyterian. It is not necessary to trace the several strands of history of Reformed Presbyterians, or Covenanters, Associate, Associate Reformed and what not—I never did have head enough to untangle the coils and kinks and get it straight, so I merely say that when James Dawson came here in 1839, and found Seceders scattered here and there toward Crawfordsville, they sent in to an eastern Presbytery for a preacher. It was the rule that before a man could be a full-fledged minister he must serve a year as itinerary missionary. George C. Vincent was licensed in Ohio, June 30, 1840, and was offered all of two hundred dollars to come here. W. J. Case, the only lawyer here, subscribed ten dollars toward the fund, and got a like pledge from every man in town, tho' several were rather loud infidels. However, in that age of Jeffersonian simplicity, no one thought the money of such kind, helpful men was tainted. Brother V., wife and two children came overland, in a buggy, and the ozone did them all good. On February 7, 1841, he preached the first sermon ever given here. Text, discourse, all rumor and tradition of them, have gone down stream into oblivion, irrecoverable. He began his pastorate July 4 following. As no fireworks were allowed, there were no accidents and no casualties—it was a safe and sane Fourth of July. The congregation was organized October 14, by Revs. Wm. Smith and D. G. Bullions. We know nothing about these clerical gentlemen. Smith, Smith, that is a familiar name—we have heard it somewhere before, but can't place him; very likely he was a descendant of Captain John Smith whom Pocahontas saved from the Big Stick of Roosevelt Powhattan. Bullions is a good name—probably some kin, this minister, of Thomas H. Benton, alias "Old Bullion." Any way, they started the first congregation in this good town, and we all thank them for it. They were only eleven, but that is neither the number thirteen nor twenty-three, and we have reason to be glad they escaped those rocks. Let us record their names here: James and Elizabeth Dawson, George and Jane Dill, Wm. and Rosanna French, also Jennet French, Mrs. Thomas Ritchie, Mrs. Electa Conger, Mrs. Jane Jackson. Mrs. M. C. Vincent. The ruling elders were Dawson and French. Installation, November 24, '41; first communion, August 6, '42, held, like other public meetings, under the biggest of the group of elms on Gospel Ridge, on the lot where now stands Frank Stewart's house on West Washington street. The former owner wished to raise a few cabbages and things, and slew that giant tree, and he and his memory deserve as decoration a string of hen's teeth. At that meeting, thirty-five were received, twenty-eight by certificates from churches in Pennsylvania, Ohio and Indiana. So many joined, the court house would not hold them, and in '44 a church, twenty-four by thirty-six, two stories, was built, and the loft used as a school, taught by the pastor as long as he staid. The building cost eight hundred dollars, but the labor and materials were donated. Mr. Vincent served till September 8, 1847, when the Lord, having the same habits then as now, "called" him to another field, to

George C. Vincent

Pennsylvania, and in a year Rev. W. H. Andrew came, also in a buggy, from the east, was installed September 14, 1848, and remained till April 10, 1851. The church grew, and building No. 2 was erected for three thousand dollars. A financier can spell town prosperity in those figures. But after a while this structure lapsed into what is now a mournful house, mis-named music hall, and it degenerated still farther into theater, barracks, skating rink, basket-ball gymnasium, under the ownership of Dr. Chilcote, Colonel Scofield and A. H. Wallace. The latter being the sole surviver is probably the one custodian of a lapsed dedication. What he does with the dedication I can't make out. He might stuff or can it.

Pastor No. 3 was W. H. Wilson, serving with ability from the fall of '53 to September 9, '69, when he went to Salinas, Cal., thence to The Dalles on the Columbia. In '64 the church had let him serve as chaplain in the army.

The present church was built for sixteen thousand dollars under his reign, but it has been twice remodelled at nearly as much expense since, and is now the finest auditorium in the city.

Rev. W. C. Williamson came April 19, '71, a Revolutionary anniversary, and stayed till July 21, '85. It was unfortunate that differences as to such non-essentials as instrumental music resulted in his withdrawal to Keokuk, then to Burlington. He was able, dearly beloved, full of sweetness and light. Whenever he has returned, series of affectionate ovations have overwhelmed him, but he liked them as the feeble, aged Voltaire enjoyed being "smothered under roses" when he returned to Paris from Geneva, a fortnight before his death. Far different from Montezuma's finish on "a bed of roses."

Rev. A. L. Davidson served from June 11, '89, to September 9, 1902, yielding to Rev. F. O. Ross, an odd genius, who came in 1903. He was at once a book-worm, a student, a scholar, and a man of the world, all wrapped up in politics. Indeed, as to that taste, he was more Methodist than United Presbyterian, and a distance like the diameter of the solar system separated him from a Covenanter who will not vote, tho' a critic. How Ross did like to read out the election returns, national election nights, making funny remarks, and leading the hip-hip-hurrah with all of a noisy boy's relish. He was a bully fellow, if that language is parliamentary. Alas! He died of ptomaine poisoning in July, 1909.

Rev. W. O. Fisher, is the present pastor, a handsome, cultivated gentleman who seems likely to stay a long while. He has a fine stage presence, indeed, he looks, acts and carries himself like Senator Cummins, is fluent, thoughtful, a hard worker, but is not robust. If he cares for his health with a sort of religious devotion, he should be with us many years, with profit to his congregation and to the entire community.

There is not room to detail even the sketchiest history of all the local churches. But the First United Presbyterian merited an outline, as it was Washington's first, that is, historical church.

The Second United Presbyterian church was originally the Associate Reformed, but went into the union in '58. The first Associate Reform sermon preached in the county was earlier than Mr. Vincent's, viz., during the week between the first and second Sabbaths of July, 1835, by Rev. Alex. Blaikie, who was appointed by synod for that service. This happened within the bounds of Brighton congregation, long since dissolved. In '40, Dr. Samuel Findley and Benj. Waddle were sent out to visit mission fields, and the former preached the first Associate Reform sermon in Washington at Wm. Wallace's home, June 10, 1840. Then came ministers Samuel Sturgeon, Jeremiah Dick and J. B. Clark in '53-4. An Associate Reform church was organized either in '53 or '55, and Pastor Sawhill compromises on September 11, 1854, when J. A. Donaldson and I. N. Smith were chosen ruling elders, and among the charter members (the record prior to '58 is missing) were Mrs. M. M. Young, Alex. Young, Samuel and Mrs. McCloskey, Mrs. A. Adams, Mrs. Rebecca Norwood, Samuel R. Palmer, Sr., the colonel's father. The first communion was on September 24, '54; the first pastor was S. F. Van Atta, ordained and installed June 14, '55. He also had the Brighton charge, giving each a Sabbath about. This relation lasted till the fall of '63 when he was appointed by synod member of the Christian commission and went south on a gun-boat, with his wife. Below Vicksburg it was fired on by guerrillas in ambush. The captain bade all lie down flat on deck, but before the Van Attas could obey, a cannon ball virtually decapitated Mrs. Van Atta and a minnie ball lodging in his hip killed him the next day. He had served from June 14, '55 to May, '63. Then came, in turn, Abijah Conner, '65 to '69; N. E. Wade, '70 to '72; R. B. Taggart, '74 to '76; H. G. McVey, '77 to '80; J. R. Logue, '83 to January 1, 1903; W. R. Sawhill began March 1, 1903, and is still making abundantly good.

A brick church was built in '57, and in '77 they bought the Congregational church. The old brick stood on the sites of Daniel Wilde and James Work's present homes, and at noon recess the folks could look across the valley and see an ex-judge's bald head shine like a tin roof in the sun, as he hoed in his garden, and they had to vacate, I take it, tho' the distance from the square was a handicap. Besides, the condition of the church they bought, as described elsewhere, was such, they had to build, and the present pretty church was erected in 1890 and dedicated January 25, '91.

Van Atta is rated a martyr, and wears a halo in fond memory. The church proudly cherishes the name of Connor. He was a free lance, stopped the

First Place of Worship

Third Place of Worship

Second Place of Worship

FIRST UNITED PRESBYTERIAN CHURCH.

slip-shod finances of the church, putting it on a cash basis, was small, sick, but plucky, afraid of neither man nor devil. Elected to the legislature after he broke down, he did not live to take his seat.

Logue held the pastorate twenty years, the longest in the church, and some say, in the city. Everybody liked, nay, loved him, as ditto Williamson. His fund of friendship availed him as much as a gift of diplomacy. He was our sole minister who went to Europe to get a wife. He did not know he had got her, when he came back here, but all unbeknownst he had caught the matrimonial microbe and the insidious thing kept gnawing till it got in its perfect work. He brought here a very superior woman, perhaps quite to the disappointment of the lovely local market.

It will not do to praise Brother Sawhill as he deserves, for he is very modest. However, I will say he is an invaluable man in this, he saves things. He would be an admirable curator for the county historical society, for he has an instinct to file away documents of all sorts, of local interest, pamphlets, programs, write-ups, things that a dozen or fifty years hence will be priceless. If you ever want to find out anything Washingtonian, just bone Sawhill for it, and he'll bring it out of the treasures of the snow, as it were.

The church celebrated its semi-centennial September 12, 1904. Mr. Logue could not get here. Pastor Sawhill gave an interesting historical sermon, the 11th, and Brother Ross added to it in the evening, and Colonel Palmer made a good sheaf of reminiscences, and the banquet was a buster of a gastronomical feat, and the toasts and responses beat even the meats and gravies, vegetables, fruits, jellies, jams, preserves, pies and puddings all hollow.

On October 2, '41, Rev. Hezekiah Johnson, with Calvin Craven, Isaac Arnold and Samuel Kite and their wives concluded to organize a Baptist church, and the next Sunday he preached his first sermon. Craven was elected deacon and clerk. Having no regular home, they worshipped from house to house, often at Judge Enoch Ross'. Their first church dates from May 17, '51, located on the present site, and it is still used as a Sunday school room. Rev. Hiram Burnett preached the dedicatory sermon.

The second church was a seven thousand dollar affair, dedicated by Rev. N. F. Ravelin, of Chicago, December 24, '71. It, in turn, was remodelled, and dedicated by Rev. S. E. Wilcox, of Boone, November 19, '99. The pastors have been Johnson, Wm. E. Elliott, H. Burnett, Charles Thompson, A. Pratt, H. A. Borden, Arthur Stall, J. M. Wood, E. C. Cady, S. M. Cramblett, A. V. Bloodgood, A. Robbins, Gilman Parker, R. J. Langridge, Dr. E. C. Spinney, and among the later ones N. B. Rairden, J. C. Greenwood, A. T. Fowler, Robert Gray, John Stafford, E. F. Lilley, Roy D. Echlin, H. D. Rodgers, present incumbent. The notable pillars of the church were Judge Ross and daughters, C. Craven, N. Littler, Deacons Smith, Babcock, Sage, Doolittle, and at present Drs. Jenkins and Wickham, 'Squire Kerr, the Eldridges, Bakers, Longs, Bowmans, Sages, and others.

Frank Smith and Kate Ackley are held in fragrant memory for their long service in the choir, and after the pipe organ came Miss Ada Jenkins, whose death will ever be regretted while memory of her remains, showed unwonted and tireless devotion to music as a powerful aid to the religious sentiment's creation.

It is remarkable, the number of pastors in this church who came from Canada or were of English descent.

Trinity Protestant Episcopal Society was founded August 1, '54, but for forty years the little band had nothing to show for it but a lot that was to revert to mother society if a church were not built on it. It lay vacant, raising weeds for a long while, tho' a corner stone was laid May 12, '56, by Bishop Lee, with imposing ceremonies. Finally, about '94, Mrs. Raguet, a bright woman, full of ginger, set yeast under things episcopal, and Trinity Chapel was built and consecrated June 16, '95. Dr. Paguet, of Muscatine, conducted services some time, followed by Mr. Fitch, a layman, and he by the first pastor, Frederick Parkinson, giving his time between What Cheer and this city, till he was drowned in Skunk river. Next layman James Shaeffer, Rev. Munro for three months, when Rev. Joseph de Forest, of Davenport, was a delight for two years. He died suddenly in San Francisco. Cameron Morrison filled the place in the summer of '93. The last pastor was the waggish Rev. R. G. Jones, but he, too, was called to Burlington, a devouring monster of a city that sucked out also brothers Schreckengast and Michels.

Catholic priests came in here very early, on horseback, to say mass in private houses, carrying all the necessaries in a grip, then passing on, as Parkman says the priestly heroes did in Canada three hundred years ago. The first star that fixes itself is Father Sullivan, in '53. Father Mann was drowned in Main creek, fording it. Slatterly, of Mt. Pleasant, came in '55 and built the first church, a frame thirty-five by sixty-five, in '61. It was later sold to Jesse Phillips. In '65 Philip Shanahan became the first resident priest, followed, next year, by M. Schiffmacher; he taught school, and married the first Catholic couple, Mr. and Mrs. James Casey, Sr. Jos. McDermott in '70, in '71 to '76 Father Harding, Dunn filling one of these years. Harding built the first school and brought the Sisters here in '74, and all his little spare time he played the flute like an angel. M. M. Tierney built an addition to the school from '76 to '78. D. J. Flannery, a jolly Pat, held forth from '78 to '82; he bought for five hundred dollars the four lots the church and parsonage

REV. ABIJAH CONNER

REV. ROBERT HUNTER
First Resident Minister
Clay Congregational Church

REV. CHARLES THOMPSON
Pastor of Baptist Church

stand on, and built the latter for two thousand six hundred dollars. J. J. O'Brien, Kirkpatrick, and Moron succeed, and the king of them, B. Jacobsmeier, arrived July 20, '93. His great work was the organization of societies as aids in spiritual work, the Rosary, Sodality for either sex, League of the Sacred Heart, St. James Sanctuary Society and Sewing Circle, with some three hundred and seventy members. The school was built for ten thousand dollars in 1901. Aside from city school taxes paid, they have spent thirty-five thousand dollars for the education of their children. The parish numbers four hundred and the communicants over three hundred. Father Walsh is in charge now—a man of ability and, being Irish, his fund of humor is up to par.

The Presbyterian church was founded September 23, '43, by Rev. L. G. Bell, then missionary, and the first Presbyterian minister in the state, it is said. He introduced Presbyterian whiskers here in that year. It was organized in the old court house by Samuel Culbertson and wife, John Hawthorn and wife, and C. B. Campbell, a prominent man here then, a courtly gentleman, brother to Mrs. A. H. Patterson, and for whom Cam. Patterson was named. He and Culbertson were chosen ruling elders. He served in the first convention to form a state constitution. He had been in the war with General Harrison, and in the battle of Lundy Lane, and was promoted to the rank of major. He was clerk of the church sessions ten years, but left us in '53 for Kansas. A more elegant Christian gentleman never breathed our air. Culbertson long kept the Iowa House and a store in it. All that first company are gone. The first church was built in '46, on Main and Green streets, the Library corner, but it and the lot were sold for one thousand two hundred dollars, in '65, and a three thousand dollar house built on East Washington street, close to the Burlington tracks, but to escape the noise, the society bought a lot east of the academy, which had long been hallowed by Mother Axtell's hashery, where such noted bachelors as Norman Everson, Colonel Scofield, bankers J. R. and Cass Richards, lawyers Lewis, Bennett, Sherman, McJunkin boarded and cut up high jinks. It became as noted, locally, as the taverns in London where Shakespeare, Ben Jonson, Dr. Sam Johnson, Goldsmith, Lamb and others put up and made immortal with their Noctes Ambrosianae.

It should have been said that B. P. Baldwin, Sarah Ross, Patrick C. McKenzie and George Brokaw also belong in the row of "pillars" in this church. This is a roster of the pastors:

Bell, McKnight Williamson, T. H. Dinsmore, W. H. Porterfield, Robert S. Dinsmore, F. A. Shearer for five years, T. D. Wallace for ten years, J. D. White till his early, untimely death, B. E. S. Ely, Jr., H. R. Stark, L. D. Young, and John Calvin Abels has lately begun his promising pastorate.

In 1858, a minority declining to enter the union forming the United Presbyterian church, organized the Associate Presbyterian or Seceder church. Matthew and Wm. Nelson and wives, Wm. Robertson and wife, Thomas and Andrew Duke and wives, H. D. Titus, Robert Boyd, James Stephenson, S. B. Coulter, Robert Martin, Robert Meek and wives, Mrs. Fleming, Mary and May Duke were of this party. In '62 they built a one thousand seven hundred dollar frame church, Rev. Samuel Hindman pastor, a profound Bible student, scholar and genius. I can see the remarkable and most peculiar man now in my mind's eye, Horatio, his figure and bearing are so unique and his dress so quaint. He should have been painted for the county historical society, he and Captain Sam Russell, the two most original, if not aboriginal, men in our history. He was followed by Rev. G. F. Fisher and, after his untimely death, by Rev. D. J. Masson, who still serves. That church is usually called "Seceder."

The Reformed Presbyterians, or Covenanters, organized a church in '64, and Rev. S. M. Stephenson was ordained and installed, serving as pastor till '71. In 1873, Rev. W. P. Johnston took charge, and in a series of years made a profound impression as thinker, writer, scholar, preacher. Eventually, he was persuaded to conduct the academy. His going to the presidency of Geneva College in Beaver Falls, Pa., caused universal regret. He was followed as pastor by Rev. T. A. H. Wylie, the sweetest, humblest of all saints, a Ben Adhem, in fact, a dear, delightful man, his soul as white as snow but as warm as blood temperature. He died of tuberculosis while in flower.

A three thousand dollar church was built in '66, and it was remodelled into a pretty structure under the pastorate of Rev. W. C. Allen. In 1907 he was transferred to a Chinese mission in Oakland, Cal. His was a delightful family, and its going was widely regretted.

In '62, our colored people pined for a church, and Geo. W. Black and A. C. Carter brought Rev. E. C. Joiner, of Muscatine here, and a church of eight members was formed, Mr. Black being the sole survivor, though Carter, a local preacher for over fifty years, kept living for one hundred and four years. The church almost petered out during the war, but it sprang up again, and over thirty pastors kept it afloat.

First and last this church furnished us as many quaint and enjoyable characters as all the other churches put together. There were Uncle and Aunty Coe; he was amusingly sincere and honest, and she had a genius for extemporizing birthdays for herself; she picked 'em right off the bushes like blackberries. Whenever she needed a birthday in her business, she grabbed baskets and sailed around to her white friends and came home laden with bits of carpet, clothing, foods, nick-nacks of all sorts. She was a canny, slick

First House of Worship.

SECOND UNITED PRESBYTERIAN CHURCH

EUREKA METHODIST EPISCOPAL CHURCH

Type of pioneer frame churches

old party, and fairly tickled the "slats" of the community. Then there was George Davis, who long enjoyed a sound lung and a mated lung that was done gone. He and his wife, dear, delightful Sallie, used to appear in concerts, in their native togs, and their voices, judged by the approving smiles of the audiences, were all the better for being cracked, and quite lumpy. When a revival was on, the house was crowded, and the whites were as deeply edified as the colored folk. Two or three of their pastors were amusing characters. That humble little church has done a heap of good here. Of the "pillars," mention must surely be made of Uncle Ned Skinner, Sam Hall and Wesley Moore. You could hardly get Uncle Ned to come out to night meetings—he was so dreadfully "skeered" of "evil sperits and other varmints," and he was deathly afeared dey would git him. He sawed wood, saved his money, holed up at dusk, and kept his eyes peeled for ghosts. If boys teased at his door at night, Ned would shiver out the night in terror of the dark and the awful creeping and flying and screeching things in the supernatural world. Probably he suffered thousands more deaths than any man that ever lived here. The church did not seem to allay his fears and give him comfort. What he lacked was the voice of George Davis and his laugh, and especially "Old Barney's" laugh. Boys used to pay Barney's way into shows to get the recompense of that tremendous laugh. Armed with those explosives of either men, Uncle Ned could have routed all the evil spirits this side of Oklahoma. And what a rich character Jeff Armstrong was, tho' not very pious!

The Methodist church was first organized at Wm. L. Harvey's home a mile and a half southwest of town, near the old Indian village, October 20, '39. The original members were Jesse Ashby, wife, and daughters Polly and Julia, Mr. Harvey and wife, William, Ann and Mary Connor and Eli Patterson. Later active ones were the Dickenses, R. H. Marsh, J. R. Davis, "Billy" Moore, the Chilcotes, Wilsons, Mother Ferguson and so forth. At first there was preaching every two to four weeks. In '40 they moved into the first log school house in town, on a lot north of the Seceder church; in '41, used the first court house; in '43 moved into a brick school house on the lot where Mrs. Col. Cowles now lives; in '47, used the court house in the square, and began building their first church, a frame twenty-eight by thirty-eight, near the Commercial Club, dedicated by Presiding Elder Reed. In '55 a two-story brick was built on the corner of Second and Madison streets, the site of the present church; the lower story was finished for use in '56, and the whole structure was dedicated June 27, '57, by Dr. L. W. Berry, at a cost of six thousand nine hundred dollars. The present church, already quite out-grown, the Methodists grow so fast, cost twenty-three thousand dollars, and was dedicated April 10, '92.

The pastors have been Kirkpatrick, Hayden, Reeder, Nichols, Case, Twining, Jamison, Butt, Hardy, Teas, Dennett, Harris, Lucas, Banner Mark, H. W. Thomas, Power, Miller, Frank Evans, Reineck, Morrison, Jennis, Wells, Spaulding, Chaffin, the evolutionist, Coxe, McDonald, Stafford, Kemble, Stryker, Wing, the humorist, Boatman, Thorn, Schreckengast, U. S. Smith now in charge as a free lance and bold preacher. How many do you clearly recall, their foibles, whims, idiosyncracies, etc? As this church has always made a specialty of the Sunday school, let the superintendents be named—Jesse Ashby, R. H. Marsh, Isaac Ditmars, Dr. Chilcote, W. Wilson, Jr., Judge J. R. Lewis, Mrs. Margaret Wilson, Prof. D. W. Lewis, Tom S. Dougherty, C. H. Keck, Martin P. Miller, J. T. Anderson, S. W. Neal. The school stacks way up above the thousand mark in numbers, and every kid always knows the golden text—except when they forget it. They are a gay bunch on a fine spring day, as pretty as a garden of sweet peas or Wordsworth's spot of daffodils in March.

From the first, it was an enterprising, kindly society, aggressive withal, advancing from glory to glory in architecture, zealous in music, putting in a pipe organ about the same time as the Presbyterians and Baptists, and before there were opera houses or adequate halls, the Methodists were hospitable to lecturers, etc. In the winters of '66-67 and '67-68, the church before the present one echoed with the wise, eloquent voices of Emerson, Wendell Phillips, Theodore Tilton, P. T. Barnum (the wise, shrewd, canny Ben Franklin of the whole group, tho' a mere showman), Fred Douglass, Beecher, Abbott, Anna Dickinson, Mary A. Livermore, Susan B. Anthony. Washington has never had such splendid courses since, for the raw material is gone.

The church has entertained the annual conference four times; in '62, Bishop Baker; '73, Bishop Bowman and under the same in '86; in '92, Bishop Andrews. Perhaps this is neck and neck with the United Presbyterians, who entertained the general assembly thrice. And nobody and nothing in Washington or vicinity was more keenly aware of the presence of these seven stately bodies than the—chickens.

A Congregational church was started August 1, '56, D. P. Sturges, D. P. McConahey, Albert Allen et al. being pillars in it, and, years later, Ed. Cleaves, Jackson Roberts, Norman Everson, George and Bill Hale, and Burrell, though lay members and sort of nephews to that branch of the local Zion, put their shoulders under the crumbling old thing, but it went dead, and this scribe has always felt sore since that all the "remnants" went pell mell into the Presbyterian church.

Its last church was a frame "catacornering" from the Joseph Keck home, and when the Second United Presbyterians sought a place nearer town, they

BAPTIST CHURCH

PRESBYTERIAN CHURCH AND PARSONAGE

bought our church and put an annex or appendix on its rear, making the structure look like a dachshund, as long as three Pullman cars tandem, and the under-pinning was so infirm, the floor under one's tread worked up and down like a bad-fitting set of store teeth. Delicate folk got sea-sick walking on it, it was such a choppy sea. Several times Colonel Palmer reeled on it, en route to the choir loft. It needed an operation for appendicitis.

I think Rev. M. K. Cross was the first pastor of our church. He had to fight nerves all his days, and nerves are as exasperating as fleas. The next preacher was Rev. Philo Canfield, a shrewd, genial, merry, witty, sarcastic, ironical man, but disabled by bad health. The world furnished him a good deal of amusement, and he passed it along or shared it. George M. Langdon was the last clerical sigh of the Moor, the best story-teller who ever struck this town, not excepting Wing, or Kellogg, or Fred Smith, or Henderson Walker, superb as they are, but George was king. He had been a soldier, knew the world, played with it as a kitten with a ball. He ought to have been a vaudeville actor. Fine scholar, too, whose secular bible was The Nation paper, edited in heaven, since nothing on earth ever suited its finicky nibs. After a year, Langdon went back to his native Michigan, became a lawyer, married, and may heaven have mercy on his soul. He was a fine fellow. His irradiating presence often gilded the dusty cobwebs in the Press office.

The Congregational church disbanded July 20, '77. R. I. P.

What became of that old Congregational meeting house? It was a snub-nosed, ugly, squatty, homely thing, nothing but a dry goods box. It had no more beauty than a cross-eyed, flat-nosed, shovel-teethed, freckled, awkward girl. It was an architectural crime, and it was an insult to God to dedicate such a nightmare to Him. It has puzzled me always, what becomes of the dedication of a church that lapses into a dance hall, music hall, barracks, barn, etc. The holy effluence seems to go down the vale like morning smoke from a chimney and fade utterly out. As communities get rich enough to build pretty churches, they tear down or move off structures, usually forgetting to photograph them for curios in later times, and the dedication evaporates. It should be canned.

The United Brethren fell into line in '59. The leading men were Wm. G. and Nelson Stewart, Henry Lease, W. Poland, Michael Nelson, Wm. Baker, Rev. R. Thrasher. A one thousand dollar church was dedicated by Bishop Markwood. The church failed.

Of the other churches, brief mention should be made of the Church of God, lasting from '68 ten years; Christian Science, July 15, '97, established in the prettiest little gem of a church in town; St. Paul's German Evangelical church, started July 12, '03, the church built three years later, the first pastor being Rev. K. Michels, an interesting man, but he was called to Burlington and the present minister is Rev. Conrad Sprenger.

Perhaps it is not profitable to go farther into detail. We have gone far enough to show that the earlier settlers made sacrifices of money, time and service to supply religious education.

A various fate has been that of the rural and village churches, as well as of the provincial schools. Deaths, removals, the coming in of foreigners and alien sects and cults, have depleted the rustic churches, as the gradual enlargement of farms and the flight of young folks to factories and cities have reduced country schools to their lowest terms, as if they were vulgar fractions.

It is plain all through the tracings of the several church histories, that the Sunday school was the feeder of the church, some churches laying more stress than others, but all aware that it had a nursery office and value. There was a vigor in this impulse, like the pulse of horseradish in spring, for it was a force but recently discovered and applied. When these Washington county churches began, the Sunday school was hardly fifty years old. Robert Raikes in England had in 1781 but just pressed the button and set the wheels going, and by the time this part of Iowa was settled, every church felt the tingle in the wire.

The Sunday school has put a fresh gilding on childhood and youth. After the Sunday dawn, the beautiful musical and floral service paints a new and fairer dawn on that day. The nice clothes, the gay greetings, the beauty in which the morning swims, dip the world in cool dew. With it all, children pick up here and there a bit of fact or fancy, a truth that has worth; and there is innocent merriment, which is, perhaps, as good a service as any, as, when a teacher asked a little girl what Noah's dove brought back at last after the water fell, she said, "A pickle, please." Important, if true, and if not true, pleasing and funny, and harming nobody by error. When I was a youth, my Sunday school teacher in an Ohio county-seat, the eloquent Methodist minister, was also dealing with the flood, and said all the animals, birds, reptiles were drowned, save those in the ark, nothing remained alive, not a thing. I ventured to ask if the fishes did not live—"No," he roared, "all the fish were drowned, too." He did not know quite as much as Huxley. Roosevelt would have called him either a nature-faker or a later Ananias. Nevertheless that Sunday school was of distinct use to me, and no doubt every pupil in this county gets value received for the time spent, and the study, and perhaps for the idleness and day-dreams also. I got good also, esthetic good, from a teacher whose bay hair curled tightly and as close to his head as ivy to brick walls. I fell in love with him at Sunday school, and felt it in my bones that

ST. MARY'S CHURCH, RIVERSIDE

if I could ever get reddish hair as curly as that, I, too, might be beautiful and a satisfaction to myself if not to any one else.

I do not know why Congregationalism does not flourish very well in this county. One would think otherwise, for as a polity that church is absolutely its own boss—no czar of a bishop, no high tycoon of a presbytery, general assembly, general conference, or other generalissimo lording it over common democrats and republicans. Who is not at times in the mood to knock the lightning rod and weather vane off from those tall, stuck-up things so full of pride and oftentimes of arrogance? But out here Congregational churches are not apt to last. Some bad element in the soil here? The beech tree will not flourish in this county, or in Iowa as a whole—some soil condition adverse. There are but two beeches in this county, and they are runty.

People now have lots less veneration for and awe of the clergy, but far more affection, than a generation ago, for the cloth is a much less high and mighty and awful creature. Time was here, an old settler told me, years ago, when parishioners would stand uncovered in the street, no matter how inclement the day, while talking to their pastors. Luckily, they did not remove their shoes and stockings and catch their deaths of colds. And the pew now is almighty independent, and does not necessarily let the puplit lead it by the nose as to politics, amusements and the like. The pew-man does his own thinking and his own acting also, praise be!

Churches are now run on business principles, and pay as they go, the only safe and sensible rule in all of our economies, for it is moral. It was not moral, was not common-honest, to cheat the minister out of his pay, and try to dress the scales by giving him donation parties that kept him poor, tho' possessed of boundless junk. The present day Sunday pay envelope is as moral as a bank's daily balance sheet. Such museums of truck as folks did bring to the preacher once or twice a year, and call it benefaction. It was calamity. It was insult added to injury.

Members and clergy are more jolly and social and less solemn and pokey. They stop and visit, the pastor no sooner saying "Amen" than he hikes for the front door and shakes hands like a president at a White House reception. And the sisters come up and purr nicely and lay a soft, white hand in your honest palm and smile and tell you the nicest fairy story, how glad they are to see you here, and "please come again." Thanks! The loan of such a velvet hand would bring a fellow even if he had the "slows" like a snail. Come? I should remark. It accelerates also if there be a slight but discreet squeeze in those hands given without interest on the investment. It's about the best part of the service, and I don't care if all the clergy regard that flat heresy and look hard and sour at me. I tell you, if it were not for the sisters, of all ages and sizes, flocking there, there wouldn't be much doing in the churches. The young fellows go there to see their favorite girls, especially at evening service, to see the dear creatures safely home, don't you know—they are so apt to get lost after dark unless the spark is along. It is that variety of la grippe that fetches most of the men to church. Don't try to cure it, if you want the church to last and be enthusiastic.

The moral tone of the church has mounted on the sacramental wine question as it did on the slavery question. It uses now only the unfermented juice of the grape—tirosh, not yayin. There is not a taint of booze in it, as formerly. And then the good folks are onto germs and say skiddoo and twenty-three to germs by using individual cups. Churches, however, have not yet succeeded in carrying hygiene so far as to stop kissing. Microbes—well, every body knows where their favorite rendezvous is. But it is great gain to install the separate cups.

The churches seem to be through with their infantile troubles, something like mumps, measles, whooping-cough, chicken-pox, etc., I mean the fuss about instrumental music, stoves in meeting houses, buttons, hooks-and-eyes, the abolition of tokens, etc. I mind when the Catholic church in Ohio was rent on stoves in church, have 'em or not? Mad as blazes, old moss-backs said "No," in horror; young folks said "we'll be blanked if we come here to freeze." People nearly fought over instruments, and about whether clothes should be fastened with buttons, or hooks and eyes, or just common honey-locust spikes. A local antiquarian lately showed me two tokens, one a circular disk, metallic, with a dull, leaden look, the size of a nickel, "R. P. C." on one side, an apparent wreath on the other. The second was three-quarter inch long, half an inch wide, stamped with "G. C. S.," plain on the obverse. Long ago, in troublous times in Scotland and Ireland, these tokens were precious, as certifying the owner's right to a place at communion table. Naturally, by the operation of the law of relation and association, these trinkets became fetishes—sacred, holy per se, idolatry, in fact. People almost unavoidably became superstitiously attached to them, and probably did not discern that the token was a virtual idol. Brother Williamson refused point blank to use them, when he first came to the First United Presbyterian church. and no doubt many of the older members felt a sharp shock of grief. It was vandalism, profanation, but all have got over it, and no one is left to see spiritual value in these curious things.

Ministers have an easy time now, comparatively; get good pay, and promptly, needn't preach over twenty to thirty minutes, and dilute the thinking as much as they like, and the pure food law can't touch 'em. Mr. Vincent in the '40s never got over three hundred dollars a year, and often hadn't

METHODIST EPISCOPAL CHURCH, 1909

METHODIST EPISCOPAL CHURCH
Second Place of Worship

money enough to buy a postage stamp. Once he drove far to marry a pair, and was paid in a big wad of tobacco leaves, and no one knows that he so much as smoked or "chawed." Hard lines, indeed.

The thing most conspicuous now is the amazing division of labor in the churches; they are organized to death. Some time, when I have a day off, I mean to sit down beside some nice sister in each church and copy her dictation of the various subdivisions of her church, the prayer meeting, missionary societies, leagues, endeavors, B. Y. P. M., "What I Can," circles, mothers' jewel band, Y. P. S., Sr. and Jr., King's Daughters—that's what I want to join—Helping Hand—is that the sort of hand spoken of above as velvet? if so, count me in—Ladies' Barefoot Society, if we mistake not the reference, and many more. Of course, this rather hits my funny bone, but no doubt these organizations stimulate interest in church work and keep all the members, young and old, on the qui vive or a-humping for "the cause."

Our every early church had some fad, whim, oddity, or bete noire, such as tokens, prejudice to bells, or to stoves, or secret societies, or to musical instruments, etc. Our Methodists were alone in this—up to the coming, in 1861, of Pastor Hiram W. Thomas, who afterward became famous through a heresy trial, the sexes sat apart in church right here in Washington, a fashion that George Fox, the leather-breeched founder, set for Quakers in England and America. The absurd theory was, the sexes couldn't be trusted, even in church—shame! Thomas hoped that families might sit together in their spiritual home as in their real homes, and all gladly fell in with it, rather sheepishly wondering why they had all these years done so silly a thing. There was, however, one nice thing about that custom of sitting opposite—admirers and lovers could cast sheep's-eyes and throw significant glances full of elegant and costly freight across the space, without rubber-necking a bit. Eye-beams, heavily laden with love, shot nimbly over the neutral territory, and the innovation was not popular with the "spoons." They had had a perfectly lovely time under the old regime.

Our people have enjoyed many crack preachers from abroad, at conferences, general assemblies, etc., the United Presbyterians pleased by such Rev. D. D.'s as Moorhead of Xenia theological seminary, McNaugher, R. D. Miller of the United Presbyterian, Harper, J. G. Carson, and the Methodists were built up by Bishop Charles Elliott, president of Mt. Pleasant university, and long before that president of Madison college in Uniontown, Pa., and Sam Russell went to his school. Sam was so diligent a hunter of turkey nests and eggs, he once absented himself a whole week. A mischievous chum of Sam's put Prexie on Sam's haunts,—for one, a secluded barn of the log variety, that could be entered by a ladder leading to the loft. The next time Sam visited it, there in the middle sat Elliott, looking grand, gloomy and peculiar, a veritable turkey gobbler. The quick-witted Irishman said, "My bye, we'll say nothing about it—you come to school," and Sam did, and never skipped a session after that. And in our time were Bishops Baker, '61-2, Bowman twice, in '73 and '86, Newman, Andrews, '92, McCabe, finest of all. He was here four times, twice as lecturer on Libby Prison, once at Chautauqua, the year before his death. Then the other day, Bishop Anderson.

In late years two delightfully artistic men preached for the Presbyterians, Wilbur Chapman and S. D. Gordon, the latter a gem of purest ray serene, and beautiful as a god, with a voice that was entrancing music.

Easily comparable with any of these is our own Charles R. Brown. On the Pacific coast he stands in the king row of preachers. He gave a series of lectures in the Yale Lyman Beecher Lectureship. Surely, the most eloquent tongue we may boast of and delight in as a home product.

There is a miracle about this preaching business. How can a man talk in the pulpit thirty minutes and manage to say nothing interesting? How can he dodge all the fine corners? How can he avoid saying something that one can carry away in the hand, as it were, like an orange? Many do it, but it must be awfully hard work.

I must not fail to mention an almost divine talk in the Baptist church by Conwell, the incomparable lecturer on "Acres of Diamonds."

An eastern man, father to a townsman, chanced to hear Bishop Bowman here on "Peter's wife's mother lay sick of a fever." Returning home, he heard the bishop twice more on the same theme, at different conferences. After the third rendering, he heard a bell toll one morning, and when his companion asked what that meant, he said, "Peter's wife's mother must be dead." I hope he attended the funeral.

Speaking of funerals as a means of grace, there was a woman goaded by a passion to go to every and any funeral, near or far, whether she knew the mourners or not. She was sure to go early to be sure of a seat, and she warmed a chair in every house of grief. Finally, she herself died. A witty Montana girl, back here visiting, said of "the remains," "so many came to return her many, many funeral calls, the floor sank, and all slid into the cellar." Fact, too.

As showing the scarcity of money, as late as the early '60s, collections in our churches were called "penny collections," even as evening holy time was known as "early candle lighting." Before that, there was no cash to throw into the hat, bag or saucer. Judge Charles Negus, of Fairfield, who has published much about early times, says at a Methodist quarterly meeting there, not a cent was taken; no one had ready money; but they threw in hams, bacon, corn, etc. At least one hundred and fifty were present; some had come from long distances, afoot, horseback, in wagons, men in buckskin clothes, women in lindsey, handkerchiefs on their heads instead of bonnets, or wearing hoods and sun-bonnets. What they threw hams, etc., into he does not state, but, certainly, not into hats or plates—must have been bushel baskets and coffee sacks. Now that all have money, they are bored to death for holy backsheesh at every service by church beggars—they call it an "offertory," if they want to be stylish, and the parson solemnly prays over the long-handled sacks, telling the Lord it is only returning to Him His own funds lent to us as trustees, whereas the fact is, the Lord never coined a silver or gold bit, or issued a paper bill, or put out a shin-plaster from the beginning of eternity. It must have been nice to live in a time when currency was so shy, that one had to hit the plate with a panfull of home-made sausages or a ham not sugar-cured.

CHAPTER XI.

SCHOOLS—EDUCATION.

The pioneers believed in schools, too, but the building of better schoolhouses did not become an industry till '46 when Iowa became a state. The settlers would make claims, build log cabins, break sod, scratch in corn, sow wheat, and then break out in a rash of schools and churches. It was as inevitable as children's mumps, measles, chicken pox, etc., just had to have them, for they were catching and every settlement was exposed sooner or later.

Schoolhouses of logs, of course, at first, and communal built. Logs unhewn; notch the ends and lay the logs at right angles, each log having a neck rest like a victim in the groove of a guillotine; floor of split logs smoothed with an ax, called puncheons; cracks between the logs battened and chinked and daubed with mud; windows rare, but holes left and stopped with greased paper to admit light and keep out rain, wind and cold; fire places built up of logs several feet, lined with rock, and gormed with mud, and the upper chimney a stick-and-mud affair, quite as if the swallows had done it, or it was laid up with blocks of sod like adobe; benches of slabs without backs, standing on pegs—split a log, smooth it, stick four or six pegs under it, set it level side up, clap a boy on it, and the fattest boy had the softest seat; put a book in his hand, tell him to dig in, keep a g'ad in full view, and that was primitive education.

The pupils did not wear near as many spectacles as ours now. Probably there was not a child in the county wearing glasses prior to '60 or '70, and they did not complain of headaches. Is this talk of non-focusing a graft?

The benches did two bad things—made crooked backs and sprained the cords in the kids' legs. Lincoln said one's legs should be just long enough to reach the ground. Children's feet in these early school houses did not touch the floor, nor in the churches, either, and they got knee-sprung and had a shambling gait. This defect is noticeable among people who make their children sit in church at an early age, their feet dangling. When they grow up they have a plunging walk, as if the knees were giving way at each step. It is also due to sprained cords. Seats should always allow the feet to rest on the floor. Please notice this defect—you'll be more apt to see it in the families of United Presbyterians, Covenanters, Seceders, and Catholics, than in those of other denominations.

Let's trace this school rash. There is quite a strife among claimants as to first schools and first teachers, and I do not mean to umpire the game and run the Hague Tribunal here, but just state the claim.

First Schools and First Teachers.—Eldridge Reed taught the first school in Brighton, in a log cabin in the east part of town in 1840. The next year the whole settlement built a school house in the west part.

Ralph Dewey, father of Seneca, taught the first school in Clay, in a school house a mile west of the east line of Clay, date not given, but it must have been near this time. In '48 a three hundred dollar school house was built at the first cross roads west of Brighton.

Clarissa Vance, later Mrs. Dr. Yeoman, taught a school in Clay at one dollar and fifty cents per week, and boarded round. She had twenty-five pupils. The school was on the southwest corner of section 35. Then, as now, school ma'ams would throw up a school any time to marry, train and educate a man.

Andrew Wentworth, living on the John Horning farm, moved Fairview school house from the east to the west part of the district, using several yoke of oxen.

George Waters in '42 taught the first school just over the west line of Clay in Keokuk county. It was a subscription affair. He had formerly taught in Louisiana.

Clay and Crawford ran neck and neck in intellectual athletics. Clay produced ninety-five teachers, nine clergymen, nine doctors and seventy-five soldiers. Crawfordsville, or the township, sent thirteen argonauts to California in '49, five abolitionists to the John Brown border ruffian war in Kansas, and furnished twenty-three preachers, thirty-three doctors, eight lawyers, fourteen editors, sixteen druggists, ten statesmen, six county officers, one hundred and sixty-five soldiers. With this last item couple the fifty soldiers that the Second United Presbyterian church in Washington sent out.

I doubt the statement that Crawfordsville built their first school house as late as '48.

The first school in Marion was taught by John Reed, on section 19, for three months, at two dollars and fifty cents per pupil, date not given. At the close, when paid off, he had to treat the school, or be ducked; it was the custom to do so. He returned to Ohio. The first school house was built on section 30 by S. Van Wagener for his home, but Franklin district bought

OLD HIGH SCHOOL BUILDING OF WASHINGTON

HIGH SCHOOL, WASHINGTON

it for thirty dollars. There were no independent districts in Marion, but she has eleven school houses.

The Snake Hollow school was one of the first, if not the first, in English River and Allen Thompson taught the first school there; the house was built and equipped by the voluntary aid of the whole Hollow. He charged two dollars per head for twenty pupils, in '42. Hon. David Bunker furnished the glass for the windows.

Lime Creek's first school was in a log cabin on section 26, and dates from the winter of '43. Nancy Pinkerton taught it, and the rate of pay was left to her patrons. An eighty dollar school house was built on section 25, near Taylor's.

The first school in Dutch Creek, in a log cabin, on the creek of the same name, was taught by Mr. Barker, but there is no date. A second school house was built on John Iam's farm.

Herman S. Guy, of New York, taught the first school in Iowa township, on section 26, as early, probably, as '41, a three months' school of twenty pupils, at two dollars per head for the term; "or its equivalent in trade." A school house was built in common that year by all the people.

In '43, Harry Craven taught the first school in Cedar, in a log cabin on section 29, fifteen kids at so much per head, sum not stated. In '44 the Youngs and Cravens built the first school house in that township on section 28.

Mr. Emmerson taught a school in Harrisburg, Highland, in '54. The Kentucky school house, built on section 11 in '59, was the first in the township.

Mrs. Garret Meek taught the first school in '76, in her own house—six kids. The first school house was built on the northeast corner of section 14, in '60, for fifty dollars.

Not till '79 did Ainsworth get a five hundred dollar graded school.

The Old Schools.—The motto in the old time "deestrict" schools was: "No lickin', no larnin'." The summer schools were taught by girls, and, if they were pretty, they had no trouble, nor in winter, either, for the mean traits of the big, mischievous, ugly boys dissolved in their beauty. But the men teachers wolloped the big boys unless, indeed, the latter basted them. Always a battle. Teachers were hired for their prowess. They had the worst time with the big girls. How can a fellow disarm a bunch of gawky girls who sit, grin, and smile at him, and moon and dawdle around and chew gum and ogle? I don't know what General Sherman would call their tactics of war. The unhappiest six months of my life were those spent in teaching two winter terms in Ohio backwoods. Oh, the bother of grinning girls! You can't punish 'em, they have not violated the constitution; you can't make love to 'em all at once, can you? What can you do?

The old schools were about as savage as the old navy, merchant marine and army life, as savage as the old creeds and theologies. Pupils, apprentices and the like were penalized. Teachers put in a deal of time whaling pupils with g'ads, beech and hickory boughs, ferules, straps, fists. They made boys shuck coats, and raised welts on them and drew blood. Boys got education, as their parents got religion, by the slaughter house routes. All was as bloody as altars of ancient sacrifice, including human sacrifice. Without blood there is no remission. No wonder the big boys turned, like animals at bay, barred teacher out, or defied him, and licked him if they could. Shambles in religion, in war, in cut throat business, why not in education? A large per cent of it was lickin'. The old maid teachers, crossed in love and their milk of human kindness clabbered, and mad about it, would thump us kids on the skull with heavy thimbles and raise ant-hills under the hair. Still, we'd sag on their laps as they pointed with hairpins at our letters, and say, "Gosh! is that W?" People in Paris danced, dined, and were gay even during the Reign of Terror, and pupils managed to get fun out of their persecutions. A bench full of louts at the red hot dragon stove in the center of the room would lunge side ways and shove a clown off six feet onto the floor, his slate jingling like the armor of Homer's heroes as they fell at Troy. Can't you smell yet the oxydized stove and the stogey boots redolent of stable and hog pen? Of course, some one got licked for that shove—still, it paid!

There was respite also in two going for drinking water. They would spill half of it en route, and water the live stock with the rest, out of tin dippers or gourds. Every kid would drink as much as an elephant, and laugh, strangle, spout and cough. Then, too, the crooked pin had its innings. A lob of a boy would yell out "Ouch!" and lunge forward on the desk and fumble for the dart. Another lickin',—yet it paid!

In February and March there were always sugaring-offs in the maple camps and syrup-coolings and spelling and kissing bees, and those joys made us forget our school woes. It was compensation, too, when teacher was paid off, to make him treat all, or be soaked. That was law, though unwritten. There were consolations also in spelling schools, singing schools, anything to fetch boys and girls together to ogle and lalligag and be hooks and eyes. Bringing one's dinner for noon recess was a fair stand-off for a lot of abuse,—a basket or tin pail full of figure-8 fried cakes or doughnuts, apple pie, sandwiches, hard boiled eggs, a pinch of salt, an apple, pear, peach, etc.

Lots of hardship was atoned for by the stated afternoon for "speakin' pieces," and especially by the closing night exhibition, when the curtain was sure to stick. It was not near as bad as we let on it was to sit on the dunce block, a paper cap on, for didn't we make up faces when the teacher's back

BRICK SCHOOLHOUSE BUILT IN THE '40S
Torn down to give place to high school

was turned? Nor was it real punishment to be seated with the girls, though we pretended it was. We didn't really hate it more then than we did a few years later. A good deal of smart was taken out at nooning, by stoning frogs in the creek, tying tin cans to dogs' tails, and tying up cats' feet in wads of rag, and stealing into the orchard at the brow of the hill and plugging with apples the honest yeomanry driving below. Besides, we could stucco the ceiling with wads of paper pulp, that the flies soon inked. It had to be sly work, to carve on seats and desks names, faces and phallic symbols, and in playing Pom-pom-pull-away, Hi-spy, Crack the Whip, there was alleviation for lickin's. The smallest boy was the cracker, and in sprawling in the dog fennel among the Dutchman's razors, his clothes were likely to be more picturesque than Joseph's coat of many colors. Can't you see tow-heads whose hair was sun-burned to terra cotta color, and whose faces held freckles as big as ginger snaps, with the inevitable letter in the post office, walking on the ball of the foot or heel, owing to stone bruises and stubbed toes tied in rags, rolling there in the weeds, shot off at a tangent? It was not half bad to be a country school boy in the days of Auld Lang Syne.

There was one discount—the visits of school directors, parents, and especially the minister. These old granny men had to make a few feeble remarks, of course, and it was a bore. The school ma'am was pinked-cheeked with embarrassment. What hypocrites the kids were! every one so still, good, nice, angelic, as if raised on Pious Row. We took our medicine when the preacher talked shop. He would ask a lot of fool questions out of the catechism, and in answering, the boys would fall down hard, as, "Who was the meekest man?" Some ignoramus would call out "Samson," "Goliath," "Judas Iscariot," or "Zaccheus." The average kid could not pronounce the names "Jehoshaphat," "Methusalum," "Abimelech," et al., and they got "Dorcas," "Sapphira," "Magdalene" and "Jezebel" all mixed up. They hated to have their ignorance exposed. They had no use for the cloth.

The teacher soothed his chronic irritation by that blessed custom of boarding round. If he hadn't the digestion of a hippopotamus, he very likely got dyspepsia also.

There were no two text books alike, but pupils managed to learn as much as now. If a strange boy came to school, he had to run a gauntlet of challenges, and have a series of fights, to settle his rank. Just the same thing happens when a new cow or other animal comes into pasture, or a new dog shows up. Nature will have it so. Boys and men belong to natural history as truly as other animals.

The old country schools may be parodied but can't be caricatured. We tried to caricature it here in a play, in which Add. White, Deacon Hood, and

Mrs. Col. Scofield were immense and teacher Kellogg great, but that drama merely approximated the truth of the drollery and fun. The boys nowadays don't know what fun is, going to school. Houses now are so nice you don't dare track in mud, and can't whittle desk or seat, or upset ink, and have to walk softly and mind the bell, and refrain from shoving a pin in to the adipose redundancies of the fellow ahead in line, or tread on his heels and trip him, by mistake of course, and can't wink without permission, and one has to raise an arm, jiggle a finger, snap fingers and ask, "May I g'w'out?" The Golden Age of school-going is surely way back yonder. Don't pity the pioneer kids. They had fun to burn. Those old back woods schools started as smart men as the schools do now, if not smarter. Right or wrong, I believe they got better elementary training then than now. More style now, more show, but not better or fuller substance.

City Schools.—Martha Crawford taught the first school in this city, in a log cabin on Tom Baker's claim, in '40, followed that year by Martha Junkin. Others say that Polly Ashby has the distinction, and got fifty dollars for three months' work, but no one tells what she did with so much opulence. Before this, our children went just over the Henry county line to a school taught by a Miss Smith of New England. Sarah Young taught in the court house in '42, followed later by Norman Everson and Caleb Campbell, and Franklin Everson taught in a school house on the Frank Brindley corner, and all the girls fell in love with him, he was a character so sweet. But that was not what killed him, I hope. He lies in the city cemetery, and violets and pansies spring from his dust. He was a younger brother of Norman.

Hugh Kendall went to a brick school house on Mrs. Col. Cowles' lot in the early '50s, and recalls as schoolmates Joe Dawson, Robert S., John N., and Jas. A. Young, children of John, Robert, Jas. H. and Letetia, children of Harvey Young, Calvin, Robert, David, Joseph, Belle Kilgore, Nancy, Patience and Caroline Hayes, Wm., Elza, Jos. Guzman, J. G. and C. N. Stewart, Burney, Fulton and Adaline Donahey, Gerelza and John Yockey, John Mather, Roena Moore, Andrew and Robinson Barnes, Sam, Nancy, Mary and Josephine Mealey, Margaret Orr, Mart Whitcomb and sister, Cordelia Ross, Roll, Geo. D. and Nettie Organ, Alex. Lee, Jas. Terry, Gus, Belle and Dode Wright, Samantha and Margaret Curry, Wm. Woods, Alex., Caroline and Susannah Meek, Jos., George and Martha Dawson, John Brokaw, Arthur R. and Anna J. Kendall, Byron and Lee Parker, Irving and Mary Keck, Emma Anderson, Morris Spillard, Edward Covert. Some of the teachers were Tracey, Parker, brother to Dr. M. C. Parker, Henry, Anderson Duke, Woodstock, Miss Belle Campbell, now Mrs. A. H. Patterson.

Prof. W. P. Johnston
Principal Washington Academy

D. W. Lewis
Supt. Washington Schools 1868-1893

Prof. S. E. McKee
Founder of Washington Academy

J. R. Doig
President of Washington College

PIONEER EDUCATORS

The first school house, a one-story brick, still standing as a part of a dwelling, was built in '43. In '56 "the old brick" was begun, and finished in '57, a two-story on the site of the present high school. Rev. Mr. White was principal in the upper room in '56-7, his wife his assistant, and Margaret Melville was principal below and her sister Lu was her assistant. In '58 Margaret Melville and Celia Chipman taught above and Amanda Fairbanks and Lu Melville below. From '58 to '62 these were the principals, above and below: Messrs. Milliken, J. A. Henderson, V. W. Andrus, Chriswell, Nort P. Chipman, G. G. Bennett and Misses Yates, Axtell, Clara Allen, Helen Chipman, Ellen Israel, Williams, Hattie Everson.

In '62 Samuel McLane became superintendent and graded the schools; his high school assistants were Lila Ziegler, Jennie Cleaves, Jennie Hogan. J. K. Sweeney followed him as superintendent from '64 to '68, Mary J. Hamilton being his assistant. In '66 a six room building south of the square was built for thirteen thousand five hundred dollars. D. W. Lewis took charge of the schools in '68 and served them twenty-five years, excepting the years '71-2 under T. H. Smith, Mr. Lewis during that time taking charge of an Indian school on a reservation near Omaha. Mr. Lewis revised the course of study several times, and changed the grading and distribution of the pupils. The enrollment went to eight hundred and twenty. The Centennial and Heights schools were built at a cost of eight thousand dollars each.

Geo. H. Mullin succeeded as superintendent in '93, and served seven years. The Wallace school was built for eight thousand dollars, and in the spring of '99 the South school, which then was the high school, and which also cost eight thousand dollars, was burned. A new high school was built on the site of the old brick for twenty-six thousand dollars. Mr. Mullin increased the teaching force from fifteen to twenty-one, and changed the course of study, making it a full four years' course.

W. A. Pratt became superintendent in 1900, and served three years, conforming the high school course to college requirements, and started a school library which now has four thousand six hundred volumes.

R. B. Crone came in 1905, staying three years, and Bruce Francis succeeded in the fall of 1908, but will leave us at the end of this school year, Lovell Anderson being principal of the high school, with this battery of teachers for 1909:

HIGH SCHOOL.

Margaret J. Safley, Stena Hansen, H. E. Case, Ella Woodford, Mary Bryant, Ethel G. Nichols, Jeanette Jamison, Martha Reckling (the latter teaching music and drawing in all the schools)

SOUTH SCHOOL.

Minnie Conner, principal; Lucy Meacham, Elizabeth Klein, Annie C. Rehmel.

WALLACE SCHOOL.

Rate Montgomery, principal; Emma Buxbaum, Mary D. Hatch, Edna Detwiler.

CENTENNIAL SCHOOL.

Etha L. Purvis, principal; Katherine Stichter, Gertrude Kendall, Nannie Laughead.

HEIGHTS SCHOOL.

Margaret Young, principal; Gertrude Smith, Louie Harding, Maud McCreedy.

KINDERGARTEN.

Laura B. Noyes, principal; Verne Ashby, Carol F. Forgy.

Since this cast was set there were resignations and elections, thus: Prof. A. C. Fuller succeeds Superintendent Francis and Mr. F. G. Robb follows Anderson as principal; Martha Hutchinson takes Miss Safley's place; Wilma Row, Miss Reckling's; Kate Montgomery, Miss Rehmel's; Myra Shaffer, Miss Detwiler's; Margaret Doolittle, Miss Purvis'; Effie McCreedy, Margaret Young's; Vera Alberson, Miss Ashby's.

JANITORS.

High—Henderson Walker; South—Chas. R. Guzeman; Centennial—Oliver Hicks; Wallace—I. K. McKenry; Heights—W. H. Greer; Kindergarten—Lewis H. Wallace.

SCHOOL BOARD.

A. H. Wallace, president; Dr. E. T. Wickham, Thos. J. Berdo, Frank R. Sage, C. C. Cunningham, J. W. Morton, secretary.

Mr. Wallace is this year serving his thirty-eighth year on the board, and the thirty-third year as president. He and the late Mr. Wilson, Jr., are the most altruistic men in our city's history—glad to serve for nothing and find themselves. Of such also is the kingdom.

The valuation of the city's school houses is sixty-five thousand dollars; of apparatus, five thousand seven hundred and fifty-nine dollars.

The last enumeration in the city was six hundred and twenty-three boys, six hundred and sixty-nine girls. In the county the total is five thousand eight hundred and thirty-five.

The amount of tax levied in '08 to support all the schools in the county was eighty-five thousand fifty-five dollars and twenty cents.

The city district this year asked for fourteen thousand dollars for teachers, five thousand dollars for contingent, and one thousand five hundred dollars

BRICK SCHOOLHOUSE SOUTH OF WASHINGTON

JACKSON CENTER SCHOOLHOUSE

A type built in the '70s

for the bond fund. A school statement for '72-3 asked for one thousand six hundred dollars for teachers and one thousand one hundred dollars for contingent; and in '74, one thousand one hundred dollars for each of these funds.

High school graduates have averaged thirty plus the last half dozen or more years. The trend for several years is to make the high school a sort of university or academy at least, a feeder to the university, and its graduates enter the State University and the Chicago Northwestern University without examinations. The scope is indicated by the chairs: History and civics, literature, English, mathematics, Latin, German, music and drawing. As yet no Sanscrit, Hebrew, or theology, but in four years from now there will be a chair of Agriculture, and pupils will no doubt learn how to raise chipped beef, smoked hams, boneless turkey, scalloped oysters, etc.

Academy.—In May, '54, a Washington academy was projected by trustees L. G. Bell, S. C. McCune, T. B. Dinsmore, James Beatty, B. P. Baldwin, N. Chipman, W. H. Jenkins, Hugh Lee, A. H. Patterson.

No one knows aught of this. Rev. Mr. Dinsmore and Miss Florilla King taught a school on the Frank Brindley corner, but it was not an academy. It may have been a private school, and "academy" stuck on it to gain it prestige. It may be dismissed, but there was an incorporation, it seems.

Academy of Sciences.—On December 14, '80, the Washington Academy of Sciences was incorporated by Capt. Kellogg, W. H. Hott, Chas. Hebener, Jno. W. Zaring, Geo. E. Story, W. N. Hood et al. They gathered geological and botanical specimens, collected eggs (not hens'), and stuffed birds and animals. Kellogg also canned a good many stories and jokes. The members caught most of the birds and animals by sprinkling salt on their narratives.

The Real Academy.—On February 29, '72, the Academic Association was incorporated with twenty thousand dollars capital, by Joseph Keck, Norman Everson, Nathan Littler, Dr. Chilcote, Michael Wilson, J. H. Bacon, Col. Bell, John Bryson, W. Wilson, Jr., Jas. Dawson, J. F. Henderson, Dr. McClelland, A. H. Patterson, John Graham, G. G. Bennett, J. P. Huskins. A sixteen thousand dollar building was erected in '74. The school has graduated four hundred and ten of both sexes, some of whom have made shining marks in many places. It has been in the care, in turn, of Prof. S. E. McKee, twice; W. P. Johnston, two years; Martha Rudd, one year; J. C. Burns, two or three years; John T. Matthews, W. C. Allen, C. S. Dodds, R. D. Dougherty, seven years.

For several years there has been an average attendance of one hundred and fifty, and they have spent two thousand eight hundred dollars per year in tuition and as much more for rent, board, etc. And several families have moved here to educate their children. The school has been of distinct economic value to the town. The present faculty is R. D. Dougherty, principal and teacher of Mathematics and Sciences: Margaret Doolittle, A. B., Literature and English; Nora Corette, A. B., History and English; Mame Jericho, Shorthand and Typewriting; Flo Parish, Piano and Harmony.

Trustees.—A. H. Wallace, president; Ab. Anderson, treasurer; F. L. Wilson, C. M. Keck, H. M. Eicher, Col. D. J. Palmer, R. D. Dougherty, secretary.

Prof. Dougherty has been an indefatigable worker and has done a great deal of good. The modern high school trenches on academic grounds, and academies have hard sledding. But Prof. Dougherty has done thorough work, and put graduates into the second and third year of the university.

Washington College.—In April, '54, the Associate Presbyterian church resolved to found this school. Nine acres were bought for a seat and campus on South Marion street, a lovely elm grove on the rising ground one might have then seen closing the vista looking south from Cook & Sherman's drug store. School began September 1, '55, in the third story of Wm. Blair's block, and in '56 it occupied the First U. P. church, now music hall, and in two years it had one hundred and ninety-three students. In the third year there were five ready to enter the junior year. The faculty was: Rev. Dr. J. R. Doig, president and teacher of Moral Science and Greek and Latin Literature.

Rev. Dr. W. H. Wilson, A. M., Professor of Mathematics and Natural Science.

Miss M. S. Walsh, principal female department and assistant in Mathematics.

Jno. K. Sweeney, A. B., and L. F. Sherman, tutors; James Dawson, treasurer.

One account says the endowment was forty-five thousand dollars, another fifty thousand dollars—both absurd. It was ten thousand dollars, and in '64, Rev. David A. Wallace, president of Monmouth College, took it over to his school, saying he would take care of our professors and return the money fund whenever the Iowa synod called for it. It never returned. Long-headed Wallace! He did take Dr. Doig and Sweeney to his crib.

In the meantime a brick building, three stories high, fifty by seventy-five feet was put up, but only the first floor was ever used. In '61 there were five graduates—J. F. Graham, a fine singer; Wm. H. McMillan, Matthew Robb, John H. Walker, Geo. Mitchell. "Why does Nature love the number 5 and the star form repeat?" All five became ministers.

It was a co-ed college, and its main function or industry seemed to be to turn out grists of romance and weddings, a failing of all such bivalve schools.

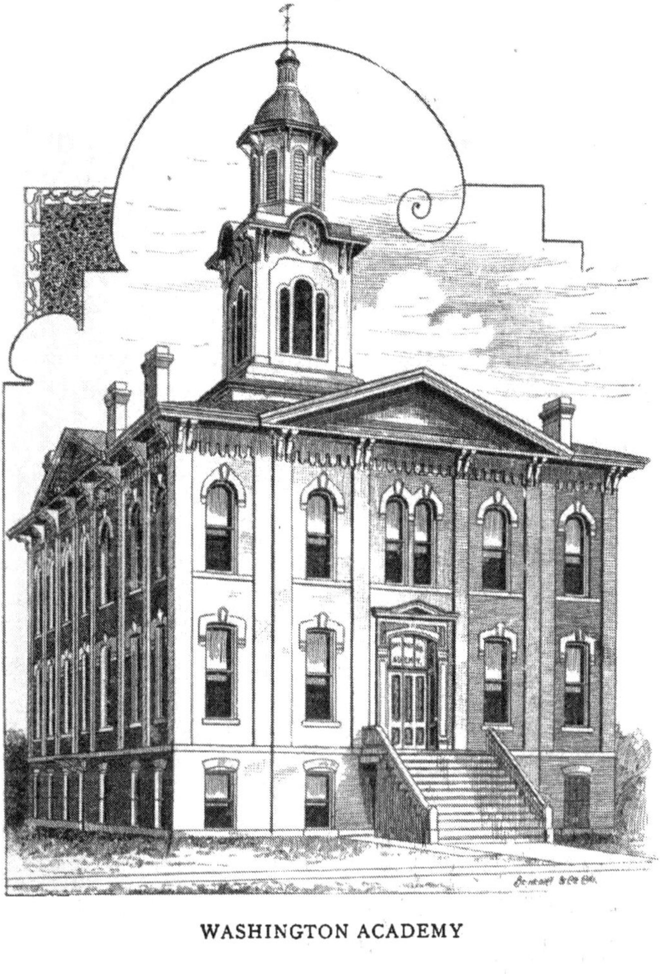

WASHINGTON ACADEMY

Mary Cowden married W. H. McMillan, and Said Oburn, Graham. And there were plenty more affinities. There were no walks down there, and the imaginative reader can guess what perfectly lovely times smitten swains had helping the nymphs on the less muddy sides of the roads and over the stiles into the leafy campus. I can distinctly see not only pink and blue ribbons around slender waists, but hooks that looked much like manly arms clasping the aforesaid as tightly as iron hoops on a sugar barrel. And not a single filly kicked. The town fellows caught on, and frequented the paradise. Howard Holden captured Mary Oburn, Bachelor Everson thought the school was a fine pasture-run for fairies, graces and muses, nor was Cadwallader a slow coach at hops with those student girls, groups of angels in vivid sashes. Granville G. Bennett, Nort. P. Chipman, John H. Walker, Granville G. Cowden, John Dawson, Dave Palmer, Dave and Bob Kilgore, Wm. Burnside, Matthew G. Hammill, "Pap," "Big-footed Barber" McCutcheon, a giant who shaved all the boys, were gay and festive gamboliers and high-stepping bucks. Dr. M. C. Terry and Miss Israel, of Brighton, whom he married, were students there, and Sarah Kinkade, now Mrs. Hon. B. F. Brown, and her brother Milton, Daniel Harris, who became cloth and still lives, an invalid, in Cuba, where he lost a son.

In '62, the graduating class was Granville G. Cowden, Andrew McMillan, Luther Winter, brother to Mrs. A. H. Wallace, Mollie Cowden, Helen Chipman, Clara Allen, Jennie Cleaves, Ellen Israel, Sallie Jenkins, later Mrs. Erk. McJunkin, Marietta Conger (Mrs. Pay Master General T. H. Stanton), Cordelia Ross.

Class of '63, Celia Moore (Mrs. Prof. Currier), Jno. A. Donnell, Margaret Orr.

The class of '64 was Mary and Rhoda Craven, Mary Lindsey, later Mrs. D. W. French, Mary Bradford who became Mrs. John G. Stewart. So the school became a real alma mater.

And then a storm smote that house, and it was condemned as dangerous, and was torn down. Many of its rocks are in the foundation of the Joseph Keck house, and don't know the difference. That wind, and the war that sucked out students as by the electric vortex of a tornado, gave the college its coup de grace. Nathan Littler bought the tract years later and built on it, and now there is not a trace of the ancient academe.

Wm. A. Cook used to attend the commencements under the elms in August, and can yet see the graduates sweeping off gestures like condor's wings, and reeling off yards and rods of jargon in Latin and Greek orations, stunts that had about as much vital relation to modern life as Elijah's chariot of fire would have to a red devil of an automobile.

After ten years in harness, Dr. Doig resigned in '64 the prexyhood and went to Monmouth College, and so closed our college incident.

Postscript on Schools.—The old court house in the square was a very accommodating building. It found room for the shoe shop of J. C. Conger and the tailor shop of R. W. McElroy. There sat Mac, with a face as austere as that of a terra cotta god, and cross-legged like a Turk, with needle, shears and goose. It also served as a school house till one was built, the court room up-stairs being the school. Where now is the roar of the stamping up and down those stairs? Gone, gone, beyond the back stars. In the fall of 1842, Miss Sarah M. Young taught a three months' school there, paying six dollars rent. In winters, Norman Everson and Elder Caleb B. Campbell taught there. One pupil was Nathan Littler. The Elder, it seems, was not up in grammar, and for a wonder some pupils clamored to take that study, which is usually esteemed a bore. So the Elder hired Rev. Albert Sturgis, later a missionary to the South Pacific islands, to do the Lindlay Murray act. At Christmas time the boys warned the Elder they would bar him out if he did not treat, and they bawled "Chrismus gif'" as calves bawl for skim milk. Before daylight, Christmas morning, they gathered in the school room and locked the door. Before nine a. m., they got very hollow and faint, having skipped breakfast. The Elder came, and they became tense. Parley—Elder: "I demand admission." Boys in chorus: "Chrismus gif'," bawled the rebels, and stated the terms, viz.: "Money to buy a gallon of whisky and a bushel of eating apples." Elder went away. At one p. m., ditto, ditto. Hunger gnawed; this thing was getting stale, very old, decrepit, sway-backed, and as no backsheesh was forthcoming, the besieged were bored to the limit, and felt sold. The next day the Elder penalized them by inflicting a long temperance lecture.

No school house here till '44. In the summer of '40 Polly Ashby taught, perhaps, the first school here in a room in southwest Washington, near the line of Orr's addition, for fifty dollars a term, money raised by subscription. Among the pupils were Elmira Moore (Mrs. Mather), her sister Julia and brother Marion, James and Mattie Jackson, Geo. A. Stone and sister Augusta, the teacher's four sisters and one brother, and N. Littler. In later years, Stone met Martha Jackson, and she rallied him on her spelling him down, and he gallantly said "you were the only one who could do that." He became colonel of the Twenty-fifth Iowa, and came home a brigadier general. Littler thinks her school was in '41, not '40.

In the winter of '45-6 teacher Reed whipped a merchant's boy for spelling a word badly. The lad stood the torture as long as he could, then fought back. Reed was sued before E. Ross, justice of the peace, and acquitted, but

HEIGHTS SCHOOL, WASHINGTON

CENTENNIAL SCHOOLHOUSE, WASHINGTON

the public sided with the boy. Sam Joy, uncle to the lad, made Reed kneel in the street and apologize and beg pardon. In the trial, Baz. Williams assailed Reed's lawyer, Churchman, but the court ordered him out of the house. One day when Crooked creek was high, overflowing the bottoms, Baz. ran a rude ferry. Two men and said lawyer were passengers. Baz. threatened to drown Churchman, and he begged piteously. He was dumped on a stump in five feet of water, one hundred yards from shore, and for a long while was as solitary as Stylites on his pillar—"grand, gloomy and peculiar."

School held ten years in the little brick on the Cowles lot after the court house was abandoned. As late as the winter of '51-2 Littler taught there some of the pupils Hugh Kendall names a few pages back.

M. Goodspeed came in '59 and started the first nursery in Cedar township, and taught school in the winter of '62-3, and one morning after a sleet storm he thawed out a lot of quail whose heads were incrusted with ice. Sam C. Gardner was the first teacher in Lexington, and licked the big boys, but not the big girls. He had seventy pupils. He turned out one big girl, but she rather turned the tables on him by gravely going around and shaking good-bye hands with every mate, with mock solemnity. It tickled the scholars, and Sam grew red and sweat behind the ears.

Hannah Pinkerton taught the first school in Yankee Diggins in Lime Creek, and a relative of Hon. Hod. Willson also taught there. Marsh W. Bailey says Horace was also a teacher, and one of the best, the most tactful, he ever knew. Horace will please step down in front with bouquets.

The first select school was taught by Rev. Dr. Geo. C. Vincent in the upper story of the Associate Presbyterian or Seceder church, and he was followed by Joshua Tracy, a student at law, who afterwards became a judge, and was a locally famous songster.

CHAPTER XII.

INFORMAL EDUCATIONAL INSTITUTIONS.

A half century ago the County Agricultural Society was a sort o' people's college, combining amusement and instruction with the advantage of a market for live stock and other farm products. An "agricultural hoss trot" is educational, and keeps the blood from coagulating.

The Washington Agricultural Society was organized in '53. The premiums were small. In '58 the entries rose to two hundred, and two hundred dollars were lavished in premiums. H. A. Ball took a first on draft stallion, Morgan Hart two dollars on a matched team, Calvin Craven three dollars on a jack, Ed. Clemens four dollars on a Durham bull, and took five other premiums; F. H. Hutchinson's sheep won everything; Wm. G. Stewart had the best hogs; C. N. Stewart the loudest quacking ducks; Geo. Hayes' chickens laid the most eggs, but Bill Knox's could cackle the loudest; Mrs. John Dawson's quilt took the cake for the most patches; Jacob McFarland spun the best yarn, while Mrs. M. Palmer knocked the socks off from all rivals in knitting the same; Mrs. Wm. Anderson made the best cake, Mrs. Morgan Hart the best gooseberry jelly. Calvin Craven was president; Nort P. Chipman, secretary; Joseph R. Lewis, treasurer; directors, John H. Palmer, Jesse Pearson, F. T. Loveland, J. S. Reeves, Jas. Vincent, H. Taylor, Jason Thompson, J. T. Sales, J. G. Melvin, D. R. Carnahan, N. Littler, S. E. Hawthorn, F. H. Hutchinson, Jno. S. Beaty. The grounds were on the Mt. Pleasant road, the site of the home of the late John M. Wagner.

In '75, another society was formed to supersede the earlier one, and it bought a tract on the Brighton road, not far from the present Chautauqua grounds.

The fair in '79 took in one thousand seven hundred dollars, and paid all premiums, sold fifty shares of stock, and chose these officers: E. F. Brockway, president; J. G. Stewart, vice president; G. G. Rodman, treasurer; Andy Duke, superintendent of grounds; B. F. Brown, marshal. Directors: D. Mickey, Ed. White, Fin. McCall, A. B. Rose, B. F. Brown, M. Bradford, R. Anderson, J. H. Laughead, Wm. Billingsley, S. E. Woodford, H. Ingham, Hugh

Draper, David Wilson, E. W. H. Ashby, Dr. Joseph Brockway, J. A. Cunningham.

Fairs were fine things to break bad droughts with. Many and many a time maidens radiant in white gowns and pink sashes went home bedraggled with flood and mud, garments clinging like bathing suits.

People got tired, after fifty to seventy-five years, seeing the same old afghans, ottomans, crazy quilts, etc., shown in Art (?) Hall, and fairs came to an end in 1897, under the presidency of James A. Cunningham.

These fairs were awful bores to editors—to set the list of premium awards in solid nonpareil was a task. We coralled the secretary and compiled the list on Sunday afternoons. There are thirty-seven annual Sundays that I thus broke into splinters—that many, anyhow. But the fairs did one good thing: by means of the agricultural hoss trot enough sports were lured to the fairs to see the live stock, and from that chance sight sprang the great industry of fine stock breeding in this county, an interest that ran into many hundreds of thousands of dollars. Nelson Stewart and Ed. Clemons brought in from Kentucky, via Illinois, the Henry Clay big white cattle; P. R. McMillan ran wholly to hogs; B. F. Brown and brother and Ol. E. Brown and many others dipped into Vermont sheep; J. R. Crumpacker, J. G. Myers, John G. Stewart and his brother Wm. G., and later Milt Yard, boomed short horns; the Singmasters developed heavy horses, and Ol. Brown introduced the Old Champ and Sleepy Joe trotting stock, and our fast nags to-day trace back to them. Ike Wagner's Bashaw came thence. These breeders, perhaps, did not make much money, but they did immense good in raising the standard of profitable breeds. The old fairs stimulated this desire for better stock of all kinds, and it was the trotting horse that kept life in the fairs—they would, else, have utterly failed.

Washington County Old Settlers' Association.—It was founded in 1877, and the first annual meeting was held in Washington, September 6, of that year, and drew an enormous crowd. The procession was five miles long, required one and a half hours to pass a given point, and said point was not a saloon. There were one thousand two hundred vehicles in line, averaging seven persons to the wagon. The first pioneers, dating from 1836, viz., Adam Ritchey, Richard Moore, David Goble, Sr., were represented by the sons George and Simpson Goble, Amos, William and Jesse Moore, Ritchey by his daughters Mrs. Sarah McCully and Mrs. Elizabeth Williams. These old persons registered: Jesse Ashby, eighty-eight years; John McMakin, eighty-seven years; Mrs. Baalam Anderson, eighty-one; Mrs. Peebler and D. H. Drake, each eighty-four years; Geo. W. Deveeman, eighty years.

D. J. Norton, Sr.

J. H. Stewart

George Brokaw

Robert Fisher

PIONEER MERCHANTS

Many antiquities were shown—a quilt fifty-two years old and still "crazy"; two glasses one hundred and fifty years old; fruit dishes that had escaped the knocks and shocks of half a century; fire shovels or "slices," as the New Englanders called them; an English two cent piece dating from 1442, before America was discovered, tools for working flax, books printed in 1768, etc.

The dinner was a reincarnation—johnny cake, honey, pies, chicken, roast ham, pot-pie, biscuits, slices of bread eight inches long and two inches thick, pickles a foot long, and one johnny cake measuring seventeen inches. Prof. S. W. Mountz sang Auld Lang Syne, Rev. Wm. Poston prayed, and Hon. Sam. A. Russell made an eloquent talk. Dr. Abram N. Miller recited a poem on the flax scutcher, written by a Quaker girl. Father Drake sang one of his own songs, that had only sixteen stanzas, eight lines to the verse. It was quite a while passing a given point. Jas. Dawson, Uncle Billy Moore, and others spoke. It leaked out that 'Squire Everson married Uncle Billy, and the latter has been grateful ever since.

Officers elect: Jonathan H. Wilson, president; J. S. Mapel, Dr. O. H. Prizer and W. J. Eyestone, vice-presidents; N. Littler, secretary; Jas. Dawson, treasurer; J. L. L. Terry, Ed. Deeds, J. S. Reeves, C. C. Hasty and Wm. Moore, executive committee.

The second annual meeting was in Brighton, four thousand people attending. Meeting number three was held in Washington on August 28, '79, and two thousand came. Hon. C. W. Slagle, the orator.

The meetings lost popular interest after a series of years, as the same old hard luck stories were told, and the last meeting was held in the fall of 1898, in which W. Wilson, Jr., was seized while making his speech.

Society of Natural History.—In April, '59, it was organized by these officers: T. H. Dinsmore, president; N. Chipman and N. Everson, vice-presidents; J. G. Cowden, secretary; N. P. Chipman, treasurer and keeper of cabinet. Members lost interest in bugs, rocks, etc., and ceased to do much at it, and the collection went to the junk-pile, and the society evaporated.

Free Public Library.—Washington owes her library to Dr. D. Scofield more than to any other one man. He put the yeast in the sponge. In August, 1878, the project took shape. The city council, justified by citizens, levied a half mill tax which produced five hundred dollars, which was invested in new books, to keep company with the donations of books made by Dr. Scofield, Mrs. Wm. Scofield, Judge A. R. Dewey, C. T. Jones, H. A. Burrell, and many more. Everybody served gratis—James A. Thompson as librarian, Geo. G. Rodman as secretary, and Dr. Scofield, Dr. J. D. Miles and Prof. D. W. Lewis as trustees, with all the volunteer helpers needed. John W. Templin followed as librarian, then Frank Graves, his capable wife Julia A. Graves being the real officer. She was succeeded by Miss Nannie J. Springer, who, with her nephew, John Springer, until recently judge in the Philippines, appointed by Gov. Taft, now president, and her nieces, Mrs. Laura Stichter and Mrs. Anna Huskey, served with credit fifteen years. Miss Eva Denny now holds that post.

Until the city hall was built in 1883, the library occupied the front upper room in the Press building several years.

Mrs. Jane A. Chilcote, widow of Dr. A. W. Chilcote, willed her home property to the city of Washington for perpetual use as a free city library, and it was so occupied in October, 1901. It is so far the sole public benefaction in our history. Her domestic life had been so happy in that home, she wished it to be used henceforth in a public, not a private, way. The property is worth twelve thousand dollars, and the house is quite well adapted to library use; changes are under consideration to make it still more serviceable.

This library of well selected books on all lines—history, biography, fiction, poetry, science, travel, belle-lettres, youths' miscellany, religion, philosophy, cyclopedias and other reference—has been, now is, and will long continue to be of immense educational value in this city. Books—all things are in books. Any one, every one, can give themselves a liberal education by browsing in good libraries, and amuse and entertain themselves, besides. And the library has been a Providence to the children of those too poor to buy books. No institution in the city or county has done more good, given the many so much pleasure, yielded them more instruction and innocent delight.

There are now seven thousand volumes, and several hundred new books are annually added. The aim is, to keep reasonably well up with the best, the cream, of the issue of books in all the departments. In the reading room are all the leading magazines and other periodicals and journals. And the library is rich in government publications and documents, over three thousand volumes.

The board of trustees comprise: H. A. Burrell, president; Mrs. Orville Elder, secretary; A. H. Wallace, Marsh W. Bailey, Cordelia Ross, Rev. W. O. Fisher, Mrs. Ida Nicola, Chas. H. Keck, Frank L. Wilson. Mrs. Nicola resigned, and S. W. Livingston was elected her successor.

Study Clubs.—For a generation now, Washington women's lives have been much modified by clubs. Mrs. Judge Dewey, a prominent club woman, assured me that more than thirty years have elapsed since what is believed to have been the first club was formed here. So unobtrusive was the coming of the shy light of the dawn.

In the autumn of 1878 a band of twelve courageous women stepped out from what was then their accorded sphere, and claimed one afternoon out of seven for the pleasure and profit that associated study might bring.

JANE A. CHILCOTE
Donor of Jane A. Chilcote Free City Library

JANE A. CHILCOTE FREE CITY LIBRARY

"History Class" was the name assigned. These women were earnest seekers of knowledge, and delved with eager persistence to the very bottom of authentic history, and even peeped some distance into its myths. Such heroic names as Asur-bani-pal, Tigleth Pileser, Shalmaneser, etc., became pet household words in the homes of some of the first families of the village.

Patience and determination work wonders, in this instance quietly laying a strong symmetrical foundation of facts, with its cornerstone properly squared ready for the superstructure sure to follow.

Just at this time the great Chautauqua movement sprang up to meet the Macedonian cry, in America north and south; in Europe, Asia, Africa, Australia, Japan, were millions hungering and thirsting for a knowledge that seemed far beyond their reach, now brought to their very doors, and hailed with joy as supplying a want widely realized.

Chautauqua Literary and Scientific Circle.—The idea of this circle first arose in the mind of its founder, Rev. John H. Vincent, D. D., in his early ministry, starting as a Sunday school assembly in 1874. During a session in Chautauqua, N. Y., in 1878, the circle was instituted—a course of reading and study covering the principal subjects of a college curriculum, which an individual could pursue alone, if necessary, yet adapted for associated study. It was a four years' course, embracing history, science, literature and Bible study.

The C. L. S. C. of Washington was organized in October, 1882, under the leadership of Rev. C. L. Stafford, the resident Methodist minister, who held the office of president. Prof. D. W. Lewis succeeded him as president. This local C. L. S. C. flourished a number of years; for some time it was necessary to hire a hall to accommodate the large membership. The history class quickly merged itself into this new educational movement. As to the beneficial results there is no question; it breathed an atmosphere of culture around many homes, relieved the dull round of woman's never-ending work through worthy themes of thought and conversation, and enabled middle-aged people to supplement the deficiencies, keenly felt, of their early education.

The first graduates were Mrs. Norman Everson, Mrs. Wm. Scofield, Mrs. C. H. Wilson, Rev. C. L. Stafford (the only man thus far), Mrs. Frank Graves, Miss A. E. Buchanan, Mrs. Albert Phelps, Mrs. R. M. Ackley, Mrs. P. P. Ink, now Mrs. Ab. Anderson, and Mrs. A. R. Dewey, and is known as the class of '86.

Post Graduate Reading Class.—In the spring of 1887 this class was organized at Mrs. Norman Everson's, to do more thorough work along particular lines, and also to win seals to adorn the much prized C. L. S. C. diplomas. It was composed of the class of '86 and two others, Mrs. H. A. Burrell and Mrs. Dr. A. W. Chilcote; later, women graduates from the classes of '87, '88, '89, '90, etc., became members of this post graduate class. viz., Mrs. A. H. Wallace, Mrs. Dr. Meacham, Mrs. Jackson Roberts, Mrs. Dr. E. R. Jenkins, Mrs. Chas. M. Stinson, Mrs. J. C. W. Coxe. These special seal courses, made out by the parent C. L. S. C. board, were adhered to for a number of years and found to be interesting and profitable, were systematic and kept local circles in touch with Mother Chautauqua. Meanwhile, the diplomas were being sprinkled with variously colored seals, the color denoting the particular course finished. Later, however, the reading class selected the books for perusal, at present reading and discussing the new Emmanuel movement. One unique feature of the class is that from the start it has had neither officers nor written laws of any kind. Webster's Unabridged, however, always occupies the center of the floor during the meetings. Countless books of recognized high order have been used and discussed, and the end is not yet. The "Old Reading Class," as the members fondly, even caressingly, speak of it, has held weekly meetings for twenty-two years; every Wednesday afternoon practically, winter and summer, rain or shine, found the faithful ones assembled. Seven have moved away and six have passed beyond, but neither distance nor death can sever the bond that time, association, common pursuits of enlightenment, common topics for conversation and discussion, have created and sealed.

Present membership: Mrs. Dr. Jenkins, Mrs. J. T. Anderson, Mrs. H. F. Steck, Mrs. Wm. Edgington, Mrs. Mary Simons, Mrs. J. B. Merton, Mrs. Ab. Anderson and Mrs. A. R. Dewey, the two latter the only ones remaining of the original membership.

Nineteenth Century Club.—It was organized by Mrs. H. A. Burrell and Miss Anne Burrell, now Mrs. Dr. M. C. Terry, October 12, 1894, with a membership of fourteen. That number was not exceeded, and was maintained by filling vacancies. It joined the State Federation in 1896, the General Federation in 1902. Chosen color, lavender; flower, pansy.

From the beginning, each member has been loyal to the club, keeping a live interest in its stated object, the study of chosen historical and literary subjects as well as current events.

Twelve members have removed, and death has taken Elizabeth Winter Wallace, November 25, '97; Jane Ballard Chilcote, March 3, 1901; Mary Beard Wilson, March 2, 1903; Bessie Babcock Bovee, January 16, 1907; Martha Jackson Burrell, July 2, 1908.

William E. Chilcote

John A. Henderson

E. T. Hebener
At death oldest marble cutter in the United States

James A. Thompson

PIONEER BUSINESS MEN

The officers for 1908-'09 are: President, Mrs. A. R. Dewey; vice-president, Miss Margaret Doolittle; secretary and treasurer, Miss Anna M. Henderson; corresponding secretary, Mrs. Carl Roberts.

Twentieth Century Reading Circle.—It was organized in 1899 with these charter members: Mesdames Elizabeth Anderson, Martha Dawson, R. P. Lewis, R. T. McCall, Susan McClelland, L. D. Robinson, Josie Smith, Winfield Smouse, W. A. Wilson, J. H. Stewart, Harry Shrader, Walker Skinner, M. Morehouse, J. Titus, Dr. Burroughs and Misses Mary Johnston, Belle Smith, Mide Lewis and Fronia Lamphere.

Fortnightly Club.—On November 28, 1896, Mrs. H. Scofield, Miss Cora Scofield, Mrs. J. C. W. Coxe, Mrs. D. H. Ballard, Mrs. E. R. Jenkins and Miss Ada Jenkins formed a woman's study club, to be unlimited in number and meet once in two weeks. On January 16, 1907, a year's course of study was entered upon by the club numbering twenty members: Mesdames D. H. Ballard, B. F. Brown, J. C. W. Coxe, C. B. Daugherty, G. H. Eiskamp, J. A. Harwood, Aaron Hise, W. N. Hood, Emma C. Ink, E. R. Jenkins, Chas. H. Keck, James R. Logue, J. Albert Phelps, Hiram Scofield, Frank L. Wilson, and Misses Ada Jenkins, Cora Scofield, Anna Springer, Katherine Stichter.

On October 1, 1908, the plan of beginning the year's course with the club, instead of the calendar, year was adopted and has since been followed.

The club now has one hundred and thirty-five members, with departments and leaders as follows: President, Mrs. Lorle Cook; vice-president, Mrs. Carolyn Elder; recording secretary, Mrs. Nettie McLaughlin; corresponding secretary, Mrs. Hallie Hull; treasurer, Mrs. Florence Patterson; department of literature, leader, afternoon section, Mrs. Ida Nicola; evening section, Miss Ethel Nichols; Bible study, Mrs. Harriet Wilson; current events, Miss Laura B. Noyes; music, Miss Myrta Jeffrey; household economics, Mrs. Etta McCall; child study, Mrs. Bessie McLaughlin.

The following ladies have been president: Mesdames Coxe, D. H. Ballard, Hiram Scofield, Frank L. Wilson, W. C. Allen, B. W. Nicola, W. R. Jeffrey, Elizabeth G. Beamer, Mrs. Minnie Keck, Mrs. Lorle Cook and Misses Cordelia Ross and Myrta Jeffrey.

March 9, 1897, the club was admitted to the State Federation, January 18, 1906, into the General Federation.

In addition to the literary and social features the club has been active in the betterment of the city, as by furnishing fine pictures and casts to the schools, assisting in the work of recataloging, by card system, the Jane A. Chilcote library. For the latter work it gave about one hundred and fifty dollars, and the services of several members. Two fine art loan exhibits were given, and the proceeds, about one hundred and fifty dollars, expended for pictures to be given the schools. Two chrysanthemum sales have been held, the proceeds used to aid in beautifying the parks.

The club is constituted like the two great English universities, each a cluster of colleges, as this is an array of independent sections, or departments, of literature, Bible study, current events, music, household economics, child study. These are severally officered, and each runs its own affairs, but all come together to celebrate their anniversary on November 6, in various ways. Literature has afternoon and evening sections, and this year both "do" Tennyson, the Brownings, Dickens. The Bible course seems to be elaborate, and the meetings are held at Mrs. Hattie Wilson's, the leader's home, while the other sections are peripatetic. The current events class traversed topics from Dan to Beersheba. Household economics deal with the satisfactions of the inner man—pies, pastry, cake, puddings, sauces, etc., an endless parade.

Sunshine Club.—About 1905, it was formed by these girls, ranging from nine to fourteen years of age—Lydia Eicher, Ruth Wilson, Dorothy Wickham, Elizabeth Bell, Margaret Godfrey. Out of their pin, caramel, chocolate and soda fizz money, they have sent from fifty to seventy-five dollars to help support the orphan asylum in Des Moines. At their meets they have devotional exercises, read the Bible, sing hymns and psalms, say the Lord's prayer, then play.

Academy Societies.—There are two, Aurora and Magnet. The rivalry is keen, and they strive to hold the honors even.

Chautauqua.—This is one of the jolliest things yet invented. For ten days each year in August, we hark back to nature, and tent, in a grove, do housework at an amusing disadvantage, learn the virtue of a garbage barrel, dispense with private bath, grab a cushion or two and a rocking chair and rush to a big tent and start a fan in a crush of sweating humanity, and listen to things grave or gay, to music, to jokes with chin whiskers more or less gray.

For six years now, this festival; Sam Jones, Gov. Taylor, Billy Sunday have tickled us; Charley Brown, Prof. Wilcox and other Bible and historical students have edified us, and a great variety of entertainment has been given us. Several notable characters have appeared. On the whole, no more generous programs have been served to our people since the great days of the lecture or lyceum which offered such men as Emerson, Phillips, Curtis, Douglas, King, Chapin, Gough, Beecher. And for this source of profitable pleasure, Washington is most largely indebted to the good offices of Alex. R. Miller, editor of the Democrat. There is a temptation to introduce yellow features, and flaunt the sensational, as two or three vast attractions are not always available, to make great financial days.

Edwin Cadwallader

R. T. Wilson

H. F. Steck

J. Albert Williams

PIONEER BUSINESS MEN

Newspapers.—But of all educational agencies, the papers lead in widespreading influence. They are thick as leaves in Vallombrosa, and treat every conceivable subject. All the other professions combined, preacher, lawyer, doctor, teacher, do not exert so great an influence as the press, in the aggregate. You cannot pick up a sheet that has not at least one good item in it. The editors have been called the Fourth Estate, and truly. No matter how weak a sister many an individual editor may be, the mass of them are as infinite and irresistible as a school of fishes. And yet, probably no other profession has so many mortalities as the press. The grave-stones of Washington county newspapers whiten the night of the past and yield a ghastly effect.

The Argus was the first paper in the county, started in Washington in '54; Lewis F. Waldin, publisher; J. F. Rice, editor. It made a hard live of it for two years and "went democratic," its politics being that kind. It was two dollars a year, cash, or its equivalent in pumpkins, whetstones, etc. It took all of its namesake's one hundred eyes to see any income. Its motto was funny—"Devoted to the Interests of the Country." That was cutting out a lot of work. Its last croak in the throat was, "The Press will fill out copies due." A. R. Wickersham bought and turned it into the Press.

But the Press was not launched in 1856 just to fill over-paid subscriptions to a paper that had more eyes than a butterfly. It came to become the patriarch of all the county papers. A. R. Wickersham owned it and ran it ten years, with the aid of Thad. Stanton and A. S. Bailey. The two former are no more, but Sim. Bailey has still the cheerful habit of being alive and kicking on a Shenandoah paper, setting nonpareil type without glasses at the age of seventy-six or more. He was a capital writer, a thoughtful and gentle soul.

Howard A. Burrell bought the paper in 1866 and staid by it thirty-seven years, selling it in 1903 to Ralph L. Livingston who, in a short time, sold a half interest to Charles K. Needham, of the Sigourney News and three or four more weeklies in Iowa, and is now sole proprietor. He put in a linotype and made the whole equipment of the office practically new. There is not a better newspaper plant in the state, and he is a capital business man. Livingston is a Cincinnatus on Col. Palmer's farm, and now that Burrell has quit lying and is striving to lead an honest life, his health is at par.

E. B. Bolens started "The Washington Democrat" November 22, 1860. After many ups and downs of fortune, including sundry temporary suspensions, filling the intervals with able-bodied swearing, he took the plant to Wisconsin. I have the impression that he died, and has been an angel for several years.

But it is hard to kill a 'possum. On August 14, '78, Joe Biles, a printer, bricklayer, and fine fellow, revived "The Washington Democrat." Charley

Chrisman had in Riverside a "Times" paper bought of Geo. Trumbo, or Gumbo, and wanted some one to help him let go. Joe bought the plant, moved it to Washington, took in Capt. J. J. Kellogg as partner, but in May, '79, they sold to Kell & McCracken, of Des Moines, and wags changed the "K" in Kell to an "H." In September they sold to Waters & Hood. Lobana Waters was a merry youth, and it took all the gravity of Deacon Wm. N. Hood to anchor this aeroplane. Both are dead, alas!

Geo. G. Rodman bought Waters' interest in the "Democrat" and acted as editor, with Hood, several years, and won the post office from Cleveland. George sold his half interest to A. R. Miller, and he took over the whole thing after the terrible death of Mr. Hood, and is still its master. He gives it individual flavor like horse-radish, and makes a lively, racy, readable paper, with a slap dash spirit that many at home and abroad like. The paragraph is his forte, and he makes a rattling paper that is appreciated at home and elsewhere, tho' sometimes criticised for a censorious tone and an occasional dash of uncharitable spirit.

And aside from the paper, he is an useful man for a town, in the lines of running Chautauquas and lecture courses, farmers' institutes and the like, and bringing to belated knowledge and honors heroes like Timothy Brown, the Revolutionary soldier buried in this county many years ago, getting a legislative appropriation to secure a characteristic Continental bronze bust of the patriot and a pedestal for it to rest on. All these are meritorious offices, and the public has appreciated his public spirited services in such ways.

John Wiseman was a briefless lawyer, but a lovely singer. He Andy-Johnsonized, hankered for Wickersham's post-office, and to get it started a barrel-organ, "The Washington Gazette," December 24, '68, as a Christmas gift. He kept on till '77, with his alleged "independent" paper, but it felt like a sliver in a finger. He sold to "The Gazette Printing Co.," and Rev. Alex. Story edited it. Eventually it fell into the hands of D. H. Logan, and S. Wake Neal bought in, but they sold to Livingston of the "Press" and Elder of the "Journal," both the weekly "Gazette" and the "Morning Herald" that Hugh McCleery started, and re-named it "Morning Gazette."

It must have been in the early '70s that A. S. and S. P. Bailey published "The Record," a semi-agricultural paper, but it suspended before 1877 when A. S. B. moved to Brighton.

Way back in 1857, Washington college pupils put out a paper named "The Bower of Literature." "Bower" is good, also "literature."

Daily journalism began in Washington February 15, 1893. While working on the "Gazette," Wm. V. McCausland had long contemplated starting a daily, but lacked money. He later had a job office in the Temple and men-

CHARLES EVANS

WILLIAM WILSON, JR.

tioned his project to Harry Keister, and on the above date they launched "The Hustler," and Mac staid in eighteen months, selling his interest through Harry to Wm. Fitzwilliams and Narris ("Nate") Black, February 15, '94. They ran it a year under the name of "Washington Printing Co.," and re-named the paper "Evening Journal." G. Logan Payne bought the plant February 15, '95, and developed a remarkable talent for soliciting patronage of all sorts. His daily manna was eagerly devoured, and the evening chit-chat was as relishable as the fresh-plucked things from a garden.

On May 15, 1900, Orville Elder bought the office, and has made the purely local paper a phenomenal success. No daily paper in any Iowa town the size of Washington has had anything like "The Journal's" vogue, remunerative patronage and circulation, the latter having increased from eight hundred in 1900, to two thousand, and nearly all of it local. It is non-partisan and has great advantage in that, making no antagonisms. Elder is a wise editor, winning more by instinctively knowing what to leave out, and absolutely ruling it out. It is what is put in a paper, that is apt to give offense—never what is left out. The paper is clean, enterprising; strives to be accurate and fair; is newsy, timely, and it is timeliness, freshness, early morning dewiness that give charm to news as well as to flowers, fruits and vegetables. The object of the management has been to make it a sort of a public utility, a household necessity. There is an investment of about fifteen thousand dollars in the plant, and twelve people are employed in the business, reportorial and mechanical management of the publication.

Since this was written, Mr. Elder has ordered a web-perfecting press and a linotype—a ten thousand dollar to fifteen thousand dollar improvement.

Brighton had a worse murrain among papers. Robert H. Moore started the first paper, "The Pioneer," in the '60s, and in 1871 Hatton & Snyder ran "The Register" eighteen months. Then Astronomy set in and the village had celestial sheets. In March, '73, a joint stock company launched "The Western Star." Col. L. B. Fleak, the great character of the town, and Ed. Deeds edited it for a year, when the Colonel bought it and called it "The Brighton Star." In January, '77, he sold it to A. S. Bailey who made it shine two years with rare brilliancy, for he was an admirable writer. It shot down the sky into darkness in '79. In January, '78, Fleak & Son created "The Brighton Sun," which blazed till April, '79, when C. C. Heacock turned it into "The Greenback World," that finally lapsed into "The Enterprise," in 1882. Heacock has run out all the other papers there, and no man in this county has shown more editorial genius than he. He has developed that intangible thing called "style" in thinking and writing, a very rare but a charming and unique property, and he has the "art of saying things" plus. Individuality stamps every squib he writes. He is not a "mush of concession," and he is working out of certain foibles that rather handicapped him in his editorial apprentice and amateur years.

In 1880, Laban Fleak conducted "The Reporter" a while, but it reported itself out into limbo, as did Kellogg's detective paper in Washington.

Geo. H. Frasher ran "The News" in Brighton, followed by Rev. J. Dolph and his son Herman, but the year cannot be stated. In '77, Geo. A. Matlock tackled it, and made the "News" newsy, but it, too, went to the boneyard. Hic jacet. That's right—"here lies"—did they always "lie," writing marriage notices, obituaries and puffs about candidates and in campaigns? No, indeed, but they were educational forces, all of them, carp and criticize as one may, and they did more good to their communities than the latter ever did to them.

Wellman has had two papers, one now dead. Albert A. Townsend started "The Reporter" December 21, '85, and in August, '89, Wm. Reed and W. F. Reinert issued "The Advance," and Coffey now keeps it up to Billy Reed's high standard. It is one of the most prosperous of the country weeklies. Its peculiarity is its loyalty to Wellman business men, rejecting advertisements from competing places.

Reed's father, Geo. L., let loose "The Keota Eagle" in 1875, and his boy got his first taste for types there. Richardson Bros. keep the bird in fine trim. It is neatly made up and printed and well edited.

Riverside had "The News," run by S. C. Bruce, but it has utterly evaporated from my eye and memory and from the records.

"The Leader" was started, was it not? by Dennis Flynn in 1883. He drifted to Oklahoma, and became delegate to congress. He is rich; Ellery Foster and John Cherry say he is a smart campaign speaker. Altogether, he seems to have soared higher than any other Washington county editor. Charley Beverley followed him, then Mr. McIlree, but now Wm. J. Kueneman is putting it thro' its best paces.

Crawfordsville's best things came in her old age—a railroad and "The Imprint" paper started and run by Frank Wolf in 1894, and now, after a suspension, conducted by O. L. McCleery.

"The Ainsworth Clipper" was founded in 1883 by John H. Pearson, and he still makes it a very welcome weekly visitor. He is called "Old Clip," but there was never anything real "old" about John except his cob and clay pipes. For many years they were extremely aged, fully ripe, yet fierce, and pulling on them industriously made him as lantern-jawed as Don Quixote, and as generally "lean" as Dante said his poem made him in the composing of it. However, John has lately sworn off, and virtue is fattening him. I am

JOHN WISEMAN

A. S. BAILEY

W. N. HOOD

A. R. WICKERSHAM

glad to record in this veracious history, for a lesson to all the future generations that may read it with a child-like confidence, this instance of righteousness. Rise and sing, "While the lamp holds out to burn the vilest sinner may return."

The Kalona "News" completes the list of luminaries that constitute "the light of the world," or of this part of the world. It was started in 1891 by U. B. Smith (?). He was a clever little man. He sold to D. C. Miller, who is making a very enterprising paper.

I salute the craft, and wish all "the boys" well. I have been something of a liar myself. Nothing draws, pulls, hauls me like the magic and fascination of the types, and the aroma of roses and carnations and violets is to me not near as ravishing as the scent of printer's ink.

Washington Telephone.—People do not stop to think what an educational factor the 'phone is. Really, we do not learn so much, so many things, from any other preacher, doctor, teacher, editor, etc. A ring, two helloes, and then the cunning thing begins to leak information as a hoop-loose barrel or bursted hydrant hose gushes water. Of course, it has done a lot of damage to our healths, by depriving us of the wholesome exercise of walking. We used to do a lot of mileage, chasing people on errands. The 'phone saves all that, economizes our time, and in a day it tells us many things. Especially the rural lines. They say when a ring thrills the country wires, it is just like pleasing sensations vibrating our bodily nerves. Every receiver is clapped to an eager ear in each house on the line, and to listen to the gossip as to the sick, the loves of this pair and that, the sales, market, parties and all the other neighborhood news, is equal to a liberal education.

L. D. Robinson started the service here November 4, '94, associated with Thomas Dupuis and D. H. Logan, with a capital of ten thousand dollars. A sketch of the plant appears elsewhere. This is merely to claim the telephone as a popular educator.

Rural Mail.—A like claim may be made for rural mail delivery. Farm life had been isolated, dull, dreary. The 'phone was "company." The daily mail carrier was a messenger as from heaven. These two agents revolutionized the conditions of life on the farms. Nine carrier spokes radiated from Washington as a hub. This county was one of the first in the district to be threaded with routes, thanks to the energy of our congressman, Hon. Thomas Hedge, under the efficient administration of Postmaster James A. Cunningham. At first, three routes were established, later two more, still later four more. The first rural delivery dates June 1, 1901. The first three lines were about thirty miles long, and ran north-east, north-west, and south. The length now is twenty-five miles. The salary started at five hundred dollars, advanced to six hundred dollars, and now is nine hundred dollars a year, excepting on one shorter line, which is docked to eight hundred and sixty-four dollars. The carriers have off fifty-two Sundays, five legal holidays, fifteen days' vacation on pay, in the year. Free city delivery was started with two extra country routes in 1902, and the mode of delivery of mail to five thousand to six thousand people was changed over night.

This governmental scheme for landing letters, papers, magazines in every home in this county nearly every day, is as truly a part of popular education as are school-houses, blackboards, chalk, text-books and teachers—it is apparatus, means to ends. Uncle Sam never did a humaner stroke, not even in providing homesteads. In all there are thirty-five to forty routes in this county, so laid out that no farm house is over a half, or at most, a full, mile from a line. Practically, every house-holder in the county is served daily. The Paul Reveres who bring the printed tidings on horse or in carts are like an enriching tide, feeding all the creatures glued to the coast.

Loan and Building Association—This is another educator, as practical as Ben Franklin, as wise as Poor Richard's Almanac—teaching people to save, to profit by saving, and enabling themselves to get homes on an easy monthly instalment payment plan. It was organized here in May, 1886, has loaned three hundred and twenty thousand dollars, and four hundred and thirty loans averaged seven hundred and fifty dollars per loan. It thus aided in building or buying three hundred homes in this county and other counties. During the last ten years, under the present law, it has not operated outside our county. It never had a loss worth mention. It set aside yearly two and one-half per cent from net earnings to meet losses, and this more than covered "accidents." The conduct of the association has been conservative. J. M. Denny has served wisely as president from the first. F. H. Graves was secretary one year, and Hon. C. H. Wilson ever since, and there have never been more than one or two changes in the directorate. The stock has always been at par, or above, and in demand.

I had forgotten one institution—a home lecture course. You may not credit it, but we had about all the big talent in the country here in two or three courses—Philips, Emerson, Douglass, Barnum, Tilton, Beecher, and many more, and it occurred to some that we could lay those fellows in the shade, so this home course, some thirty or thirty-five or more years ago. G. G. Bennett spoke of Stay-at-Home Travels, Wiseman on Tree Toads, Burrell on The Good of Evil, and Drs. Fraser and Scofield and Revs. Johnston and Chaffin on subjects I have forgotten. The strange thing about this effusion of eloquence, with chunks of wisdom in it like oysters in a soup, was that not one of those orators was asked to take the general platform and give dust to the men of national fame. It seems Washington was not a city set on a hill, and its light did not reach farther than that of a June bug.

CHAPTER XIII.

COURT, BAR, CRIME, ACCIDENTS.

As stated elsewhere, the first court in Slaughter, afterward Washington, county, was held at Astoria, on David Goble's farm, May 7, 1838. Half of his double cabin was devoted to the records. The weather being warm, the honorable court sat under the trees and the grand jury perched, like bumps, on a log, in a slough nearby. David Irwin, judge of the second judicial district of Wisconsin territory, presided. Thomas Baker was clerk under two thousand dollars bond. A nameless federal marshal summoned the jury. An old-style dime piece was made a seal. Some lawyers came, but no clients; no cases presented, no indictments found. The august court masticated tobacco, ordered one day's allowance for officers and jurors, and adjourned till the next term, beginning October 22, '38, Joseph Williams, judge; Baker, clerk; G. A. Hendray, deputy marshal; but this session, too, was a water-haul, "no person appearing, either parties, attorneys or jurors," the record says. The sole incident of interest was the meloning of the court, as related in another chapter. Simpson Goble, who carried the sweetened water to the elephant, and received a dime for it, could not rest until he had spent the hot cinder in his pocket, and as there was no store nearer than Burlington, fifty miles away, he went there with his father, walking half the way, and bought a—jewsharp!

The third court was held near Washington, Washington county, June 17, '39. The grand jurors were Wm. B. Thompson, Thomas Wilson, Wm. Ayres, David Goble, Sr., Wm. Basey, M. Moorhead, Richard Moore, J. W. Neil, Thomas Ritchey, Abraham and John Hulock, Wm. L. Harvey, Nathan Griffith, Geo. Parks, John Grimsley, Harrison Goble, Daniel Powers, David Goble, Jr., Ira and John Maulsby. No petit jurors that term. The costs in the first two cases were under eight and twelve dollars respectively. He who became U. S. Senator Grimes got a divorce for John Woods against Elizabeth. Nearly all the women were named Elizabeth, probably in honor of the red-headed and fiery-tempered Queen Bess.

On the grand jury for 1840 were no well known men but David Goble, Sr., and Hugh Smith, while the petit jury for that whole year held James Dawson, Wm. Essley, John J. Jackson, Jonathan Wilson, Michael Hayes. Nearly all the indictments were for illegal sales of whisky, that is, by unlicensed sellers.

Judge Williams was a brilliant talker, a ventriloquist, a story-teller, a singer, fiddler; indeed, he could play many instruments. He was odd, humorous, variable, and got much of his fun by ventriloquial feats and practical jokes. One of his strangest eccentricities was making temperance lectures—he was a democrat!

The first court held in the court-house opened November 8, '41.

As late as '45, the county attorney got an annual salary of twenty-five dollars. It may be worth noting, that at the second court session two attorneys came here, who afterward became governors and one of them a U. S. senator of great power and of a courage so splendid he voted against the impeachment of President Andrew Johnson, viz., James W. Grimes and S. P. Lowe. We cannot lasso prospective governors and senators as easy as that in our courts now.

On the 31st day of May, 1841, in Clay, Elijah Seacy murdered Peter Perry with a club, was arrested, indicted, but the case was so manipulated that he escaped. The case was not tried.

A Mahaska county murder case, Job Peck the murderer of Wm. Johnson, came here on change of venue September 9 '43. It was a melodrama; a cultivated Canadian revolutionist, a beautiful girl Kit claiming to be his daughter, horse thieves, etc., being the personae dramatis, and elopement and kidnapping constituting the action of the piece. The Canuck was shot in his cabin and a lover of Kit was held for the crime. Kit was spirited to Pittsburg, Pa., and the lover proved an alibi. He had married Kit near Fairfield. While in jail here, he did not know his bride's whereabouts, nor for several months after, but he finally found her with fine people. They lived near Oskaloosa for years, then went to California. Who she was, was never known; she denied that Johnson was her father; he may have been her husband. After Peck's death, she married again, and had a noble family, and was called the "Queen of a Thousand Isles"—in the oil business? Johnson was the subject of state correspondence between England and the United States. A British subject, he revolted, turned renegade and spy in 1812, and robbed the mails to get information. Both countries offered a reward for him, and he fled to the "Isles."

NORMAN EVERSON

SAMUEL A. RUSSELL

HIRAM SCOFIELD

J. F. McJUNKIN

And still we had no public execution. Courts are tedious without gallows attachments.

There was a double murder. Wm. McCauley was indicted for shooting Don Ferdinand Coffman in English River, Aug. 4, '44. The victim's wife was the alleged woman in the case. There were not enough women in the world, it seems, to go round. The rival men had threatened each other often, and Mac ambushed himself in a fence corner, and, as Don rode a horse by, not over eighteen feet away, carrying a child in his arms, fired, killing both. The case was tried in Van Buren county, Mac was convicted and hung, but we were cheated out of a spectacle we had earned. Mac said he did not mean to kill the baby; also that Mrs. Don put him up to the crime.

A fourth murder.—John C. Herriman was indicted for killing David H. Miller, on A. J. Disney's farm in Marion, August 9, '48. Herriman was an ex-Ohio convict, ~~and was violent~~ when drunk. Talk of challenging his vote enraged him. He was not challenged, but was mad anyhow. Miller riding up with a child, dismounted, and Herriman voided profanity and obscenity on him, and when Miller asked "What are you going to do about it?" drew a gun and shot him dead. After one continuance, the case was tried, he was convicted and sentenced to be hung November 17, '48. On that day there was an Apocalypse of Human Nature in the raw, with the bark on. Sheriff Jonathan H. Wilson had erected a gallows on amphitheater ground east of and adjoining the city cemetery, that a vast crowd of rubber-necks and morbid folk might have a nice roost from which to see a man die like a rat in a trap. Folk came for miles and miles all around, men, refined women, tender children, and camped out, cooked rations, slept overnight in the open, to be sure of having a good place to see the tragedy. When a messenger came dashing up on foaming horse with a stay of execution, that crowd suddenly filled themselves with Helen Blazes, and cussed the welkin blue. Sweet populace, wasn't it? Christian? Civilized? Noble humanity! The upshot was, the supreme court reversed the judgment of the court below; a new trial, in Fairfield, was granted, and a judgment of manslaughter was reached, and he was sentenced to eight years at Fort Madison, but after three years Gov. Hempstead pardoned him.

Marion had another killing, July 15, '59,—Jonathan Dewees, the corpse. Near the Crooked creek ford at Van Doren's mill was a red light house, that a dozen decent citizens set out to abate as a nuisance, the night named above. In the attack, the inmates, two men and two women, fired, and

Dewees was hit in the neck, Arnold Custar was suspected, but he escaped, and, though indicted, nothing came of it.

The tragic scene shifts to Brighton. Dr. L. E. Hogue, dentist, shot Dr. J. T. Sales, August 18, '68, and he died in a week. Hogue escaped, and that was the end of it. Sales and others had given Hogue a letter of credit for three hundred dollars to a Chicago house for goods, that Hogue sent to Fairfield, and he decamped. He was brought back and the goods attached. He returned to Brighton, paid costs of suit, and had team ready to escape. Sales and Hogue had hot words, and when S. shook H., the latter drew a gun and fired.

In October, '69, John McNally was tried for the murder of Thomas King. Mac had borne a grudge for twenty years, and when full of booze it became as hot as a poker. In the summer of '68, Mac had been hitting the bottle and called to settle the trouble. Invited into the house, he stabbed King. Verdict, murder in the second degree, a life sentence imposed. Supreme court ordered a new trial; defense, insanity; sent to Mount Pleasant.

John O. Dayton was shot in a West Chester billiard room August 19, '76. He was playing with J. K. Dayton, waiting his turn, when a man fired through the curtains of a raised window. Ed. C. Clemons was arrested; marks in the soft soil tallied with his boots; his enmity to Dayton since he was a witness for his wife in a divorce suit, was well known. He was convicted of murder in the second degree. There were several trials, resulting fruitlessly. Clemons went to Colorado, ran a sheep ranch several years, prospered, and set out in a late fall to drive here for a visit. He was overtaken by a blizzard in Nebraska, and perished of cold.

In '78, Wesley Miller was shot from ambush as he was walking in the road near West Chester. Tom Dayton was arrested on suspicion and bound over in eight thousand dollars bond. The case was continued from time to time, and finally petered out and was dismissed.

The last murder case tried here was imported from Oskaloosa. Phil Conklin, a large handsome man, was indicted for wife-murder. The case was sensational, and the court-house was packed for days by people eager to see and hear the flower of the Mahaska bar, men like the county attorney, Geo. W. Seevers, Senator and Judge L. C. Blanchard and Mr. Malcolm, assisted by local attorneys, C. J. Wilson, H. M. Eicher, et al. An acquittal resulted, and then tears flowed, flowers were dumped on Conklin, as he floated in a sea of emotions.

Since then, no murders, no blood, and the county was quite free of crime, and for years the jail was empty and did not pay expenses. All told, about a dozen murders in our history, at least two of them committed by insane men, which is not an awful record for seventy odd years of white occupancy. Probably, the Indians did far worse. In every one of the murder cases, the cause can be traced either to bad whisky or bad women, or both. Moral, abolish whisky and women—what's the use?

John Ashworth was Highland's first criminal, and was convicted of forgery in '55. He enlisted and was killed at Shiloh.

Judge Irwin was a Virginian, and was appointed to the bench in Michigan, then to that in Wisconsin. He was a bachelor, returned to Wisconsin, was removed in 1841 by President Harrison, went to Texas, was a hard rebel, and at last accounts was still a Dave Hill—a democrat.

The year 1879 was thick with suicides and murder. Oliver P. Hull murdered his daughter Emma, in Lime Creek and suicided, and John Strahkirk in Marion and Geo. Hill near Ainsworth shuffled off. But why turn the spiggot to let loose the endless stream of suicides? Or why trace the fatal accidents by flood and field? Frost made icicles of many a man in this county, lightning transfixed several victims, fire cremated others, horses ran or kicked many into kingdom-come and slew them, and machinery and railway wrecks crushed our fair average, but probably, more went by the water route than by all other modes of violent elimination. Mammals are not amphibious. It would be dollars in our pockets if we were armed with fishes' air bladders as life-preservers. If mankind had been created on as fair terms as the one-half of living things were, viz., the plants, which subsist on food held in solution in the atmosphere; that is, if our food had also been stirred into the vital air, and we, too, could breathe it as a sort of aerial soup, then our entire disgusting interior apparatus and economy could have been left out—stomach, liver, viscera, etc.,—and the cavity filled with air-bladders to make us buoyant in water, and the chief cause of human mortality would have been abolished. If we except earthquakes and wars, from Noah's flood down to date, water has killed more creatures of air-breathing habit than all of the combined agencies of earth and air and gas. More people, by far, drown than go hence by all other violent deaths. If I were to name all of the victims of creeks and rivers in this county, the list would be as formidable as a mortuary roster on Memorial day.

The officer who sentenced Herriman was Judge Geo. H. Williams, who, it is said, became U. S. senator from Oregon.

When news of the bombardment of Fort Sumter came here, Judge Wm. Stone, who, after the war, became governor of Iowa, adjourned court to enlist. He signed up several blank court records for the clerk to fill in, and some of these are still extant in our clerk's office, though the veteran deputy, Teller, never saw them.

Clark Hoskins took into his home, in Clay, Harry McClain, a convict who claimed to have been converted. He fell in love with Ruth, Clark's sister, tho' several years Harry's senior, but she repulsed him, and he left, but returned in the night, struck Clark on the head with a club, his mother also, but he told Ruth he would not harm her. Florence Baker, a domestic, rolled under her lounge and escaped. Ruth ran to a neighbor's and gave the alarm. Harry supposed he had killed Clark and his mother. He was never heard of, though long searched for.

I have known the courts and bar in this county since 1866. A few judicial faces stick in my memory. Judge Sampson was ideal. He had been a soldier, was as modest as a woman—that is, some women—was a hard student, as honest as truth itself, and he should have stayed on the bench, but was seduced into politics, into congress, for which he had no fitness.

There was never a keener blade on our bench than Judge Winslow. He died too young.

Perhaps Judge J. C. Cook, shifty in politics and a bit slick and agile in affairs, was the most resourceful judge in the list. Years later, he tried a railway case here, and the revelation of his power, adroitness, knowledge, his ready equality to every development of the case, were mental feats wonderful to see.

Judge L. C. Blanchard was a "horsey" and sporty judge, but later rose to prominence as state senator and was rated a strong man; but he indulged a sneering, sarcastic, acrid habit, which marred his character and career.

Judge W. R. Lewis was a mechanical genius, a philosopher, a muser, and, perhaps, a dreamer, a man of eyes as soft and sad as Lincoln's, and a face truly beautiful. Eyes like pansies, all velvet and dew. If one could only see just how the world and life globed themselves in his fine brain and soul! One could love that man, somewhat like a woman. Not less could one love his perfect opposite, the burly, irascible, warm-hearted, impulsive Judge John Scott. He was a delightful old fellow.

In the '60s, the strong men at our bar were J. F. McJunkin, Col. Hiram Scofield, Joseph R. Lewis, Granville G. Bennett. The last two were appointed federal judges in Dakota, Idaho and Washington. Lewis got rich in Seattle, after he was cunningly "resigned" out of office by forged letters. He used to laugh over the cute, shrewd trick.

McJunkin was rated the best advocate at the bar, and he quoted Scripture in his jury addresses like a preacher. He became attorney-general of Iowa and state senator.

L. F. SHERMAN

ANTIS H. PATTERSON

J. F. BROWN

J. R. LEWIS

Everson did not do much at law, and ill health half disqualified A. H. Patterson from practice. Somewhat later he took in as partner John Rheinart, but he was more financier and man of the world than lawyer proper. Born in Alsace, educated in Paris, steeped in the fine arts and literature, he was, on the whole, the best all-round brain and the most entertaining and versatile companion I ever knew here. He was a true Epicurean, with just enough Stoical ice in his philosophy to keep it from getting soft and rancid. He set his stakes at a fortune of fifty thousand dollars, and said that, when he touched that point, he would quit business, and he kept his word. He alternated between our little Washington and Paris, living there months on end; his residence in Milwaukee was heaven, as he beat everybody at whist; he finally moved to Los Angeles, and there I last saw the sadly broken old man in 1892. Not a great lawyer, but the juiciest and most agreeable man of native parts and varied culture who ever lived here, so far as I know. He had the art of living down finer than any one in my acquaintance.

Sam Russell hung on the fringes of the court, and was "nuts" to the humorists and wags. No other man tickled to the core so many of our people.

Another amusing lawyer was a Thersites named McGuigan. He was wont to hit the booze hard, and it made him a snarling hyena, and he used to refer sweetly to me as "that damned Bur-rell," accent on the last syllable. Being a democrat, he had it in for Scofield, or any other democrat. He particularly resented Col. Scofield's intrusion into the councils of the democratic party after he Greeleyized in 1872. The Colonel used to tell in high glee and with a fine apopleptic red on his face and neck, of a scene in a convention that proposed him as a delegate to a higher convention. He begged off, as he was a novice as yet in democratic politics, and Mac, with a nice snarl, agreed with him for once, and moved to rule him off the list, as "we have too much of that d——d truck in our party now." Scofield would here explode buttons and seams.

Judge J. F. Brown was a curious member of the bar. Master of intrigue, wonderfully fluent, masking his humor under a severe manner put on for a joke, he always cleverly managed to act as a sliver festering in the other fellow's flesh. He got as much fun out of such sallies, as a monkey does in roiling a stream above a group of drinkers.

Do not think I am going to spoil our present bar by making them severally and singly objects of the fine arts. They are alleged modest men—H. M. Eicher, C. J. and C. C. Wilson, S. W. Livingston, M. W. Bailey, S. W. and J. L. Brookhart, W. H. Butterfield, C. A. Dewey, E. D. Morrison, Mort Keeley, Clifford Thorn, J. J. Kellogg, A. S. Folger, Peter Hanley,—who would resent my effort to make them picturesque as portraits on the wall. With the exception of the Dean, the venerable J. F. Henderson, who is eighty-three years old, our bar is made up of young men, at least, men under middle age. Well read, shrewd, honorable, striving to settle cases rather than to promote litigation, they are as fine a bunch of lawyers as ever yelled "I object—it is immaterial, irrelevant, incompetent, impudent, insolent, leading, calling for the conclusion of the witness, not the best evidence," etc. Folger has been handicapped by ill health ever since the war. Patriotic, heroic service in his case meant irretrievable damage to his constitution, robbing him of stamina, energy and endurance in mental work.

Our bar was not the wet bar you are thinking of.

Our brigade of High Foreheads, that is, of baldheads, have had a world of fun at court. It was quite like the stage, which serves up, in turn, tragedy, comedy, melodrama, farce. A breach of promise case, if the letters are ripe and juicy, is the funniest entertainment on earth. You can hear the smacks, feel the thrills, see them "set up" till 2 a. m., hear them say "good night," "good bye," plumb forty-five reluctant minutes by the watch. So absorbing, that housewives hurry breakfast, to get to court; skip noon lunch, or take a cold bite, or stack the dishes to be washed later, or let the dog or cat lick them clean. The whole town is in the court room, and till the case is over folks forget religion, politics, education, finance, business, and loaf all day in the Temple presided over by an eye-bandaged goddess playing blind-man's-buff with sword and scales.

And the High Foreheads rock back and forth and wiggle with tickle that trickles tears in laughter, and think of the days in Auld Lang Syne, when their knighthood was in flower, and they were practicing, every one of them, the fine art of Lalligag with their select and elect bits of calico.

A bar association was formed February 9, '05, H. M. Eicher president, Col. Scofield vice, C. C. Wilson secretary, M. W. Bailey treasurer. On April of that year they arranged for the funeral of Judge A. R. Dewey, adopted a memorial and spread it on the records. On June 10, there was a like meeting respecting the death and funeral of A. H. Patterson, and on November 18, '05, they took suitable action concerning the death of the mother of President Eicher, and sent representatives and flowers to her funeral.

If ill health spoiled a lawyer in A. S. Folger, it made of him a notable manufacturer of sorghum, and the growing of cane that he stimulated in this county and region and the developing of sugar and syrup became a very considerable industry. His connection with the sweetening art began in Indiana two years before the war. Coming here in '75, he made in that year two evaporators for Christian Eicher and Elijah Noble. The culture continued till '85-6, when it almost entirely ceased. This year he is making two evaporators for large manufacturers in Nebraska and Missouri, and he expects that one will make thirty-five gallons per hour and the other one hundred and seventy-five gallons in twelve hours, and he may get an order for one that will make one hundred and fifty gallons per hour, tho' this is problematical. In the '70s, he thinks the local culture of the cane averaged one acre for every farmer in the county. He did realize a syrup that was smooth and wholly free from all acrid quality, a very nice dope or spread on bread and butter, that would slickly glide off and nicely trickle through the fingers and require finger bowls. Folger's sweetnesses competed successfully with those of girls. It originally cost two thousand dollars to introduce sorghum seed from China and France into this country, and the annual crop is still valued at one hundred millions of dollars, and grown on land generally unfit for aught else.

It was over-sight—Eardley Bell, Jr., of Wellman, should have been included in our bar. He was county attorney two terms, and covered the intervening eighteen miles in his own big auto, one of the earliest buyers.

The late R. S. Mills, once a legislator, was for many years a familiar figure in our courts. He attained high age, but was blind the last years of his varied career.

There were several ancient lawyers of whom no satisfactory knowledge can be gleaned. Mr. Bailey says there are papers on file in the court records that indicate he was a trained and clever lawyer in Auld Lang Syne,—a Mr. Harrison. And also a Mr. Conkling, Mr. Compton, Mr. Dinsmore, brother to the preacher. But their "I object" is fainter than the ocean's voice in a shell.

Churchman was the lawyer who got scared at Wassonville when there was an armed demonstration to rescue a white maiden from the Indians. He did not need to skedaddle home, for the Reds offered to surrender her if she wished to go and they would be good to her, and she did not want to go. Besides, he was the lawyer that Baz. Williams left stranded on a stump amid the wild waves of over-flowed Crooked creek.

W. J. Case, it is said, was the first lawyer here, in '39-40, and he pledged the two hundred dollars of untainted money, needed to bring here for a year Rev. Dr. Vincent, the first pastor. That was for that time equivalent to pledging one thousand two hundred dollars now. Who of our present bar would assume that obligation? Not one, O ye of little faith. If, perchance, there is even one, Charley Wilson would be the most likely one.

He was not a member of our bar, but had been a lawyer in Burlington, a partner of his brother, and both members of the territorial legislature there in '37-8, and he became a Methodist preacher here and elsewhere, and so I may name him here, the eccentric man, Geo. W. Teas, father to our Lush. While a statesman he seemed to fall from grace, for he published this metrical card in the Burlington Gazette:

"Be it known from shore to shore
That I'm a Methodist no more."—G. W. Teas.

Years later he went to preaching again, and some guy printed this on him:

"Know ye from Georgia down to Maine,
That I'm a Methodist again."—G. W. Teas.

Can't you see heredity sticking out of Lush?

Among the many activities of the late Jackson Roberts was the practice of law. Born very poor in a now deserted log house on a Vermont hill, that I saw a few years ago, he had been teacher there, a mercantile clerk in Boston, a miner and county judge in California, speaking but not walking Spanish, a grocer here and dealer in wild animal skins, broker, discounter of notes, buyer of tax titles and low wet farms and one of the first of the men sagacious enough to see that tiling would make them the most valuable farms, etc. But he never felt quite at home in the law, probably because he did not give his whole mind to it. He was a student of finance, a telling stump speaker on economics, a racy story-teller, humorist, a wit, a good mixer, and in a few years he made a fortune counted large for this section. Take this many-sided man all round, he was the ablest, most versatile man in this county in the last forty years.

A great lawyer is the most signal man in the professions. A man in wide and varied practice should, must, and does know nearly everything, must be a constant student of all the 'ologies—psychology, physiology, anatomy; be an alienist, a specialist in neurotic diseases; he must know everything that is likely to reveal the secret places where motives start and lurk, and the secret springs of conduct and conscience. A much narrower and more scantily furnished man may make a creditable preacher, doctor, teacher, editor, etc., but a great lawyer must have vast learning. Rufus Choate for two to three score years had a habit of buying one strong book per week, and mastering it, and remembering it, to apply its facts and principles in his amazing practice. In the clerical ranks there was no man to match him as an omnivorous reader but Theodore Parker, and in the other professions no equal. In any community, where you find an exceptional lawyer, he is easily the greatest man there, having no intellectual peer in pulpit, clinic, university chair, sanctum. Take a home man like attorney McJunkin,—what other man in Washing-

JAMES DAWSON'S ELEVATOR

BUNKER MILL AFTER HAIL STORM

ton, city or county, had a tithe of his tireless, incessant mental activity? His restless brain fairly oxidized his tissues—he burnt up long before his time.

A year before his death, after an illness, Col. Scofield discounted the tedium of a convalescent chamber, in Seattle, by writing on a tab, on his knee, in bed, his Reminiscences of our Bar, and they were published in the Washington Journal. The manuscript was not left with the clerk of the court, nor with the curator of the historical society. If the family survivors have it, it would be gracious in them to put it in the custody of one of those officers. His personal, actual and traditionary memory would well nigh cover the whole legal line. I do not recall the writing, but there was wide opportunity for happy characterization, for sketches graphic, gay, just, true, all embodied in forms of literary charm.

Since the last paragraph was written, C. C. Wilson, secretary to the bar association, hands me that manuscript. The Colonel came here in '56, and covers the time thence to '61 when he enlisted. The lawyers here in '56 were Everson, Patterson, Jos. R. Lewis, county attorney, and John T. Burris, county judge. All had offices in the court house but Everson, and he had been there, too, but had moved into the little brick shanty on the Temple site. Besides the county officers, the said lawyers, tailor and shoe shops, Argus print shop upstairs, the Press office later, etc., that court house must have had a "bosom" as capacious as Abraham's bosom, and its tenants were as thick as six in a bed. Clients being scarce, and the county rats not over-worked, all sat in the lower hall, fanned by the south breeze, and swapped lies and stories and stuffed the pin-cushion of leisure with yarns, personal confessions, experiences, and with talk of old times and earlier men.

Lyman Whitcomb told of the old shooting matches; there was no money, and they shot for county orders that were well nigh worthless; each marksman had a hole in the ground to stick his won orders in.

When J. C. Conger was a shoe-maker in Ohio, he "allowed" that if he ever managed to get one thousand dollars ahead he would be content, his life not a failure. He earned honestly one hundred and fifty times that stake.

Joseph Keck owned to fifteen thousand dollars made in the cabinet trade, and said he was content. Was he? Scofield says he reached three hundred thousand dollars, but he "did worse than that." Before he began to distribute to children and grand-children considerable chunks of money, one who knew pretty well his status, said he could count up over four hundred thousand dollars, and that was not all of his stuff, either.

A. H. Patterson had come in '46, but went with his father to California in '49, the latter dying there. Joe Lewis had come in '55, McJunkin in '57. Nort P. Chipman had been a partner of Lewis, but G. G. Bennett took his place in the '60s. In '56 there was a genteel lawyer named E. D. Ludington, a society man, and the ladies thought he was too sweet for any use, but he couldn't cut the legal melon, and went back east. In Highland was a lawyer, Fairchild by name, who was so cross-eyed he could see both sides of a case, very likely, tho' Scofield does not say so. He does say, however, that there were seven murders committed in this county, only one conviction, and no one punished. Patterson & Scofield had a collection on Ed. Clemons, whose titles were so clouded they could not fasten on anything. Finally, Clemons entered a lot of fine stock at the county fair, in his own name, and Patterson levied on them. Ed was mad, sought A. H. P., knocked him down, and beat him sore, and had the pleasure of paying fifty dollars for the fun. He thought it paid.

It was to Scofield, and perhaps not to Michael Hayes, though it might have been to both, to whom Everson got off his famous politico-ethical mot, when accused of lying, "this is a free country, and a man has a right to lie."

An Early Court Trial.—In '63, before 'Squire R. H. Marsh, suit was brought by Missouri slave owners to replevin a team that run-away slaves had fetched here and sold to John H. Bacon. Four of the jury, it is remembered, were Isaac Ditmars, P. R. McMillan, C. H. Wilson and Isaac Wagner. The jury could not agree. The case hinged on the point—Are these slave-holders traitors? Lincoln had proclaimed amnesty if southerners returned to allegiance in ninety days. It was figured that there were just eleven days of grace left, and while the lamp holds out to burn, the vilest sinners might return, don't you know? They were not technically traitors quite yet. So a jury in a tuppeny court of the justice of the peace gave the horses to the Pukes who could "show" they were "l'yal," as Mr. Dooley says. They did not care a tuppence for the "niggers," they said, but must have the team. Just what Bacon thought of it is not known, but he was never known to swear.

Accidents.—Among the shocking railroad casualties were the death of W. N. Hood; the rush of an engine into the buggy containing John Graham and his boy Sammy; the collision of a locomotive with the vehicle in which John Vincent and wife and Mr. Gilmer were riding home; the sinking of the bridge near Ainsworth, killing several soldiers who had served thro' the war only to be destroyed in a creek within seven miles of wives, sweethearts and relatives; the recent killing of Mr. Myers in a closed carriage on the tracks.

In the burning of the Richmond brewery May 3, '74, Mrs. Zahn was cremated. A worse calamity was the burning of the first county infirmary December 8, '78, when five poor creatures lost their lives, viz., Mrs. R. P. Disney, Mary Krofta, Henrietta Hagan, Anna Haberlick and Susie Hardy.

Several of the deficients kept running back into the fire, while others were locked in a cage, cut off from rescue by smoke and heat. A snow storm was raging at the time. There were twenty-three patients in all. The institution had been running four years. The buildings cost seven thousand dollars, were insured for four thousand two hundred dollars. The people voted for a fifteen thousand dollar brick building, the present structure.

On the 22d of May, '73, a tornado ravaged Jackson township. In the morning rain fell in torrents; the air was sultry; clothing stuck to flesh. At 2 p. m. angry clouds formed mob-like in the southwest and northwest and approached in whirling volumes, black, yellow, glaucus in color; hail fell; there was a roar like heavy freight trains; suddenly a black cloud, dirty as if filled with sucked-up dust, illumined by vicious lightning jabs, formed in the shape of an enormous pollywog, and its prehensile tail reached for stacks, trees, buildings, like an elephant's trunk, lithe and snaky. It got what it went for. The dwellings of A. McKee, John Maughlin, Geo. Gilchrist, Wm. Caldwell, Thomas Waters, Alex. Gibson, J. M. Davidson, and the Puddleford school house were destroyed, and Mary Rathmell, Mrs. Waters and child, Davidson and Laborn Housel were killed, and twenty-five more were seriously hurt. The property loss was seventy-five thousand dollars. Poultry were plucked clean; wooden debris stuck as splinters and darts in fields for miles; scantling were driven endwise into tree trunks; stoves were carried many rods and set down in pastures, hardly broken, the fuel burning, ready to cook; people and cattle were sucked into the air, and made temporary angels, though without wings; there were all sorts of modes of transportation; live stock fell out of the air and broke bones and necks; the freaks were endless. Love letters, etc., were picked up miles away. What kind of a pickpocket is this electrical prehensile tail, that creates a vacuum as it passes over buildings, sucking out the contents, bursting the walls outward in a spiral whorl, or collapsing them inwards? It impresses one as a devil like Mephisto, a busybody full of malevolent wit, delighting in mischief and cruelty. The houses of J. P. and N. L. Babcock and many others were twisted, knocked off foundations, and more or less damaged.

Nothing is more distressing than people, especially children, getting lost. In the summer of '59 Jackson Patterson's seven-year-old boy was lost, crossing the prairie. The next day he reappeared in front of his home, so bewildered by terror that he did not recognize the place or his parents.

On Sunday, August 25, '72, Wm. Scranton and his little boy were visiting at John G. Stewart's home in Franklin. The boy toddled away unnoticed, and by night one hundred people were searching. On the next Wednesday he was found in wretched plight under the brow of a bank of a slough, hidden in tall grass. Mrs. Wm. Clark, an invalid, had seen the baby in a series of dreams the stormy night before his discovery; so vivid was her vision of boy and locality, she urged her husband to ride a horse to the spot. He pooh-poohed it as a case of nerves, but at last he yielded to her passionate entreaties, and rescued the baby from the habitat she had so accurately pictured. The whole county thrilled to the joyful signals of "Found" that rang from church bells. One touch of nature makes the whole world kin, hearing the plaintive cry of the woebegone child,—"I knew you would come, papa."

James Burch got lost, returning from Washington, and on March 27, '44, his frozen body was found near the head of Goose creek. He lived in Richmond. Nature cares no more for a man than for a worm or weed.

Skunk river at McMartin's mill, later known as McKain's, and at Brighton and Coppock mills, as well as English river at the mills in the northern tier of townships, were veritable dragons, devouring boatmen, bathers, forders. Pearl Hutchinson, Robt. McCaleb, David Sharp and Mr. Nichols were bathing victims. Jones and Hibbs and boy were drowned, crossing the swollen river. When found, Hibbs still had the child in his arms. They were buried by torch-light.

Samuel McKain and Thomas Philips were drowned March 4, '67, and Madison McKain escaped by clinging to a shelf of ice left as a collar round a tree when the water fell, but he was so chilled by long exposure that he died when taken into a warm room.

John Pennington, freighter from Burlington to Brighton, came near perishing in a blizzard Nov. 8, '42. He left his wagon, unhitched the oxen, tied himself by the wrists to an ox's tail, and was dragged to Lewis' store, insensible, badly frost-bitten.

Wm. Hickenbottom, from the Robinson place in Clay, started for Oregon with his father's family, resolved to kill an Indian. He shot a squaw. The Reds demanded his surrender, or they would massacre the party, and they skinned him alive and burned the body before the white train. The shock killed his mother on the trip, but the father married a widow in the party before arriving. Seems to have been a nice family.

John Kyle, a Scot, got so mad at a cow that ate his garden truck at night, that he walked eight miles to the river, went out on a log overhanging the water, jumped in and drowned. It did not restore the vegetables, but he did get even with that blamed cow all right. Funny lot, those pioneers.

In the '50s, Smith Thompson was accidentally shot at Hasty's farm by parties shooting at a mark. He was hauling lumber from his mill to Richmond. He died at Hasty's house.

GRANVILLE G. BENNETT

JUDGE A. R. DEWEY

Would it be too cruel a joke to classify as accidents the mis-carriages of mining companies organized here, with the net result that the stock holders and victims of assessments were made "men of sorrows and acquainted with grief?" On April 15, '76, nine men organized the "Iowa State Mining Co." First and last, they blew more coin into it than out of the mines. Of the dead say nothing but good.

On June 14, '87, there was the "Washington County Prospecting Co.," to find oil, gas, coal, and any old thing except pearls, rubies, diamonds, etc.

Then on March 21, '99, the "Hawkeye Gold Mining and Milling Co." was organized. None of these declared dividends. I put them in the category as accidents, because they made "lame ducks."

In the same category let me place, say "The Jackson Pipe Organ Co.," and several other sells like that. I still have a certificate, No. 11, of five shares in that delectable thing. It was one of the nuttiest things I ever did fall into, as into an open well in a dark night, and there are others who struggled in that same Black Hole. The various attempts to get factories here have been sad, tearful things. It is jollier to nurse sickly twins and triplets than to raise "infant industries" on bottles of protection. Pause right here, gentle readers, and let the dupes weep into cuspidores.

In July 1854, Brighton had an epidemic of cholera. Nothing is said about it in the prints, yet it is more than a tradition. The old settlers say a little girl member of the Wm. Trine family traveling through had the disease, and the infection spread. At least twenty-five died; terror aggravated the conditions. The medical profession had more courage than anyone, and helped all they could. Everson was a volunteer nurse. The contagion ran its course, the germs got exhausted, lay down, and quit, and did not appear elsewhere. There has never been a county-wide pestilence, not even of la grippe; "malaria," whatever that may be, spread the broadest mantle. The early population shook their teeth out with ague.

In June, 1902, a fierce tempest raged southward from this city, spending its intensest energy down Eureka way. The artillery limbered up in the early evening in the southwest and northwest, and it looked twisterish, but we got grandeur only, not disaster. Hail went through greenhouses like bullets, rain fell two and eight one-hundredths inches deep; the top knot on the Presbyterian church was wrenched to the south, and rubber-necked; two of the "five points of Calvinism" on the First U. P. church were knocked off, and the tall phallic M. E. steeple vibrated itself out of plumb enough to provoke payment of insurance. The storm waxed vimful as it sped south. Nineteen high school graduates, chaperoned by County Supt. Cora Porter and teachers, had picnicked at Coppock, and were gripped and blown and soaked, and sixteen of them wounded, on the way back; one buggy capsized; all ran to a brick school house at Eureka, smashed in the locked door, when away went the roof, down came the walls, a youth's arm broken several times, a collar bone broken, heads so cut and mauled as to cause delirium, faces disfigured, teeth knocked out and skin scraped off, girls hit in the back with missiles, shoulders dislocated, clothes gormed with grime. The McCunes took in the sorry crowd, and one hundred and five dollars and fifty cents was raised to compensate them.

This item should find place in "crime." One night Dr. A. A. Rodman was wakened by a burglar holding a gun near his face, demanding money, and he threatened to return and kill him if he gave an alarm. The sheriff caught the desperado at the station. Court was in session. The next day he was indicted, tried, convicted, sentenced to state prison, and on the way thither, all within twelve hours. Never another case of such rapid transit in our court.

In 1845, Ezra C. Clemons brought into Marion a black boy named Henry Hanna, and C. L. Hendricks got possession of him. People fancied he meant to take the lad to Missouri and sell him for a slave. Remarks about going to Mormon Nauvoo still more excited suspicion. Mr. Yockey and Rev. Mr. Vincent drove to Hendrick's place. As he was not at home, they took the darkey to Houston's, two miles away, and that night Houston's son-in-law Ritchey took the boy to his father's house in Winfield. He was secreted here and there till the next term of court, when liberty was secured to him.

A Municipal Stain.—Like the eloquent snake in Eden, whisky was the trail of the serpent over us all from the first. Licensed persons were allowed to sell it, and the earliest courts were mainly engaged in prosecuting liquor-license jumpers. From the organization in 1839, we had whisky, like the poor, ever with us. But the old settlers did not mind it specially. It was pure and almost as cheap as water. There was no object in adulterating it. It cost so little, merchants kept barrel, faucet and gourd cup on the free list, and customers thought no more of taking a copious nip then in the stores than now of going to the ice-water tank. Washington was full of saloons as late as 1866 when I came, to observe the customs and manners. They seemed to belong to the order of nature, certainly to the order of society, as truly as sun, moon, rain, frost, and banks, shops, etc. There had been little popular education along the line of temperance. The council licensed saloons as a matter of course. There were joints on each side of the square and on each spur of street from the corners of the square, vile, stinking holes, full of Low Brows carrying round sloppy, tobacco-stained mouths and eyes like boiled gooseberries and the eyes of dead fish. The temperance crusade started in an outraged esthetic sense, and not in morals—in sheer disgust at the spectacles—men reeling, vomiting, swearing, voiding obscenity, lying helpless in their filth like hogs in a fence corner, embalmed in stucco from a mudhole. All decent instincts revolted at such sights, and for several years there was a see-saw of license and no-license issues in city spring campaigns. The temperance sentiment grew, and with it a detestation of the insolent manners of liquor-dealers and the vile habits of their victims. The prohibition constitutional amendment carried in county and state in 1882, and, though it was thrown out by the supreme court, on a technicality, statutory legislation had followed, and our powerful county temperance league came in collision with Wm. Jugenheimer who owned a brewery and supplied three of his own saloons here and elsewhere with beer, as well as rival saloons, perhaps. In '84 the Jugenheimer places were declared nuisances. Years before, when he built the brewery, and sold its product, there was no protest, popular or individual. He was not molested or even questioned when he invested several thousand dollars in the plant. But by '84, and earlier, there was a strong sentiment against his works. On April 20, '85, steps were taken against Jugenheimer before 'Squire J. H. McLaughlin. Just a year later the trouble culminated in an order to Sheriff M. O'Loughlin to seize and destroy the liquors in the brewery, and six and a half hogsheads and nineteen kegs of beer were spilled. Of course, the plant was paralyzed, virtually confiscated, and many men thought that, in spite of all just provocation, a just valuation should have been put on the old German's property and fair remuneration made him. I confess that I have so held, and felt, and still feel, that the harsh confiscatory action was and is a stain on our city record. It could, and should, have been managed in a better and more rational temper. Passion having long since subsided, the people would now pay the old man, were it to be done over. Any reader, curious to trace the action, may do so on page 192 of the docket from November 24, '82, to September 20, '87.

It may be added that J. P. Spittler had run a brewery here, and there was one in Richmond, no protest launched at these concerns at their inception. There was not a kick against planting any of them; therefore, when public sentiment recognized them as nuisances, we should have given Jugenheimer a fair price for his products, machinery and buildings, that could not be converted to other uses, as a condition of their effacement, for by not protesting against starting them, we were in a sense, a moral sense, silent partners in the plants. Jugenheimer sued for damages in federal court, but never recovered.

Heresy Trial—Indignation Meeting.—Let this chapter end with something personal, though the incident of Burrell's heresy trial in 1868, I guess it was, belongs neither to court, crime, bar, nor accident. It turned out so ridiculously, it was such an utter abortion, it might be classed with amusements. Under the M. E. church pastorate of the late Frank Evans, he and a few others who had worms took foolish umbrage at a squib, intended solely as pleasantry and badinage, on a certain church choir, and the cabal started in to do the editor in an indignation meeting, and boycott his paper both by stopping it and withdrawing advertisements. Perhaps said editor's penchant for fun and his disposition to be a free lance, had made him seem all sorts of a fool to the unco' gude. Perhaps he was a mustard poultice on this, at that time, straight-laced community (it has changed mightily since), and may have needed discipline, but that was not the way to get or give it. Anyway, one evening, "at early candle-lighting," in the First U. P. church—what is now Music Hall—a big crowd gathered, some to penalize the culprit, but, as it turned out, lots more to see the fun at a bear dance, and to vote for Satan when the time should come. Entering a half hour late, "a chiel amang them, takin' notes, and faith he'll prent 'em," he knew he had the situation by the top-knot, by the way those miserable sinners "stomped" and ovated "the cuss." Some one stated the object of the meeting, amid snickering. A few feeble remarks were made by several saints and Pharisees. Rev. Dr. Doig spoke kindly, saying the editor seemed to have a considerable knowledge of the Bible, and was, perhaps, a bit too unconventional in quoting it. One brother, a merchant, in a fiery moment, advised all to take out their ads, but as the whole thing was an amusing fiasco, he was the first business man to get into the band-wagon with alacrity—early the next Monday morning, the day before publication, he brought in a column ad., and thus heaped a whole hod full of live coals on the editor's exalted head. In fairness, the meeting asked the defendant to speak in self-defense. He said he was no speaker, had merely come to report the proceedings, and would make his speech in the next Press. At this, several insurgents swallowed so hard they came near losing their cuds and Adam's-apples. A committee of three was sent out to draft resolutions of censure, whereupon arose a little fellow named Rev. 'Bije Conner of the Second U. P. church, and told the meeting they were doing a very foolish thing; he believed in free speech and free press, and wanted no such snap-judgments taken, like this. He added, the editor merely saw the funny side of things, and if there was anything ridiculous going, he was sure to fasten on that, as it loomed up in his eyes as big as a barn in a fog. The plucky little fellow enthused the hoi polloi and threw several ponds of moisture on the pseudo saints. The resolutions were read; they were quite mild, and limp under Conner's cold water douche, and when the motion was put, just three men were brave enough to say Aye, while the Noes sounded like hail on a tin roof.

And how the congratulatory letters did come in, with subscriptions unsolicited! Editors and publishers, if you want to get a circulation, manage to get foolishly "indignated." An indignation meeting is trumps, and a bully good hand. It was the best piece of newspaper luck that ever happened to yours truly, and the net result of it must go into the pot with the usufruct of three libel suits for ten thousand dollars each, by which he made in clear money thirty thousand dollars—by beating them all.

CHAPTER XIV.

FRATERNAL AND OTHER ASSOCIATIONS, ETC.

Secret societies attract many minds and give them satisfactions via instruction, sociability and amusement, especially those that have a goat annex. A goat is like Artemus Ward's kangaroo, "a most amoosin' little cuss." And, then, the idea of having a secret that not even wife or sweetheart can share, though curiosity breaks their necks to find out, and they sort o' suicide into the Eastern Star auxiliary to get even. Besides, it is a certificate of good fellowship and personal popularity, to escape a blackball. And, then, if there is opposition to the society, particularly by a church, as there used to be here thirty years ago, that stimulates recruiting. There are probably over five hundred straight Masons in this county, not counting men in the sub-divisions called, I believe, capitular and cryptic Masonry, etc. Washington Lodge, No. 26 A F. & A. M. was founded June 13, 1851, by N. Chipman, R. W. McElroy, J. F. Sales, E. Clemmons, G. H. Jamison, Wm. Fisher, J. K. Walker—all dead. Chipman was W. M. till he moved from the county, McElroy was tyler, as well as constable, for ages, being as permanent as the axis of the earth and the Pole star.

The lodge met first in the Iowa house, on the Crail corner, and is now handsomely lodged on the third floor of the Temple. Among the more noted Masons were Dr. Rousseau, Hon. and Rev. G. W. Teas, S. G. Owen, John Chilcote, James Thompson, Wm. Wilson, Jr., Dr. Scofield, A. H. Wallace, Judge A. R. Dewey, Hon. A. N. Alberson, 'Squire Terry and Rev. Dr. Coxe, and one will have to call nearly the entire roll of M. E. ministers, who had as brisk appetites for Masonry as for chickens.

Cyrus Chapter, No. 13, was chartered June 1, '56, and Col. Crabb shone in that. Cryptic Masonry was established in '59 and ran till '78 when there was a consolidation of Council with Chapter degrees. Leon Mayer, Milt Barrett and J. S. Allen were conspicuous. The Chapter has now one hundred and twenty members.

The Knights Templar have here Bethlehem Commandery, No. 45. The charter was granted in '83. It is the only one in the county, and has one hundred and four members, and they are the gay, shining boys, in their glad rags and plumes, swords and gauntlet gloves, and their resplendent shapes are mirrored splendidly in all maidens' and women's eyes, like trees in clear rivers.

Richmond Lodge, No. 96, was organized June 4, '57, by J. L. L. Terry, the Rownds, Benns, Maples, Scotts, Van Pattons, Bunkers, Gallaghers, O'Loughlins, Gwinns; it has forty members, and was long ago transferred to Kalona.

The Fleaks, Prizers, Aulds et al. chartered Lodge No. 64 in Brighton June 6, '55, but differences arose and it dissolved, but it may soon revive.

Dayton Lodge No. 149 was chartered June 6, '60, and now flourishes with sixty members in Wellman. Riverside's Victoria Lodge No. 516 is fifty strong, and was sired by the Beardsleys, Druffs, Otts, Godloves. Ainsworth's Orient Lodge No. 365 has forty-five members, and was founded by the Mickeys, Parkinsons, Andersons, Hulls, Matthewses, December 9, '75. Crawfordsville No. 4 got in early, June 8, '54, and has twenty-one members.

As auxiliary to the Masons, the sisters who, for some mysterious reason can't possibly be Masons, founded Eastern Stars, one each in Washington, Wellman, Riverside, Ainsworth.

I. O. O. F.—Odd Fellowship is strong in this county. Washington Covenant Lodge No. 101, was chartered January 1, '56, by Col. Cowles, O. H. Graves, Fred Vogt, J. M. Schilling, J. H. Harrington; Judge Dewey, Col. Rodman, W. V. Mason, John Yockey, Hugh Kendall, J. F. Henderson were later noted members. They once lodged on the west side, their property was burned, and for many years they perched in Blair's third story, but now they own the Crawford block, paying six thousand two hundred and fifty dollars for it. There are about eighty-five members. Washington Encampment No. 43 was started in '69.

Brighton, Riverside, Richmond, Wellman, Kalona, Dublin, Crawfordsville, Ainsworth have I. O. O. F. lodges and encampments and auxiliary Rebekahs.

Fraternal Insurance.—Several secret societies were organized with that purpose, as the A. O. U. W. Our Hawkeye Lodge No. 1 was the very first dating January 14, '72. It split into two factions. It cost four dollars a year at first, but after long years, if one did not, as Dante said, "have the hope to die," it cost so much that many quit, unable to shoulder the dollars they had sunk. But the dying ones were lucky—their families got two thousand dollars each. C. H. Dixon's home was the first to realize the benefaction. On the whole the society did much good. The Legion of Honor went the same way, as all such societies must go as members age—recruiting stops, since new organizations come up to attract younger people. The Legion started April

E. B. Bolens	W. G. Simmons	S. Thornton	Irv. A. Keck
M. Bradford	E. Crandall	G. S. Eddy	Leslie Parker
Florian Balzer	Wm. Ditmars	Daniel S. Eicher	G. W. Hull

WASHINGTON'S FAMOUS BAND, ORGANIZED IN 1866

15, '79, succeeding the I. O. M. A., which ran a year. Then there was the Pioneer Relief, appearing in November, '79, which paid as much for sickness per week, either six, or ten, or twenty dollars, as members paid per year.

The Knights of Pythias belong in this list. They came on the carpet in '83, Judge Dewey being the first Chancellor Commander. There are one hundred and forty members. The objects are endowment, sick benefit, social pleasures, etc. The dues are five dollars a year, and a sick member gets three dollars a week and the service of a nurse.

There are here two hundred and seventy-five to three hundred Woodmen, the Court of Honor numbers one hundred and fifty, the Brotherhood of American Yeomen sixty, the Fraternal Aid Society, the Modern Brotherhood of America perhaps fifty members, Home Guards fifty—all flourishing, fraternal insurance being the main thing, plus sociability.

The Pythian Sisters are auxiliary to the K. P.'s, the Royal Neighbors ditto to the Woodmen, Degree of Honor to Workmen. The Sisters, Rebekahs and Eastern Stars initiate men, and each order keeps an agile goat for the men to ride, and as the critter bucks the illuminated motto is stuck up, "Let joy be unconfined—go it!"—and the goat does. All of the above last named orders, except the Woodmen, are co-ed, so to speak. You can't keep the sexes apart, not even with a club.

P. E. O.—This order started in a school in Mt. Pleasant, January 21, '69, and was the dream of seven maidens, one of whom became our Mrs. Rev. C. L. Stafford. They never thought it was contagious, but it was, and cities and states "took" it. Our Chapter J was organized February 6, '85, by Mrs. Julia Baldwin-McKibbin. Charter members—Mrs. Hattie Williams, Eva Denney, Ida Cunningham, Sara McJunkin, Belle Patterson, Anna E. Buchanan, Helen Sturgis, and seventy joined. The meetings are fortnightly. Our chapter has business, literary and musical programs, then runs to sociability and good cheer. An annual tea, a real banquet, is served February 6, and every woman who is unfortunate enough to be married may bring hubby by the hand. "Feed the brute!" This is, perhaps, intended as a bribe to marry P. E. O. girls. Then there are doings on Hallowe'en Night, to which the single lass, who wishes to escape her hated singularity, may bring her solidity or incipiency, as the case may be. All a scheme of hooks and eyes and affinities. All right—go it!

For some years all chapters owed allegiance to the supreme chapter, but when chapters became numerous they made obeisance to a state chapter organized in 1893. Mrs. Sarah Dewey was president of the supreme chapter, also vice president later, and was historian; Mrs. Ola Miller is now president of the state chapter; Eva Denney was vice president of the supreme, and Mrs.

Winnie Richards Durland has been organizer. Mrs. Lulu B. Patrick was very prominent. The "Lives" of that lady and of Mrs. Dewey and many more are published in a pretty book loaned me; there's one queer thing in it—hardly one "Life" gives the subject's age! Why is this thus, girls? You can't fool us all the time, that is, unless you have store teeth. You might as well have given the birth year, for we can tell your ages by your natural teeth—when you smile, laugh, talk, eat.

Our chapter has had one convention each of supreme and state chapters, and entertained them well.

The name P. E. O.? what does it mean? No man really knows, and many have lost their minds trying to find out, years ago, but now every body is pretty certain what the three initials stand for, hence all is now quiet on the Potomac.

Our chapter has done a lot of good in esthetic ways. On one Thanksgiving day it sent baskets of goodies to the poor; in 1901 it had a Christmas tree and invited in two hundred poor kids to get, each, a sack of candy, popcorn ball, book, doll, knife or toy; next year it grew a Christmas tree for the kindergarten tots, and it helped many a poor child to attend that school. So, three cheers for the P. E. O.!

Rest Room Association.—This room in the court house basement was one of the best institutions ever invented. Rest and relief it has brought to thousands of women in the last eight to ten years.

Card Club.—In 1906 Mesdames Rothschilds, Dr. Stewart, Rude Warfel, Frank Stewart, Guest, George Stewart, Harry Montgomery, C. J. Wilson, Archie McCulley, Ernest Lemmon, Ed. Bowman, Crail, and Bratton, and Misses Esther McGugin and Lou Cunningham organized the Afternoon Card Club, and had a world of fun, I guess, slapping the cards down hard on their fair knuckles and laughing, squealing, talking all at once, and no one missed a word that was said! They gave prizes of china and cut glass, and games were as strenuous as Roosevelt's lion-hunting in Africa. The churches, when in revival heat, slapped card-playing, looking severely at this club, perhaps, and perhaps not, but the sisters went right on cutting bread and spreading butter just the same.

Cooking Club.—One was started in '96 by Kate and Myrta Jeffrey, Alice Samson, Maud Hott, Anna Henderson, Anne Burrell, Doll Daugherty, Emma Miller, Mame Stewart, Cora Bell, and it is running yet. The girls met at each other's homes, and the hostess had to cook and serve the meal. Tradition says some suppers were divine, and others were certain death. Cupid kept picking 'em off, but the club recruited. Six married, and some went away permanently—to escape the meals? You can't keep anything taut, that has girls in it, they are so fluid and erratic about men!

Commercial Club.—Half a dozen years ago a lot of men formed this club and bought the Win. Smouse-Ed. Blair-C. H. Wilson brick house east of the opera house, and built a long annex, and serve up billiards, bowling, reading room, gymnasium (only the apparatus is not used), and dances on the hardwood floor. The ostensible object was, to promote anything that would help the town. It could be made of far more good use than we have yet seen.

W. R. C.—There are about a hundred members of Washington Women's Relief Corps, and they have done for many years, and are still doing, a blessed work for the poor in soldiers' families, nor restricting their service to that class alone. Their committee is vigilant in finding the destitute and in getting supplies to them.

G. A. R.—I. G. White Post has been recognized as a worthy institution for many years. The scope of the work it and the W. R. C. do, and have done, is so well known that space need not be used for encomiums. Most every town in the county has a Post.

D. A. R.—Who would have believed there were so many Daughters of the American Revolution hereabout? These were the charter members of the Chapter organized in Washington, November 19, 1906: Dr. Cora Smeltzer Allen and Nellie Smeltzer Juzeler, Dr. Ida Bailey, Hallie Berdo, Gertrude Stewart, Lorle Rickey Cook, Ella Corbin, Mrs. Everson, Mrs. Harwood, Anna Henderson, Mrs. Mary Lemmon, Maud Morton, Mrs. Laveria Stewart, Mrs. Owen Wilson, Mrs. E. A. White.

Since then, these joined: Josephine Babcock, Mrs. Ola Miller, Mrs. Col. Palmer, Florence Parrish, Mrs. Mame S. Smith, Mrs. Josephine Smith and her daughters Kate and Gertrude will join when their "naturalization" papers are perfected, as well as Mrs. C. J. Wilson and Mrs. Archie McCully.

The chapter meets monthly and discusses Colonial and Revolutionary history themes. The colors are red, white and blue.

Mrs. Harwood was privileged to be a delegate to the national body in Washington city since the inauguration of Taft. His wife's first reception was to these ladies, and the big fellow enjoyed it more than did his wife, apparently. She seemed bored, but he had his famous smile with him. That body has a half million building just across from the presidential cow pasture, and Mrs. Harwood vouches for that noted Jersey that has browsed all through the American journals. Each of the thirteen original states sent a tall marble column. It is a splendid structure, and some way the Daughters coaxed the funds out of breeches' pockets all right. It's not the first time their fair, soft hands have found their subtle way into said cavities and fetched up valuables.

It was through the untiring efforts of Mrs. Ella Wilson Corbin and Mrs. Dr. Bailey that the organization was completed. They worked all the summer of 1906 to help the members get their application papers from the national chapter at Washington, D. C., as each member has to belong to that before joining a local chapter. Dr. Bailey was appointed regent here by the state regent, and elected president the second year; Mrs. Corbin treasurer, Anna Henderson vice regent, Mrs. Bowman recording and Miss Berdo corresponding secretary, Mrs. Cook registrar, Mrs. White historian.

Some wanted to name the chapter "Timothy Brown," for the Revolutionary soldier, but "Washington" prevailed. The object is to promote patriotism, reverence the flag, mark Revolutionary soldiers' graves, study colonial times. They celebrate June 14 as Flag Day, and meet at some member's home: the first year at Mrs. H. M. Letts', next at Mrs. Ernest Lemmon's, the next at Mrs. Cook's, and this year at Mrs. Juzeler's. Each year prizes of five dollars and three dollars are given the grammar grade to stimulate study of U. S. history. The chapter gave fifteen dollars to the Iowa room in Continental Hall. Two members have died—Mrs. Everson December 13, '07, and Mrs. Brown May 2, '07.

The Automobile Club is the drollest of all. The ladies are not cynical or vixenish, but just humorcus, and meet once in a while to "run over every body." It is an expansion or extension of the private club that Artemus Ward's mother and a neighbor woman organized, to b'ile soap together and "aboos their neighbors." They have so much fun, they do not need a goat.

Then there are the Rose Club, the Navajo Club, a basket affair, the Bachelor Maids who hate to stay maids, the Ready Maids, ready for anything romantic, and for sodas, ices, flirtations, perhaps, I don't know, the A, B, C's for girls, and the Ready Bats for boys, etc. I hope I have got 'em all now, but will not gamble on it. We are organized to death, both society and church.

Yes, there was an Eczema Club, that was full of business and activity when the rash burned and itched. A. H. Wallace was president, H. A. Burrell vice, Elmer Mason treasurer to pay for dopes, washes, salves and other fakes and frauds, and George Griffith chaplain. Its sessions were as lively as those of a squad fighting seven-year itch, or bedbugs or mosquitoes.

After the surgical fad of opening people with prayer, to cut out the vermiform appendix, got well started, the victims, who were minus that pendant, organized an Appendicitis Club, and had a museum where each one's bottle of vermiform, pickled in alcohol, was labeled and on exhibition, or the trophy was dried, like a strip of mummied venison or jerked buffalo.

There was once a Y. M. C. A., but in the presence of so many churches there seemed to be no need of it, and it languished and quit. But just now an effort is making to reorganize on a popular scale and erect a worthy building.

It wasn't exactly a club, but a rifle team that did wonders. It was organized about 1885 by Bill McCutcheon, D. S. Cole, A. A. Rodman, Chas. Hebener, Alex. Coffman, Gola Hise, 'Phon Sheets, J. J. Kellogg, Mart Whitcomb, C. J. Wilson, A. H. Wallace, Will McClean, Tom Teller. They used old muskets, not even the improved Springfield, and they beat all rival teams, the Denver Rifles, Minneapolis Rifles, two or three matches, Chicago Lake View team, Davenport Rodman Rifles, Muscatine, West Liberty, Columbus Junction, etc. The Rodmans had never been beaten before. McCutcheon shot in shirt sleeves and breeches bagging both at seat and knees, and after he shot he went behind the house, hutching up the slack in his pants. The fastidious and chagrined Rodmans said by way of explanation of their defeat, "He (Bill) is a damned old trapper from the Rocky mountains!" Our boys always carried the badge of the brigade, never lost it. They were as expert as the squirrel hunters in the South Carolina war. Capt. Kellogg was secretary and treasurer of our team.

A W. C. T. U. would seem to be superfluous in this county any more, but it endures. Washington, city and county, is thirty years ahead of the wonderful temperance wave-movement that has swept over the country the last two or three years, especially thro' the South, the old slave states, and that part of the northern states that is covered with brush, that appears to be the native lair of the drink habit. We have had no saloons since '84. Railways and many large business corporations will not use drinking men. Folk are tired of this relic of barbarism—booze. It fosters crime, domestic misery, poverty, and is the worst sort of economy, no matter how much revenue it creates. Whisky is tabu. But it is amusing to hear local humorists, who used to wet their whistles, tell of the hard times after the adoption of the constitutional amendment, the expedients that drinkers resorted to, to titillate the beer and whisky nerve. All of a sudden there was a great run on certain easy drug stores for bitters. The damp brigade would send this one and that one to buy a bottle, till the club had enough for an inward bath. They could get a variety of bitters—Boreheaves Holland Bitters, Drake's Plantation, Loback's Bitters, Hop and Vinegar Bitters, Centennial, Red Jacket, Yahoo, etc., each containing fifteen, twenty, thirty and forty-five per cent of alcohol. Every brand had a fang that squirted poison. The club sent in a farmer to buy for them. He didn't know what to ask for. "Hostetter," they prompted. "I can't mind that name," he objected, and called for Hostile Bitters. Another granger emissary forgot the name and said, "The kind that —— buys."

Dusty, parched were the gullets in those days. Too much alum, and it took the boys a long time to get used to the new ways of reform, and not one of them believed that virtue is its own reward.

Altogether, there are some seventy-five societies, orders, clubs and what-not where our people may go for solacement, amusement and edification. And they are outside of church sub-divisions. Churches are wonderfully organized and sub-organized. All have Sunday schools. The Methodists have four foreign and three or four home missionary societies, Epworth League, ladies' aid society to procure funds for wise use. The U. P.'s have the Senior and Junior Endeavors, Ladies' Missionary Society, King's Daughters, a dual affair of Golden Rule and Helping Hand circles, men's league. The Presbyterians have a brotherhood, Senior and Junior Christian Endeavor, Ladies' Aid, Women's Missionary Society, and the Baptists have a missionary society, What I Can, ladies' league, B. Y. P. U., men's league.

Hold on—there is a Junior Cooking Club, formed some ten years ago, by the two Misses Shearer, two Meachams, two Parrishes, Maud Moothart, Louise Wilson, Mrs. Morrison, Mary Massey, Anna Wells Truesdale.

Halls, Etc.—Akin in aim and service to the above seventy-five organizations are the public places where people gathered for all sorts of purposes,—the several court houses, Corette's hall, Everson's hall, Music hall, Smouse's hall, the churches, the first Graham opera house that was burned, and the present structure bearing the same name, etc. In these, or in all but the churches that limited their accommodations to lectures, concerts and festivals of a semi-religious but amusingly hold-up nature, we were treated to magic, phrenology, plays, exhibitions, music, home talent shows. Two five and ten-cent shows opened in 1907-8, and Brinton built an Air-dome late in 1908.

In December, 1883, roller skating became so absorbing a passion that a rink was built, and its roar at night was like the pounding of surf on a lee shore. The fad passed, but now that cement walks are so general, skates have come back, but the streets are the rink. We have had all kinds of locomotor ataxia. In the early '60s, or late '50s, we put away oxen and tried horses. It was about forty years ago that Irving Keck introduced a velocipede, not the tall kind, but with the pedals so far in front that the rider looked like a reversed flying shitepoke, and acted like a cantering broncho that had caught his hind feet in the stirrups. Henry Clarke and Irv. bought that absurd thing in cahoots, to get exercise—they got it—plus. About twenty-five years ago Cloyce and Ralph Dougherty brought in two velocipede concerns some sixteen hands high; they had to climb the neck of a giraffe, or its equivalent, to mount one. Ira Sproull and Mort Keeley also indulged. The things cost only one hundred and twenty-five dollars each. The principle of the machine was dead wrong: the drive wheel should have been the high one, not a low one. All swift animals are well set up behind to give the big push. The velocipede had a short hind leg. In due time bicycles appeared and were modified until the perfect safety was devised. It took a long time to educate country horses not to shy at them. Rev. Mr. Stryker imported the first one, or at least he was the first "cloth" to ride one for his daily constitutional, and some men in his church chided him—it was "undignified," but now that riding habit is rated as orthodox as for girls and ladies to ride horses astride, as they do.

Over fifty years ago, the venerable Jacob Dodder, father or grandfather to Charley, a very ingenious mechanic and patternmaker, who was always evolving some idea or another, invented an automobile. The motive power was steel springs. His shop was between Cook & Sherman's drug store and the alley. The first trip was disastrous. He started down South Marion avenue lickety-cut, and below the tavern the thing wouldn't gee and mind its rudder, and he and it went into the ditch, and it busted. He was hurt in the mix-up, and that was the last of the auto business here for half a century.

For many years there were no carriages, buggies, phaetons, etc., just lumber wagons, not spring wagons, and not even spring seats. J. C. Howe and Dick Houghland were early wagon-makers. Folks would pile straw into a wagon box, and women sat in it, not tailor or Turk fashion, but with feet straight out, and rode along smoothly in sleds or bumpy in wagons. They came to market and church that way, sitting broad-based and secure like statues on firm pedestals. Much later Wm. Ditmar and Bell Brothers, and still later Mr. Sage in the Washington Buggy Co., made fine rigs of various names. You can't keep a young fellow on the farm any more unless he can own and sport a top buggy, rubber tire, and the girls all know when he gets it, and they, one by one, sit closely to him in its proper dedication. And even the hired man stipulates that he is to be furnished a rig once in awhile, if not twice and thrice in a while, to go to town or give his girl an airing. But these rigs got passe. In 1901 Dave Donovan drove in an Olds automobile, the first mobile seen here. It made a sensation. Not long after Dr. M. C. Terry brought one into Brighton, to do his practice in. How the country folk did fear and hate that "Red Devil!" How the old rural nags did dance and snort and run away! Not only were their necks clothed with thunder, but the sound and smell of an auto fired them with unwonted ginger, and they went straight up; they became bipeds, and were on their hind feet most of the time, talking sign language with their fore legs. In 1904-5 there were perhaps twenty-five machines in this city. The yeast got into the farmers, and twenty of them use these machines as runabouts, and Wooley Bros. say eighty to ninety more are under conviction, and will buy autos of some make this summer. Last fall there were one hundred and forty-six machines owned in this county, and by this June 1 there will be one hundred and seventy-five, if not two hundred. The young fellows have discovered that the glamour is all off of buggies so far as the girls are concerned, and that no one can make a capture henceforth unless he drives a chugger and loud smeller.

Have we now reached the limit in locomotion? Nay, wait for aeroplanes —they're coming, sure. They alone can solve the good roads problem. The only way to escape mud—in some slovenly districts where King drags are not used and the roads are not worked. When we get these winged planes, every fellow will be a "bird," if not an angel.

How antiquated that makes navigation in old settler days! Before railroads the rivers were the routes of travel, coming and going. Thousands were employed in boating, even as in Canton, China, and the captain was the great man, if he had oaths enough in him. St. Louis got the trade of the up-country merchants, as she was head-quarters for skins and furs in the still more ancient days. Before 1820 there was not much river traffic above the Des Moines rapids. In 1827 a boat was forty days from New Orleans to Keokuk. The Panama canal may right the big river and restore its prestige, but just now the traffic on the Ohio river from Pittsburg down greatly exceeds that done on the entire Father of Waters below St. Louis. Everybody now works but Father. A report just at hand, as I write this, says the business on this river from St. Paul to the Missouri river in 1908 exceeded that on the lower stretch. Over two million passengers were carried and over thirty-three million dollars' worth of freight, and yet the traffic fell off far from that of the previous year.

The Washington County Historical Society was organized June 6, 1905, and officered thus: Marsh W. Bailey president, C. H. Keck vice, A. R. Miller secretary, J. A. Young treasurer, C. J. Wilson curator. Directors, H. A. Burrell, A. H. Wallace, Frank Stewart, Col. Bell, S. W. Neal, C. H. Wilson. The other members are H. M. Eicher, J. O. Elder, A. Anderson, Dr. Hull, Col. Scofield.

The society has a room in the court house and has gathered some materials,—diaries of pioneers, their letters back east, account books, property lists, old addresses and sermons quite dry by this time, but not incendiary, papers, magazines, photos, pictures, maps, books, pamphlets, MSS., documents, souvenirs, curios, and county histories by Nathan Littler and Irving A. Keck, etc. In the winter of 1908-9 the society authorized the preparation and publication of a History of Washington County, Iowa, in two volumes royal octavo.

Temperance.—The fight was long and had ups and downs. The first fighting force was the Sons of Temperance in 1850, followed in '65 by the Good Templars; in '67 the Blue Ribbon movement. In '77 and '78 beer was voted out, but, like "nature when driven out with a fork comes running back," as the ancient poet said, the tide came back in '79. In '82 the constitutional amendment swept the county, and it has not had a saloon since 1884.

On February 12, '09, Brighton formed a Fellowship Club. Religious service via sermon, lecture, talk, etc., Sunday p. m., by home or foreign talent.

There have been many musical associations round the county, resulting in various bands. And park, detective, anti-horse-thief, cemetery and opera house associations, and the Chautauqua formed November 26, '02. Kalona got a Pavilion association in '03. The list of these affairs is well nigh endless. The cemeteries round the county have a mournful interest. Many graveyards were abandoned. Oregon had two cemeteries, one in James Long's cornfield, the other "Old Camp Ground." Cedar had the Patterson, Highland the Davis Creek, Lime Creek one near H. B. Taylor's, Clay the Smith, Riverside formed an association in '82, Brighton in '67, Washington got Elm Grove in '87, and a Revolutionary memorial for Timothy Brown November 23, '03, and a bronze bust of an ideal Revolutionary soldier was set up in the Circle to his memory, the legislature appropriating five hundred dollars for it.

Endowed, as we are, with so many, many clubs, circles, societies, etc., we have had about every thing in the way of culture except mothers' congresses, composed, as they usually are, of childless ancient maidens who look all right in the dark. We are a cultivated community. I believe it is that serious Mr. Geo. Ade who rose to remark in one of his slang books, that "home is not a lecture bureau. I don't blame any man for marrying a woman who has got the intellectual bulge on him. In these days of clubs and reading circles, it is a cheap grade of wife who hasn't got the he-end of the outfit beaten to a pulp. Nearly every woman knows more than her husband, but it helps some if he has enough gray matter to enable him to chip in now and then, if only to give her cues. But thirty years should be a long time to sit at one end of the dining room table, feeling about the size of a cockroach."

CHAPTER XV.

BANKING, INSURANCE, ETC.

Money makes the mare go. Its effect on oxen is nil. Yet it depends much on the quality of the money if it makes even the mare go. All through our Colonial and Revolutionary periods, and even down to the Bryanese '90s, the currency pestered us It would not stay put. It wobbled and was erratic. The circulating medium in colonial days was amusingly various. In Virginia tobacco, wheat, peas, Indian corn, barley, oats, silk competed with gold and silver. Massachusetts, mother of brains and culture, used Indian wampum. "Legal tender" was various, and all of it fluctuated. In 1619 the general assembly of Virginia fixed the rate at which tobacco should pass current, but the inconstant stuff had to be doctored by legislation in the years 1633, '42, '55, '66, 1727, '30 and '55. The weed, and the certificates issued in its name, constantly depreciated, and the partial destruction of stocks and the enforced suspension of planting, were no cures. Conditions were similar in Maryland, in New England and other provinces. Massachusetts issued bills of credit as early as 1690. Rhode Island put out one million two hundred thousand of these bills. Assemblies rivaled each other in debasing the currency, and in every case depreciation and repudiation ensued. The wiser mother country opposed this speculation, and that was actually one of the "grievances" that led up to the Revolution—our cranks could not freely "wild-cat." Not till the middle of the eighteenth century were gold and silver plentiful enough to form a basis of currency, but even then the colonial legislatures strenuously opposed any improvement in its quality. In 1779 the Continental Congress issued two hundred forty-two million dollars in paper, and in two years it was worthless. The foreign coins were flaunted, and shin-plasters, stump-tail, wild-cat were preferred.

Barter was pretty near as good and handy as such money. An ox was for ages the standard of value in antiquity, when the word "pecunia," meaning flocks and herds, was coined. But in traveling, it is not exactly convenient to drive an ox along, instead of carrying a purse or check-book, and then it is difficult to make change in calves, yearlings and two year olds, or in goats, kids and doves, as in the Mosaic period. But that was what all the great fur companies did in John Jacob Astor's day, and before and after that— a beaver skin was the unit of value. It did not fluctuate, for the market could not be glutted with skins.

Up to 1850 money was scarce here, and little of it was good enough to make even the mare go, let alone the oxen. Good money was saved to buy land with. Why have banks in an ox age? Barter, on the basis of a standard price for muskrat skins, sufficed when wages were but forty to fifty cents a day; fifty cents for splitting one hundred rails; corn, six to ten cents a bushel; wheat, twenty-five to thirty-five cents; cows, ten dollars; yoke of oxen, forty dollars to sixty dollars; breaking prairie, two dollars per acre, done exclusively by oxen, three to five yoke to a team, swearing thrown in. No driver could lead a consistent Christian life. Engineer Theo. P. Shonts' father, a pioneer, coming west with an ox train, told a clergyman in the party, who had the best ox team, but they were always getting stuck, "Parson, you've just got to learn oxen talk. Damn 'em, sir. Cuss 'em right and left; it's the only language they understand."

When things began to look up here in '55, with the sure prospect of the railroad coming in in '58, Norman Everson opened an Exchange and Deposit bank, June 1, '55, in the little one-story brick shop on the site of the Temple building. It was jerk-water, but the beginning of banking here, and the end of barter in Washington. Everson would fry eggs—I saw him do it in the spring of 1862—on the top of a small stove in the back room, and take in money and loan it in the front room, and between whiles he would trace Dr. Rousseau's Bertillon finger tip marks in the dust on the shelves, fumbling for Norman's apples. Later, Mayer & Rich ran a clothing store, in both the old and the new building, on the northwest corner. That bank ran till the branch of the State Bank was established.

In March, '57, Shaw, Rigour & Co., started the Washington Deposit bank, in a small frame on the northeast corner, but they were succeeded in '58 by W. H. Jenkins & Co., who ran till the branch bank came. A. H. Patterson and Col. Scofield were the "& Co." On July 29, '58, notice was legally given that books would be opened for subscriptions to stock in a branch of the State Bank of Iowa, at Jenkins' bank August 19, '58. This application failed, but on March 15, '59, fifty thousand dollars were subscribed thus: G. C. Stone and J. A. Greene, two hundred shares each; Patterson, four; C. Craven, five; Jos. Keck, ten; J. W. Quinn, six; Jas. Dawson, ten; L. Whitcomb, five; S. G. Owen, four; Thos. Walker, five; Wm. Wilson, Jr., four; G. Brokaw, five; Thos. Wilson, two; Robert Dawson, ten; Jenkins, thirty. The directors were, Greene, Stone, Holden, Keck, Jas. Dawson. In August, '61, Keck

J. R. Richards

Joseph Keck

J. H. Young

took Greene's place as president, and held it through the bank's existence. In that year also one J. Richardson was assistant cashier, whoever he was. The Branch began business April 19, '59. Howard M. Holden succeeded Stone as cashier till February, '61. W. H. Hubbard took the place a year, giving way to Holden who stayed till '65.

The first monthly statement, May, 59, gives assets as forty-three thousand fifty three dollars and thirty-six cents, and the balancing liabilities embrace such items as capital, twenty-five thousand dollars; deposits, eight thousand five hundred fifty-seven dollars and thirty-five cents; surplus, three hundred twenty-five dollars and forty-one cents. Statement May 1, '65, assets, three hundred eighty-eight thousand eight hundred five dollars and ninety-one cents, holding such items as specie, legal tender and bank notes, one hundred thirty thousand fifty-six dollars and seventy-five cents, notes and bills discounted, one hundred fifty-six thousand three hundred nine dollars and fifty-four cents; U. S. bonds, thirty-five thousand six hundred dollars; revenue stamps, one thousand five hundred dollars. And the balancing liabilities show capital, fifty thousand dollars; notes of circulation, fifty-nine thousand eight hundred fifty-six dollars; deposits, two hundred forty-seven thousand forty-two dollars and thirty-eight cents. There were but three other banks in Iowa that did more business than this one. On April 30, '65, it was merged in the First National bank, with these stock-holders: Keck, one hundred and twenty-eight shares; Holden, one hundred and forty-five; Dr. Chilcote, thirty-three; his wife, seventeen; Shep. Farnsworth, thirty-four; Owen, forty-five; Brokaw, twenty-eight; Mrs. E. A. Banta, eight; C. Craven, eighteen; J. M. Craven, twelve; Jas. Dawson, three; John Moore, eleven; Hugh Smith, eleven; J. M. Rose, six; Robert Dawson, one. The First National was organized in April, '64, but did not begin till May 1, '65. J. Keck, president; Holden, cashier; directors: Keck, Holden, Owen, Chilcote, Jas. Dawson. The capital stock of fifty thousand dollars was doubled October 22, '70. In '66 Owen was cashier, Farnsworth assistant, but before the year was out, Owen became vice-president, Farnsworth promoted. The next year Everson was elected vice-president; in '68, Irving Keck was assistant cashier, Farnsworth resigned, and Henry S. Clarke served as cashier five years. Irving resigned in '69. In '71, R. R. Bowland was assistant cashier, and was promoted in '73, and the next year Wayne G. Simmons was his assistant. Bowland resigned in '82, and Simmons served in his stead, and on August 7, Frank Knox was made assistant.

On February 25, '83, the bank burned, with full half of the west side of the square, and the bank took temporary quarters in the Press building. This made Burrell a National Banker—in his mind, but he didn't "bloat," for on

August 6, the bank moved into its new building. The old vault had proved fire-proof, but for a few days, while it was cooling enough to be opened, there was much anxiety as to the condition of its contents.

In '84, Simmons resigned, and Chas. H. Keck became assistant cashier, and in '85 S. A. White succeeded to the cashiership and held the post till January 19, 1902. Frank Knox had resigned, and in '90 C. H. Keck became vice-president of the First National. This is a list of its presidents: Jos. Keck, Everson, A. H. Wallace, Wm. Blair; and its vice-presidents were: Calvin Craven, Holden, Owen, Everson, James Dawson, Hugh Smith, Leon Mayer, Wm. Blair, C. H. Keck, Sol. Rich.

At the close of the renewed twenty year charter, in 1903, the bank took the name Citizens National Bank; C. H. Keck, president, Carl M. Keck, vice, Frank R. Sage, cashier.

As the First National was our first considerable bank, our historic bank, it seemed fitting and just to go into quite full detail.

The Citizens Savings Bank was organized in Washington, May 7, 1892, with twenty-five thousand dollars capital, which was later increased to thirty-five thousand dollars, and in 1902 to fifty-thousand dollars, and in 1908 to one hundred thousand dollars. The Citizens National Bank went into voluntary liquidation June 1, 1908, and the Savings Bank took over its business. The officers of the Savings were C. H. Keck, president; C. M. Keck, Frank Stewart and Ira Sproull, vice-presidents; Frank R. Sage, cashier. Its last statement, May 18, 1909, gives loans, eight hundred twenty-three thousand six hundred dollars and ninety cents; and deposits, eight hundred nineteen thousand nine hundred eighty-five dollars and forty-three cents; total footings, nine hundred twenty-eight thousand nine hundred fifty-five dollars and sixty-nine cents. It should have been stated that the first officers of the Savings Bank were Jos. Keck, president; Frank Stewart, vice, and Chas. H. Keck, cashier.

J. R. and L. C. Richards and A. T. Green opened a private bank in Corette's corner in '65, and ran it two years, but on June 11, '67, a corporation was formed, The Farmers and Merchants Bank, by John A. Henderson, I. N. Laughead, Dr. McClelland, Joe L. Rader, Richard brothers, Dr. Chilcote, Owen. Henderson was president; Dr. Richards, vice; Owen, cashier. They opened in the Yellow Brick. In July, '70, Dr. Chilcote took Henderson's place. December 26, '70, they decided to merge the bank into the Washington National, with fifty thousand dollars paid up capital. Chilcote served as president till his death; Wells became vice-president in January, '79; Dr. Richards was cashier till July 1, '78 when he resigned and John Alex. Young was elected, and still serves with ability and success. In '74 Cass Richards resigned as assistant cashier and Young took his place and had four years' apprenticeship. The bank building was erected in '71. In April, '74, the capital was doubled. W. W. Wells succeeded Chilcote as president and held the place till his death in 1908, when A. H. Wallace was chosen. W. A. Cook is vice-president; J. A. Young, cashier, and Walter F. Wilson, assistant.

Two balances will show the growth of this bank. On April 28, '71, the deposits were eighty-four thousand two hundred fifty-seven dollars and sixty-six cents; the loans, one hundred four thousand one hundred thirty-four dollars and ninety cents; capital, fifty thousand dollars; total assets and liabilities, two hundred twenty-five thousand six hundred three dollars and sixty-eight cents. The last statement, April 28, '09, shows deposits, nine hundred thirty-one thousand three hundred eight dollars and forty-one cents; loans, seven hundred sixty-five thousand seven hundred twenty-six dollars and seventy-three cents; capital and surplus, each, one hundred thousand dollars; total assets and liabilities, one million two hundred fifty-six thousand seven hundred six dollars and fifty-nine cents.

The original stock-holders were: Dr. Chilcote, Michael W. Wilson, Wm. Wilson, Jr., W. W. Wells, S. G. Owen, J. A. Henderson, I. N. Laughead, J. R. and L. C. Richards—all dead, and per cents interest them no more.

The growth of all our banks was quite slow till very recent years; it has been rapid the last ten years, and very swift the last five. For general business was good, money plenty and of the best, farmers had bumper crops that sold at top prices, and they got out of debt, got rich, and they began slowly fifteen to sixteen years ago, to deposit in bank. Before that, when they sold stock and grain, they tucked a roll of bills in their pockets, paid their bills, and if anything was left, took it home and hid it. Now they slip it into banks, and carry checkbooks like real city business men. In mid-May this bank had eight hundred and sixty-eight check accounts, and about three-fourths of these were farmers. Same ratio in all banks, probably. Folks have never been afraid of our banks; there was never a bank scandal, or even the suspicion of one, in either city or county. It is a remarkable testimonial to the probity and integrity of our bankers. Their conduct has taught morals as truly as our pulpits.

The rate of interest began to go down years ago. In '74 it was ten to twenty per cent, ten and a third, or thirteen, being the usual. By '80 it was down to eight and ten, and stayed till '92 or '3, dropping to six on large loans. Six per cent was legal on debts where no interest was specified, and twenty per cent was legal in contracts. Our people in late years have been flush with money, as the bank deposits show.

I might as well state here as later, that in June, 1909, there was on deposit in the banks in this county, exclusive of the banks in Keota, that accommodate many of our farmers in the western part of the county, the enormous sum of four millions two hundred and thirty-six thousand four hundred and fifty-nine dollars and ninety-two cents. And the loans were four million ninety thousand nine hundred seven dollars and ninety-eight cents. And the capital stock was three hundred fifty thousand dollars.

In the pioneer period it would have been hard to scare up thirty cents.

The Washington County Savings Bank was organized October 7, '76, with fifty thousand dollars capital. Wm. Rowan, president; W. R. Jeffrey, vice; Jas. H. Young, cashier, and they were directors with T. S. Rowan, J. C. Ferguson, B. F. Brown, N. Littler. It began business in October, '76, south of Cook & Sherman's drug store, with twenty-five thousand dollars capital, paid in, and in January, '78, the rest of the stock was paid up. The statement for January 11, '78, shows a balance of assets and liabilities of sixty-five thousand five hundred ninety dollars and fifty-six cents, the deposits being fourteen thousand fifty-eight dollars and sixty-nine cents. A contrasting statement for May 24, 1909, gives said balance as three hundred seventeen thousand twenty-seven dollars and eighty-seven cents; loans, two hundred sixty-two thousand one hundred eighty-two dollars and forty-three cents; deposits, forty-nine thousand nine hundred eighty-three dollars and eighty-seven cents.

Jas. H. Young served as president from October, '84, to October, '99; W. R. Jeffrey was promoted from vice-president to president till October, 1903, when Jas. A. Cunningham was elected. A. Anderson had been vice-president, was assistant cashier a year, and was cashier till April 1, 1907, closing by resignation of that post a good, continuous service in the bank of twenty-three and one-half years, and his brother, J. T. A., who had been assistant cashier since October, '87, was elected cashier, but resigned April 1, '09, and A. W. McCully, who had been second assistant cashier, since October, '99, was chosen cashier, with R. B. Bèrdo as assistant. The vice-presidents have been A. Anderson, Hon. B. F. Brown, A. Harvey. The present directors are Cunningham, Harvey, Brown, Dr. H. C. Hull, A. Anderson, Col. D. J. Palmer, T. J. Berdo. From the first the bank has not once failed to pay semi-annual dividends.

The Farmers & Merchants State Bank of Washington was organized June 5, 1902, with fifty thousand dollars capital, divided among fifty-seven share-holders. The first directors were Chas. Ohngemach, David McLaughlin, H. E. McCollum, Sam Thompson, J. C. F. Wead, J. T. Matthews, S. W. Brookhart, E. G. Wilson, S. A. White. The first officers were: Ohngemach,

R. R. Bowland

A. W. Chilcote

Shep. Farnsworth

PIONEER BANKERS

president; D. McLaughlin, vice; S. A. White, cashier; E. G. Wilson, assistant. Business was begun August 20, '02. The first statement, September 5, '02, showed assets, seventy-two thousand two hundred four dollars and eighty-three cents; loans eighteen thousand six hundred ninety-nine dollars and forty-nine cents; liabilities same as asset total, and deposits, twenty-one thousand thirty-four dollars and ninety-six cents. Statement February 20, '09, tells a contrasting story: Balance of resources and liabilities, two hundred thirty-five thousand four hundred ninety-eight dollars and seventy-three cents; loans, one hundred eighty thousand seven hundred fifty-eight dollars and fifty-five cents; deposits, one hundred seventy-nine thousand one hundred twenty three dollars and thirty-four cents; surplus, six thousand three hundred seventy-five dollars and thirty-nine cents.

Present Officers.—S. A. White, president; S. Thompson, vice; R. L. Coulter, cashier; W. A. White, assistant. Directors: D. McLaughlin, McCollum, Thompson, Brookhart, Matthews, H. A. Baxter, E. G. Wilson, D. A. Boyer, S. A. White.

The West Chester Savings Bank was organized in 1900 with twelve thousand dollars capital, divided among twenty-one stock-holders—D. A. and W. S. Boyer, G. C., W. J., A. L., and J. C. Mayer, C. A. Snyder, David Fisher, R. S. Warfel, O. F. Laubach, D. Bennett, Jas. Daniels, J. L. Corman, S. J. and E. H. Statler, J. B. Crayne, R. F. McFarlane, S. C. Lewis, J. N. and M. E. Eyestone, J. N. Phillips, Thos. Shulty.

The statement of February 20, '09, gives the balance of assets and liabilities as one hundred forty-seven thousand three dollars and ninety-nine cents; Deposits, one hundred twenty-one thousand two hundred nine dollars and seven cents; loans, ninety-four thousand five hundred sixty-four dollars and twenty-one cents.

D. A. Boyer is president; L. P. Jackson, cashier. The bank is a great convenience to two of the heaviest stock shippers in the county—Fisher and Munro.

The Ainsworth Savings Bank started with twenty thousand dollars capital, January 28, '90; E. W. White, president; T. Y. Wickham, vice; A. E. Spalding, cashier; G. R. Parkinson, assistant. Directors: White, S. D. Miller, D. P. Van Horn, Wickham, W. A. Walker, J. F. McCall. On October 27, '91, the authorized capital stock was increased to fifty thousand dollars, and fifteen thousand dollars more stock was sold, making a total of thirty-five thousand dollars, which the bank now has. Balance of assets and liabilities June 30, '90, was forty-one thousand five hundred nine dollars and twenty cents; loans twenty-eight thousand five hundred and eighty dollars; deposits, twenty-one thousand five hundred nine dollars and twenty cents.

Balance of same, February 20, 1909, was two hundred one thousand two hundred sixty-seven dollars and thirty-nine cents, of which loans were one hundred forty-four thousand nine hundred ninety-six dollars and seventy-three cents; and deposits, one hundred thirty-five thousand two hundred eighty-nine dollars and eleven cents; surplus, thirty thousand dollars.

Present officers: W. A. Walker, president; I. L. Colthurst, vice; A. E. Sands, cashier. Directors: Walker, Colthurst, S. C. Pearson, W. W. Moore, C. C. Raymond, T. H. Barns, Sands.

The Brighton National Bank was organized in '72 with fifty thousand dollars capital; R. C. Risk, president; W. H. Lloyd, vice; J. W. Prizer, cashier. It changed to a state bank in '94. The statement in '75 shows the balance of assets and liabilities as one hundred thirty-eight thousand seven hundred fifteen dollars and fifty-eight cents; loans, fifty-two thousand five hundred ninety-one dollars and eighty-nine cents; deposits, thirty-eight thousand five hundred sixty-one dollars and thirty-nine cents. The contrasting statement for 1909 gives a like balance at three hundred seventy-two thousand seven hundred and twenty-one dollars; loans, two hundred ninety thousand seven hundred ninety dollars and sixty-three cents; deposits, three hundred ten thousand five hundred seven dollars and fifty-four cents; surplus, twelve thousand two hundred thirteen dollars forty-one cents.

Present officers: C. H. Lloyd, president; A. E. Horton, vice; W. H. Lloyd, cashier.

The National Bank of Brighton, Brighton, Iowa, was organized in 1900 by C. H. and C. M. Keck, M. C. Terry et al; chartered August 25, 1900, opened for business December 1 following, with Dr. Terry, president; J. L. Downs, vice; Frank R. Sage, cashier. Downs was succeeded by J. H. Bull, who served till his death in '06, and Geo. Savage became vice-president, and A. B. Endicott followed Sage in '02. Henry F. Tracy was cashier a few months in 1903-4 while Endicott was absent. Original capital, twenty-five thousand dollars, paid up. On December 24, '06, the stock-holders voluntarily liquidated and turned the business over to The Savings Bank of Brighton, Brighton, Iowa, December 31, '06. Said Savings Bank was organized in 1906 by the interests then owning the National; capital, twenty thousand dollars; surplus, five thousand dollars, and began business January 2, '07, officered thus: M. C. Terry, president; Geo. Savage, vice: Endicott, cashier, and they still serve. Directors: Terry, Savage, R. E. L. McClintic, J. A. Lemley, G. P. Madden, D. F. Berry, Carl M. Keck.

First statement December 13, 1900; loans, two hundred ninety-seven dollars and ninety-four cents; deposits, six thousand eight hundred forty-one dollars and thirty-eight cents. Last statement, March 18, '09; loans, one hundred ten thousand four hundred seventy-eight dollars and sixty-three cents; deposits, one hundred thousand three hundred sixty-one dollars and twenty cents. The bank owns its building and equipment, worth over five thousand dollars.

The Farmers and Merchants Savings Bank of Haskins was organized about 1903 with thirteen thousand dollars capital. Its statement, May 18, '09, shows a balance of resources and liabilities of seventy-two thousand nine hundred thirty dollars and thirty-four cents; and the loans are, sixty-four thousand nine hundred nine dollars and eleven cents; and deposits, fifty-six thousand three hundred forty-five dollars and eighty-five cents. J. C. Jones is cashier, and three of the directors are L. F. Woodburn, W. F. Gardner, S. A. Sands. This bank failed to respond to a call for a statement in this history, and the above is all we could get.

The Rubio Savings Bank was formed July 2, '06, with ten thousand dollars capital. F. H. Feltz, president; H. A. Luithly, vice; L. B. Luithly, cashier. Directors: Jos. Augustine, Marsh W. Bailey, C. B. Morgan, F. R. Feltz, H. A. Luithly, J. H. Ramge, J. L. Stein. The footings in the last statement were fifty-three thousand seven hundred seven dollars and thirty-three cents, of which loans were twelve thousand eight hundred thirteen dollars and seventy-one cents; deposits, forty-three thousand seven hundred seven dollars and thirty-three cents.

The Wellman Savings Bank, on May 1, 1888, began a general banking business under the supervision of H. G. Moore. For a year it was a private bank. On September 1, '89, it was organized as a savings bank with ten thousand dollars paid up capital. C. O. Nichols, president; J. W. Gemmill, vice; H. G. Moore, cashier; Chas. Grassell, W. P. Gardner, W. A. Downing, W. A. Shepard, directors. The deposits then were twenty thousand dollars, loans about the same. The business increased so that more capital was needed, and on July 26, '99, as deposits were one hundred eighty-seven thousand three hundred sixty-two dollars and twenty-seven cents, with total footings of two hundred twenty-four thousand four hundred seventy-five dollars and eleven cents, the capital was made twenty-five thousand dollars. At this date the deposits are four hundred fifty thousand dollars, with total footings of over half a million; loans and discounts, three hundred eighty-five thousand dollars; surplus fund, twenty-five thousand dollars. The bank has paid thirty-two dividends. Present officers: J. H. Romine, president; H. W. Deuker, vice; H. G. Moore, cashier; W. A. Downing, W. P. Gardner, Jesse Longwell, I. N. Carr, W. W. Sigler, directors, with these additional stockholders—J. B. Lloyd, J. H. Crawford, J. F. Romine, H. M. Eicher, J.

M. Shomberg, C. C. and R. W. Yoder, J. V. Hoefert, M. L. Webster and Wm. Nuttall, trustee for the L. W. Nuttall estate.

Cashier M. C. Struble of the Wellman Security Savings Bank did not respond to either of three invitations to give his bank's status and history, and I am sorry that this bank exhibit is somewhat crippled by a very partial statement, gathered from the bank's last statement, which reveals that its capital is twenty-five thousand dollars; deposits, two hundred thirty-two thousand six hundred four dollars and sixty-two cents; loans, two hundred twenty-four thousand nine hundred ninety-six dollars and thirty-two cents, footings of assets and liabilities, two hundred sixty-one thousand eight hundred ninety dollars and thirteen cents each. W. T. Hamilton is president; C. B. Hamilton, vice, and among the directors are J. H. Klockenteger, W. B. Darnell, N. B. Gardner. The bank dates from June 15, '96.

The bank has always paid its entire earnings to its stockholders each year, and they have received an amount equal to the paid-up capital.

Wm. H. Palmer began a private banking business in Kalona in '89, and in '92 he and B. F. Allen, Chas. Liebig, A. Mellinger, S. E. Parker, Phil. E. Shaver, and W. H. Smith organized the Kalona Savings Bank with ten thousand dollars capital. Shaver was president; Mellinger, vice; Palmer, cashier. The present officers are: L. G. Shaver, president; B. F. Allen, vice; Palmer, cashier; Geo. A. Eglin, assistant. Directors: Allen, H. A. Mellinger, Palmer, Eglin, Shaver and John P. Wagner. The last statement gives balances, two hundred ninety-seven thousand nine hundred forty-eight dollars and eleven cents; loans two hundred eighteen thousand nine hundred sixty-one dollars and seventy-two cents; and deposits, two hundred eighty thousand nine hundred forty-seven dollars and thirty-six cents.

The Farmers Savings Bank of Kalona issued a statement the first year, whose footings were forty-one thousand five hundred twenty-nine dollars and eighty-eight cents; loans twenty-one thousand eight hundred sixty-three dollars and sixty-five cents; and deposits, thirty thousand three hundred seventy dollars and eighty-eight cents; capital, ten thousand dollars. The contrasting statement of May 18, '09, gave said footings, two hundred three thousand eight hundred eleven dollars and twenty-four cents, of which loans were one hundred sixty-three thousand five hundred seventy-six dollars and forty-two cents, and deposits, one hundred eight-five thousand five hundred thirty-six dollars and fourteen cents. The bank began business in September, '99, with ten thousand dollars capital. The officers are: C. M. Keck, president; L. E. Edmondson, vice; F. E. Skola, cashier; and Wm. O'Loughlin, assistant.

The Citizens Savings Bank of Riverside, organized in '92, began business May 23, the stockholders being John Mentzer, John Lohberger, Joseph, Albert

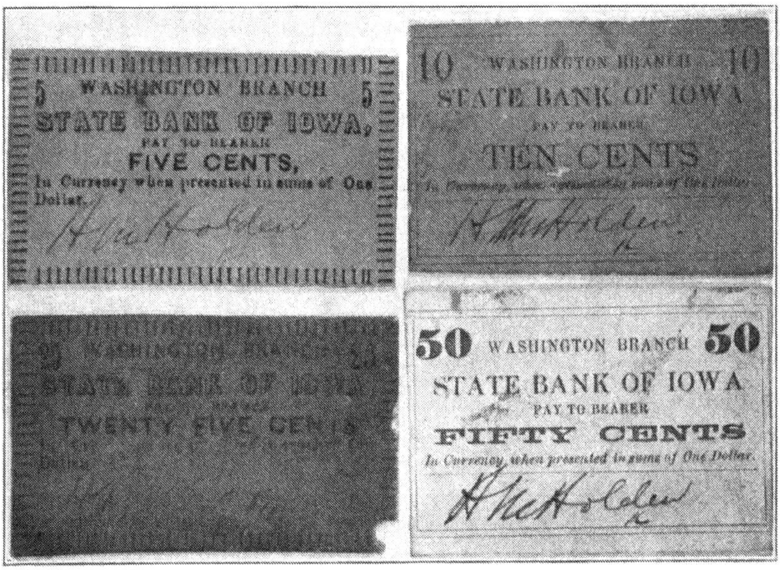

CURRENCY CHECKS IN 1862

and Frank Critz, F. J. and Gregory Schnoebelen, Moses Dawson, G. F. Wieland, Nicola & Harmon, Peter Gerot, John and F. X. Scherrer, W. H. Cress. First directors: Joseph Critz, Mentzer, Lohberger, Dawson, F. J. Schnoebelen. The capital stock always, fifteen thousand dollars. First statement, October, '92, footed up in assets and liabilities, twenty-nine thousand eight hundred forty-nine dollars and nine cents, the loans being, twenty-one thousand thirty-seven dollars and ninety-two cents; and deposits, twelve thousand ninety-nine dollars and three cents. The first officers were: Mentzer, president; Lohberger, vice; S. F. Critz, cashier. The present officers are: G. F. Wieland, president; Anthony Yeggy, vice; Frank Critz, cashier; Leo C. Critz, his assistant. The directors now are: Wieland, Leo Critz, Yeggy, Richard Heitzman, A. Lear. The last statement, May 18, '09, gives a balance or footings in assets and liabilities of one hundred sixty-seven thousand nine hundred ninety-two dollars and sixteen cents, in which figure loans one hundred forty-five thousand three hundred eighty-one dollars and eighty-one cents, and deposits, one hundred forty-six thousand ninety-six dollars and seventy-five cents.

The Riverside Savings Bank was established in '88. W. B. Boyd, president; John Mentzer, vice; Jesse Boyd, cashier; D. A. Fesler, assistant. Directors: Mentzer, W. B. Ford, F. A. Druff, D. A. Fesler, F. P. Davidson, The first statement gave bills receivable, thirteen thousand nine hundred seventy-three dollars and fifty cents; deposits, four thousand eighty-two dollars and fifty cents; cash, two thousand six hundred twenty seven dollars and thirty-three cents; due from banks, one thousand four hundred eighteen dollars and forty-one cents; undivided profits, two hundred twenty-four dollars and sixty-nine cents; capital stock, ten thousand dollars. Present officers: D. A. Fesler, president; J. S. Bailey, vice; H. F. Griffin, cashier; Victoria Saforek, assistant. Directors: Fesler, Bailey, Wm. Tener, M. W. Truxaw, Jos. Kiefer. The statement for October 1, '08 gives bills receivable, one hundred thousand six hundred seventy-five dollars and fifty-seven cents; deposits, one hundred thirty-seven thousand, five hundred sixty-three dollars; cash, three thousand five hundred forty-four dollars and forty-two cents; due from banks, thirty-six thousand six hundred seventy-two dollars and thirty-four cents; undivided profits, four thousand five hundred sixteen dollars and eight cents.

The First Savings Bank of Crawfordsville was organized September 28, '08, with fifteen thousand dollars capital. The officers are: Elias Williams, president; M. D. Maxwell, vice; J. R. Rickey, cashier and Trude Rickey, assistant. Directors: Williams, Maxwell, G. W. Nickolaus, A. A. DeLong, W. P. Davidson, J. H. Huston, H. E. Davis, A. S. Lunquist, W. K. Wooley.

First statement, October 26, '08, gives the footings at ninety-four thousand five hundred eleven dollars and eighty-five cents, of which the loans were forty-five thousand six hundred forty six dollars and ninety-seven cents, and the deposits seventy-nine thousand five hundred eleven dollars and eighty-five cents. Statement, June 18, '09, gives growth in the footings, one hundred fifty-five thousand three hundred and thirteen dollars and forty-three cents; loans, one hundred one thousand four hundred ninety-four dollars and fifty-one cents; deposits, fifty-five thousand eight hundred ninety dollars and ninety cents.

The lack of money made small difference and little inconvenience to the pioneers and later old settlers. Out here they were ahead of civilization—ahead of railroads, canals, telegraphs, steam navigation, scientific agriculture, markets, telephones, daily mails, etc. Letter postage was twenty-five cents, but they rarely wrote letters anyhow, nor did they travel, and why telegraph? There were no local bucket shops to swindle themselves in, and no board of trade in Chicago—why jerk tamed lightning juice thither? Civilization long since caught up with people, and went ahead of them, and will never lag behind again. Railroads now run through vast areas of country scantily populated. They have distanced emigration. What did the pioneers need money for? If a farmer drove stock or wagoned grain to Muscatine and Burlington, and exchanged them for provisions to haul home as ballast, that was barter, and it was plenty good enough for such slow coaches and slower cold molasses as the pioneers were, compared with their hustling descendants. Or they could get goods "on tick" for a year, till they could drive and haul down more stock and wheat. Local merchants were trusted a year. Credit is just as good as cash to the debtor, isn't it? Our merchants did not buy goods in Chicago till 1858, when railroad and telegraph came in, and no exchange was issued till Everson opened his small jack-pot in '55. About '62, Howard M. Holden issued a little less than one thousand five hundred dollars in shin-plaster small change, in five, ten, twenty-five and fifty-cent cards, green, yellow, red and pink colored, respectively. The Press printed all but the twenty-five's, E. B. Bolens of the Democrat printing those, and they were out till April 1, '63, when they were redeemed on presentation, the government at the latter date issuing postal currency. Specimens of Holden's fiat money are sent by Irving Keck to our county historical society.

Insurance.—In July, '67, the Home Fire Insurance Co. was organized in the Farmers and Merchants Bank. J. H. Wilson, president; John Bryson, vice; C. H. Wilson, secretary; S. G. Owen, treasurer, with these other stockholders: J. A. Henderson, Wm. Wilson, Jr., J. R. Davis, Dr. Chilcote, Hugh Smith, Judge Brown, V. W. Andrus, Robert Dawson, Dr. McKee, J. F.

McJunkin. It lasted perhaps a half dozen years and was not a marked success. One of its agents was Rev. Father Twining, a dry humorist. When asked if he had to lie a bit in the business, he said, "No," but added with a shrewd grin, "we have to prevaricate some now and then."

On February 20, '83, the Washington County Farmers Mutual Insurance Association was organized, and it was re-incorporated February 11, 1903. This proved popular, and from the first it knocked out, in the country, the agents of all the town and state companies. Rates were very low in the Mutual, and most farmers sought its protection to buildings and stock, and losses were promptly met. An immense business was and is done, at small cost.

Most of the stock losses are due to lightning. In storms, stock go before it to the limit of the wire fences, huddle there, and the bolt follows the wire till it leaps thence and strikes animals. Farmers could easily ground the wires and ward off such accidents. Barbed wire fences have much evil to answer for.

Old time life insurance companies have been crippled, in towns, by fraternal societies offering co-operative insurance. Probably nine-tenths of the policies carried in this city and county are in these societies.

CHAPTER XVI.

HOW WOULD YOU LIKE TO GO BACK THERE?

Say to universal horseback riding, sitting on saddlebags, as all doctors and travellers did?

Or to the early time when horse-racing was the main means of recreation, dissipation and gambling, a passion we got from the Indians? And when men wore moccasins to meetings, or went barefoot or in ox wagons?

Or to the old-fashioned winters, say those of '55 and '59, when snow lay deep and for long, and mercury went to thirty-five and forty-five below zero and stock perished in barnyards and humans had to be brisk in thin houses to keep blood in flow; when farmers discharged a hand if he could not skin cattle as fast as they froze; when snow was too deep to allow passage to the cemetery, and coffins were in some places put in the cold storage of drifts till spring; when in the sleazy cabins men got out of bed, mornings, to crawl from under a snow bank or dig through a drift on the floor to start a fire in fireplaces or stoves; when by New Year's ice was fourteen, sixteen, even thirty and thirty-two inches thick.

To a time when boys wore stogey boots, heavy and coarse, the hides tanned at home, made up by a cobbler coming to the house, who sewed with a wax-end and bristle and held the pegs in his mouth. Boots wet by day, drying out at night, and stiffer than dried codfish in the morning; you couldn't get into them until they were greased with tallow. Ever try to black 'em, Sunday, over that tallow? Fine calf boots were worn by men who could afford them, and they had high heels and the tops were ornamented with moons and stars, and colored silks were stitched in, in fancy patterns, and perhaps there were flossy tassels. The cobbler shod the whole family. In summer all went barefoot. The man measured the foot with a twig or stick that was stepped on and had a notch cut at heel and toe, and the boot had to fit then. Heads were measured with a string for caps, and the size marked by knots. The boys and girls could braid hats up to twelve straws wide, and they made their head-gear.

Or to the pewter age when folk wore buckskin, jeans, linsey woolsey, hoops, tilters, sunbonnets with pasteboard slats, brocaded shawls, ruffled shirts, stocks as ties, plug hats of queer shapes, when a house without spinning wheel, loom, etc., was not furnished, where women spun wool on a flax wheel, and carded wool, wove cloth, measured, cut goods, sewed garments, and they could look a sheep serenely in the face. Whir of wheel, bang of shuttle, click of knitting needles, were the domestic music. Families made their own clothes. Women spun and wove. Mrs. John Brier, in Brighton, in 1838, worked a rude loom her husband made with a broad ax. In Iowa township, in '42, Mrs. Catherine Marling was weaving carpet, jeans and linen. In Seventy-six township Mrs. Jane Patterson did the first weaving. Women's work was never done—eternally cooking in pots on cranes in fireplaces, or in Dutch ovens, or in brick ovens outside. If nothing else to do, scour tin ware with sand, scrub puncheon floors and scatter sand on them and work odd designs in the sand with brooms made of hickory saplings doctored as they knew how. If all else failed, they could make dry or jug yeast, dry sweet corn, apples, pumpkin strips, in the sun, braid onion tops, string red and green peppers, gather medicinal herbs to hang on rafters, make soft soap, getting lye from wood ashes to cut grease and boil to a jelly in a big kettle out doors, near a line fence beyond which another woman was doing likewise, the eyes of both smarting with smoke and their noses dripping sap. If still there was nothing to do, they could rest themselves patching quilts, and now and then neighbor women came in to a quilting bee and all talk at once, gossip, turn up a rough seam of conduct in somebody, remark "la," winding up with a tea, each drinking several cups hotter'n blazes and strong enough to hold up a brick. Really they wobbled home quite jagged on the cup that cheers and does mildly inebriate. They saved the spools to make What-nots. Girls were brought up in the belief that all that was proper life, and they were ashamed to marry before they could cook, sew, spin, make their wardrobes and quilts and b'ile soap. Then wed, have a dozen children, work like slaves, age prematurely, and at last go to heaven—to rest. No illusions along that path? What fun was there in so much of that?

Let's amble back to the early candle lighting era. Ever make tallow candles, cut wicks, pour, make the cooled candles crack in the moulds? Ever make a tin lantern by punching holes in it? If candles can't be afforded, use a lard dip, or put melted lard in a saucer, hang a rag over the edge, like the tongue of a lolling dog or ox, light it, and you will have an electric pear.

Or suppose we return to the malarial age when ten per cent of the settlers shook with chills and burned with fever, and men were doped with quinine, calomel, boneset tea, and kids with castor oil, sulphured molasses,

ENOCH ROSS

Member of Constitutional Convention of 1844-5

WILLIAM McGAUGHY

At ninety-seven years of age

root and yarb teas, nasty decoctions for worms and things, and their heads were daily fine-combed for creeping things and the hair plastered down with a candle-roller, and water was denied in fevers, and sick adults and sick horses were bled by the quart and gallon—do you care to go back there to live in such a cheerful, intelligent state, when doctors knew much less than they do now and did more guessing?

Now I know why you are so eager to go back there—it's to sleep in a high-post bed, corded with rope that was tightened with a big wooden or iron wrench such as the rural doctors pulled teeth with. When a jerk-water M. D. got one of those appalling things out, wrapped in a cloth, and fumbled for your sick molar, there seemed to be as much apparatus in it as in a guillotine or gallows. When a bed rope was fetched up taut, if you turned over in bed, a neighbor a quarter-mile away could hear the doleful creak. Those beds did protest too much. When the tick was crammed with straw, it was as pudgy and corpulent as a Dutch housefrau, and one needed to be scotched on either side to prevent rolling out, in sleep. Some beds had canopies and curtains, to assure ventilation, and there was always a valance that looked like a petticoat sunk too low under a dress skirt. Under the bed was, perhaps, a trundle bed for a kid, etc.

Perhaps you would like to "break" a prairie farm. It was about as severe a stunt as to clear a timbered farm in Indiana and Ohio. Hitch six to eight yoke of oxen to a plow twelve to fifteen feet long, the front end of the beam run on trucks, the share cutting eighteen to twenty-four inches. The ground was covered and matted with blue-stem grass as high as a man's head and as thick as hair on a dog, and when the driver yelled to Buck, Bright and the rest of the lolling quadrupeds and swung his g'ad, and talked anti-Sunday school jargon to the motors, they went crashing through the tule grass and hazel bushes, and robins and blackbirds had picnics in the grubby furrows. In the first years, indeed up to the coming of the railroad in '58, farmers did not need much plowed ground to grow corn on. The price of corn was too low. It was easy to cultivate, as weeds had not then got a foothold. Besides, hogs wanted nothing better or more fattening than the abundant mast in the woods, that is, nuts. A pioneer hog was abreast of the hygienists now. A nut is as concentrated and rich as an egg. Squirrels thrive on nuts. A Boston dietist says pie prolongs life, and if one eats nuts one will live a thousand years. Don't, therefore, eat too many nuts. Why raise corn to fatten hogs when mast abounds? In Florida, the best bacon in the world is cut from hogs that live on mast. Those rail-splitters have a snout, head, neck and shoulders that constitute two-thirds of the dredger animal. They are built to unheave mast, and chemistry transmutes nuts into sowbelly and "sweet ole ham" that are divine. The pioneers needed corn only for oxen and johnny-cake. With plenty of eggs so cheap they were fed to the hogs by the bucketful, and with milk and honey flowing, butter selling at three cents a pound and barrels of honey retailing at twenty cents per gallon, and wild turkeys, prairie chickens, ducks and deer galore, and an infinitude of berries, crab apples, plums, grapes, haws, cherries, all these a drug at from six to fifteen cents a gallon, women bringing them to market, barefoot, putting on their stockings and shoes at the edge of the town, and swapping them for sugar and coffee, why should men plow much? Why plant corn to raise stock, when a colt would make its good living on the common, and a three-year-old steer sold for ten to twelve dollars, fat wethers at two dollars a head, and hogs, dressed and hauled to market, brought two and two and a half cents per pound? It is odd, the only kick the farmers made then on the country was, "It would be all right if it could grow fruit and grass."

You see there was not a blade of blue grass then; that has clothed our roadsides, meadows and lawns only in very recent years, say twenty-five to thirty years, with its lovely tresses. Nor was there timothy or clover; just wild grass, blue stem, slough grass, the jungle stuff that they had to fire in the fall to make travel possible. Or, if it went over till spring, and, when dry again, was burned, the blackened prairie was white with myriads of prairie hens' cooked eggs, pearly white as if laid by a brooding hailstorm. There is but one field of the ancient wild grass in this county, it is said, on the Page place. Blue grass has taken the country, and no one knows when or how or why it came, but it came like "the kingdom of heaven, without observation."

Would you like to hike back to the ancient style of shopping? Groceries showed no novelties. There were no canned goods but oysters, peaches, sardines; nor granulated sugar, but the A sugar, like our light brown stuff, nine or ten pounds to the dollar, that would dry out as hard as stone, and New Orleans sugar, as black as the coons who made it, and as damp as Venus scooting from the bath. Coffee was not roasted; women had to parch it and grind it in a mill nailed to the wall, as well as spices; coffee so high it was mixed with rye, and was poor stuff to moisten your clay with. Most stores were eclectic, selling everything. Thus, Hugh Kendall's father, Wm. W., was the first druggist here, on the east side, selling out to Dr. Chilcote in '55. Cook & Sherman have some of his preparations yet, quite likely. He also sold dry goods, groceries, boots and shoes, hardware and other universally needed bric-a-brac.

Perhaps you would like to go back to the time when all cattle wore horns, and not a single mooley in the county, or state. In the wild state, and even on the range, they need horns for defense. A horn was always a sign of power, and that is the reason why Michel Angelo put two nubbin horns on the head of "Moses" in his gigantic statue. But domesticated cattle, herded in sheds, stables and pastures, do not need horns; indeed, horns are a nuisance and menace, and fifteen to twenty years ago Mr. Haaf began dehorning, and most all farmers dehorn now. It improves the beauty and temper of cattle, and sort o' Christianizes 'em. The act seems cruel. So dehorn chemically, with lunar caustic. The pain is almost nil. Pure bred cattle may keep their horns, as a rule, but stock for the shambles and dairy are better cropped. But the pioneers lived in a forest of horns, and crowned them with brass nuts, to prevent goring.

Perhaps you would like to be set back into that furry period when the skins of mink and otter were plentiful and stood for good money's worth. Farms were paid for in furs. Trappers, day after day, brought in ten dollars to forty-five dollars' worth of skins, each, including muskrat, when two dollars and fifty cents would buy an acre of Iowa land. It seems queer, but then counties paid a fifty-cent bounty on sand-hill cranes, as they devastated wheat fields. These birds were as 'cute as crows, knew a gun, posted sentinels, ate under guard, heeded signals. Furs persist in Iowa yet. Jackson Roberts, thirty years ago, probably made more money on skins he bought than on groceries he sold. There are still Iowa firms that handle yearly fifty thousand dollars to one hundred thousand dollars' worth of skins.

Really, I'd like to go back there for several reasons. 1. To get the prime maple sugar the Indians made. Even Chief Black Hawk, after his downfall, and his wife and daughter made sugar to sell. The girl was handsome and smart, fell in love with Joe Walsh, of Baltimore, a clerk in Fort Madison, and he went daffy on her, and spent Sundays with her, talking Indianese, but a chum disillusioned him, the engagement was broken with mutual consent, and she fitly married a red buck, and they probably lived happily ever after? The whites traded flour for Indian sugar. 2. To see the unaffected hospitality, the true democratic sentiment, the total absence of caste and class feeling. A family would in winter bundle up and visit a neighbor, staying to dinner—not a modern fashionable call, but stay all forenoon and into the afternoon till it was time to go home and do the chores. It was "a regular corker of a time," as Teddy would say. There was no big head, no one put on airs, all was simple, sincere, genuine, "the days that are no more," alas! 3. To see the parrots. What! Don't you know flocks of painted parrots came into the southern counties of Iowa in the spring, and, perching on leafless trees, clothed them with hues of rainbows? It is a fact. It is no more singular than that tropical humming birds should "Gee-whiz" about us—that is what the hum of their swift wings sing out in spelling school. That vernal scene must have been like the display of colors parrots make on the west coast of Africa. The late Missionary Charles McCleary told me that when the vast forests there bore flowers on their tall tops, parrots would feast there in myriads, the sounds deafening, but the colors gorgeous beyond description.

Would you relish going back to a time when potatoes were so scarce that no one planted a whole one, but used the peelings for seed at a cost of two dollars a bushel? To a time when the wags said the main undergrowth was rattlesnakes? To a time when a gristmill was the rendezvous for candidates, politicians, claim-traders, horse-tracers, wrestlers, swimmers, fishermen et al? All these fellows could get in their work while patrons waited their turns at grinding. A mill was a general clearing-house for gossip, axes-to-grind, jobs, etc. There were no bolts in those mills; wheat was merely cracked in them, and the grist was soot-black, and the pioneer bread was as black as a coal.

How about going back to honey-hunting, when men not infrequently found three to four score bee trees in a day? Every one of the millions of bees had the instinct to gobble honey as soon as it smelled the hunter's smoke, for they had been doing that for millions of years. It is the only way to handle them yet in hives. Take the top off a hive and puff in smoke, every insect goes to eating like mad and forgets to sting. It feels it may be a good while before it can get at another hoard of sweets, and is so intent on gorging that you could comb its hair—it will not dagger you. Early Iowa, when the cows came home, was indeed a land flowing with milk and honey. Honey, eaten by humans in moderate quantity, is a powerful food—it stands for ninety-eight per cent of pure energy. Don't eat too much, mind, but take an inch cube of comb every day, perhaps at each meal—nothing is more wholesome.

If we should visit an early Iowa Sunday school, we should likely see the teacher teaching tots their a, b, c's, and reading and spelling, using spelling books and testament as text books. More sensible, too, than teaching catechism theology, not?

An early prairie would not look like the present expanse. It was thickly covered with the bones and horns of elk, buffalo, deer, slain for meat and pelts. And in June behold an infinite carpet of blue-stem, lilies, sweet william, prairie rose, lady slipper near the woods, wild tiger lily, etc., as brilliant colors as in oriental rugs, carpets and tapestries.

Or would you prefer to see how the pioneers, who were mostly young people, amused themselves, courted, married? They went round from house to house, debating fool questions that raise no issue, such as, "which is better, art or nature?" Then picnics, spelling and singing schools, schemes devised to give the boys a chance to go home with the girls, rail-splitting contests,

ELIZABETH KIRKPATRICK BAILEY
Who returned to Ohio in 1843 on horseback, carrying James, her eight months old son. She had five sons in the Union Army

log-rollings, kissing parties regardless of germs which had not been invented then, house-raisings, men going ten miles to get a chance to lift and hit booze. As the cabins were one-roomed, the sparking was slily done in the dusky corners of the fireplaces that took in four to five-foot wood. If the old folk fussed about it, the pair eloped. If he had a pair of blue jeans and a row of brass buttons on each side of a coat front, and she had a new calico dress, that was trousseau enough—they had each other, what more did they want but a preacher who never charged a cent, for no one had money—all he wanted was a wedding dinner. The average preacher is the hungriest critter in the jungle, always was, ever will be; he is an organism built up round a stomach, just as a model house is a shelter constructed around a Webster's Unabridged Dictionary and a bath room.

Or we'll look in on a country dance back there, in a room sixteen by eighteen when the furniture is set out doors, and the Jakes and Janes grab each other and "sashay." Our Abe Essley used to fiddle for them. The girls would walk miles, chewing a gum snatched from resin weed, to a cabin, barefoot, wash their feet in a run or in dew instead of butter, as in Scripture times, and put on stockings and shoes, and the swains did likewise, then at it, and the ambition was, to hold out the longest. No fancy program, pencil, autograph, white gloves, loop for the skirt to slip on an arm—no silly "horse" of that sort, or Beau Brummell and Lord Chesterfield manners—just homespun ways and natural, spontaneous fun.

There were other forms of fun not so innocent, as card-playing by a club of bad boys during divine service in Snake Hollow church, in '53.

An amateur preacher weighing over three hundred pounds was asked, in this city, long ago, to help at an Ainsworth revival. It was a hot day, and he was in decided undress, and very dirty, but he agreed to go and stop a gap in the preaching force if given a clean white shirt and a pair of decent breeches. He squeezed into them, and held forth without coat or vest. When in full action, there was a loud crack, as if some one had split a bolt of muslin, but it was only his tight shirt. A fearful gesture, forceful enough to knock the devil off a culvert, ripped it open in the back. Though it gave the good man much needed ventilation, it was embarrassing. He was a typical pioneer exhorter. That class had so much to do, they rarely did anything well. Robert Collyer, the famous ex-blacksmith Unitarian divine, in his book, "Augustus Conant, Illinois Pioneer and Preacher," quotes this from Conant's diary:

"May 2. Wrote a sermon.

"May 3. Sunday. Wrote poetry.

"May 4. Made shelves and split rails.

"June 3. Made a table, and borrowed six bushels of potatoes to be paid back with interest in the fall.

"Made a coffin for H. Dougherty.

"Dressed pig and calves torn by wolves. Dug a well.

"Unwell, and so studied algebra.

"Made a sun-dial.

"Unwell, so wrote temperance address.

"Temperance meeting: delivered my address.

"13. Got my oration published, and paid for.

"Made a plan of a sermon on the prodigal son, a pair of quilting frames, and an argument at the Lyceum against capital punishment.

"Read the Methodist Disciple. Helped my wife to wash.

"Finished sermon. Made soap."

That fellow was a jack of all trades and good at none.

One does not have to go back far to reach this practical joke, perpetrated here some thirty to thirty-five years ago, and it was as outrageous as anything done in the reckless olden time. A queer fellow got full in a south side joint one Saturday night, and when asleep wags put him in a coffin exposed in the front window, and he lay in state all Sunday forenoon, for church passersby to look at, a horrid example.

Knighthood was in flower in Washington in 1842, but it was a chivalrous sell. At that date Indians still held a bit of land in Lime Creek township, that had not been included in the former purchases. A good many Reds camped at Wassonville, fishing while waiting the grinding of their grain. Dr. Lee reported here that they were holding a white girl prisoner. He worked on the sympathies of our leading citizens, who snatched arms and mounted thirty horses to rescue the maiden, and more men would have leaked sympathy if there had been more nags. When Mr. Churchman, a lawyer, saw the reds in force, he wheeled and ran home; he may be running yet. The others interviewed the chief. "Yes, she is white; they had taken her from the Sacs and Foxes who abused her; you can take her if she wants to go, and if you will give bonds to treat her well and educate her." In good English the girl thanked them for their interest, but she preferred to stay with her benefactors! Knighthood chased itself all the way back to town. The folks never got tired of guying the turned-down knights, among whom were such men as Joseph Keck, Jonathan Wilson, M. C. Kilgore, J. E. Malin et al.

Queer characters back there. One was our surveyor, Daniel McFarland. His plat book in the county offices is a good record. He opened it August 31, '44, with this inscription: "Now commences the labours of the Snake Charmer, D. W. McFarland." He lost his life in the streets of St. Louis, showing timber and prairie rattlesnakes. On a cold morning he hauled them out of a box rather roughly, and one fastened its fangs in his thumb. It took so long to detach it, he could not suck out all the poison. That was his remedy—he never used whisky—it is a humbug. He had an adventure at Wassonville with Iowa City armed troopers who officially came there to drive off to their boundary six miles away, a band of Musquakies who had come to the mill to get corn ground. They knew they were technically trespassers, but they were friendly with the whites and would leave as soon as they got their grist. The fool lieutenant meant to scourge them back. McFarland told the chief to toss him his blanket; he threw it round his shoulders and told the soldiers, "I am chief now, these Indians are friendly, and he would give them fifteen minutes to start back to Iowa City," at the same time raising the Indian war-whoop. The red warriors looked savage as yellow-jackets, and the troopers at once put spurs to their horses.

It was "boys" who saved the Union in the '60s, and it is young fellows who emigrate, colonize, open new country, build society, for it takes enthusiasm, hot blood, strength, hope, pluck to do those things. So it does not surprise to learn that the vanguard of the pioneers were largely single men, coming on foot or horse-back, with gun, ax, auger, etc., and at the nearest trading post buying buckets, tin cups, plates, knives, forks, Dutch ovens, coffee pots, skillets, and as much meal, bacon and sugar as they could pack, stake out a claim, build a hovel, and on going to work leaving food in the cabin for any wayfarer who might come along, hungry. He would not be a tramp, anyhow. It was an universal custom thus to make the cabin a cache. All the recompense asked for was, the autograph of the guest chalked on the door.

The first cabins were simpler than later ones, being a cross between "hoop-cabins" and tepees or bark huts. Strictly, there were no cabins till there were enough settlers for a raising with shouts of "Heave o' he," and John Barleycorn's aid. In human dens, windows with sash and glass were rare, greased paper being used. Door latches were wooden, a deer skin string hung out—pull it and come in! No electric buttons then to get out of order.

The "bull" plows were equally primitive, the mould-boards made of wood, or half wood and iron.

Before gristmills, hominy blocks were fashioned out of sections of a tree trunk eighteen to twenty-four inches in diameter, hollowed out at one end and hardened by fire. They resembled druggists' mortars. Pestles of wood with an iron wedge attached, big end down. One block served a neighborhood.

As there were few taverns, the cabins were crowded; anybody, everybody were taken in to lodge over night; the first family to arrive took the back part of the cabin, and it was a case of progressive bedding toward the door. Young men slept in wagons. Those nearest the door got up first and went outside to dress. It was handy. Meals of corn bread, fat pork, buttermilk, occasional coffee, were served at the ends of wagons. On Sundays an extra ration—wheaten bread; the grain threshed on the ground under the feet of horses or oxen, cleaned with a tossing sheet, and mashed by hand.

They say the loneliness of pioneer life made people so bashful they did not know how to behave after a good many came. Solitary herders of stock go insane, not bashful, and of late years many isolated farm women get crazed by their awful loneliness.

It is said the early settler women paid scant attention to flowers and did not have posy beds or try to keep winter plants in bloom. The woods were full of flowers, and the prairie was painted with their hues as brightly as the winter night sky with stars.

For some years horses were few, and they were kept for riding. R. T. McCall says there were not a half dozen horses in Crawford township in the early '40s. Oxen did the farm work. One man might own a horse, a neighbor another, and thus a wagon team could on a pinch be conjured up.

Let's take a look at the Indians: they sometimes dissected the bodies of their dead, if they could not be transported; they cleaned the bones, dried them in the sun and boxed them in vessels of bark. The skeleton was the unit, as with the Chinese in this country; "John" lightly regards what he calls "the meat," and loads fleets of ships with celestial bones to be buried at home where ancestral worship may be made to the "remains."

Indians and hunters fired the tall dry prairie grass annually—an impenetrable, impassable jungle, else.

Many things that were necessities way back there, long since gone into innocous desuetude, now stock museums as curios—go look at 'em and let your sore heart ache for our forebears—grain cradles, baby cradles, scythes, trundle beds, spinning wheels, hetchels, candle moulds, looms, boot-jacks, candlesticks, rude lamps, dasher churns, "slices," valises made of glazed stuff that cracked into as many wrinkles as seam the faces of Mexicans and Indians apparently a thousand years old, or made of flowered carpet cloth, trunks bound in pelts, the hair left on, studded with brass nails, but the hair worn off in use, as on the flanks of a horse worked between tugs, and the trunks seemed crying for wigs. Is there anything more doleful looking than such a lot of discards? With these might fitly go a list of abandoned practices and industries. Folk used to make their inks with logwood, etc., and dyes from

MRS. ALMON MOORE
Came to county in 1839

MRS. JESSE ASHBY
Mother of Nathan Littler

madder and the juices of other plants, but now corporations make dyes from coal tar cheaper and better than any one could do alone. And our forebears were eternally trying to substitute the products of maple sap, sorghum, etc., for sugar, now abandoned as commercially non-economical. Flax and hemp were grown and worked for clothing and cordage, but they have lapsed. Corporations can beat the individual. And foods have changed. Wild rice in Minnesota and Wisconsin feeds twenty thousand Indians, and in Oregon wet lands and marshes the seeds of water lilies nourish many Reds, and the wild berries and fruits that sustained Indians—all that we modern whites disdain, though our pioneers rated them luxuries and necessities.

We should not like to be set back there without labor-saving machinery, matches, tooth-brushes and mouth lotions, disinfectants, court plaster, breakfast foods, railroads, telegraphs and telephones, phonographs, plays, sewers, water under pressure, hospitals, nurses, "comfy" houses, nice furniture, prompt and cheap mail facilities, cheap postage, cheap books and magazines, opera houses, music, art, luxurious travel with sleeping and dining cars, hair mattresses, lawn mowers, automobiles, electric fans, billiard tables, golf, tennis, croquet, gymnasiums, gas and electric light, ready-made clothing of all sorts, street cars, refrigerators and ice, banks and safety boxes, cheap and pretty watches and clocks—O, well, why extend the list? We could not be hired to swap our lot for theirs.

About the only respect in which our pioneers held it over us was, they were not victimized as we are, were not eaten by swindlers, burglars, tramps, nor bitten by book agents, colporters, college and church beggars, lightning-rod and nursery stock peddlers, and all that pestiferous ilk. They had nothing to steal. Blessed be nothing! They had no security debts to pay. No notes were "raised" on them. They were not asked to endorse. Their hind legs were not cut off by human, or inhuman, sharks. But in thirty to forty years, when they were getting pretty well off, Vermont sharpers came here with merino rams and ewes that they sold at fabulous prices—rams with Jericho horns, alleged fifty-pound fleeces, and four million skin wrinkles, critters bound to die of hoof rot and scours. And the slick tree liars "did" them to the queen's taste, and the railroad promoters bled them copiously on subscriptions. All those rams were good for was to fight like a lot of Roosevelts. They'd back off four or five rods, run together, leap into the air, and hit heads with an impact like a railroad engine collision, then back up, licking their chops and snuffing with catarrh, run, strike again and again, till bereaved of their few feeble wits.

As to early products of our rich soil, an average yield of corn was fifty to seventy-five bushels to the acre, sometimes one hundred; wheat thirty,

thirty-five to fifty bushels; oats seventy-five; no rye or barley till 1840. Tobacco throve and sugar beets made a good crop.

"If Iowa could only raise fruit and grass," sighed an ancient. Tradition in the Hoskins family in Clay township is, that the Jonathan, best of apples, originated in Iowa, and was named for Jonathan Hoskins, brother of the late Moses H. Hoskins, and grand-uncle of the family now in Clay. He located near Salem in Henry county, in 1835, planted a seedling orchard, and one tree bore the luscious red apple they knew as "the Uncle Jonathan." It was propagated and grown by the Hoskins folk ever since. Really, that and the parrots are about the only things worth going way back there to see and enjoy. Who cares to see scythes, spinning wheels, looms, grain cradles, clumsy hoes, wooden rakes, "slices," andirons, candle-sticks, warming-pans, and all that antique trumpery, except in a museum? Our labor-savers are infinitely better.

"Better fifty years of Europe than a cycle at Cathay."

The next chapter will tell how we have ameliorated.

CHAPTER XVII.

"WHERE ARE WE AT?"

Mr. Littler's History of Washington county halted in the early '70s. The last history bears the date 1880. Thirty to forty years are to be accounted for. In that time we have come to ourselves, ceased to be primitive and provincial, have reached full maturity, developed on many lines, secured many of the good things going, become somewhat up to date. Let us strike in anywhere, not exact as to dates of realizing things, unmindful of logical order, and invoice some of our blessings.

We have a court house and jail that are models, the former fire-proof as to the record vaults, and so ornate that ever since it was built everybody in town has tried to live up to it, and every tax-payer in the county is glad he owns a few bricks in it. That building became the standard of beauty in the county-seat, and has exerted an esthetic influence on every townsman and farmer who has put up a fine house. Since then, no one cared to build an ugly house or keep untidy grounds. The court house set the pace. It is rare that a building has been such a fountain of good taste and inspiration.

The public business transacted in that building and in the city hall is carried on with the nicety of clock-work. Tax levies are made to meet actual needs; public business is intelligently and honestly conducted; the people fix the taxes, by insisting on having the so-called best schools, the best bridges, the best roads, and, in the city, the very best public utilities, such as infinite pure water, sewerage, serviceable streets, school buildings, fire departments, etc. The bridges are now of steel, and serve the people well. They were built with such sound judgment, this county has had less loss from high water than any other in this part of the state. The first steel bridge was built at Brighton in 1867.

In the city, we began the twentieth century right. George Carlin, of Oskaloosa, in 1900, laid a few of the first cement walks here. In the spring of 1901, J. J. McKeone extended the work, and later T. Minick & Son, J. C. McCartney, Cass Slocum, Horsey, Robert Gault, Hiram Johnson, Ballou pushed it, so that board walks have largely disappeared, and women can wheel cabs without running into cracks and giving babies jerks endangering their necks. The city is substituting cement street crossings for planks. It was a great day when cunning, canny men hit on God's art of making stone, and they do as good a job as He did, and do it lots quicker. He took eras and eons to precipitate the lime in shells and roll the weight of oceans over the beds, but a half dozen men can mix a square yard of cement in less than half an hour, and the stuff solidifies itself. Many a farmer has cemented his cellars, laid artificial stone walks, and even cemented feed lots. It beats mud all hollow, and saves grain.

And the making of plain and ornamental cement blocks for house foundation walls, by McKeone and the Minicks, has become a growing and promising industry.

Akin to laying cement is the laying of tiles under farms. That is probably the greatest hit ever made in agriculture. A farm well tiled has a basement story put under it. Say what you may, man's greatest foe is—water. It is likewise his best friend, when he conquers it, takes the noxious germs out of it, runs the cold stuff away from the otherwise drowning roots of his plants, and by the use of tiles makes the escaping water distil the proper amount of moisture to nourish said plant roots and aerate the soil, a function precisely like that performed by earth-worms in borings. Read Darwin's book on said worms. Draining, like frost-heaving of soil, secures a free circulation of air in the ground. The plants get food from the soil, yet they derive it primarily from the air. Carbonic acid, carbonate of ammonia, nitric acid are dissolved out of the air by falling rain, and carried into the soil. Plants get nine parts of their subsistence from the air, one part from the soil. Draining makes soil porous and ten degrees warmer, due to atmospheric circulation in the soil. Grass starts earlier in spring in drained fields; land can be worked two to three weeks earlier. Drained earth is warmer in cold weather and cooler in very hot weather. There is no sort of doubt about the utility of drainage; plants in swimming all the while do not thrive any more than boys equally immersed. England has demonstrated the advantage of ditching and tiling, and New England and the middle west also.

The Creator must have liked water or He would not have made so much of it. Three-quarters of the globe are covered with it. The oceans, lakes and rivers are factories where climates are made. Water, both fresh and salt, is good, but we do not wish to drown in it, nor do virtuous plants wish to do that, but as they are anchored, they cannot escape drowning, in a wet season, unless tiles rescue them.

Mountain farmers facetiously say it pays to cultivate a mountain—you have two sides to deal with, double acreage when the land is stacked up on

WASHINGTON CITY PARK, LOOKING SOUTHWEST, 1909

edge. A tiled farm has two sides, an upper and an under, and the latter is not a cistern. Get rid of excess water, cries the intelligent farmer; provide constant moisture for plants in a time of drouth; that string of burned clay cylinders in the field performs both functions.

James Eckles was the pioneer tile-burner in this county, beginning in 1877, and he has sold in all seventy-eight thousand dollars' worth. Mr. Swift made them later, and now the Long Bros. are making most excellent tiles by the wholesale. Eckles sold more three-inch size than of others, and threes and fours are the favorite sizes. He got tiles for cellar drains as early as '67. The size of farm tile is dictated by the fall. Tiling is said to add twelve dollars to fifteen dollars per acre to the value of a farm, and the increase or excess of the first crop after tiling pays for the laying, and that of the second crop pays for the tile, and that of the third crop and all subsequent crops is clear. Hon. A. Pearson has planted two thousand dollars' worth on his splendid farm in Jackson. John Romine is a great user of tiles, and says they double the value of a farm. A. Huber is also firm in faith and practice, as was the late Jackson Roberts, and many more.

John Shields began shipping in tiles in '84-5, and has handled a thousand cars of it. They have been sold plentifully at all our railway stations, and are made at Wellman, Riverside, Kalona, Crawfordsville, and were made at Brighton. Perhaps one-third of our flat farms have been tiled. It is believed that rolling lands will eventually be tiled also. It is pleasant to think of a time when there will be a two-story Washington county, a subway under the whole of it.

We have adequate steam transportation facilities, lines of road through the north and south parts of the county and the mid-region—the Rock Island, the Burlington, the Milwaukee, Muscatine Western, Iowa Central, etc. When trolleys come in the next twenty years, our cup of such blessings will run over. The great markets are annexed now to our shippers. Trolleys or electrics are bound to come. One line is projected, the Iowa City, Kalona and Washington railway. The company incorporated in 1903, surveys were made and estimates of cost given, but it was not financed. The trouble is, lack of dense population; Iowa has few tolerably large cities. So far, only the Des Moines system has paid well. Two of the officers live here, G. G. Rodman, president and Carl M. Keck treasurer.

Many years ago, the late Wm. A. Stiles proposed to build a horse-car line, running round Robin Hood's barn, to the cemeteries, depots, etc. The project was still-born. The people in the cemeteries do not travel; they do not want to go anywhere, but just rest, and they have no nickels to pay fares.

The County Farm and Infirmary provide generously for the most unfortunate of our poor and the mildly insane.

Few counties have ampler educational facilities, only some of the rural districts suffer, here and everywhere. There is a steady and progressive decay of country schools, and churches as well. Some districts have a half dozen or less pupils. It does not pay to hold schools in them. Consolidation of schools, on the basis of the township as the unit, is the obvious remedy. There is a tendency to larger farms. The owner of a forty or eighty can't make a living on it—must have more land, to raise stock, but can't buy our high-priced land; he sells to a richer farmer and moves out of the state. That rich farmer keeps on adding quarters and eighties till he can give each child of his a farm. This land-hunger has several times become acute, and there have been notable hegiras, to Missouri, Kansas, Nebraska, the Dakotas, to Canada, to Oklahoma, to Texas, to Colorado, etc. Partly speculative now, but hundreds of farmers have sought cheaper lands in the offings west, south, north. These movements of farmers have been interesting phenomena. People are as fluid as water and air. Illinois farmers in the last fifteen to twenty years sold out at one hundred and twenty-five dollars to one hundred and fifty dollars and even one hundred and seventy-five dollars per acre and came here, bidding up our land, that is as good as theirs, from twenty-five and thirty dollars to fifty dollars for Alex. Loughridge's farm, and to seventy dollars in the case of the late John Smeltzer. That price struck us all dumb. "Land can never go higher than that high water mark," all gasped, but the yeast has sent it to one hundred dollars, to one hundred and twenty-five dollars, to one hundred and fifty dollars, and it will go to three hundred dollars, mark that, and then some, give it time. B. F. Dixon has boosted our farm land, in the sixteen years of his residence here, more than any other man. He has operated most actively in Cedar, Washington, Franklin and Oregon townships. He has sold some farms five and six times, at an advance each time. The first farms that sold at fifty dollars per have gone to one hundred and fifty dollars. Not one buyer failed to do well on the farm picked out for him by Dixon. He has located over seventy families from Illinois, who sold at twenty-five dollars to sixty dollars more per acre than our lands commanded, but of late years there is not that disparity—our lands are as good and valuable as theirs. Restless, ever on the move, a man gets the wander-lust and cheap-land-hunger, and migrates, selling to a richer and firmer-rooted man ere he flits. It is a sort of hoboism. That movement reduces the number of families. Schools feel the depletion, churches also; can't hire a teacher, must starve the preacher, so they cut off both, hitch up the fleet team, step into an auto, go to a village or city to church, send the children off to school.

Many of the out-going farmers sold to foreigners, and there have been migrations into the county as well as out. Those industrious people, the Bohemians, have come in and multiplied so fast, they have changed the political character of townships like Iowa, English River, Highland, and Jackson, and modified the social and religious life of those communities. Another curious migration, that has helped villages while depleting the country, is the retiring and exodus of farmers to the towns. Old, well-heeled farmers fancy they would like to spend their last days in town. They rent their farms to their boys or others, come in, buy places, keep a team, a cow or two, some chickens, a dog and cat, and in a few years leave rather reluctantly for—heaven. A few years ago there was so large a colony of ex-Jackson people in this city, they formed a club and had grubfests and high jinks. As I recall, there were then sixty to seventy families. Other townships have suffered the same way. For awhile, the exile enjoys the novelty of the town; he goes to shows like Uncle Tom's Cabin, they are so moral, gardens some, drives out to the farm, but after all, it's like shutting up a bird or animal in a cage. He irks under the limitations, gets lonesome, loses his cud, mopes, gets a grouch, grows morbid, loses appetite, finds he has a slow liver, bad kidneys, develops locomotor ataxia, shuffles off, makes another widow. The women stand the change better than the men, for, as domestic help is scarce, they usually do their own house work, and that keeps them busy and contented. Really, the continuity of their exercise has not been broken, nor their domestic experience short-circuited. So it is far more apt to be a widow than a widower. On the average, they plant an old rich farmer, retired from all work, in about three years. That is, if he is foolish enough to shut off all accustomed work, and "takes life easy," as he says.

Still, there has been in the last year or two but little land money going out of the county, save to the Oklahoma pan-handle and to Missouri. The out-going stream of cash for land is almost dry—has wholly ceased to Canada and Texas.

City Utilities—Water.—The water in our wells became suspect. Many libeled God for sending typhoid fever. He could prove an alibi. Germs in water in wells contaminated with sewage did it. In '89 a few men chipped in and imported a driller to bore a deep well on Smouse's land out east. They got unlimited water, and offered to turn the well over to the city on easy terms, but the offer was declined—too far out, for one reason. In July, 1890, J. P. Miller & Co. were hired to drill the first city artesian well, and began November 5, and stopped March 12, '91, at a depth of one thousand six hundred and eleven feet and two inches. For a test it was pumped ten days, at rates from ninety-five to one hundred and twelve gallons per minute, the city requiring but eighty-three and one-third gallons. Ten inch casing was put down two hundred and forty-two feet, six and one-quarter inch to four hundred and sixty-one feet, then rock one hundred and two feet, five and one-quarter inch down to eight hundred and eighteen feet, rock five hundred and eighty-two feet, four and one-half casing to one thousand four hundred and sixty-eight feet, rock one hundred and forty-three feet, casing to bottom of well. After a second pumping, water stood forty-four feet one inch from top of casing. Quality of water good, its temperature seventy-four degrees. The cost was four thousand dollars.

Well No. 2 was drilled by O. G. Wilson in the fall of '96, and was one thousand two hundred and seventeen feet deep, with casing one thousand and ninety-four feet. The city bought the casing and paid two dollars a foot for drilling. In 1908 it was deepened to one thousand five hundred and sixty-five feet.

Well No. 3 was drilled, in 1908, by C. P. Brant, to a depth of one thousand eight hundred and six feet, costing about nine thousand seven hundred and fifty dollars. The original plant, wells, buildings, standpipe, etc., cost thirty-nine thousand nine hundred and forty-two dollars and one cent. Water rents have not yet equalled the operating expenses, cost of extensions of mains, interest on bonds, etc., but who cares? We have plenty of wholesome water for domestic use, fire protection, lawns, etc. We have about eight miles of mains, and are putting in an universal meter system, and receipts will come up. The last of the bonds, five per cent, is due in 1911. Interest on bonds for ten years, operating expenses, fuel, incidentals, street corner drinking and park fountains, watering troughs, bring the total cost of water works, exclusive of well No. 3, up to one hundred and five thousand three hundred and thirty-eight dollars and sixty-three cents. With that well added, nine thousand seven hundred and fifty dollars, the grand total is one hundred and fifteen thousand and eighty-eight dollars and sixty-three cents.

State chemist's analysis of the water is appended:

Mineral analysis of water shows as follows:

Silicic acid (SiO_2), .5599 gr. per U. S. gallon.

Potassium chloride, .6410 gr. per U. S. gallon.

Sodium chloride ($NaCl$), 6.2655 gr. per U. S. gallon.

Sodium sulphate (Na_2SO), 36.3261 gr. per U. S. gallon.

Sodium bisulphate ($NaHSO_4$), 29.1590 gr. per U. S. gallon.

Calcium sulphate ($CaSO_4$), 7.0332 gr. per U. S. gallon.

Magnesium sulphate ($MgSO_4$), 12.4800 gr. per U. S. gallon.

Sulphuric acid (H_2SO_4), 26.2139 gr. per U. S. gallon.

Aluminum oxide (Al_2O_3), .0583 gr. per U. S. gallon.

ARTESIAN WELLS WATER WORKS, WASHINGTON

Ferric oxide (Fe_2O_3), .2099 gr. per U. S. gallon.

These determinations are as would be computed in the regular manner. The iron and aluminum should be indicated as sulphate probably. The water is acid due to the presence of sulphuric acid, which with the large amount of sulphates present must indicate that the water comes from coal measures. The large amount of sodium and magnesium sulphates, known as glauber and Epsom salts respectively, would of course act as a fine cathartic agent. The presence of the free mineral acid would not be so desirable as a mineral water. This, however, could be neutralized by use of a little alkali which would then make it a very valuable mineral water.

We do not find the presence of any rare mineral in the water as first suspected. This water would compare very favorably with many celebrated mineral waters.

What is under us? That all may know what, at least to the depth of one thousand eight hundred and six feet, is below, and learn how Nature built up the globe beneath our feet during eternities of time, read this log of the driller of well No. 3:

DEPTH	FORMATION	
1— 65	Subsoil white and blue clay	Pleistocene.
65— 70	Quicksand	
70— 105	Blue clay	
105— 117	Quicksand	
117— 235	Blue clay	
235— 242	Quicksand and gravel	
242— 360	White shale	Kinderhook Shale.
360— 385	Brown shale	
385— 435	Blue shale	
435— 475	Brown limestone	Devonian Limestone.
475— 527	Gray limestone	
527— 534	Brown limestone	
534— 563	Gray limestone	
563— 605	Blue shale	Maquoqeta Shale.
605— 620	Brown shale	
620— 700	Blue shale	
700— 735	Brown shale, sandy	
735— 763	Blue shale	

763— 790	Brown limestone, shelly.................	Galena Trenton.
790— 800	Brown limestone, hard..................	
800—1028	Gray limestone	
1028—1037	Brown limestone, hard..................	
1037—1050	Brown limestone, hard..................	
1050—1090	Gray limestone	
1090—1108	Blue shale and sandstone.................	St. Peter Sandstone.
1108—1211	White sandstone	
1211—1215	Blue shale	Oneata Limestone.
1215—1230	Red limestone shells, hard................	
1230—1353	Gray limestone, hard..................	
1353—1365	White sandstone, soft..................	
1365—1375	Red limestone	
1375—1380	White sandstone, soft.................	
1380—1400	Gray limestone	
1400—1480	Gray limestone, soft....................	
1480—1590	White limestone, hard..................	
1590—1670	White sandstone, soft..................	
1670—1700	Gray limestone, hard...................	
1700—1740	White sandstone, soft..................	
1740—1803	Gray limestone, hard...................	
1803—1808	Pink limestone, hard..................	

PIPE.

14-inch extends from the surface down 256 feet.
10-inch extends from the surface down 610 feet.
8-inch extends from the surface down 1470 feet.

WATER LEVEL.

At 500 feet, 200 feet from surface.
At 563 feet, 120 feet from surface.
At 1215 feet, 110 feet from surface.
At 1365 feet, 95 feet from surface.
At 1670 feet, 83 feet from surface.
At 1808 feet, 80 feet from surface.

After fifty-three hours' pumping test, water level stood seventy feet from surface.

It is curious—water. The St. Peter porous stone and the Oneata sandstone, dipping down so deep here, crop out several hundred miles to the north of us. Rain and melting snows up there sink into these inclined planes of rock, and our artesian water was surface water filtering down those rocky sponges. It comes down to us from the surface in long cascades under ground. Our deep-seated rocks came up, like whales to spout and breathe, far to the north, just as the shales that once roofed coal beds here went into the air by erosion and the coal measures exhaled with them. Go west, said shales deepen and protect the coal deposited in Keokuk, Mahaska, Monroe and other counties.

Why have the ancient springs dried up? They have not dried up, though we mistakenly so stated. They flow merrily and sparkle and sing yet. 'Tis so here, and in Ohio, and in New England. A score of years ago, I visited my ancestral farm home in Sheffield, Berkshire county, Mass., and at the milk house the famous spring that delighted father's eyes when a boy a century and more ago, was boiling and bubbling still, pouring a stream of pure, cold, soft water as thick as one's thigh. What feeds them? Ultimately, it is the sun evaporating water from the oceans and sending the vapor clouds over the continents. For Europe is full of springs, medicinal and other. So long as sun and seas and trade winds do business at the old stands, waters will gush out of the depths of the earth as from the rock that Moses smote. Many states of our Union exploit commercially the alleged healing waters. Our federal geological survey shows that we drink over fifty-five million gallons of bottled waters each year, and fifty-two millions of these come from domestic springs. Minnesota, Wisconsin, New York, Massachusetts, the Virginias and Indiana lead. It is also queer that medicinal springs vary in strength of charge, lose their virtue or suffer a diminution of it. But, praise be, the live springs stay, and gush, bubble, sing, go on forever. "Why have Iowa rivers ceased to be navigable?" The erosion of plowed fields. Put Iowa in universal grass, with timber along the streams, as she was clothed in 1830, the creek and river beds will scour; remove dams, and boating will again be possible, and our opaque flowing waters will be as clear as New England brooks and Colorado crystal streams.

Light.—About 1879, DeGalleford, who had put in a gas plant, and struggled with it, borrowing money of Mr. Everson till he had to take the elephant, wandered elsewhere, and Everson sat up nights with the vexatious thing, the unknown business worrying even him. He used to emerge from cellars, reading meters, with a huge hat on, so festooned with cobwebs it looked like a cocoon. Still more embarrassing and distressing was this inherited business to his inexperienced widow, and in sheer desperation she sold the plant to Win. Smouse in 1895, and he organized a stock company, The Washington Illuminating Co. In 1906, they sold the works to The Iowa Gas and Electric Co. (Carson brothers) for thirty-six thousand five hundred dollars. They are this spring replacing mains, rusted by thirty years' service, with larger tubes. A great deal of machinery is now run here by electric motors, day and night, and Washington, which has no water power or coal mines, that used to be deemed essential for manufacturing, is on an equality with towns that have these old advantages.

The city put in a seventeen thousand dollar electric plant in 1902. A special hot election authorized a maximum expenditure of that sum, if needed, and a Davenport firm took twelve thousand dollars in bonds at four per cent, and would take three thousand dollars more later. Both arcs and incandescents were to be used. The bid to construct was twelve thousand five hundred dollars. In 1907 it cost three thousand four hundred and thirteen dollars and fifty-four cents to run it and in 1908 two thousand nine hundred dollars, exclusive of interest on bonds. The last four per cent bond is due in 1922. St. Clair Lewis has been the efficient head of both water and electric plants many years.

Sewerage.—Within the last ten years, a city council had sense and courage enough to hire an engineer to map a district, make a plan to drain the city, and we are trying to live up to it. First and last, it is estimated by surveyors and ex-city officials, we have, foolishly or wisely, mainly foolishly, spent one hundred thousand dollars on underground sewers, shallow drains, ditches, etc. A sewer is a municipal gut, with laterals—nasty, but a stern necessity. And, really, a big city, catacombed with sewers, hides its chiefest marvels. Ever read Victor Hugo's account of the sewer system of Paris, in "Les Miserables?" If not, don't sleep till you have with him threaded that wonderful underworld. At last, Washington has a Big Sewer, built of brick, tile, Vousir. Its general trend, like that of tornadoes, is from southwest to northeast, from Crooked creek to the water works, and beyond, tapping all that flat region covered by the pearl button factory, seed house, etc. The first section from the brickyard to Len Smouse's corner was two thousand eight hundred and twenty eight feet, built by Swift, at a loss, for ten thousand six hundred dollars; egg-shape, three feet across horizontally, five feet perpendicular, for one thousand feet; next eight hundred feet, three feet by four and a half; the rest, three feet by four; thence to the railroad, two feet by three; from the tracks, one thousand one hundred feet, a thirty-inch tile to Geo. McKay's. Roy Davis built a one thousand six hundred foot section, cost not available to me. From the brickyard to Perry Hayes' line the sewer is made of Vousir, or four-holed cement blocks, each block an arc of a circle, so that, when laid, the sewer is a perfect circle. These blocks should have been cemented, experts say; each freshet sets them awry, and some of them are now exposed. This section cost ten thousand dollars, and is a bad job, and lacks capacity, having broken during every flood. It is five

JAMES DAWSON

thousand two hundred feet from the brickyard to the creek, and that stretch is only three feet in diameter. There are many laterals, as from the court-house, North Marion and Iowa avenues, and from several directions along the route. This intestinal canal accommodates perhaps one-half of our people, together with its laterals and other tributaries. Lesser entrails take the secretions from other areas. As a result, hundreds of houses tap these arteries, and kitchen sinks, bath rooms and closets were put in by hundreds, and there are left hardly enough out-houses to go round with mischievous boys on Hallowe'en. Where sewers were not available, cess-pools have been put in, to justify bath and closet, and the sanitary conditions have greatly improved, to say nothing about the multiplication of creature comforts, conveniences, luxuries. We are pretty well civilized now, in the city, and well-to-do farmers, building modern houses, are level with us in sanitation. Many a homo, both in city and country, has realized, at last, the dream of their lives, in extending the gracious functions and services of their houses. Yes, life is now well worth living.

Telephone.—Everybody used to walk. Curiously, as the walks got good, we quit walking and "hellooed," saving time, but losing health, in non-exercise. The first telephone installed in this county dates from 1890. Thomas Dupuis put in one of his own make, and soon had several in operation. In '94 he and his son were given a franchise to build and operate a 'phone exchange. He, L. D. Robinson and D. H. Logan organized the Washington Telephone Co. with ten thousand dollars capital. Construction was begun June 1, '94; no pole line leads were constructed, but they built leads over the tops of buildings around the square, called bridging construction. The Western Telephone Construction Co. made the office equipment. The company began operations November 6, '94, with forty-nine subscribers. Rates for residence one dollar and twenty-five cents per month and two dollars and eight cents for business. In '96 part of the system had to be rebuilt, as it had grown beyond all anticipation, and rates were lowered to one dollar for homes and one dollar and fifty cents for business.

In '97, L. D. Robinson and W. A. Wilson bought all the stock, when there were nearly two hundred 'phones in town. And they rebuilt the whole system, making pole leads and installing three thousand feet of fifty-pair cable and putting in more office equipment. In October, '97, they began building eighty-one miles of toll lines to eleven of the main towns in the county, at a cost of ten thousand dollars. The material used was of the best. In October, '99, a toll line service had been installed to all the towns in the county. On July 10,

'90, the first rural line was put in, giving service to John and Charles Griffith and David McLaughlin.

In June, 1903, the company was incorporated with a capital stock of sixty thousand dollars, of which fifty thousand dollars was paid up and ten thousand dollars in the treasury. The stockholders were Robinson, Wilson, E. G. Fox, H. M. Eicher, Orville Elder, F. H. Smith, Dr. E. T. Wickham, F. L. Wilson. They made extensive improvements, adding more office equipment and putting in over four thousand feet of under-ground cable. and other extensions and improvements.

In May, 1906, additional stock of ten thousand dollars was issued to L. H. Wallace and Ralph Smith, making the sixty thousand dollar stock paid up. In the fall, Robinson and Wilson retired. In January, 1907, the stock was increased from sixty thousand dollars to one hundred thousand dollars, all paid up. In that spring the company made very extensive improvements, rebuilding the entire system, putting in approximately forty-five thousand feet of cable of different capacity, from twenty-five-pair cable to one hundred and fifty-pair cable; also rebuilding their office and adding a new complete office equipment, and building thirty-two miles of copper toll line circuit from Riverside to Brighton, meeting Iowa City at Riverside and Fairfield at Brighton.

On April 1, '08, E. G. Fox, manager and stock-holder, retired, selling his stock to C. J. Wilson, D. W. Mannhardt was engaged as manager. and on February 1, '09, F. H. Smith sold his stock to Mannhardt.

Up to this time, the telephone business in the county developed very rapidly, as shown by this data obtainable from the different exchanges in the county and some of the adjoining exchanges, as follows:

Brighton Mutual Tele. Co.	438	telephones.
Uniondale Tele. Co., Riverside	400	"
Kalona Mutual Tele. Co.	212	"
West Chester Mutual Tele. Co.	230	"
Olds Telephone Co., Crawfordsville	160	"
Mutual Tele. Co., Haskins	130	"
Wayland & Coppeck (in county)	90	"
Ainsworth Telephone Company	260	"
Wellman Mutual Tele. Co.	500	"
Mutual Tele. Co. in Keota (in county)	78	"
Richland Tele. Co.	40	"
Washington Mutual Tele. Co.	149	"
Washington Tele. Co.	1500	"
Total number telephones in county, January 1, '09	4187	

Post-Office.—This is a business that has the smallest competition known. It has cut into the banking and express business, and has them as rivals in sending money and parcels. Still, it is the sole business in every town that is not over-done. For the year ending March 31, '09, our office sent eight thousand three hundred and sixteen money orders and cashed thirty thousand one hundred and ninety-two. The department pays our nine rural carriers eight thousand four hundred and forty-five dollars and the four city carriers three thousand one hundred dollars, and gives this office for wages of hands six thousand four hundred dollars and four hundred and fifty dollars for repairs and messengers hauling mail to and from depots, and six hundred and sixty dollars for rent, and for four railroad postal clerks living here five thousand five hundred dollars, a total of money spent here of twenty-four thousand five hundred and fifty-five dollars a year. The rural carriers handle on an average sixty-five thousand five hundred pieces each month, that is, each one handles three hundred pieces a day. We ought to have in Washington a federal building for post-office, etc. A good many rural post-offices have quit. Except in the larger centers, the post-office is a vanishing institution.

Seed House.—F. B. Mills & Co., of Syracuse, New York, incorporated in that state, built here in 1907 a three-story brick building forty by one hundred feet, as a branch seed house. This is their western distributing point, but, funnily, lots of eastern orders come here to be filled, even from parties who are neighbors to Syracuse. They receive here seeds from all the states in the union and from Europe and other foreign countries, packing them and filling orders through the post-office mainly. L. D. Langworthy, the local manager, says the volume of business done this year was double that of last year. He employed ninety-two men, women and youths to do the work from December till June 1. Next year he will have in a complete printing plant, to make the catalogs, seed package inscriptions, labels, etc. The labor pay-roll was heavy this season, girls making eight, nine, and even thirteen dollars some weeks, beating domestic service badly, and it will be continuously harder to get kitchen help, as girls universally feel that such folks are looked down on and are banned and black-balled and discriminated against. The house gets so many postage stamps in payment, it does not buy here over two hundred to three hundred dollars worth, and so, thus far, is no special help to our post-office, but the office got an extra hand or two from the department, to handle the tremendous out-put. One item was a quarter million of one style of small package. The establishment gives us a certain prestige, and we welcome the big plant among our industrial factors.

Fire Department.—Every town has to burn two or three times before it gets sense. At first it depends on a bucket brigade. All come at an alarm, and those who are not yelling orders and suggestions and doing nothing else, get in line and pass buckets and spill half the water before the rest of it kisses the flames with a steamy, hissing smack. Others are toting out stuff. All manage to get soaked and muddy. For ages we did that, and could not do otherwise. We had no water works. We dug cisterns in the corners of the square, and ran water from the surrounding roofs into them. Fine places for bull frogs, "crawfish," mosquitoes and muskrats. We lacked water, but had plenty of beer.

Providence kept chiding and chastening us. In '84 half the west side turned into ashes, from the First National Bank corner to what was the Stewart drug store, occupied by Emerson Hoover. It was a seventy-five thousand dollar loss, but need not have been over seventy-five dollars if we had had any means to stand off from the intense heat, say thirty feet, and throw water twenty-five feet high. The "bucket shops" were of no avail. In humiliation we had to let the half block burn. The hoi polloi demanded a fire department. It became an issue—fire-fighting apparatus. Geo. Rodman, Burrell and two more, have forgotten whom, were elected to the council on that score. We bought for three thousand five hundred dollars a "Rumsey" brake engine, hose carts and ladder truck. That engine was a splendid gymnastic: to work it taxed one's wind, and in ten minutes one sweat three gallons. It saved thousands of dollars' worth of property. It stopped a bad fire in Harwood's store cellar. The germ of a fire department was a bucket brigade organized in '82; in the next three years after getting the engine, Charles Hebener was chief and a department was set up with 100 men. Charley did good work at fires if he could abstain from mocking 'Squire Burkholder and Gus Ross. These chiefs followed his wise lead: J. F. Curran, Hugh Kendall, E. S. Mason, H. C. Welch, Sam Hout, J. C. Ford, N. H. Jones, Scott Reister, Chas. Brown, S. R. Davis, John Little, Geo. Graff, Jake Minick, Hugh Teeter, Ralph Dougherty, John Steck, Ora Turner.

Bill Glover was foreman of the first engine company, and Kendall of the ladder truck. The boys got very expert and had lots of fun, drilling and squirting. When we got water works, the machinery was sold for a lot of hose, that was clapped on hydrants and operated by city pressure. City Hall had been built in '83, and the department occupied the lower floor with good machinery, and have a tower for elevating and draining hose by gravity drip, and the old library room upstairs, back of council chamber, is their headquarters. There are now seventy-seven hydrants. Fire alarms are operated from the telephone station. Folk now feel comfortable and safe, for the fire lads are lively and faithful boys. Their main handicap is—bad roads. They never swear except at "a defective flue," which vainly routs them out to find that its glim is doused just as they arrive after a long haul. The equipment is—two hose carts, the Jonathan Wilson and the Gazelle, twenty-five men each, a hook and ladder company of twenty-five. But one member of the fire department has died in service—Lucian Wagner, in '86.

Storage.—In 1902 Elmer G. Mason built for five thousand dollars, on two lots on the heights, a transfer and storage building one hundred and twenty-eight by forty feet, two stories, in which he also has an extensive machine shop, a very busy place. The plant is a good thing for its owner and for the public. He can lay up your furs and woolens and feathers where moth and rust doth not corrupt, and store fruit, vegetables, furniture and whatnot.

Paving.—In 1904, sixty-five years after the founding of the city, the first paving was laid down in the county-seat, a luxury shared with us by every owner of a country team coming in here. We had boated, and stuck in the mud, around the public square, for over half a century, showing how natural it is for an alleged moving body to keep on in the plane of its motion. That area was paved with vitreous brick, and the streets for a block each way from the park corners. The next year the paving was extended on north Marion and Iowa avenues to the railroad tracks and a bit beyond on Marion, on East Main to H. M. Eicher's residence, and on West Washington street to the entrance to Sunset Park, and the center of that street was boulevarded, or an island of grass, trees, dandelions and other choice weeds was washed by brick on either flank. Such a stimulus to driving, automobiling, promenading! Gospel Ridge used to be a silent street, shaded by giant elms, where lovers foregathered in the gloaming to indulge labial and other symptoms of condition, unseen by the profane; it was like a deserted village, but now the honk-honk and smoke and smell of mobiles keep us alert as a pitcherful of Egyptian vipers, all their heads reaching out nervously to see what is going on.

Hurry-ups.—Tamed lightning did not appear here as a working force till the railway came in '58. At first, service was at the depot, but stock men forced an office down town, and it used to be about where Eicher & Livingston's law office is now. There Joe Rader et al. were wont to jerk the frisky tail of a thunderbolt to get the Chicago markets.

I feel quite certain, but not dead sure, that the express business also came in with the railroad. And I think W. H. Jenkins was about the first agent. If so, after him were Norman Everson and Dr. M. C. Parker, and in more modern days the late C. F. Chester, followed by W. D. Shearer in 1900. They served the United States express. In May, 1909, Wells-Fargo came in, making E. G. Fox agent. It is said the former company covers thirty thousand two hundred and fifty miles, including electrics and steamboats, but is exceeded by the latter in a mileage of forty-eight thousand seven hundred; and the American, forty-four thousand three hundred and sixty miles; the Adams, thirty thousand eight hundred and eighty; while the Pacific contents itself with twenty-three thousand miles.

Steam Laundry.—R. F. Smith started one about twenty years ago, getting soft water from a sandstone vein one hundred and fifty feet down. J. A. Crawford opened a rival shop in 1896. Smith sold to Major Latta, he to Eddy & Howe, they to Moulton, he to Elliott, and Crawford took it over in 1903, but now sells it to Chas. Means.

Hays & Hartman constitute the Washington Ice Cream Co., formed in '09, to supply city and country round about with this luxury.

Dairy Products.—Nearly thirty years ago creameries and cheeseries had a great vogue in this county, and who can tell why creameries have quit, here and in many other sections? The old dash and dog churns and all the newer sorts of churns went into privacy in most farm houses, much to the joy of the kids who had to run them and cry that the butter would never come. But bye and bye, after one or two eternities, all of a sudden, a sort of salty, watery sounding noise would come from the churn, like the death-rattle in the throat, and butter clots showed color on the dasher like gold grains in a miner's pan. In the creamery period, a neighborhood sent its milk or cream, mornings and evenings, to the factory, which made lots better butter than ninety-nine out of every hundred farmers' wives could achieve then. More soap-grease than butter was made a generation ago. It was awful paste, threaded with woman's errant hair. Female tresses are usually beautiful—suck-eggs tie a wad of it with a pretty string or narrow ribbon, and stow the sentimental thing away in a book, but not a single hair of that tress looks sweet and appetizing in butter. No, Melissa dear, please exclude your locks from at least my consignment of the golden fleece from the old brindle cow. You hear me. The creamery product relegated the old axle-grease stuff which used to disgust grocers and consumers. Many farmers' wives make prime butter now. Many have separators, and they are up on cream temperatures and other factors. A good butter-maker can get all the town customers she wants, at twenty-five cents a pound the year round. The creameries set the pace; they were the missionaries that redeemed heathendom in butterland.

Over five hundred million pounds of creamery butter are made annually in the United States. Farmers who patronize central creameries have invested in hand separators infinitely more than all the central plants cost. In 1905, creameries, cheeseries and condenseries paid farmers thirty-one and three-tenths per cent more for milk than in 1900, but Iowa, that had nine thousand and seventy-five plants in 1900, lost two hundred and fifty-two in five years, Wisconsin and Minnesota beating her badly. Her creameries were mostly co-operative, but the central system encroached on the smaller creameries and farmers' receipts decreased heavily. Perhaps that destroyed our factories. There was one in Washington; Crawfordsville had a six thousand dollar one in '92, and so had Keota; Daytonville a butter and cheese company in '81 with two thousand four hundred dollars capital; Nira in '87 an eighteen hundred dollar factory for both butter and cheese; Dublin a two thousand dollar cheese factory in '85; Clay, in '74, a cheese company capitalized at sixteen hundred dollars; West Chester had early, and still has, a flourishing cheese house.

Cows are more plentiful and valuable than ever, but where did the creameries go, and why? The next federal census ought to tell in how many families women and girls have to "pail the cow." It never seemed right to make a woman milk, especially in wet weather, in muddy barn-yards. She cannot dress for it. She has not cowhide boots, and should she trail skirts through mud and worse filth and squat in a puddle? It is not at all fitting. And she cannot swear enough to fill the role creditably. Did you tell her, when courting her and saying all those sweet things that you very well knew at the time were confounded lies,—did you tell the angel then that she would have to slop around in an old barn-yard and milk fourteen cows, nights and mornings? Of course not—you would not have dared; but when she became your property, your chattel, about on a level with the cow, you forced her to do that nasty chore. You ought to be ashamed of yourself. Nice old growly, grouchy bear you have become since you were a fraud of a lover! You are worse than a nature faker. The average woman can't talk to the average cow as she needs to be elocuted to. A cow, like an ox, needs "talking to," as well as hammering with a milk-stool when she kicks, or won't give down, or swats one in the face with her tail perfectly solid with burrs, in fly time. Women, if you do not vote for me for president, when you get the ballot, you will be very ungrateful, like average republics.

Canned Goods.—The art of canning fruits and vegetables is a recent art. We used to dry them in the sun and elsewhere, and hang dried apples and pumpkin strips from the rafters, and swell up on dried apples, but now canning time is as regular a thing as cleaning house. Not a fruit is skipped. This dainty art prolongs summer and fall into winter and spring, and is as stately a bridge across seasons as Gibbon's History was said to be between ancient and modern ages. And it was so individual an art that all were surprised when a Crawfordsville company incorporated with fifteen thousand dollars stock in '83. Corporations can do most things cheaper and better than individuals. Planters sell cane and beets to factories, farmers sell milk and cream to creameries and cheese factories, cucumbers, onions, etc., to pickle plants, fruits to canneries, fishermen sell salmon to the all-firedest smelling chebangs, yet most house-wives sweat and burn themselves and say "Darn it" in a sort of religious way, while canning, preserving, jamming their fruit, and in this county churn their own butter. Groceries are full of canned goods —tomatoes, beans, beets, corn, peas, sweet potatoes, spinach, peaches, cherries, pear, quince, pumpkin, fish, etc., etc.

Incorporations.—It is interesting to glance through the books in the recorder's office, to note the varied things incorporated from the '70s and '80s down to date—church societies, loan and building associations, elevator, pipe organ, heating, hardware and furniture, clothing, mercantile, banana crate and hoop, harness, lumber, floral, pearl button, wagon-box, storage, seed plant, brick and tile, abstracting, city improvement companies —a long procession of them. The range is great, and the capital invested very considerable. Really, a great many things are made and done here, though no one has dignified us with the name "manufacturers" and asked us to yell for a tariff on any infant industries.

We have lost several things—as potteries, foundries, implement factories, grain-weighers, etc. It was a sad day for this city and county when the Wildes pulled out. Judge Ross, ages ago, ran a pottery here—"vere is dot bottery now?" And where are Mart Kilgore's and Wildes' foundries? And Williams & Shields' woolen mill? By the way, that last story is worth telling.

Hop Williams came here from Wales in the '40s and settled a mile south of Marshall, now Wayland, his house in Henry county, his barn in Washington county. He bought a great deal of land on Williams creek, on which Ben Goldsmith built a saw mill and worked it several years. In that time, W. J. Williams came, bought out Goldsmith, and in '66 he and John Shields turned it into a woolen mill, made cloth, spun, carded, and after awhile moved the machinery to Washington, into Tom McClean's shop. Father Polluk was interested in it, but finally John Graham took it, got one Jackson to operate it, and W. J. Williams went to Missouri.

The best properties to own in the early '40s and '50s, if big stories may be credited, were saw and grist mills. Several men assert that John Coppock paid his partner, Tommy Tucker, twenty thousand dollars in gold for his half interest in their last big mill, built in '57-8, and that Ben McCoy and some one from Brighton offered Mr. Coppock sixty-five thousand dollars for his mill on Skunk river. But the son, Wm. Coppock, says the stories are preposterous, and he does not believe the kindred story that Allen of Brighton was offered forty thousand dollars for his mill. I cite the yarns on both sides and don't pretend to say that the fables are true. Sound sort o' Munchausenish, eh? But mills were paying things in the building and wheat-growing periods. People came from near Iowa City, Oskaloosa, Fairfield and Mount Pleasant to get grinding done at Coppock's and he ran day and night, and did not work exactly and solely for his health, it may be fairly presumed. But, speaking of Tommy Tucker, he did sell out and invested in dry goods in Wayland and a grist mill, and also a saloon on the north side of our square, it is affirmed—it was no discredit in those times—he would not do it now, even if allowed to do so. He was a mighty hunter, and kept hounds. The Oskaloosa branch of the Burlington road now runs over the site of the Williams creek mill.

The grist mill business was lively and lucrative in early days. John Park's father came here in '41, and from '42 to the wet season of '47 all had fine wheat crops. Excess of water checked that industry. However, the habit of sowing wheat continued till '55, when weevil took the cereal. Ever after, it was a losing crop; we did not grow enough wheat to bread our people, and do not now. Bugs—drat bugs! As Josh Billings said sagely sixty years ago, "I hate a fli. Darn a fli!" John Coppock read the ominous writing on the wall, but tried to preserve his Diana of the Ephesians, and in the stress he paid Henry Davis two dollars and ninety cents per bushel for wheat. Lafe Stout held his wheat for three dollars and twenty-five cents, held and kept on holding, and finally sold for sixty cents a bushel, long before the days of Patten, the wheat cornerer. In '47 and '55 folks imported flour, and it was a staple in groceries as it is now, whether "knighthood was in flower" then as now, or not. Mills depreciated, and now millers are content to grind a little meal, buckwheat, feed, etc. As to land values, Park says in '45-7 it sold at ten dollars per acre; by '54 it was up to twenty-five dollars, and stood under thirty-five dollars many years after the war. When Loughridge got fifty dollars, farmers sat up and took notice, and when Smeltzer touched seventy dollars, they simply said "Gosh" in their bewilderment, and felt soda water tickles all through 'em.

Washington Manufacturing Co.—In 1902 Charles Parkinson made wagon boxes and shoveling boards in the pipe organ factory, and later manufactured gloves and mitts, but gave it up in labor discouragements. In 1905 Frank Stewart organized the above named company with an authorized capital of twenty-five thousand dollars, and eighteen thousand dollars paid up, Win. Smouse, president; Wm. A. Cook, vice; C. M. Keck, secretary; Mr. Stewart, treasurer and manager. They make wagon boxes, shoveling boards, barn floor scrapers, six to eight thousand boxes per year, employing ten to fifteen hands the season through. The total business runs to thirty thousand dollars a year. The work is done in a one-story brick building seventy-five by one hundred feet. Another, though entirely separate business, the most novel in town, is run on the same grounds. The American Pearl Button Co. had done a large business in Muscatine for six years, and Mr. Stewart and Mr. Fred Giesler brought the machinery into the pipe organ building in 1908. A new company was organized, with one hundred thousand dollars authorized capital, and forty thousand paid in. Mr. Stewart owns one-third of the stock, and the Gieslers, father Fred and son Frank, Win. Smouse, C. H. Keck and others are stock-holders. The force of seventy-five to one hundred hands turns out an annual product worth one hundred and fifty thousand dollars. Frank Stewart is president and manager; Fred Giesler, vice; C. H. Keck, treasurer; H. A. Pauls, secretary.

The supply of shells is ample, and sweet water mussels are shipped in by car loads from the Illinois, Mississippi, Arkansas, Red, White, Wabash, Ohio rivers, and, indeed, from all rivers except the Missouri. The pearl button business in the west was started fifteen years ago by a German, Mr. Doepful, in Muscatine, cutting shells by hand, as in the fatherland. The Barry Manufacturing Co. there, contractors who built our county infirmary, invented automatic machinery to cut the shells, which process cheapened buttons seventy-five per cent. The tariff on the buttons is thirty-five per cent ad valorem.

What should we do, could we do, without Elmer Keck's green houses? He and his wife have been capable professors in the chair of esthetics, and have immensely stimulated the popular sense of beauty.

Two excellent hospitals, established in the last two or three years,—what would the pioneers have thought of them? Skilful surgeons, trained nurses, where sickness is robbed of so much of its terror and suffering.

Is it logical and chronological to follow that item with this about two cemeteries? The old city burying ground, laid out by Jonathan Wilson, is populous, notwithstanding many of its graves yielded up their dead at that sort of resurrection when Elm Grove, the beautiful, opened its ample Abraham's bosom of earth as a new plantation of the bodies of those whom folks had loved and lost. Elm Grove is beautiful for situation; the prospects are superb. Sleep will be sweet in the warm soil of that elevated plateau. And then there is so much beauty in stone, and tree, and green sod, and tombs, and martial circle, and receiving vault—it is well to invest the sad ending of life's tragedy with such good taste and exquisite beauty.

The Geo. H. Paul Co., dealing in Texas land on a colossal scale, large parties going in excursion trains, living in smoking, dining and sleeping cars, processions out-distancing oriental caravans for comfort, if not for picturesqueness—well, this is the local phenomenon of 1909. Elegant office furnitures, retinues of high-salaried employees, outfits of splendid horses, harness, carriages, cavalcades—it is quite as fine and spirited as Chaucer's Canterbury

ABIJAH SAVAGE
Donor of Sunset Park

Pilgrims en route, or the Crusades in Europe, in a smaller way. Washington is quite astonished, bewildered, and talks of millionaires as if the Arabian Nights had come again, with Aladdin's Lamp that somebody is vigorously rubbing.

Parks.—A city is not a city without them. We were lucky to be able to get the twelve acres in what was happily called "Sunset Park." It lies four or five blocks from the square, down West Washington street, just beyond Gospel Ridge and its big elms and pious habitants. It was lucky, too, that Abijah Savage had a heart in him as big as a generous ox's, for he gave three thousand dollars towards payment on that lovely real estate. It is delightful to see the merry, happy crowds come and go there, to picnic, promenade, lounge, ogle, flirt, and be joyous according to their moods. About eight acres are lawn-mowed weekly; the trees already furnish ample shade; the grass is velvet; there is pure water, electric light; in half a dozen years, with care in cultivation, it will be a thing of beauty and a joy forever.

By the way, reader, do you know that in all our civic history, with plenty of rich people, only two have left the public a benefaction, a man, Mr. Savage, and a woman, Mrs. Dr. Chilcote? No, let's not use the ugly word "tight wads," but here we have been on the map ever since 1839, and all of two gifts to the city! It is, indeed, a long time between drinks. But, cheer up! the Greeks are bound to come with splendid presents in their hands. This wee bouquet I wish to lay on the grave of Mrs. Chilcote and this one in the living hand of Mr. Savage.

Wm. Smouse laid out Highland Park, a right pretty place, but it is quite a way out. The city is growing that way, and in time that will be a charming breathing space for a part of our population.

The public square, with its carpet of green, healthy trees, tame squirrels, fountains, music stand, comfortable iron seats, broad cement walks, circle of flowers set by Elmer Keck, the florist, electric light, is as pretty as the blue eyes of a baby. On hot nights many a young fellow sleeps on the grass, on a blanket, in that inclosure. Saturday nights the fine band plays there, and it is gala. Youth and beauty, maturity, families, lovers meet there to hear the music, play, talk, court, enjoy, and promenaders saunter round on the sixteen foot cement walks, and jostle amusingly, while the wide brick pavement is thronged with vehicles. It is quite like the gala, festal nights in the plazas of the City of Mexico—innocent, decorous, picturesque abandonment to the gayeties of life in their most alluring forms and colors and spirit. City and county empty humanity into that green bowl of bright sensuous existence.

It is a great convenience to have three such machine shops as Tom H. McClean's, Ed. Carris's and Elmer Mason's. Tom is an indispensable mechanic, and a very ingenious man. Carris invented and makes a one-match delivery box that has a great run, and he does a variety of job work.

Cal. Long, blacksmith, invented a wagon brake that brings him good returns. Geo. G. Rodman devised a photograph holder, a neat addition to our repertory of inventions. Geo. Black, blacksmith, improved on a machine for sharpening lawn-mowers, by which he puts on a razor edge that lasts. Mr. A. S. Meek hit on a window sash ventilator that stays put.

Daniel Wilde is probably our most resourceful and miscellaneous inventor —his brain is a hot-house for the development of ideas. His grain-weigher scheme was his master-piece, a fruitful germ that makes for him a fine income, and is putting his son Walter to the fore as a capable business man in Peoria.

Charles Hebener and the Neiswangers are excellent marble-cutters, and have put out designs that are indeed works of art.

From small beginnings, W. S. Reister has built up a remarkably large trade in eggs and poultry.

Wooly Bros. have a big garage, and hustle the automobile trade. B. F. Dixon has a private garage to store the two machines he handles. The Bardens had one on North Marion avenue, but it is now used by Clyde Brown for carriage refitting, painting, etc.

Frank Bell conducts successfully a very large carriage factory, and turns out admirable work in great variety.

Three elevators, Whiting's on the Rock Island, Chalmer's on the Milwaukee, and H. A. Baxter's on the Burlington, suffice to handle the grain delivery.

Standard Oil has a large supply station here. Oil of the best quality now sells at fourteen cents per gallon, that thirty or forty years ago, was quoted at sixty and seventy cents. Thus glides the greased world away.

Indeed, we have about all that heart could wish, except, say, a public swimming pool, street cars, buggies run by that electric storage battery that Edison eternally promises but does not offer, and a federal building for post-office and other uses.

We have so many blessings, so common and matter-of-fact, we do not note or appreciate them, as, for instance, matches in place of steel, flint and punk; ready-made yeasts, baking powders, ready-to-wear clothes for both sexes and all ages and sizes; breakfast foods, ready prepared, probably worthless, but as the Frenchman said, "varee pla-zant;" handy machines for sewing, mowing, raking, hoisting, refrigerating—we used to hang milk, butter, meat, etc., down the well—heatless gas and electric stoves, bicycles, automobiles, and so on with hundreds of labor-savers and comfort-bringers. Just take screens, for instance. We used to be eaten alive with flies and mosquitoes. Doors and windows had to be open, and these insects filled the house and paid not a cent of rent. Folks made whips of paper strips tacked on sticks, or flourished bushes with leaves on, or waved a stately feather affair when company came. Flies defiled with filth and disease germs slices of bread and cake, mashed potatoes and all they alighted on, swarmed into the sugar bowl and blew down the cream pitcher. They had been on the stable dung-heap, but when the horn blew or the bell rang, they knew what that meant, and rushed into the dining room, never stopping at the pump to wash off their feet the germs of tuberculosis, scarlet fever, diphtheria, typhoid. It was a fright. They inked everything that was white; if there was a crack in the plastering, they etched a mourning border round it. In the early morning, when sleep hung in festoons round your head, they woke you by crawling over your countenance, tickling your nose, blowing in ears and nostrils, and complacently braiding their fore and hind legs on your alabaster brow. What flies skipped, mosquitoes took. Where the skin was exposed, they raised colonies of muskrat cones. The baby, next morning, seemed to have old-fashioned hives on face, neck and arms. Just strips of fine mesh wire stop all that old torment. There is nothing happier in the sanitary line than screens.

Then houses were stifling hot in summer, cold in winter. Bare floors were as austere, half the year, as oil-cloth or cement. Men and boys had no under-clothing or night gowns, and got into beds of ice—no woolen sheets, but cotton ones, and they spooned, or hutched up cold feet to get warm, and radiated their body heat to warm the bed—the bed should have warmed them. Bed rooms were as frigid as the ice section in Dante's Hell, where sinners from the tropics eternally froze, while Eskimos fried in the boiler rooms. Gen. Sherman can talk about war being hell, but war is not a circumstance with domestic conditions sixty years ago in this climate. But now furnaces give houses the winter climate of Cuba—it is jolly to go to bed, and to get up, mornings, is heaven. Under the old regime, to pull on a pair of frozen breeches and stockings and shoes was like drawing on sections of stove pipe and slippers of frosted metal. And there were then no easy chairs and lounges—the sick could not be made restful on furniture that was contrivances of torture. And no such thing as a rest room, a warm bath room and closet in the house. How did folks endure it when mercury ranged twenty-five to forty degrees below zero, and the air going as many miles an hour was full of icicle poniards? That old order of things for whites was hardly above the barbarism of Indians. The truth is, the earth has not been a comfortable and decent place to live in till the last fifty, perhaps forty, years.

The one respect in which we have lost ground is, the dearth of good hired help in house and on farm. Girls decline to work in kitchens, as they feel they are looked down upon and disgraced by doing menial work, and they go into factories, stores, millinery shops, etc., deeming that employment more genteel, and in the end get less net recompense than in the old, hated places. But it is not disgraceful to be a good cook, a neat house-keeper, a deft server at table. Nevertheless, in the personal equation, their thinking so makes it so —for them.

Well, somehow we have grown, and let me show how:

Additions to City.—The original plat of Washington was very small—just a little huddle of land around the square. The trouble in all pioneer settlements, in Illinois and Iowa, seventy-five to one hundred years ago, was, no one had faith in the outcome of the west, nor provided for the future with any prevision, wise or otherwise. In laying out towns now, folk forecast and anticipate all things possible. Daniel Webster, giant intellect as he had, scoffed at the vast Oregon country—"would never, could never be settled, worth nothing," "supreme folly." Our pioneers had the same scant notion as to the rich Mississippi valley. It was hard getting here, there were no advantages, comforts, conveniences when they got here, the prairie would never have habitants—freeze, blow away—absurd! Not an optimist among them, unless it was Norman Everson; every one a pessimist, a knocker, had a grouch, had it in for the country. Everson came in '41, and believed that folk would be glad to skip the heavily wooded lands in Ohio and Indiana and take this rich land ready for the plow; it would enrich any man who settles on it, cultivates it, stays by it. He was right, but few shared his views. So they laid out a picayune town, anticipated not a single need of a village bound to expand, provided no sewerage, no water, no light, "no nothing." Every man dug a shallow well and scuffled with the noxious germs in it; his wife threw the slops on the ground for the sun to take care of, if he would; shallow drains carried off the rainfall; folks had no walks, and wallowed in mud; in a civic way they lived from hand to mouth, and were wasteful. In the matter of sewerage we have sunk enough money in shallow ditches and drains —one administration ripping up what another had put down—to have now the best sewered city in the state if an engineer had given us a system and we had worked it out in detail. But no one believed the town would ever be any thing but a measly hamlet—why monkey with sewers and things? People were not up in sanitation then. Let us not blame them. The people perish from lack of knowledge.

The early ones had claims near the town site, and as the burg grew these were platted, that is, they crumbled into the "city," as farms drop into the Missouri river, and re-appeared as additions. There is a south, a south-west, an east Washington, a west addition, a north-east, a Chilcote addition, eighty acres in the last in the south-east; Wm. E. Chilcote laid out a few blocks as a sub-division; Ashby's addition had four blocks, Crandall's sub-division a few blocks, Conger's addition, but it was never platted, left in acre tracts; James H. and Margaret Young each made a twenty-acre addition in the north-west; James Dawson, McConaughy and Len. Smouse each laid out two blocks, Cunningham and Knupp two, but the big things were these:

One of Dr. Chilcote's strokes of humor was calling the flat frog land north of the Rock Island tracks "The Heights." The name stuck. In 1875 he and J. M. Denny, Col. Cowles and John A. Henderson paid to the Chet Weed estate six thousand dollars for sixty-eight acres there. They laid off fifteen blocks, eight lots, four by eight rods in size, to the block, though a few lots were smaller. That plat took about half the land. Lots sold at one hundred to two hundred dollars, and in later years as high as six hundred dollars. The growth of that suburb was astonishing. In '66 I rode horse all over that fenceless expanse, cumbered with only one homestead, the Botkin, afterwards the Thomas, one hundred and sixty acres. That is now the most attractive part of the city.

Win Smouse is "the Little Giant" of city real estate, and has done noteworthy things, that enriched himself and benefited and beautified the town, enhanced it, enlarged it. In 1882 he created "Eastside," the twenty-eight acre tract where the Wallace school stands, that he turned into ninety-eight lots. He paid seventy dollars an acre for it. It was an impulse, a sudden whim, almost a caprice; when he rode horse out in the mud that wet spring to the auction sale, he had no notion of buying, but a swift vision flashed on him, he obeyed the call of the wild, and realized a lovely suburb. To the east was a tract of forty-nine acres, that he paid thirty-eight dollars an acre for in '84. It continued across the tracks, and Jackson Roberts bought twenty-seven acres at thirty-seven dollars per acre. Smouse turned his tract into one hundred and thirty lots, and they made his "Second Addition." In developing these two city adjuncts, he gave us his first fine object lesson in the construction of streets, making walks, planting trees, etc. He was and is a real landscape gardener. Those two tracts, being close in, were quickly sold and covered with a superior class of houses.

In 1892, he created Highland Park addition of four hundred and thirty lots, laying out a six-acre park and an artificial lake of three acres, with boats, boating house, etc. This was formed from the one hundred and forty Thomas tract, that cost him one hundred and five dollars per acre. Win and brother Len. had bought of Mrs. Everson twenty-five acres at three hundred dollars per acre, north of the railway tracks, and Win bought of her forty acres at two hundred dollars per acre, where the pipe organ factory stood, also twenty acres from Ab. Anderson at one hundred and ten dollars per acre, twenty acres from Parkinson at eighty-five dollars an acre, and six and a half acres from Frank Graves at seventy-five dollars an acre. These tracts, together with the Everson tracts, made the Columbian addition, two hundred and ninety-six lots. He improved them, set out hundreds of trees, graded streets, etc., and the big sewer headed that way.

West of Highland Park he bought of Geo. S. McKay fifty-three acres for six thousand dollars, and sold it in acre bunches. From Bowland he bought five and a half acres for three thousand dollars. It lies between Highland Park and the Heights, and is called his north-east addition. Sighing for other worlds to conquer, he expended twenty thousand dollars and a lot of Napoleonic energy on the town of Haskins, in 1902, a one hundred and twenty-acre town site covered with structures. Withal, he has been our greatest builder of blocks, stores, houses, and his trading enterprises have extended from Dan to Beersheba. In '82 he put up the Columbian block, in '93 the ornate house the Commercial Club bought, and houses no end. As a sagacious man of affairs he might truly say, as Danton said at the Revolutionary tribunal in Paris, "I was known tolerably well in the Revolution, I did not lack energy."

Well, all these additions pushed out the bounds of the city till now the corporation embraces one and a half square miles, and commercial travelers and other visitors say it is one of the prettiest little cities in Iowa. It is, indeed, a comfortable and comforting place to live in.

CHAPTER XVIII.

POLITICS, CAMPAIGNS, ELECTIONS.

Men love to fight—perhaps women, too. It is an instinct we inherited from our forebears, the animals we ascended from. An animal at bay will fight till it dies. It must, in self-defense. Men never become so highly civilized and angelic that those combative lumps behind the ears entirely disappear. At bottom, we are fighting animals. In the natural state human tribes were ever at war. It was the great merit of Rome that she stopped the tribal wars that were decimating mankind. She would have world-wide peace if she had to fight for it. She conquered a peace. Those reduced tribes she brought into her vast empire, let them bring their mob of gods along and set them up in her Pantheon and worship them in perfect toleration—they could do as they pleased, only fighting had to stop. Politics is the modern substitute for war. It is exciting, it is cruel, it lets you break heads and smash noses once in a while—it is quite satisfactory. Washington county has had her share of this rude fun.

The record of our elections for the first decade of our history from 1839, is as hopelessly lost as certain of "the lost books of Livy." No great loss. In that decade there was no political interest, as local offices were without enticing pay or held in honor. Salaries were ridiculous, mere shrimps. Party lines were not drawn till '46 when the territory came in as a state. The county was generally anti-democratic; whig and republican had it their own way. Pro-slavery men, that is, democrats at that day, naturally emigrated to Missouri, a slave state, while anti-slavery folk as naturally came to Iowa, a state that expressly came in as a free state to balance Florida, a slave state that was admitted at the same time, to maintain equilibrium. And yet Iowa was democratic quite a while, four times electing Gen. A. C. Dodge delegate in congress, and sending him and Gen. Jones to the United States senate, but Kirkwood beat him for governor.

The first spirited local contest was over county judge in '57, and its temperature was about two hundred and fifty degrees in the shade. S. P. Young had seven hundred and seven votes, Dickey, democrat, seven hundred and ten;

E. Ross, three hundred and thirty-five. By throwing out the irregular vote in Cedar, arbitrators J. R. Lewis, Jas. Dawson and Duke Story declared Young elected, he having six hundred and ninety-four votes; Dickey, six hundred and ninety-two; Ross, two hundred and eighty-seven. Heat under many collars. Suppose we count Cedar and toss out Jackson that had given Young, nine; Dickey, eighteen; Ross, sixteen? Young proposed another election—he did not want to serve on the present basis. But he did serve, and so well, he was twice re-elected.

All agree that the campaign of 1860 was primus—nothing like it, before or since. Iowa was too raw and infantile to have taken part in that most unique of all campaigns, 1840—Tippecanoe and Tyler too, log cabins on wheels, hard cider aboard, coon skins nailed to the doors, and Tom Corwin playing the immortal oratorical clown. The campaign of '60 was pitched on a higher note. There was moral flavor in it, that raised it in dignity to a high mathematical power, as it were, and even to heights of moral sublimity. Country, liberty, the rights of man were involved in it, and over it all lay the dread shadow of possible civil war. So there was a verve about it that distinguished it as sui generis.

Who can ever forget the vast mass meetings, where earnest orators addressed acres of passionate people, and literally converted men by the acre, scooping honest, generous democrats into republican ranks as Billy Sunday dragoons sinners. That art of oratory has long since lost its charm and power. Editorials may now and then change votes, but stump speeches do only this—confirm a man in his political faith, which may be but a prejudice—warm him up like left-over potatoes for breakfast, interest the average voter enough in the campaign to go and vote.

Who can forget the bands, the singing of the Lombards, the thrills of fine speaking, the wild beauty of torch-light processions, the stately march of the Wide Awakes with hats and capes that needed to be ample to protect clothes from dripping kerosene lamps hung on sticks slung over the shoulders. In the tread of those illuminated hosts a keen ear could hear the tramp, tramp, tramp of hundreds of thousands of armed men a year later; a prescient eye could see armies hurrying southward, the sun glinting on myriads of gun-barrels. It was a prophetic campaign, and a thing inspiring awe.

The Lincoln electors had one thousand seven hundred and twenty-six votes in this county, the Douglas democrats, one thousand and fifty-seven; Bell, fifty-seven; Breckenridge, twenty. The population was fourteen thousand two hundred and thirty-five.

The Granger campaign in 1873 was a hot tamale, nay, a desperate thing. That was the year of the alleged "Great Crime," that we did not know any-

WILLIAM SAID

JOHN W. PRIZER

WILLIAM WILSON

thing about till 1896 when Bryan and Coin's school discovered the mare's nest. With a catchy cry of "Anti-Monopoly" and with a club for exacting, discriminating railroads, the Grangers fought like fury, and whipped the Grand Old Party out of its boots. B. F. Brown and E. F. Brockway beat David Bunker and Wm. Allen for the legislature by three hundred and seventy-eight and three hundred and twenty-six, respectively. Editor A. S. Bailey defeated John Alex. Young for auditor by sixty-seven, and John thought chaos and old night had come again, not seeing that it was the best thing that ever happened to him. Clara Harris led E. R. Eldridge for county superintendent by three hundred and three, and John W. Anderson beat Capt. Woodford for treasurer by four hundred and eight, and so on. Some of the Granger laws stood the test in the United States supreme court, and on the whole their agitation and legislation did good. But with their workable notions were ideas that never could be operative, and they made so many promises, no doubt in good faith, that they could not make good, reaction set in, and the next year the republicans vaulted back into the saddle and stayed there ever after, though the broncho bucked pretty hard sometimes.

The Granger movement was like la grippe,—you could not predict how it would leave a republican who had seceded. In fact, many republicans never came back, but lapsed from one fad and heresy into another, like a man caught in quick-sand,—descending into greenbackism, into socialism, into free silver, democracy, and may the Lord have mercy on their souls!

The greenback campaign in 1879 was a desperate thing, too. But the gracious Nemesis that came to the aid of the grand old party in 1874 intervened again, and the elephant tore his way through the fiat jungle at great rate, trampling down the dreamers. Republican majorities in '79 ranged from five hundred to eight hundred odd.

Then came the constitutional prohibition amendment canvass of 1882, which was no less fierce for being non-partisan. Sentiment swept the county by a big majority.

The Blaine-Cleveland campaign of 1884 was watched here with great anxiety. It was pitched low. Mugwumpism was born. Nasty stories were told of both nominees. Beecher, who had been there himself, gave Grover a character, and many thought it a case of pot calling kettle white. Malignity, scandal, Ananiasism, a swarm of lies, and finally Old Burchard of rum, Romanism and rebellion fame, pursued Blaine, and republican journals deserted him only less numerously than democratic papers repudiated Bryan in '96. It was a Sheol of a time. Things were so muddled, that The Nation newspaper, which was the weekly edition of the New York Evening Post, and the most scholarly and critical journal in the country, though edited in heaven, proclaimed two standards of morals for the sexes, and said it was vastly more important to the universe for Marie Halpin to have been chaste than for Grover Cleveland, her alleged paramour.

Well, Blaine went down under four thousand votes cast in New York city for Gen. Ben Butler, greenback nominee for president, his votes being fraudulently counted by Tammany for Cleveland. It was the first time the grand old party had been beaten in the nation since '56, and who does not recall the perfectly sickly feeling republicans had? It seemed as if the bottom had fallen out of the whole secular order of things—the universe had gone to everlasting smash—only it hadn't. We were not used to defeat, and couldn't take it with any grace at all.

From time immemorial any sort of a ballot had been used here. Ballots were left in stores, in election booths, in saloons, and peddled on the streets by candidates and their friends and partisans. The electioneering was funny, and if a vote was bought, buyer collared buyee, took him to the booth and saw that the ballot went into the box. In factory towns and slummy cities the vote was debauched. America went to the antipodes to get a corrective in the Australian ballot. It was as big as a barn door, but it did business by freeing the voter—he could in secret vote as he pleased. We used that ballot first in this county in 1892.

Then it occurred to a good many that we had a surfeit of politics in annual elections. Hundreds of indifferent and bored voters would not go to the polls if the weather or roads were bad—they would rather go to prayer meeting or recite the catechism. So, to get rid of redundant politics, we got biennial elections in 1906, and right off we had more politics than ever—had politics to burn, only it wouldn't burn any more than clouds in a thunder storm.

Nor was that the limit—the dear "Peepul" had no show, some said, in nominating conventions—the politicians euchred them—we must have primary elections, and we got the first one on June 2, 1908, on the U. S. senatorship, and Allison won by some ten thousand majority in the state. As Allison made the mistake of his life by dying the next August, it all had to be done over at the general election on November 4, '08, and Cummins beat Lacey decisively. All the state, district, judicial and county officers submitted to the same ordeal. The last senatorial primary in this county stood for two thousand two hundred and fifty dollars expense, but the state paid half of it.

What the next political fad may be, no one can guess.

Some famous men have talked politics in this county—Wendell Phillips, Fred Douglass, U. S. Senators J. C. Burroughs, James Harlan, J. W. Grimes, Jas. F. Wilson, Allison; Governors Kirkwood, Shaw, Cummins; Generals

A. C. Dodge, J. B. Weaver, Fitz Henry Warren; Bryan, Henry Clay Dean, et al.

Here is another version of the Dean-Morgan incident. Hon. M. Goodspeed sat by Morgan and heard it all, and his memory is good. His version is likely to be the correct one. In the fall of '60 Dean spoke to an immense crowd on the east side of the court house in the square. He was a comical looking man, short, rotund, dirty, small sunken piggy eyes, who carried everything in front of his spine, hardly a thing about him to indicate his striking individuality, mother-wit and powerful intellect. He had just been chaplain of the U. S. senate, and was bragging about the democratic party, the big things it had done, it had never made mistakes or mis-appropriated public funds, and he challenged any one present to cite an instance of the latter. Up piped Morgan's squeaky treble voice, "I can tell you."

An electric thrill went through the crowd.

"When? Where?" asked Dean.

"When congress paid you for your prayers."

Crowd: "Put him out!"

Dean: "No, no, let him remain where he is. I thank God I never shall pray for you till I pray for the redemption of the brute creation."

Goodspeed says the crowd, mostly democrats, thought the retort was sharp, but Dean himself admitted, years after, that he was never so gravelled and neatly and effectively winged by a critic's shot.

The funniest political incident in our county history came as an inspiration to the humorist Jonathan H. Wilson—his bringing of Kirkwood to town. Kirkwood and Gen. A. C. Dodge were rival nominees for governor in '59. The men were utterly unlike in appearance, temperament, spirit—Kirkwood a slovenly man, careless in dress, common as daylight, while Dodge was by nature an aristocrat, dainty in dress, dignified, proper; very chesty, traveling on his shape, courtly in manners, a gentleman of the old school. These men, in joint debate, were coming here from Sigourney. Geo. D. Woodin was driving Kirkwood. Between 2 and 3 p. m., John H. Bacon drove a swell barouche out to bring in Dodge, in style. Brother Jonathan saw John and divined his purpose. In the same instant he saw two yoke of oxen and a wagon with an empty hay-rack, standing on the square, and a picture flashed on him. He found the owner of the rig, easily negotiated the rental of the uncouth outfit for two hours, when the tickled farmer learned the object of it, and grabbing the g'ad Wilson whoa-hawed 'em down to the creek on the Sigourney road. Bacon swelled by, Dodge inside, and John wondered what Wilson was doing down there. He found out about an hour later, at the hotel. Jonathan introduced himself to Kirkwood, and said, "I want you in there." "In there?"

grinned Kirkwood. "Yes, in there, Governor." He caught on "immegit," and climbed aboard and chuckled clear to the square at the homespun humor of it. Jonathan kept pace with the oxen and chariot, followed by a retinue of shouting folks, and he whoa-hawed the motors up to the Yellow Brick corner, and by this time the whole town was onto the joke, and as Wilson plied the g'ad on the leaders and the wheelers and made 'em squirm and crowd and loll out their tongues, the people yelled and laughed and screamed, and gave Kirkwood the greatest ovation ever. He stood up and bowed acknowledgments, and grinned, and expectorated tobacco juice, and he couldn't have worn a larger smile unless his face had been enlarged and his ears set back on the rear of his neck. Dodge and Bacon saw the ridiculous spectacle with emotions, Dodge knowing that his egg was hard-boiled, and as for Bacon he was so chagrined he said then and there he would never vote another democratic ticket, and he kept his word. One circuit of the square was not enough to satisfy the people and take the tickle out of their funny bones, so Wilson sailed round again, nothing loath. He was having the time of his life.

In '61, Senator Harlan ordered an election for postmaster here. Andrew Kendall, C. H. Wilson and Vint Andrus ran, and Kendall won. But Lincoln appointed Editor A. R. Wickersham of the Press because it was his settled policy to stimulate the papers to stand loyally by the government. Wickersham held into Lincoln's second term. After Andrew Johnson came in, John Wiseman, a briefless lawyer but a delicious tenor singer, sought the post office, was named, but the senate would not confirm him. A little secret plebiscite here settled his case. Harlan wired Lewis & Bennett and a merchant I will not name, "Shall Wiseman be appointed?" "No." "Shall Horatio Anderson?" "No." "Shall Col. H. R. Cowles be confirmed?" "Yes." And it was done before Cowles knew a thing about it. He had not sought the place. It was a genuine surprise party to him. One of the trio said to him on the street, "You are P. M." "The —— I am," he exclaimed.

Usually, a school director election is tame, but now and then it was great fun, and astonishing votes were recorded. One of the most amusing was engineered by Joe Rader, the most humorous and persistent tease ever. I forget the issue—probably there was none—but it was the personalities that lent piquancy to the contest. "Billy" Wilson, Jr., as he was affectionately called by everybody, for he was one of the most useful men in our history, had been nominated for director, when Joe trotted out Maggie Axtell, a "character" in petticoats. The populace did not care a bawbee, but saw a chance for fun, and snaking men to the polls became a riot of mirth and a jolly jamboree. All day electioneerers and laughing fans pulled and hauled voters to the booth. The vote was unprecedented, exceeding that at a national

HORACE H. WILLSON

JOHN P. HUSKINS

D. B. PARKINSON

WILLIAM B. LEWIS

election. Maggie came in first under the wire by a few votes. Wilson saw the fun of it—a few days later.

Dr. W. F. Rodman was a democrat of mild manners, and enjoyed getting Dr. Chilcote in a crowd and telling a remark he made during the first Lincoln campaign. At a night spectacle fire balls, soaked in turpentine, were safely thrown by hand if one were quick about it. Chilcote grabbed one, but he had a woman's defective clavicle and couldn't throw any straighter than a cross-eyed man, but he did slam the fire ball into an open building. Rodman screamed, "Doctor, you might fire the house." "D—— the building, hurrah for Lincoln!"

The Wide Awakes went to every town in the county, and to Fairfield, Mt. Pleasant, Muscatine, etc. One night about sixty rode horses from here to Pilotburg, and as many of them had not been on a horse for years, there was so great a demand for arnica and court plaster, the drug stores were bankrupted. It was the sternest reality of the campaign.

'Squire Anson Moore, of Brighton, had striking individuality and keen humor. A townsman had been elected to some office, and came to the 'Squire to "qualify," as he said. Moore said, "I can swear you in, but all —— can't qualify you."

The Greeley campaign, though it had a pathetic, tragic sequel, had amusing local features. Not many republicans flocked to Uncle Horace's standard, and many democrats flouted him. Gen. A. R. Z. Dawson, a republican, was made chairman of the democratic county committee, and one rainy day, after much advertising, and a day of wallowing in mud, and the slick hickory pole slipping back several times, Dawson and Lyman Whitcomb finally got a flagstaff set up on the south side. Many times it had slipped and sloshed around, and the gallant general in hip boots addressed many pungent remarks to "the god of things as they are." Republicans meanly joshed the toilers a good deal, but they had bad luck with their own taller pole on the north side. The flag ropes were cut one night. Whitcomb, though a democrat, was furiously mad, offered ten dollars for the discovery of the "galoot" who did it, and paid for a new set of ropes.

It hardly fits in here, but it has to go "sommers." There was to be a celebration here in honor of some foreign hero, whether Kossuth or Garibaldi, no matter. Howard M. Holden was chosen to respond to a certain toast. When called, he rose, appeared greatly surprised and flustered, prefaced his off-hand remarks with a long apology for not being prepared, but he would do the best he could under the circumstances, but he was sorry, both for himself and the audience, that notice had not been given him, etc. A good while after, in hoeing and cleaning out the bank where he served as cashier, the manuscript of his extempore speech was found, verbatim as he had reeled it off, when he "fulmined over Greece." The town laughed over his extemporaneity. They say he had a hard time explaining it to his solid girl.

In the Blaine-Cleveland campaign the republicans missed out once or twice on night parades. The democrats matched our displays, if they did not exceed them, in numbers and brilliant pageantry, particularly the equestrian show-out, with torches. We led off in that, and fancied that the spectacle was as brilliant as Vauxhall. But the country, not the city, raises horses, and the democrats brought in a caravan of them. The entire space around the square, Cleveland night, was solid with Centaurs. Every horse's neck was clothed with "O thunder," as the envious, jealous republicans said. Many rustic horses "raired" and pitched and snorted, and waltzed on hind legs, in a panic of fear of the lights, noise of drums and the shoutings of the democratic captains. This veracious historian has to admit that for once the democrats kept us busy in this county.

This recalls a ludicrous incident on a Memorial Day when Judge Dewey was marshal. He wanted a white horse. Humorist Sheriff Tom Johnson loaned his, knowing how very touchy it was about martial music. When the band struck into a dirge, the splendid steed went into the air, and wished to shake hands with all and sundry. It turned and faced the band till it came near with its throbs and muffles, then wheeled and ran like the wind several rods, and turned again to watch the dreadful thing. Again and again it cut that caper, much to the irritation of the gallant rider. As all knew the judge was a clever horseman, and could not be thrown, they enjoyed the fun, which rather destroyed the solemnity of the day.

It was worth the price of admission to see and hear Everson and Patterson discuss politics on the street. There was no attempt at argument, and logic and fact and courtesy were interlopers; they'd raise their voices to the highest pitch, shout, scream, gesticulate violently; pay no attention to each other's statements, but yell and sweat. Nothing more absurd was ever seen in our politics.

Some thirty years ago we tried a primary system of nominating county tickets, for two or three years. The country fancied the city beat them to base in nominating conventions, but the country was the first to tire of the new scheme, as the plan was expensive, costing lots of time and mileage to buttonhole voters, and all gladly went back to the old system. Van Doren was running for auditor or treasurer, but being an absent-minded but really a very able clerical man, he strolled, unawares, over into Keokuk county, and was working those aliens hard before he learned by their grins and winks that he was beyond his bailiwick. He took a few more turns of his inevitable comforter around his neck and hiked back to his jurisdiction.

A republican orator was speaking in Uncle John Iams' school house, and voided the stale hot air about poor boys in this country having a chance to be presidents of the United States, and he punched this hole in the doughnut—"who knows but some boy in this audience may become president." This convulsed Iams, and he slapped his knees, roaring with laughter, and shouting, "Hell! think of a president from Dutch Creek."

At this date, the summer of 1909, the general aspect of politics leads one to remark that there is no politics visible to the naked eye or even to high magnifiers. The tariff debate in the special session blots party distinctions. Democrats are as keen for "pork" as are republicans. Even the holy insurgents want to snatch chunks of pork here and there, as La Follette on paper and wood pulp, since his state makes paper; southern planters for sugar, rice, pineapples; California for lemons; Tillman for a few cups of tea; Dolliver prefers pork without cotton or woolen fibers in it as butter without hired girl's hairs in it. Cummins wants pork in the guise of free tapioca pudding, and gives small hunks of pork to Iowa farmers on hides, while saying that the tariff does farmers no good, or hardly any good. Republicans, democrats, insurgents are practically all alike.

What reduced political parties to this common, neutral paste or mush? It was that glacier Roosevelt operating in the last four strenuous years. He triturated parties into pulp, into drift. Every thing he did was done in a way either to tickle the people by its outlandishness, as his spelling reform that fell flat, his undignified swatting of nature fakirs, his storm-day horseback ride to shame lazy army officers, his absurd hunts of bob cats and black bears, his going down in a sub-marine boat, etc. Or to enthuse the Hoi Polloi by attacking corporations, by assailing judges who did not decide his rash way, by vigorously punching Judge Parker, Gov. Haskell, Senator Foraker, Bryan. Or to electrify the people by his original and meritorious proposition to conserve national resources, etc. Or to stampede timid business by throwing populace and banks into a panic. He won partisans from all parties. His ideas, manner and spirit were solvents in which parties literally dissolved. Naturally, he was so spectacular, he made more adherents than enemies. He won many thoughtful admirers and friends, but alarmed the fewer conservatives, and attracted all the undiscriminating crowd of jealous, envious folk who like to see more prosperous people assailed and put in soak, whether justly or no. Certain types of people are beginning to murmur because President Taft does not do things in Roosevelt's frantic, half crazy way. When folk get used to high seasoning, a chief magistrate who does not shake peppers, salve with mustard, dope with tobasco, and drench with vinegar, seems tame, and splits observers into factions or parties. Roosevelt disintegrated parties; Taft may re-establish party lines. But at present, republicans, democrats, insurgents are as like as peas in a pod.

CHAPTER XIX.

WASHINGTON COUNTY IN WAR.

We do not claim Timothy Brown, the soldier of the Revolution, who died in this county and was buried in Elm Grove with honors and with oratory by Federal Judge McPherson, nor do we claim any soldiers in the war of 1812. But we may properly count on volunteers in the Mexican war, who settled here after it. One was Capt. N. A. Holson, of Cedar township, who enlisted in March, '47, in Company D, Fourth Ohio Infantry, when sixteen years old, and was mustered out in '48, and became captain of Company E, Tenth Iowa, in the Civil war.

Thomas C. Scott, of Iowa township, was another. He went out with the First Louisiana Battalion, Company B.

Elias Leynard, of Riverside, was a third. He enlisted in the third New York, and served two years, and was wounded in the fights around Mexico City, but he got a land warrant in compensation for his services, for one hundred and sixty acres, as did Mr. Scott.

Daniel Mickey, of Oregon township, served fourteen months, and located near Brighton his one hundred and sixty acres.

Phillip Haynes, of Lime Creek, was another Mexican war soldier. Perhaps there are others.

Wm. Corbin came here from Kentucky in '41, locating four miles northeast of Washington. He served in the Black Hawk war in 1832.

But what would one think of this true statement? This county in 1860 had but fourteen thousand two hundred and thirty-five population, but under Lincoln's calls of 1861-2, she furnished one thousand two hundred and forty men, a surplus of five hundred and fifty-four. So says a report of the adjutant general and acting quartermaster general. Her quota was six hundred and eighty-six men. Think of a township like Lime Creek giving one hundred and thirty-eight men, sifted through twenty Iowa regiments and the First Connecticut Cavalry and Bird's Sharpshooters.

But remember that war is the greatest of the spectacles and illusions, and therefore the most popular, soul-stirring, brain-stimulating, character-building thing that ever came down the pike. Of course, we say it is horrible, but it is an incontrovertible fact of history, that war has been the one sovereign educator of mankind. People are bound to suffer and die, anyhow—be mowed down by the pestilence that walketh in darkness and the destruction that wasteth at noonday—if it is not the ravage of war, it is calamity by famine, by cholera, by bubonic plague and Black Death, by tuberculosis, typhoid, syphilis, etc. As compared with "germs," a battle is a quite safe place to be in.

Nowadays, a nation must give the world a good reason for declaring war. Whatever the ostensible reason, the real reason is, the nation is mad. When the south shot at Fort Sumter on April 12, 1861, and Cubans sank the Maine, in 1898, we just had to let our people fight—they would have it so, they were so mad. We call the impulse of such uprisings "patriotism"—no matter what one calls it, it comes anyway. It is hard to analyze patriotism, it is so composite, has so many elements, is so subtle and elusive a sentiment, but at bottom, when all is said, we organized armies and "went hell-bent," because we were mad through and through.

In obeisance to that fit of righteous indignation, as the north would not stand for a divided nation—one government is bad enough, two governments would be intolerable—President Lincoln, three days after Sumter was fired on, called for seventy-five thousand men to save the Union. That number looks ridiculous now. The truth is, Gen. Sherman, by long odds the greatest genius of the war, was the only noted man who appreciated the gravity of the political and military situation, and when he told how many men it would take and how long they would be re-establishing national authority, people said he was "crazy," but he was the sole sane man in the whole bunch. In contrast, Seward, secretary of state and dreamer-in-general, with his silly "ninety days" as the limit of the war, seems like an idiot. One regiment was enough for Iowa. Gov. Kirkwood called for it April 17. His match touched off a keg of powder here. A war meeting was held that night in the court house in the square, and Capt. H. R. Cowles of the Washington Light Guards, organized in '58, pledged twenty-five of his men as a basis of a company of eighty-four officers and men. It was the germ of the first company for this county. Cowles was its captain, A. L. Thompson and N. P. Chipman first and second lieutenants. They were ordered to report at Keokuk May 25. A dinner was given them in the square the 23d, and the occasion was crammed with emotions, you may imagine. The boys became Company H, Second Iowa, and were destined to have fighting plenty, getting their baptism of fire and blood at Fort Donelson.

The second company was the Kirkwood Guards, B. Crabb captain, W. P. Crawford and G. G. Bennett lieutenants. The quota being full, they were

Col. Henry R. Cowles

Major S. E. Rankin

Gen. N. P. Chipman

OFFICERS OF THE REBELLION

not accepted then, but in July they were ordered to Burlington, and became Company H, Seventh Iowa.

The Washington Rifles, W. B. Bell captain and S. E. Rankin and A. A. Rodman lieutenants, was the next company to leave for Davenport, August 20, '61. Just before marching to the depot a member named John Morton, being probably insane, shot himself through the heart, but no G. A. R. post was named for him, poor fellow! upset by excitement. This body became Company C, Eighth Iowa.

The Richmond Guards were the next, becoming Company E, Tenth Iowa, N. A. Holson captain and R. J. Mohr and W. W. Purcell lieutenants—four companies enlisting in '61. Later companies were recruited, in whole or in part, in this county, as F, Eleventh, Capt. Moore; I, Thirteenth, Capt. Elrod; K, Thirteenth, Capt. Woodford; I, Eighteenth, Capt. Blanchard; C. Nineteenth, Capt. Stanton; A, Twenty-fifth, Capt. Palmer; I, Twenty-fifth, Capt. Russell; E, Thirtieth, Capt. Burgess; K, Thirtieth, Capt. Cook.

But one draft was made in this county, in October, '64. By special effort Iowa, Lime Creek, Cedar, Jackson, Washington and Seventy-Six townships raised their quotas, but English River was stuck for ten men, plus ten alternates; Brighton for four of each; Dutch Creek ten; Oregon four; Marion six; Clay three; Crawford seven; Highland two; Franklin six.

I have copied from the adjutant general's reports a complete roster of the soldiers credited to Washington county, and have gone over the lists carefully with Cols. Palmer and Bell, Captains Boyer, Young, Cocklin and Gray, and with J. W. Morton, Porte Lewis, Marion O'Loughlin, D. J. Eichelberger, Tom Allen et al., and tried hard to make it accurate. This county raised fourteen full companies, had twenty-three staff and field officers, thirty-two captains, thirty-four first and forty second lieutenants—one thousand two hundred and forty men, all told. But Tom Allen makes one thousand four hundred and six. He checked the names of our boys in the adjutant general's report, correcting errors therein; for instance, he found there a dozen or score of his Lime Creek men were credited to Dayton, Bremer county, who belonged in our Daytonville. Anyway, it is a great showing. Read this list of Homeric heroes:

SECOND IOWA INFANTRY—COMPANY H.

H. R. Cowles, Capt., Lt. Col.; N. P. Chipman, Adj.; J. M. Porter, Capt.; A. L. Thompson, 1 Lt.; Lem Donovan, 1 Lt.; Hiram Scofield, 2 Lt.; J. M. Davidson, 2 Lt.; J. H. Stewart, 2 Lt.; D. M. Williams, 2 Lt.; J. W. Harper, S.; W. G. Hamill, S.; Wm. Wright, S.; J. M. Miller, S.; C. T. Jones, S.;

G. W. Neal, S.; J. W. Wilson, S.; S. A. Maley, S.; I. G. White, C.; Wm. Dawson, C.; James McKinney, C.; J. A. Easton, C.; Wm. McCurdy, C.: Hugh Amarine, Moses Amarine, J. W. Andrews, C. J. Arnold, Fred Ault. D. L. Aughey, Hervey Bell, A. J. P. Barnes, H. Barton, D. S. Beaty, A. Brawner, Jos. Belville, R. M. Boyd, J. C. Blue, Peter Boggs, John Brokaw. J. R. Budd, Stephen Callvert, E. Cochran, J. S. Carson, R. H. Coe, Andrew Condon, A. Crawford, J. N. Crawford, Thos. Curran, J. M. Currie, Levi Crouch, W. B. Compton, S. L. Corbin, G. W. Corbin, T. S. Coppock, Wm. Creath, W. H. Cahail, F. M. Cahail, J. R. Cooper, J. M. Dick, J. H. C. Dawson, M. G. Davidson, A. M. Easton, James Embree, Robert Easton, Benj. Edwards, S. M. Eicher, F. L. Elliott, J. C. Eichelberger, Daniel Eckerman, D. C. Eckerman, R. B. Funston, Marvin French, S. A. Frisbee, J. S. Funk, H. C. Fleak, G. B. Farley, J. R. Fullerton, James Gilmore, J. W. Griffith, Robert Glasgow, Alex. Graham, R. A. Hamill, J. N. Hamill, Wm. Hudson, B. H. Hammond, J. M. Haynes, J. T. Husband, D. H. Hainer, W. I. Herritt, J. A. Hight, Ed. Hoxworth, W. V. Johnson, G. C. Kelley, Moses Kettering, Aaron Lindsley, C. W. Lease, C. W. Lemon, Jas. Murkin, W. S. Matthews, J. H. Matthews, W. T. Matthews, I. J. Moore, Wm. Minick, P. L. McKinne, Thos. McCutchan, Joshua Murray, J. W. Miller, Albert McLane, James McAvoy, James McAbbey, J. S. McClelland, L. O. Montgomery, Oliver Montgomery, Jesse Malone, Ananias Miles, L. W. Neiswanger, O. P. Neal, Henry Nichols. W. C. Oburn, Mark Oats, Finley Paxton, B. R. Parker, F. M. Parish, Sol. Peak, O. S. Pickens. Theo. Pyle, P. Peters, D. N. Robb, H. C. Russell, Jesse Rogers, Michael Reinert, J. H. Romine, Wyatt Ragden, J. S. Risocker, Elbert Sisson, J. T. Shaw, Sebastian Shaffner, Phillip Swisher, W. A. Stiles, E. B. Stewart, C. N. Stewart, M. V. Smith, John Stephenson, Amos Swan, B. R. Stickley, Monroe Shepard, Sam Swick, Jas. D. Swick, L. L. Teas, W. A. Tedford, C. H. Tarr, Richard Taylor, W. E. Varney, John Van Sant, W. J. Vincent, J. J. Van Nostrand, W. H. H. Van Dyke, J. W. S. Van Dyke, J. S. Williams, T. Y. Williams, R. R. Williams, Wm. Wallace, J. B. Young.

First regiment of three year men enlisted in the state, May, '61, mustered in at Muscatine, re-organized and veteranized in May, '64, mustered out July 12, '65, at Louisville, Ky. It had fighting plus, and then some.

THIRD IOWA INFANTRY—COMPANY G.

Silas Coryell.

FIFTH IOWA INFANTRY—COMPANY C.

Milton Campbell, J. A. Farris, John Graham, Charles Keating, D. S. McCampbell, David B. Moore.

SIXTH IOWA INFANTRY—COMPANY F.

B. F. Adams, R. B. Davis, T. L. Elliott, R. W. Elliott, R. J. Jones, W. M. Richardson, Geo. S. Richardson, W. H. Samson, A. T. Samson, John Wait, Company K, —— Berrie.

NINTH IOWA INFANTRY.

T. J. Jones, David E. Love, Joseph Powell.

ELEVENTH IOWA INFANTRY.

H. R. Anderson, Thomas Black, A. B. Taylor.

TWELFTH IOWA INFANTRY.

Wm. A. Coulthurst, Renaldo C. Taylor.

FOURTEENTH IOWA INFANTRY—COMPANY B.

Gaspar T. Husband, Jesse D. Clary.

TWENTY-FIRST IOWA INFANTRY.

Cyrus McLane, Company F.

TWENTY-SECOND IOWA INFANTRY.

Thomas Carr, D. N. Connelly, James Cornell, I. R. Grimes, W. M. Kimberley, C. W. Lowder, John Miles, J. W. Radebaugh, Simon Taylor.

SEVENTH IOWA INFANTRY—COMPANY H.

Benj. Crabb, Capt.; J. B. Hope, Capt.; W. P. Crawford, 1 Lt.; T. L. Montgomery, 1 Lt.; H. S. Kinsey, 1 Lt.; G. G. Bennett, 2 Lt.; R. N. Graham, 2 Lt.; L. C. Dawson, S.; J. H. Lewis, S.; P. H. Dayton, S.; J. M. Glasgow, C.; S. M. Logan, C.; P. R. Dick, C.; A. J. Shephard, C.; W. S. Riggs, C.; W. L. Woods, C.; S. M. Rickey, C.; A. D. Reed, C.; Alfred Gilson, C.; M. M. Stone, C.; W. A. Boyd, C.; J. A. Abbey, Hugh Andrews, Lewis Austin, W. R. Austin, W. C. Arnold, S. S. Arnold, W. W. Baninger, C. T. Bush, Swayne Beaty, S. L. Black, Charles Bloom, John Batterson, J. O. Brins, W. A. Bailey,

E. J. Badger, W. H. Carlyle, Michael Crowner, S. C. Crowner, Joseph Carr, J. R. Clark, J. D. Clause, S. S. Calhoun, I. A. Dean, Charles Evans, Charles Evans, Jr., J. F. Elliott, W. W. Edmundson, S. S. Ellsworth, Theo. Ferree, Burton Fuller, R. S. Glasgow, H. C. Gilleland, A. S. Gray, W. E. Gregg, Franklin Gregg, George Glider, Phillip Gladwin, Matthew Gordon, James Gerthoffer, Jacob Hare, G. W. Hoag, A. M. Holmes, John Holmes, Nathan Ireland, J. B. Jacobs, A. F. Johnson, E. P. Jayne, B. L. Kinsey, H. S. Kinsey, August Kensing, G. A. Logan, W. H. Lamb, D. K. Larimer, Gilbert Lowe, J. M. McConnahey, John Moore, Wm. Moore, T. J. McConnell, J. T. McConnell, J. V. McLaughlin, J. L. McDowell, G. S. McKay, T. O. Mann, J. E. Moorman, A. S. Moorman, J. S. W. Matthews, J. C. Nelson, J. O'Brien, J. S. Periton, E. A. Peckover, Wm. Phillips, Jeremiah Phillips, John Perkins, Leander Richey, W. H. Robertson, C. D. Rickey, J. D. Robinson, T. C. Robinson, W. H. Ray, Alex Ralston, W. S. Smith, George Smith, James Shields, Ambrose Shaw, C. M. Simms, W. N. Sowash, D. C. Troup, J. D. Tansey, S. R. Tansey, George Tennant, J. C. Temple, J. A. Van Atta, W. R. Van Atta, Isaac Werts, G. W. Wells, Sam Warren, J. P. Warren, W. A. Wallace, R. S. Young.

SEVENTH IOWA INFANTRY—COMPANY K.

Otho Bonser, 1 Lt.; J. E. McIntyre, S.; John Trine, C.; H. M. Starrett, C.; C. C. Strohm, C.; John Ashton, Asst. Sur.; J. H. Atwood, T. B. Atwood, C. E. Birge, H. L. Bosworth, E. J. Badger, Wm. Frame, C. F. Hessletine, W. O. Hessletine, J. W. Hall, Alfred Harvey, Asa Mendenhall, Job R. McKain, J. H. Morris, Isaiah Miller, John Roedolph, J. F. Snow, F. B. Statts.

SEVENTH IOWA INFANTRY—COMPANY I.

Joseph Abbey, J. T. McConnahey, Thomas Randleman, J. M. Temple.

S. A. Wilson was in Company A, also Chas. Evans.

Regiment mustered in at Burlington, July, '61, and mustered out July 12, '65, at Louisville, Ky.

EIGHTH IOWA INFANTRY—COMPANY C.

W. B. Bell, Capt.; S. E. Rankin, 1 Lt.; J. C. Maxwell, 1 Lt.; E. B. Plumb, 1 Lt.; A. A. Rodman, 2 Lt.; J. A. Boyer, 2 Lt.; G. W. Marsden, S.; S. T. Crawford, S.; J. G. Hight, S.; Wm. Carris, C.; S. R. Mather, C.; D. J. Palmer, C.; R. M. Kilgore, C.; J. A. Duke, C.; R. S. Young, C.; Abe Critser, C.; C. Harper, C.; S. D. Cook, Sur.; Wm. Poston, Chap.; J. E. Bailey,

REV. S. F. VAN ATTA

MRS. S. F. VAN ATTA

First pastor Second U. P. Church, Washington, shot on a gunboat by rebel guerrillas below Vicksburg

Caldwell Bailey, D. H. Bailey, David Braden, G. W. Braden, H. P. Bosworth, J. F. Boyer, Levi Barton, S. S. Cook, Ed. Carris, Seth D. Carris, J. R. Crawford, A. N. Calvert, A. F. Craven, J. H. Carl, R. J. Campbell, J. B. Dawson, John P. Dawson, Geo. F. Dawson, G. J. T. Dillie, T. W. Fosdick, J. E. Grooves, J. D. Glasgow, J. D. Goble, Henry Glider, Sam Gordon, N. R. Hall, David Helliger, W. H. Harding, Andrew Johnson, David Kilgore, D. A. Knowles, D. E. Lowry, Henry Lightner, James Marshall, John Miller, M. Mac Whinney, T. H. Maxwell, A. J. McCutcheon, J. J. McClelland, Michael McLancey, Sylvester McKinsey, John McMurray, Gideon McHenry, Marion Neal, M. L. Orr, David Parrish, S. R. Palmer, Nelson Payne, H. N. Rust, W. T. Randall, H. M. Reid, John Shaw, U. B. Smith, W. T. Smith, F. H. Smith, L. A. Stephens, C. S. Scott, Wm. Smiley, W. H. Tripp, R. C. Thompson, Leander Tilton, S. W. Thornton, Martin Van Vleit, R. O. Watson, J. Bruce Young, Jas. H. Young, Richard Young.

EIGHTH IOWA INFANTRY—COMPANY D.

Wm. A. Elliott.

EIGHTH IOWA INFANTRY—COMPANY F.

G. W. Embree, Josephus Kritey.

EIGHTH IOWA INFANTRY—COMPANY G.

J. A. Rose, F. H. Wilcox.

EIGHTH IOWA INFANTRY—UNASSIGNED.

Spencer Parkhurst.

Regiment organized in summer of '61, mustered in at Davenport, mustered out July 12, '65.

TENTH IOWA INFANTRY—COMPANY E.

N. A. Holson, Capt.; J. H. Terry, 1 Lt.; W. H. Parcell, 2 Lt.; Jas. Tustison, S.; Hiram Tatman, S.; L. M. Phillips, S.; J. A. Marling, S.; J. M. Haley, S.; Abe Dawson, C.; Jasper Cox, C.; Joe Glosser, C.; Jacob Dawson, C.; S. S. Maple, C.; N. H. Parkes, C.; M. G. Cooper, C.; G. M. Nedro, C.; C. Page, C.; Adam Kloos, C.; Willis Arnold, Fred Able, John Allen, James Bailey, Henry Barger, E. N. Bell, Oliver Berry, Charles Bradway, Abe Bunker, James Bower, Wm. Bear, Jesse Brown, Thad Britton, Martin Cummins, Samuel Curry, Benj. Demherst, John Endfield, Samuel Endfield, Solomon Endfield, Nathaniel Fulton, Wm. Gallagher, Ed. Garland, Wm. Garver, Joseph Gilbert, B. J. Godlove, Wm. Hammond, August Hemmenn, John Hare, John Hatton, Guy Hulrey, L. A. Iden, J. W. Kinney, Fred Klockentager, A. V. Lane, Ed. Loomis, C. H. Louder, Wm. Lutz, E. S. Marsh, Wm. Marsh, Alex McIlree, G. C. Montgomery, H. P. Nelson, Adam Page, Daniel Page, W. G. Parker, T. J. Parsons, M. J. Pierce, Daniel Prindle, Levi Pool, L. S. Potter, N. M. Raridaugh, T. B. Roberts, D. A. Rice, James Rogers, Wm. E. Rogers, C. J. Rose, John Santchi, John Smeltzer, I. C. Stark, V. R. Stone, J. N. Tatman, Elias Tatman, John Tatman, Phillip Thoma, S. P. Ulch, G. F. Wilson, W. L. Woodburn.

TENTH IOWA INFANTRY—COMPANY B.

Solon Shockley.

TENTH IOWA INFANTRY—COMPANY D.

Thomas Lane.

Regiment organized at Iowa City September 6, '61, mustered out August 15, '65, at Little Rock, Ark.

ELEVENTH IOWA INFANTRY—COMPANY F.

I. G. Moore, Capt.; M. Lemon, Capt.; J. D. Miles, 1 Lt. and Asst. Sur.; H. B. Trotter, 1 Lt.; W. J. Williamson, 1 Lt.; J. B. Dawson, 2 Lt.; N. L. McKinney, S.; Geo. Palmer, S.; E. G. Jackson, S.; I. N. Carr, S.; G. J. Borns, C.; R. McConnell, C.; Eph Stephens, C.; M. A. McLain, C.; Jack Coulter, C.; John Gibson, C.; B. F. Brown, C.; D. M. Anderson, David Andrews, David Black, Thos. Black, F. M. Beauchamp, Theo. Campbell, W. C. Crill, J. R. Crouch, Alex Capen, E. W. Carpenter, W. B. Crawford, John Cochran, J. G. Dickinson, G. B. Dawson, G. V. Dawson, Alex Dawson, E. R. Eldridge, D. P. Espey, J. M. Ferguson, Joel Farley, Daniel Gibson, Samuel Gordon, Jabez Hitchcock, Wm. Huffman, J. S. Hood, Jabez Hawk, Jesse Jackson, R. C. Jackson, J. J. Jackson, D. W. Jones, Thos. Jordan, James Kennedy, John Keating, S. S. Lytle, Stephen Layton, D. M. McConnaughey, Jas. McCahon, R. W. McConnell, Isaac Martin, Jas. McGowan, T. A. Morrow. Benj. McConnell, R. D. Nelson, J. R. Paxton, Henry Purrington, H. H. Riley, John Riley, John Rolston, Wm. Rickey, A. J. Scott, Wm. Smiley, Wm. Steadman, G. W. Swift, T. M. Souter, T. J. Thomas, Perry Van Winkle, W. E. Winter, W. J. Williamson, J. B. Wallace, John Williams, Wiley Whicher.

ELEVENTH IOWA INFANTRY—COMPANY B.

C. H. Best, Alonzo Butler, Sandford Carder, L. J. Dickerson, Wm. Harp, Alex Hamlerson, Alex Henderson, E. C. Housdm, Thos. Hickman, Geo. Longstroth, Philip Longstroth, W. H. C. Michael, J. A. Miller, M. L. W. McBride, Theophilus McKinnie, J. F. M. Postlethwaite, G. W. Peters, Daniel Page, Newton Printz, Geo. Shaw, E. R. Street, J. W. Sands.

ELEVENTH IOWA INFANTRY—COMPANY I.

Geo. Clinton.

THIRTEENTH IOWA INFANTRY—COMPANY I.

D. E. Cochlin, Capt.; John Elrod, Capt.; C. T. Young, 2 Lt.; J. A. Brown, 2 Lt.; W. S. Beatty, S.; J. T. Beatty, S.; Marcus Humphrey, C.; F. M. Adams, H. R. Anderson, Jacob Blick, Thos. Black, Thos. Brown, H. H. Burham, H. H. Beatty, A. L. Cochlin, F. G. Chesley, R. R. Cox, Zachariah Cox, Sidney Curtis, David Creath, G. V. Dawson, T. C. M. Dayton, J. C. Dayton, J. E. Delong, T. H. Elrod, D. J. Eichelberger, F. H. Farley, J. W. Farley, F. H. Garley, L. D. Gray, J. H. Gray, Tobias Hites, Josiah Housel, Samuel Hartzler, Hezekiah Harvey, J. E. Johnson, R. F. Kyle, Nimrod Long, F. M. Marvel, Benj. McConnell, Samuel Marvel, D. W. Mount, Jos. McKee, Sur., Henry Nichols, J. E. Ogden, Simeon Polen, David Park, W. C. Pattison, Jos. Park, David Park, J. B. Romig, Win. Romig, M. M. Runyon, Wm. Rickey, V. B. Story, Wm. Southard, G. W. Snyder, E. G. Stephens, S. P. Stephens, A. Sewall, James Sewell, A. B. Taylor, M. Whetstine, G. H. Wilson, F. Wisenaud, Stephen Werst, E. G. Whetstine, Solomon Waters, Thos. Young.

THIRTEENTH IOWA INFANTRY—COMPANY C.

Abraham Garver.

THIRTEENTH IOWA INFANTRY—COMPANY K.

S. E. Woodford, Capt.; V. W. Ambrose, Capt.; Leslie Bassett, 1 Lt.; S. D. Cook, 2 Lt.; J. W. Eyestone, 2 Lt.; J. S. Rice, 2 Lt.; W. H. Allen, 2 Lt.; J. P. McQuestrian, S.; W. L. Rogers, S.; J. M. Smiley, S.; Dan Coryell, S.; Cyrus Cox, S.; J. W. Marrell, C.; W. E. Hawthorn, C.; Jacob Hutton, C.; Harmon Cox, C.; J. C. Howe, C.; J. Mel Armstrong, C.; D. Anderson, D. H. Armstrong, W. D. Armstrong, M. J. Armstrong, John Ashworth, S. S. Atwood, J. W. Atwood, Geo. Black, Elisha Brown, Wm. Brown, J. R. Beasely, Wm. Couger, James Casey, Patrick Casey, James Clancy, D. S. Cole, O. W.

Creath, J. W. Donovan, Walter Dillon, H. E. Day, W. J. Erwin, J. H. Evans, Simon Gongever, Wm. Gemmell, Adam Hoag, S. J. Hartman, John Hicks, John Hutson, Edward Jayne, Michael Kelley, W. F. Kremer, N. M. Kinney, Samuel Krause, A. J. Krause, David Krause, John Law, W. W. Leach, B. F. Lamb, T. D. McElroy, F. B. Myers, Wm. Myers, J. W. Moore, S. C. Moses, John Neal, Drury M. O'Loughlin, Ezra M. Organ, A. Peaseley, W. W. Robison, G. G. Robison, Reuben Riley, N. Rhoads, W. M. Roland, D. A. Robertson, S. S. Smith, W. H. Snyder, Jacob Seacrist, Jacob Spainhower, W. H. H. White, J. M. Wood, Jason Wilson, Ben T. Welch, Chas. M. Wilson.

Drafted men and substitutes assigned to Thirteenth Iowa Infantry. Draft made October 24, '64:

M. D. Anderson, Benj. Ayres, Wm. Armstrong, Absalom Buckstone, E. F. Badger, Theo. Bryan, Montgomery Clark, A. P. Cavit, M. F. Childs, C. C. Cummins, J. D. Cramer, Robt. Coe, Wm. Clark, Albert Diggs, M. P. Miller, J. W. McGregor, Jos. McCorkle, Wesley Miller, Allen Meacham, Williston Plumb, Wm. Shepherd, N. B. Sayer, Larkin Stucker, W. H. Smith, Henry Scott, Wm. Sample, J. W. Taylor, F. C. Townsend, T. W. Wilson, Allen Wheatley.

The regiment was mustered in November 1, '61, for three years, veteranized in February, '64, for three years more, mustered out July 28, '65, at Louisville, Ky.

SEVENTEENTH IOWA INFANTRY—COMPANY D.

Lot Davis, Levi H. Davis, Abe Freak, J. T. Fitch, J. G. Hibbs, Isaac Herring, Wm. B. Hibbs, F. M. Henderson, D. C. Johnson, A. Mead, A. Meacham, J. D. Pickett, Abe Strayer, W. M. Spanhower, M. D. L. Spanhower, Michael Shafer, W. H. Stephenson, Wm. M. Wilson.

SEVENTEENTH IOWA INFANTRY—COMPANY F.

Wm. A. Laydick.

Mustered in at Keokuk April 16, '62 and out July 25, '65 at Louisville, Ky.

EIGHTEENTH IOWA INFANTRY—COMPANY I.

Thos. Blanchard, Capt.; S. A. Wilson, 2 Lt.; B. I. Kinsey, 2 Lt.; J. P. Wait, S.; B. D. Allen, S.; H. V. Ferguson, C.; W. H. Morgan, C.; J. R. Winders, C.; H. L. Beardsley, C.; G. W. Crawford, Jos. Demar, H. O. Evis. E. S. Gallagher, John Goodwin, Wm. Harvey, W. V. Johnston, Denton

Col. Benjamin Crabb

Col. D. J. Palmer

Col. William B. Bell

OFFICERS OF THE REBELLION

Leasure, S. N. Matthews, Israel Martin, E. O. Mitchell, Michael Myer, Jas. M. McKain, H. H. Nordyke, D. K. Patterson, J. B. Plumb, Wm. Rickey, David Roche, J. D. Rhoads, David Royer, Patrick Sugrue, Samuel Squires, A. J. Treadwell, John Whetstine, M. Whetstine, R. Whetstine, P. Whetstine, S. S. Welch.

Organized July 4, '62, at Keokuk, out July 6, '65, at Davenport.

NINETEENTH IOWA INFANTRY—COMPANY C.

B. Crabb, Col.; G. G. Bennett, Adj.; James Bennett, Ord.; T. H. Stanton, Capt. and Pay M. Gen.; J. S. Gray, Capt.; E. O. Woodford, 1 Lt.; L. B. Cocklin, 1 Lt.; Geo. Johnston, 2 Lt.; S. Farnsworth, S.; T. McCannon, S.; W. G. Simmons, S.; W. R. Jeffrey, S.; L. C. Limbocker, C.; L. W. Osburn, C.; R. M. Glasgow, C.; J. I. Durgan, C.; W. A. Smith, C.; A. H. Young, C.; T. E. Johnson, C.; Geo. Temple, C.; J. S. Anderson, Samuel Atwood, D. C. Anderson, H. W. Anderson, J. W. Anderson, Aaron Abbott, J. W. Abbott, W. A. Bailey, S. P. Beard, S. A. Black, F. Bivans, James Bennett, I. N. Brown, N. L. Babcock, J. G. Bowman, Wm. Blair, G. W. Cosner, G. D. Collins, Cyrus Condit, E. C. Condit, L. W. Carson, M. G. Davidson, Jos. A. Dawson, W. E. Dawson, Isaac Draper, J. R. Doig, S. T. Easter, John Essley, G. W. Fling, David Gilleland, L. S. Hall, N. G. Hessletine, John Hulick, J. J. Helwick, E. B. Helwick, Amos Helwick, S. B. Houston, Udolphus Johnson, W. W. Kendall, Alex Kirkpatrick, J. S. Kirkpatrick, Jacob Kime, J. M. Lytle, Wm. Lytle, R. H. Lewis, W. J. Lewis, Wm. Lea, J. T. Long, D. K. Larimer, George Maier, Charles McDonald, J. W. Morton, W. N. McConnahey, Wm. McDowell, C. M. McKenzie, Wm. McGregor, R. J. Moore, Andrew McCampbell, C. H. Nichols, G. D. Organ, Jim Porter, Wm. C. Porter, A. B. Powers, A. P. Randall, J. C. Richey, August Robinette, Talbert Russell, M. S. Russell, J. T. Robertson, G. M. Stultz, N. C. Southard, P. B. Shafer, W. M. Smith, Abe Snyder, J. M. Snyder, George Stump, Ralph Shatto, Leander Smiley, Abner Stephens, P. Swartslander, Joseph Skinner, W. D. Sherman, Israel Trostle, M. A. Tenney, S. W. Taylor, T. J. Talbot, James Van Winkle, Marshall Wilkin, John Wilson, W. A. Wallace, J. S. White, E. Worthington, J. S. Winter, J. L. Winter, Nicholas Wilkin, B. F. Wideman, J. N. Young, Jas. H. Young, R. H. Young.

Regiment mustered in at Keokuk in August, '62, mustered out at Davenport, August 1, '65.

TWENTY-FOURTH IOWA INFANTRY—COMPANY D.

J. B. Casebeer, Capt.; Daniel Ott, 2 Lt.; Elijah Brown, C. F. Channell,

Samuel Godlove, G. W. Harbin, Justus Henderson, J. W. Iden, N. C. Miller, Thos. L. Sims, J. F. Yennkin.

TWENTY-EIGHTH IOWA INFANTRY—COMPANY H.

Robert Manatt, Martin Shelly, Aaron Wilson.

TWENTY-FIFTH IOWA INFANTRY—COMPANY A.

D. J. Palmer, Capt.; J. M. Dick, 1 Lt.; M. B. Anderson, 1 Lt.; J. A. Young, 2 Lt.; Marion B. Anderson, S.; J. G. Vincent, S.; R. B. White, S.; G. H. Hale, S.; D. A. Boyer, S.; H. M. Robertson, C.; Daniel Jaynes, C.; B. F. Warfel, C.; S. S. Cherry, C.; Samuel McKee, C.; D. R. Miller, C.; S. E. Stewart, C.; W. G. McClelland, C.; G. V. Allen, B. J. Barton, John Burnside, Wm. Burnside, Jerome Beach, M. T. Baker, John Black, M. L. Bishop, Wm. B. Bishop, J. W. Baker, G. W. Baker, Robert Bennett, J. W. Cherry, Elisha Coon, John Clary, G. V. Currie, W. W. Cook, G. T. Cavit, T. F. Cochran, John Copeland, A. P. Donahey, C. L. Davidson, A. L. Demarce, Moses Demarce, Eugene Dunlap, Martin Dennison, John Eldredge, Simeon Fawcett, S. C. Gardner, J. R. Hammond, J. A. Hammond, J. A. Hamilton, Wm. Harvey, J. M. Hatcher, Egbert Horth, James Jones, H. H. Johnson, J. M. Kilgore, J. C. Kilgore, Patrick King, Isom King, James Kain, Mark Keating, Jacob Kopp, S. H. Kirkpatrick, J. B. Lane, Alex M. Lane, John Leffler, R. P. Lewis, George McDonall, Thomas McDonald, M. S. McDowell, J. T. McKee, N. McVicker, M. M. Messick, W. H. Marquam, Charles McBride, J. A. McCorkle, John Myers, D. R. Miller, L. C. Marvel, Peter McDole, Wm. Nelson, B. W. Nash, Wm. Nash, Michael O'Koeff, Hiram Payne, Thompson Palmer, J. M. Patterson, D. P. Quinn, Wesley Rickey, R. H. Roach, G. W. Roberts, Benj. Rich, J. F. Royer, W. H. Shields, W. A. Shannon, Benj. Showalter, J. M. Stewart, J. W. Swift, Richard Stevens, Wm. Steedman, L. C. Sitler, Alex Scott, Jesse Sanders, B. F. Tipton, George Thompson, M. D. Townsend, W. W. Wheatley, A. W. Wheatley, H. B. Whittell, R. E. Wilkin, Joseph Wallace, Leonard Werts, J. M. Wright, C. L. Woods, J. L. Woodburn, John Wolfe, J. L. Wallace, J. P. Work, J. M. Winders, Charles Wortley, Wm. Wortley.

TWENTY-FIFTH IOWA INFANTRY—COMPANY E.

Jas. M. Neal.

TWENTY-FIFTH IOWA INFANTRY—COMPANY F.

Jonathan Supplee, T. E. D. Selders.

Regiment organized in August, '62, mustered out at Washington, D. C., June 6, '65.

TWENTY-FIFTH IOWA INFANTRY—COMPANY I.

S. A. Russell, Capt.; J. W. Harper, Capt.; T. Y. Williams, 1 Lt.; R. F. Strain, S.; Geo. Harter, S.; Andrew Ferguson, S.; J. A. Harper, S.; L. B. Carll, S.; J. H. Taylor, S.; T. M. Neal, C.; A. H. Mintier, C.; David Twinam, C.; Isaac Gross, C.; J. S. Colville, C.; E. N. Cochran, C.; Henry Spears, C.; G. W. Gates, C.; A. Morehouse, C.; W. I. Neal, Mus.; E. F. Daine, Mus.; A. Seber, Wag.; Hiram Alexander, W. V. Alexander, D. L. Allen, J. W. M. Allen, Chris. Arthaud, Jos. Adams, A. H. Benson, R. E. Bennett, Henry Black, T. M. Brown, W. P. Carlin, John Cherryholmes, F. M. Crawford, J. R. Crawford, Jos. Chiquet, S. P. Coe, A. J. Davidson, W. D. Davidson, Mark Dill, H. M. Edwards, J. W. Fullerton, Henry Fisher, G. W. Hunt, A. C. Holmes, Jos. Huston, E. H. Hipwell, Andrew Jackson, W. F. Johnson, J. M. Johnson, Wm. Johnson, D. K. Kell, Wm. McCall, Robert McCall, J. C. McConnell, J. J. McClelland, Jas. McCutchen, J. R. McElroy, T. H. Maxwell, Vincent Maxwell, Pulaski Maxwell, Thos. Matthews, W. C. Mayhew, J. A. McKee, E. C. McMillan, A. I. Mitchell, S. J. Moore, W. H. Moorehead, J. P. Mize, S. W. Neal, J. H. Neal, Thompson Palmer, W. I. Neal, B. A. Portèr, James Porter, George Porter, J. W. Rankin, G. W. Riley, T. S. Rowan, J. G. Rowan, W. H. Ray, W. C. Schwaebe, S. C. Scott, J. G. Smith, S. B. Slaughter, James Strain, Samuel Strain, D. P. Strain, Samuel Thompson, W. D. Twinam, W. J. Walker, Eleazer Wolford.

THIRTIETH IOWA INFANTRY—COMPANY E.

W. T. Burgess, Capt.; Jos. Smith, Capt.; D. S. McCannahey, Q. M.; M. W. Parker, 1 Lt.; I. S. Drummond, 2 Lt.; J. W. Middleton, 1 Lt.; Robert Blair, S.; Robert Beaty, S.; J. N. Coffield, C.B. Smith, S.; T. W. Hyde, Chap.; H. B. Jordan, C.; A. M. Bosworth, C.; L. W. Pringle, C.; E. C. Hobson, C.; David Horton, C.; Jas. Pollock, Mus.; W. B. Shephard, Mus.; B. F. Wight, Wag.; J. L. Bales, Henry Blick, Wm. Bridges, L. Bramer, D. C. Boers, W. I. Brayhill, Benj. Bowman, Sr., Benj. Bowman, Jr., O. P. Cauffman, Jas. Cregan, H. G. Connor, David Clapper, Wm. Donovan, W. C. Easter, C. S. Eddy, Wilford Ewen, Samuel Fox, Geo. Fowler, Henry Gilmore, W. W. Gayton, P. F. Hemmenway, W. H. Heaton, J. W. Harvey, G. M. Jacobs, Otto Kraken, D. E. Kendle, Jos. Lyon, O. M. Miller, Jas. McIntire, Ephraim McIntire, J. A. McIntire, Session Melville, G. D. McCarty, Jas. McCoy, J. J. McCarty, Samuel McCulley, T. D. Pollock, Thos. Parshall, W. M. Painter, Daniel

Pickens, Mount Peaseley, D. M. Robison, G. W. Reed, John Ralston, H. C. Sales, Albert Spencer, J. D. Shorer, Perry Stoker, L. G. Stanley, C. L. Smith, J. R. Snyder, J. P. Smith, James Smith, A. M. Smith, Josiah Smith, W. M. Snyder, I. Schreffler, B. B. Swisher, W. E. Townsend, B. F. Thorn, Allen Tupper, Jefferson Wilks, B. F. White, H. B. Wissenger, J. M. White, Newton Williams, P. C. Wilson, W. G. Watson, A. J. Wentworth, J. W. Wilson, Enos Whitacre, James Wiles.

THIRTIETH IOWA INFANTRY—COMPANY K.

S. D. Cook, Capt.; J. D. Gallagher, Capt.; N. A. J. Young, 1 Lt.; Frank Critz, 1 Lt.; Virgil Chipman, Mus.; W. M. Stover, Mus.; Jas. McCanna, Wag.; Leonard Benn, S.; W. H. Fulton, S.; A. B. Young, S.; Jas. Bailey, S.; J. W. Haigler, S.; H. N. Lane, C.; J. M. Criswell, C.; D. E. Bush, C.; Jacob Bishop, C.; Isaac Novinger, C.; J. R. Blackwell, C.; R. S. Merchant, C.; W. W. Looney, C.; S. C. Benn, J. C. Bunker, Elijah Bailey, Thos. Brown, John Bear, Jas. Brawner, Thiewbaut Bouquat, Wm. Brown, J. J. Bottger, L. M. Coover, John Carpenter, W. T. Coffman, C. H. Davis, S. R. Darnell, J. L. Davis, C. S. Edmondson, I. S. Edmondson, Lorenz Escher, Jr., D. C. Fritz, John Farley, T. J. Foster, Jas. Figgins, D. J. Gregory, Jas. Gilbert, T. C. Hand, Jas. Hole, Wm. Hollenback, Miles Hasty, Josiah Harter, J. M. Haigler, J. C. Haigler, S. C. Loomis, John Lohberger, Levi Lane, J. M. Louder, J. G. Louder, T. C. Mapel, C. B. Mapel, S. G. Mapel, S. S. Mapel, J. G. McCree, N. T. McIlree, Jas. McIlree, A. C. Marsh, Elias McMullen, Wm. Merchant, A. C. Minor, S. E. Parker, J. L. Patrick, A. B. Purrington, H. L. Rehkoff, F. C. Robinson, Murat Rickey, Thos. Rickey, Jos. Reiner, Wm. Strabley, J. J. Streber, J. N. Stratler, Barthold Tatman, Daniel Thurman, S. B. Ween, E. C. Williamson, Gilbert Yoeman.

The regiment was organized in August, '62, mustered in at Keokuk September 23, and mustered out at Washington City June 5, '65.

THIRTY-THIRD IOWA INFANTRY—COMPANY H.

Jas. A. Coffman, R. M. Hall, Jas. M. Wilson.

THIRTY-SEVENTH IOWA INFANTRY—COMPANY G.

Cyrus Cox, Capt.; Josiah Allen, D. P. Cole, J. D. Haley, Alfred Keeney, Thos. Little, D. T. Lee, J. R. Mitchell, Andrew McKay, Nathan Riley, Phillip

IOWA NATIONAL GUARD ENCAMPMENT AT WASHINGTON, 1897

COMPANY D, FIFTIETH IOWA INFANTRY, APRIL 26, 1898
En route to Des Moines, Iowa

Smith, David Zuck.

THIRTY-SEVENTH IOWA INFANTRY—COMPANY H.

Daniel Crugan, W. Frame, Alfred Keaney, A. M. Lyon, P. A. Tenney, Phillip Smith.

THIRTY-SEVENTH IOWA INFANTRY—COMPANY K.

Ed. S. Brinton, John Kerr, T. P. Shaw, John Van Vlist.

This was the Graybeard regiment, ages ranging from thirty-nine to sixty-four. Organized in October, '62, mustered in December 15, and mustered out at Davenport May 24, '65.

FORTIETH IOWA INFANTRY—COMPANY I.

D. W. Cox, Wm. Hornish, S. W. Reynolds, A. W. Reynolds.

FORTY-FIRST IOWA INFANTRY—COMPANY B.

Josiah Duer, Merton McIlvane, A. L. McLoud, C. L. Wakelee, David Wells.

FORTY-FOURTH IOWA INFANTRY—COMPANY D.

Jasper Cox, Leander Darling, Hugh R. McClelland.

FORTY-SEVENTH IOWA INFANTRY—COMPANY G.

James McClough, A. J. Mitchell, E. D. Whitacre, J. F. Williamson.

FORTY-SEVENTH IOWA INFANTRY—COMPANY H.

Geo. A. Black, Mus.; W. W. Abraham.

FORTY-FIFTH IOWA INFANTRY—COMPANY B.

J. B. Hope, Maj.; J. P. Dawson, Quar. Mas.; W. H. Allen, Capt.; S. E. Hawthorn, 1 Lt.; E. R. Eldridge, 2 Lt.; Samuel Stutson, Asst. Sur.; M. M. Runyon, S.; David Mitchell, S.; J. B. Nelson, T. M. McKenry, J. H. Fleming, S.; J. D. Robinson, C.; A. J. Duke, C.; C. C. Rodman, C.; J. V. Anderson, C.; W. C. Smiley, C.; Zach. T. Lindsey, C.; A. L. Williams, C.; Martin Whitcomb, C.; E. W. Allen, Luther Allen, H. C. Atwood, R. H. Armstrong, R. A. Boyd, A. R. Barnes, G. D. Brinton, W. B. Bishop, Abe Beanblossom, F. M.

Collins, A. M. Collins, Alex. Curran, B. F. Cherry, J. R. Compton, A. G. Cunningham, Hurlbut Darbyshire, Pat. H. Dayton, Hiram T. Dayton, Jeff. P. Dayton, John A. Donaldson, John C. Donaldson, Geo. Dusenberry, Jas. Fleming, T. A. Ferguson, L. O. Gallop, J. M. Gibson, E. W. Gowey, T. H. Hawkins, Henry Harris, B. F. Hillis, John Johnston, R. O. Johnston, A. N. Keister, D. M. Lydick, W. J. Maxwell, W. T. McCune, W. L. McClelland, T. E. McMillan, J. M. McNay, E. T. McGregor, C. B. Morehouse, J. M. Miller, W. H. McGeier, Wm. T. Neal, C. W. Neill, Asher F. Pay, R. H. Pattison, Milo W. Patterson, Thos. Pyle, G. R. Reas, W. N. Ritchey, W. G. Richardson, J. A. Robertson, G. W. Sison, Bigelow Story, Wm. Vincent, J. C. Wilson, Z. T. Winder, E. W. Wright, W. K. Wallace, S. P. Young.

FORTY-FIFTH IOWA INFANTRY—COMPANY F.

T. H. McFall, J. F. Meek.

Regiment organized for one hundred days, mustered in May 25, '64, mustered out at Keokuk, September 16, '64.

FIRST IOWA CAVALRY—COMPANY F.

N. H. Browner, C.; Wm. Hunter, C.; H. W. Shaver, C.; T. J. Browner, C.; S. M. Hines, C.; J. S. Baker, C.; E. H. Wilson, C.; Wm. McClure, C.; Robert Allen, J. S. Allen, L. W. Austin, Allison Bunker, Jesse Bunker, W. R. Bolding, Balt. Bollinger, James Boston, J. W. Baxter, D. B. Boyd, John H. Boyd, J. W. Crawford, Chas. Casteele, J. B. Doran, Alex. Doran, F. A. Druff, Ellery N. Foster, Elisha Gray, John C. Gerrard, Henry Grayson, John Hamilton, O. P. Hull, C. A. Housell, C. H. Housh, J. W. Horn, Charles McCoy, G. N. McCowan, Wm. McAllister, George Maier, Charles Mayer, John Noringer, C. L. Nurse, Albert Powers, Benj. Parsons, Amos Prindle, Hildebert Perry, Wm. Powers, G. W. Reilley, Samuel Sewall, Cleophas Smelscer, M. J. Simms, W. E. Snodgrass, O. A. Stillings, M. G. Troup, Wm. Tatman, Alpheus Titus, Samuel Van Norman, Ira Williams, Chalmers Woodruff, J. D. Wilson, Josiah Wilson, R. A. Williams.

FIRST IOWA CAVALRY—COMPANY K.

Melvin E. Mann, Farrier.

SECOND IOWA CAVALRY—COMPANY A.

D. J. Ferree, 1 Lt.; Samuel Havens, P. E. Leach, Otis Legg, Isaiah Miller,

Milton Sweet, B. F. Snider, L. I. Washburn, A. W. Woodford, Benj. Wagoner.

SECOND IOWA CAVALRY—COMPANY H.

Jonathan Duer, G. P. Philips, Jos. McCord, W. N. Rogers.

SECOND IOWA CAVALRY—UNASSIGNED.

Addison Brown, Samuel Furter, J. H. Givens, Henry Hildebrand.

THIRD IOWA CAVALRY.

T. J. Maxwell, Assist. Surgeon.

FOURTH IOWA CAVALRY—COMPANY C.

Wm. Coppock, Henry Fishburn, M. J. Rhodes.

SIXTH IOWA CAVALRY—COMPANY A.

Nicholas Geye, Horace King.

SIXTH IOWA CAVALRY—COMPANY E.

J. W. McCormick, J. H. Perkins.

SEVENTH IOWA CAVALRY.

Sanford Anderson, Dan. W. Cox, A. F. McLoud, T. F. Powers, David Wells, C. F. Wakelee.

EIGHTH IOWA CAVALRY—COMPANY F.

Wm. D. Harris.

NINTH IOWA CAVALRY.

J. F. McCutchan, Capt.; Marcus Allen, G. W. Braden, G. W. Benson, A. W. Bailey, John F. Blanden, G. C. Barnes, T. B. Brown, F. G. Chesler, Jas. Carmichael, Josiah Campbell, Hugh Craig, J. W. Clinkenbeard, D. B. Clouse, W. J. Durfey, J. S. Davidson, S. S. Ellsworth, C. H. Ellsworth, A. M. Easton,

T. L. Ferree, S. W. Goble, J. M. Gormley, Robt. Grover, W. O. Hessletine, John Hardy. F. E. Johnston, John Jones, Wm. Kenan, Thompson Laine, J. S. Leeper, Jesse Longwell, C. W. Lyon, A. A. Marling, D. A. McAnulty, Albert Phillips, Wm. Pierce, F. T. Russell, Jacob Stotts, F. N. Seeber, Archibold Stewart, Edward Sims, M. Tompkins, W. S. Tilton, J. M. Tripp, J. D. Tansey, E. B. Tripp, S. D. B. Welch, J. D. Welch, J. Whitlock, James Young.

SIXTIETH UNITED STATES, COLORED—COMPANY H.

G. W. Black, Jos. Dancy, Jerry Franklin, John Johnson, Henry Johnson, Josiah Leeper, Jas. Weeks, Caleb White.

The boys enlisted for two years, but stayed twenty-eight months.

ELEVENTH UNITED STATES, COLORED.

Oliphant Carter.

WASHINGTON COUNTY BOYS IN OTHER REGIMENTS.

B. F. Parker, First Battery Iowa Light Artillery; John A. Swan, Twelfth Illinois Cavalry, Company E.; Parker Hoover, Thirtieth Illinois Infantry, Company F.; also Martin Melvin, Company K.; Frank Ford, Thirty-third Illinois Infantry, Company K.; Jos. Shockley, Thirty-ninth Illinois Infantry, Company H.; T. P. Gibson, Eighty-sixth Illinois Infantry; Frank Cramer and Herman Behr, Forty-third Illinois Infantry, Company E.; Arnold Twiggs, Sixteenth Iowa Infantry.

The local camp for the city recruits was at the old fair grounds, covering the present home of Mrs. John Wagner, on the Mt. Pleasant road.

By way of "friendship garland," be it recorded that all through the wonderful political campaign of 1860, and for all the recruiting and war meetings, and the leaving of companies for the front, and for martial and political visits to other towns, E. T. Hebener, a Douglas democrat, played the fife for the escorts. He charged nothing for local night meetings, but was paid for services that took him from his daily work. He was a superb player, a mild-mannered, merry, broad-gauged man, in every way a comrade and desirable citizen. Let a republican scribe, but not a Pharisee, lay a simple nosegay on that man's grave.

Of course, our people ran the gamut of emotions in those five stirring years. There were many heart-breaks, many sobs and tears, many tragedies. Many a poor fellow did not come back, or came, darkling, in a rude box. When

Gen. T. H. Stanton
The "Fighting Paymaster" U. S. Army

Gen. Hiram Scofield
Taken when A. A. G. on Gen. Lauman's staff

OFFICERS OF THE REBELLION

the companies left us—well, no one has painted the scene like Col. Ingersoll in his immortal piece of rhetoric and pathos, the Indianapolis Memorial Day speech—

"The past rises before me like a dream. Again we are in the great struggle for national life. We hear the sounds of preparation; the music of boisterous drums; the silver voice of heroic bugles. We see thousands of assemblages, and hear the appeals of orators. We see the pale cheeks of women, and the flushed faces of men; and in those assemblages we see all the dead whose dust we have covered with flowers. We lose sight of them no more. We are with them when they enlist in the great army of freedom. We see them with those they love. Some are walking for the last time in quiet, woody places with the maidens they adore. We hear the whisperings and the sweet vows of eternal love as they lingeringly part forever. Others are bending over cradles, kissing babes that are asleep. Some are parting with mothers who hold them and press them to their hearts again and again and say nothing. Kisses and tears, tears and kisses—divine mingling of agony and love! And some are talking with wives, and endeavoring with brave words, spoken in the old tones, to drive from their hearts the awful fear. We see them part. We see the wife standing in the door with the babe in her arms—standing in the sunlight, sobbing. At the turn in the road a hand waves—she answers by holding high in her loving arms the child. He is gone, and forever.

"We see them all as they march proudly away under the flaunting flags, keeping time to the grand, wild music of war— marching down the streets of the great cities, through the towns and across the prairies, down to the fields of glory, to do and die for the eternal right.

"We go with them, one and all. We are by their side on the gory fields, in all the hospitals of pain, on all the weary marches. We stand guard with them in the wild storm and under the quiet stars. We are with them in ravines running with blood, in the furrows of old fields. We are with them between contending hosts, unable to move, wild with thirst, the life ebbing slowly away among the withered leaves. We see them pierced by balls and torn with shells in the trenches, by the forts and in the whirlwind of the charge, where men become iron, with nerves of steel.

"We are with them in the prisons of hatred and famine: but human speech can never tell what they endured.

"We are at home when the news comes that they are dead. We see the maiden in the shadow of her first sorrow. We see the silvered head of the old man bowed with the last grief.

"These heroes are dead. They died for liberty, they died for us. They are at rest. They sleep in the land they made free, under the flag they rendered stainless, under the solemn pines, the sad hemlock, the tearful willows, and the embracing vines. They sleep beneath the shadows of the clouds, careless alike of sunshine and storm, each in the windowless palace of rest. Earth may run red with other wars; they are at peace. In the midst of battle, in the roar of conflict, they found the serenity of death. I have one sentiment for soldiers, living and dead: Cheers for the living, tears for the dead."

But who would have missed it? We do not live in level, prosaic years—we merely exist. We really live, as the torch fiercelv burns, only in stress of revolution and weather.

The war was the heroic ballad of our boys' lives, their one great, signal romance. Forty and more years after, they vividly recall the battle days and speak of them as mothers mind the birth-days of their children. Both mothers and soldiers were there and have a right to remember the agony, yea, and the aftermath of joy, if they survived. By that wonderful gravitation and purification, that we see but do not understand, all the ugly things that at the time annoyed and pained, sink out of haunting memory, and the boys remember the glad things, the funny things; even the ugly things are transmuted into raw material for jest and fun. At re-unions yet, they josh and laugh and tell stories, the gayest of humorists, the most pardonable of "cheerful liars." The little brown button long since became a fetish, like a church token—it has good right to stand as a semi-sacred thing. It is the symbol of the heroic, romantic period of their lives.

It would have been billions in our pockets and hundreds of thousands of lives saved, had we bought the slaves at the owners' appraisement. Elihu Burritt demonstrated that mathematically in addresses all over the North. Sambo and Dinah and the pickaninnies caused the war. The planters would not sell them; they were mad, and we were mad, and it had to be an inevitable fight to a finish—with Dinah and Sambo and the ebonies freed. From the southerners' stand-point, it was a war of utter and supreme folly. But there was no help for it. When anger comes in, sense and reason take a vacation.

How much did this county suffer in the civil war? Scan this table of casualties in the several companies:

Co.	Reg.	Men killed, wounded, died.	Officers.
H	2d	817	70
H	7th	880	73
C	8th	731	57
E	10th	728	58
F	11th	601	47
I & K	13th	819	65
I	18th	445	33

Co.	Reg.	Men Killed, wounded, died	Officers
C	19th	549	36
A & I	25th	556	49
E & K	30th	644	58
B	45th	19	00
	1st Cav.	543	
	4th Cav.	583	

This list of deaths was prepared by Lieut. Smith W. Brookhart of Company D, Fiftieth Iowa, in the Spanish war, and read on Memorial day, 1902:

COMPANY H—SECOND INFANTRY.

Geo. W. Neal, 2 Lt., killed at Corinth; Sergt. Wm. Wright, September 25, 1861; Corp. Samuel A. Mealley, killed at Donelson, February 15, 1862; Corp. Henry Weaver, February 17, '62, of wounds; Corp. Geo. W. Johnson, September 10, '64, of wounds; Drummer Samuel M. Eicher, wounded at Donelson, died April 1, 1862; Hugh Amarine, November 8, 1863; Jno. W. Andrews, October 28, 1861; Jos. H. C. Dawson, September 28, 1861; Robt. Easton, March 24, 1864; Marvin French, killed at Corinth; Wm. Hudson, January 10, 1862; John R. Fullerton, March 30, 1862; Finley Paxton, January 16, 1862; James M. Porter, wounded six times October 3, 1862, at Corinth but would not leave field; Benjamin Edwards, at Altoona, Ga.; John Bowen; Robert McCuhen; David F. Eckerman, wounded, August 5, 1864, died; I. G. White, first man from Washington county to lose his life, August 31, 1861.

COMPANY H—SEVENTH IOWA INFANTRY.

Robt. S. Glasgow, died November 8, 1861, of wounds received in battle; Samuel Rickey, October 12, 1862, from wounds at Corinth; Wm. L. Woods, from wounds at Belmont; Jos. A. Abbey, from wounds at Belmont; Wade C. Arnold, from wounds at Belmont; Charles Bloom, killed November 7, 1861, at Belmont; Darius Bush, killed at Belmont; Hugh C. Andrews, killed at Corinth; Lewis Austin, killed at Belmont; Samuel C. Crowner, January 20, 1865; Wm. W. Edmondson, killed at Corinth; Phillip Gladwin, killed November 7, 1861, Belmont; Joseph Gerthoffer, December 9, 1864; Geo. W. Hogue, April 20, '62, wounds, at Savannah, Tenn.; Alexander M. Holmes, August 26, 1864; George A. Logan, killed at Belmont; W. H. Lamb, at Paducah, Ky., January 13, '62; John F. McConnell, at Paducah, April 16, 1862; John L. McDowell, killed at Belmont; John W. Matthew, prisoner at Corinth, died December 14, 1863, at Jefferson Barracks, Mo.;

William Moore, at Newark, N. J., May 14, 1865; John Perkins, killed at Belmont; Jeremiah Phillips, at Corinth, March 7, 1863; Anderson Ralston, September 26, 1864, at Rome, Ga.; Wm. S. Smith, November 5, 1861, St. Louis, Mo.; Ambrose Shaw, killed at Belmont; George Tenant severely wounded at Belmont, mortally at Corinth, died October 19, '62; John C. Temple, killed battle Belmont; Thomas P. Vincent, of wounds at Belmont, at Mound City, Ill., November 19, '61; Geo. W. Wells, killed in Shiloh, April 6, 1862; Reuben Worthen, killed at Belmont; Jesse P. Warren, died November 25, 1861.

COMPANY C—EIGHTH INFANTRY.

Caldwell Bailey, died December 29, 1861, Sedalia, Mo.; Sergt. James G. Hight, wounded at Shiloh, taken prisoner and died of wound October 22, 1862, Annapolis, Md.; John A. Duke, died at Macon, Georgia, of starvation and ill treatment while prisoner, October 5, 1862, captured April 6, 1862; Robert S. Young, captured at Shiloh, April 6, '62, died October 21, '62, of starvation and ill treatment; Edward Carris, February 28, 1862, Sedalia, Mo.; Martin Gentzler, killed on Tennessee river by Guerillas from ambush; James D. Glasgow, December 11, 1863, at Pocohontas, Tenn.; David A. Knowles, August 6, '62, Jeff. Bks., Mo.; Joseph F. Kelley, February 9, 1865, R. I., Ill.; James Marshall, April 20, 1862, of wounds at Shiloh, at Keokuk; John McMurray, May 18, 1862, at Mobile, while prisoner, wounded and captured Shiloh, April 6, 1862; David Parrish, wounded April 6, 1862, died of wounds April 20, at Indianapolis; James Robertson, July 31, 1862, Mound City, Ill.; John D. Roberts, September 11, 1865, Tuskegee, Ala.; Wm. Smiley, July 8, 1863, Memphis; Wm. H. Tripp, wounded August 24, 1864, Memphis, died September 24, 1864, was also captured April 6, 1862; Robert C. Thompson, September 8, 1863, wounded and prisoner at Shiloh; Robert O. Watson, May 23, 1864, Davenport; James H. Young, killed April 6, 1862, Shiloh.

COMPANY E—TENTH INFANTRY.

N. J. H. Terry, killed at Champion Hills, Miss., May 16, '63; Hiram Tatman, died at Birds Point, Mo., Feb. 19, '62; Joseph Glosser, killed November 25, '63, Chattanooga; Abraham Dawson, died at Birds Point, Mo., February 11, '62, from wound received in ambush near Charleston, Mo.; Henry Barger, of wounds, at Champion Hills, Miss., May 20, '63; Lewis C. Stark, killed November 25, '63, Chattanooga, in battle; Charles Page, of wounds in battle of Corinth; John Sanchi, June 6, '63, of wounds at Champion Hills; John G. Albin, May 28, '63, of wounds in battle of Champion Hills; Ephraim N. Bell,

May 20, '63, at Robes' Plantation, Miss., of wounds; Wm. Bear, July 1, '63, at Memphis, of wounds; Samuel Curry, February 6, '62, at Birds Point, Mo., of wounds, near Charleston, Mo.; John Enfield, January 1, '62, at Birds Point; August Hemmenn, of wounds in battle of Corinth, on October 6, '62; John Hurt, August 29, '63, St. Louis, of wounds at Champion Hills; Thomas J. Parsons, killed near Charleston, Mo., January 8, '62; Abraham Phillips, killed January 8, '62, near Charleston, Mo.; Thomas B. Roberts, April 14, '62, at New Madrid, Mo.; Dennis A. Rice, December 11, '61, Mound City, Ill.; Wm. E. Rogers, October 6, '63, Richmond, Iowa; V. W. Stone, January 5, '64, St. Louis; Wm. W. Williamson, July 17, '62, Birds Point.

COMPANY F—ELEVENTH IOWA INFANTRY.

N. L. McKinney, November 28, '62, at Lagrange, Tenn.; Geo. J. Barnes, killed at Shiloh; Martin A. McClain, killed at Shiloh; T. M. Souter, July 8, '64, of wound at Nickajack Creek, Ga.; Theodore Campbell, May 8, '62, at St. Louis, of wounds at Shiloh; David Andrews, May 29, '62, at Corinth; Edward Doran, February 21, '62, Fulton, Mo.; Job Hawk, March 6, '62, Fulton; Thomas Jorden, January 20, '62, St. Louis; James Kenedy, November 12, '63, Vicksburg; John S. Martin, September 28, '64, Keokuk; James McGowan, August 20, '62, Bolivar, Tenn.; Joseph C. McNay, June 19, '62, Corinth; John D. North, January 4, '62, Jeff. City, Mo.; Elliott Parrish, September 24, '63, Memphis; Henry Purrington, killed on route home October 31, '64, after muster out; Henry H. Riley, killed at Shiloh; Moses Ross, September 16, '63, Washington, Ind.; John Rickey, December 5, '63, Jeff. Bks., Mo.; Sam L. Snooks, February 17, '65, Bufort, S. C.; Isaac N. Smith. December 11, '61, St. Louis; Geo. W. Shafer, July 5, '62, of wounds, at Kenesaw Mountain, Georgia; Robt. A. Tedford, August 1, '64, Atlanta.

COMPANY I—THIRTEENTH INFANTRY.

James A. Brown, near Corinth, June 29, '62; Stephen R. Moore, September 24, '62, Jackson, Miss.; Stephen Werts, killed July 28, '64, near Atlanta; Charles F. Shaw, December 23, '61, Jeff. City, Mo.; Marcus Humphrey, June 12, '62, Monterey, Tenn.; L. P. Aylworth, killed at Shiloh; Henry H. Burham, May 24, '62, Monterey, Tenn.; Wm. L. Beason, August 28, '63, Montezuma; Jas. E. Delong, July 22, '64, near Atlanta, wounded at Shiloh; John M. Dusenberry, killed July 22, '64, near Atlanta; Michael Faulkner, September 29, '62, Corinth; Edmund Hill, Jan. 12, '65, Chattanooga; Tobias Hites, March 16,

'65, Savannah, Ga.; John A. Lanning, captured July 22, '64, near Atlanta, died Spetember 9, '64, Andersonville; John McCall, wounded Shiloh, died July 18, '62, at Cincinnati, O.; Sam'l C. Marvel, missed in battle near Atlanta; David Park, December 18, '61, St. Louis; B. Pierson, January 16, '62, St. Louis; Simeon Polen, wounded at Shiloh, died April 26, '62, at St. Louis, of wounds; Joseph Park, killed at Shiloh; Henry Rickey, June 12, '62, near New Albany, Ind.; Selkirk Sanders, January 6, '62, St. Louis; Horace Shelley, missing in battle near Atlanta; Wm. H. Thompson, killed July 22, '64, near Atlanta; N. H. Tannahill, February 10, '63, Providence, La.; Henry Walker, killed February 10, '64, Hillsborough, Miss.; Lewis White, killed July 24, '64, Atlanta; Frederick Wilkins, November 2, '64, Chattanooga.

COMPANY K—THIRTEENTH INFANTRY.

Jas. W. Atwood, killed July 24, '64, near Atlanta; Levi M. Roberts, killed July 21, '64, near Atlanta; John W. Stanton, killed July 22, '64, near Atlanta; John Ashworth, June 11, '62, Monterey, Tenn.; Jos. W. Atwood, killed July 21, '64, near Atlanta; Elisha Brown, June 8, '62, Monterey, Tenn.; J. R. Beasley, captured July 22, '64, near Atlanta, died October 15, '64, Florence, S. C., while prisoner; Patrick Casey, June 8, '62, Monterey; Owen M. Creath, captured April 6, '62, Shiloh, died April 11, '62, at Savannah, Tenn., prisoner; Martin Casey, killed July 5, '64, at Atlanta; Daniel Coriell, wounded July 1, '64, died July 27, '64, of wounds, at Atlanta; Walter Dillon, April 7, '62, at Pittsburg Landing; Geo. Hutchison, July 27, '64, of wounds at Atlanta; Wm. A. Hart, killed July 21, '64, Atlanta; Michael Kelly, June 10, '62, at Mound City, Ill., of wounds at Shiloh; David Kanausse, killed April 6, '62, Shiloh; B. F. Lamb, died April 28, '63, at Vicksburg, badly wounded at Shiloh; Felix L. Lindsay, wounded July 22, '64, died next day at Atlanta; L. C. Neagle, February 23, '65; Newman J. Ohmart, May 19, '62; John Pinkering, February 19, '65, Louisville, Ky.; Wm. Quingley, February 19, '65, Hilton Head, S. C.; George G. Robison, killed July 22, '64, Atlanta; L. M. Roberts, killed July 21, '64, Atlanta; Jacob Spainhower, January 30, '65, Washington; M. T. Snyder, wounded April 6, '62, Shiloh, died September 16, '62; Wm. H. Smith, January 19, '65, Huntsville, Ala.; John M. Wood, October 2, '62, Jackson, Tenn.; W. L. Wilkins, April 4, '65, Nashville.

COMPANY I—EIGHTEENTH INFANTRY.

Wm. B. Green, October 8, '62, of wounds near Newtonia, Mo.; Wm. H. H. Morgan, September 5, '62, Jeff. City, Mo.; Jas. E. Vore, at Tyler, Texas, prisoner, September 6, '64; Jos. R. Winders, November 20, '62, Springfield, Mo.; Henry R. Blankenship, April 30, '65, Van Buren, Arkansas; A. D. Cordell, killed, May 7, '64, Van Buren, Ark., by bushwhackers; Jason L. Ellis, February 28, '63, Springfield, Mo.; Harry Hunt, September 16, '64, at Tyler, prisoner; Joseph A. Jones, November 18, '62, Springfield, Mo.; Chas. Johnson, July 22, '64, Ft. Smith, Ark.; David K. Patterson, November 15, '62, Springfield, Mo.; Geo. S. Perry, August 10, '64, on march between Clarksville and Ft. Smith, Ark.; Wm. W. Raney, Nov. 1, '62, Fayetteville, Ark.; Kelly Shadden, February 11, '63, Springfield, Mo.; Nathan Thornton, September 21, '62, Sedalia, Mo.; Josiah Wilson, December 3, '62, Springfield, Mo.

COMPANY C—NINETEENTH IOWA.

John C. Ritchie, killed at Morganzie, La., September 29, '63; Robt. M. Glasgow, wounded September 29, '63, at Morganzie, died January 29, '65. Vicksburg; Geo. Temple, wounded September 29, '63, at Morganzie, fell on the colors, died October 10; Aaron Abbott, died March 11, '63, at Forsyth, Mo.; Samuel P. Beard, killed September 29, '63, Morganzie, La.; L. W. Carson, December 1, '62, Ozark, Mo.; Jacob Bowman, November 5, '62, Springfield, Mo.; David Gilleland, October 25, '63, at Washington, of wounds at Springfield, Mo.; Amos Helwick, April 3, '64, Brownsville, Texas; Richard H. Lewis, October 16, '63, New Orleans; Wm. N. McConnaughey, July 22, '64 New Orleans; Geo. M. Stultz, drowned March 2, '63, at Forsyth, Mo., in White river; Elias Worthington, Nov. 22, '62, Springfield, Mo.

COMPANY A—TWENTY-FIFTH INFANTRY.

Robt. B. White, June 20, '63, at Vicksburg; H. M. Robertson, killed July 12, '63, Jackson, Miss.; Daniel Jayne, January 18, '63, Napoleon, Ark.; Samuel S. Cherry, February 4, '63, Vicksburg, Miss.; Jas. A. McCorkel, August 26, '63, Monmouth, Ill.; Wm. C. McClelland. died September 12, '63, Goodrich Landing, Miss.; Jerome Beach, April 2, '63, Millikens Bend, La.; Wm. P. Bishop, May 25, '65, Washington, D. C.; John W. Cherry, May 24, '63, Young's Point, La.; Elisha Coon, January 30, '63, Vicksburg, Miss.; Geo. T. Cavit, June 10, '63, on steamer; Eugene Dunlap, July 30, '63, Jackson, Miss.; Jacob M. Hatcher, February 23, '63, Young's Point, La.; Jno. A. Hamilton, April 6, '63, Memphis; Jno. A. Hammond, August 12, '64, Rome, Ga.; Joseph B. Lane, February 24, '63, St. Louis; Geo. McDonnald, March 16, '63, on the steamer; Matthew S. McDowell, November 27, '64, at Washington; Jas. T. McKee, May 29, '64, Dallas, Ga.; Moses M. Messick, December 2, '62, Helena, Ark.; Michael O'Koeff, August 20, '63, Vicksburg; Hiram Payne, August 25, '63, Vicksburg; Jas. T. Patterson, killed May 27, '63, Vicksburg; Wesley Ritchie, December 3, '62, at Washington; Richard H. Roach, October 18, '63, Vicksburg; Wm. H. Shields, July 5, '63, Vicksburg; Jno. W. Swift, died July 22, '63, St. Louis; Wm. Steedman, July 8, '63, St. Louis; Jos. Wallace, February 17, '63, Vicksburg; Cyrus L. Woods, killed July 12, '63, Jackson, Miss.; Jos. P. Work, March 9, '63, Young's Point, La.

COMPANY I—TWENTY-FIFTH IOWA INFANTRY.

L. B. Carll, December 16, '62, Helena, Ark.; Jno. J. McClelland, killed September 4, '64, Lovejoy Station, Ga.; Enoch F. Baine, September 8, '63, Camp Sherwin, Miss.; Hiram Alexander, wounded May 19, '63, at Vicksburg, died June 10, '63, on steamer, of wounds; Wm. V. Alexander, April 3, '63, Memphis; Thomas M. Brown, May 5, '63, Millikens Bend; Wm. P. Carlon, September 27, '63, Memphis; J. G. Cummins, December 17, '62, Helena; Jos. Chiquet, August 31, '64, Marietta, Ga.; Geo. W. Gates, February 29, '64, Cleveland, Tenn.; Jno. M. Johnson, February 12, '63, on steamer; Wm. Johnson, September 2, '62, Camp Sherman; Wm. H. Morehead, February 4, '63, St. Louis; John H. Neal, December 29, '64, Chattanooga; Warren I. Neal, August 12, '63, Camp Sherman, Miss.; Robt. A. Nickell, August 18, '63, Camp Sherman; David A. Porter, March 2, '63, St. Louis; G. M. Springston, March 3, '65, New Berne, N. C.; Samuel Strain, April 18, '63, Memphis; Alexander Seber, killed March 20, '65, Bentonville, N. C.; Samuel B. Slaughter, wounded May 19, '63, at Vicksburg, died December 5, '63, at Pleasant Plains; Wm. D. Twinam, August 29, '63, Vicksburg.

COMPANY E—THIRTIETH INFANTRY.

R. Baty, died November 9, '62, Keokuk; P. F. Hemmenway, July 29, '63, on steamer; N. R. Cole, died January 31, '63, Vicksburg; P. Thompson, December 12, '63, at Chattanooga, in battle Taylor Ridge, Tenn.; J. M. White, November 3, '63, Memphis; P. Ellis, killed in battle, May 22, '63, Vicksburg; B. F. Wright, March 2, '63, Memphis; Jas. L. Bales, August 19, '63, Black River Bridge, Miss.; B. Bowman, May 12, '63, Millikens Bend; Jas. Kreegan, June 25, '63, Jefferson Bks., Mo.; H. G. Conner, February 26, '63, Vicksburg; D. Clapper, December 21, '63, Helena; Wm. C. Donovan, August 4, '63, St. Louis; R. E. Drake, February 26, '62, Young's Point, La.; Amon Ellis, April 11, '63, on steamer; Samuel Fox, April 11, '63, on steamer; Geo. Fowler, May 27, '63, Millikens Bend; M. Graham, killed October 21, '63,

Cherokee Station, Ala.; Geo. W. Hall, killed October 21, '63, Cherokee Station; Charles Hug, July 19, '63, Vicksburg; Wm. C. Heston, November 5, 1862, Keokuk; E. McEntire, October 14, 1862, Keokuk; Geo. D. McCarty, December 14, 1863, Helena; Samuel McCulley, killed May 22, '63, Vicksburg; E. W. Nicholson, October 23, 1863, Keokuk; Wm. M. C. Painter, missing, supposed to be dead; James Smith, November 14, 1863, St. Louis; Jas. B. Shover, March 21, 1863, Vicksburg; Perry Stoker, August 1, 1863, on steamer; J. P. Smith, December 9, 1863, Memphis; Wm. M. Snyder, October 21, 1863, Cherokee Station, Ala.; Ben. B. Swisher, killed November 27, 1863, Taylors Ridge, Ga.; Josiah Smith, killed September 4, 1864, Lovejoy Station, Ga.; Robt. Shaw, August 9, 1863, Vicksburg; W. E. Townsend, January 10, 1863, Helena; J. Wilkes, killed April 10, 1864, Clayville, Ala.; Harvey B Wissinger, killed September 5, 1864, Lovejoy Station, Ga.; Enos H. Whitacre, March 9, 1863, on steamer; B. Wikoff, April 16, 1864, St. Louis.

COMPANY K—THIRTIETH INFANTRY.

Leonard Benn, died February 27, '63, Memphis; W. M. Stover, August 7, 1864, Rome, Ga.; Hiram Brown, March 4, 1863, Young's Point, La.; Ezra Bartholemew, killed November 27, 1863, Ringgold, Ga.; Chas. H. Davis, May 20, 1864, of wounds, at Resaca; J. G. Duvoa, killed June 17, '63, Vicksburg; Jas. L. Davis, August 23, 1863, Black River Bridge, Miss.; Chas. S. Edmondson, April 9, 1863, on steamer; Lorenz Escher, February 12, '63, Vicksburg; David C. Frits, November 9, 1863, Memphis; Thomas J. Foster, killed January 11, 1863, Arkansas Post; James Gilbert, March 3, '63, St. Louis; James Hole, March 30, '63, Memphis; Samuel C. Loomis, killed January 11, '63, Arkansas Post; Levi Lane, October 25, '63, Memphis; James M. Louder, October 23, 1863, Memphis; Joseph G. Louder, March 16, '63, Millikens Bend; Wm. Merchant, August 28, 1863, Black River, Miss.; Alexander C. Miner, February 5, 1865, Keokuk; Murat Rickey, December 24, '64, Annapolis, Md.; Thos. Rickey, November 16, '62, Helena; F. C. Robinson, wounded May 14, '64, Resaca, died May 16 of wounds; Jasper N. Stattler, July 3, '64, at Andersonville, a prisoner.

COMPANY B—FORTY-FIFTH INFANTRY.

Geo. D. Brink, died September 8, '64, Memphis; Henry Harris, July 10, '64, Memphis.

These names, together with Bert Huff, Ralph Conger and Fred Crawford who died in the late Spanish war, make up the entire list of those from Washington county who have given their lives in the service of their country, as shown by the official records.

OPERA BOUFFE WARS.

The story of the forlorn hope squad that went in '42 to Wassonville to rescue a white girl from the Indians, is told elsewhere in this veracious history. One can see that kind of war almost any night in a tuppeny theater. A war of more dignity, size, gore, excretion, etc., was known as the "South English," or "Skunk River war," of August, 1863. The bush in Keokuk county was a jungle for frogs, mosquitoes and rebel sympathizers. In '48 the Tally family came here from Tennessee. The son Cyphert was a brilliant preacher, but he marred his career by voiding disloyal sentiments. At length Mt. Zion church was closed to him, but he spoke in the timber. He was lionized, his head swelled and turned, and he kept enlarging and aggravating his mistakes, cutting Gospel fat with pro-slavery alcohol. On August 1, '63, he was the chief speaker at a democratic mass meeting. Arms were secreted under hay in many wagons. Republicans were hot, and erred in so tearing butternut badges from two women's dresses as to reveal their alleged charms. It probably improved their looks, but they and their friends were mad just the same. A republican meeting was being held in South English and the democrats went there, hunting trouble. Tally was shot dead, hit in the head, standing in a wagon, revolver and bowie knife in his hands. Some one hundred and fifty shots were fired, but only Mr. Wyant was wounded. Two of Tally's gun chambers were empty. The funeral was to be held next day, Sunday, and the martyr's friends sought revenge. Wagon loads of men came from Wapello, Mahaska and Poweshiek counties, and this motley mass formed the famous South English Army. Monday night two Sigourney men rode horseback to Washington, thence by hand car to Wilton Junction, thence by train to Davenport, to see Governor Kirkwood. He ordered three hundred stands of arms forwarded, then concluded to go himself to the seat of war, and he went, minus collar and tie. Troops and cannon followed. He made a sensible speech, and the warriors slunk away like mist before the sun. The fire-in-the-rear army was estimated from five hundred to four thousand. On the Union side, according to the Adjutant General's report, were the Muscatine Rangers, Washington Provost Guards, Brighton Guards, Richland Home Guards, Fairfield Prairie, also Union Guards, Abingdon Home Guards, Libertyville Guards, Mt. Pleasant Artillery and Sigourney Home Guards—eleven companies. Nearly every body went from here, on that lark, in wagons, horseback, afoot. Mr. Rose, of Kilgore & Rose, foundrymen, "drug" a three-foot-long cannon he had forged. Sedate men, like the late Senator Wm. Wilson, joined this picturesque piece of chaos. Nothing equal to it since "Our army in Flanders" won the belt and championship as swearers. There was no commissary—how they lived is not known, and perhaps it is best not to inquire. No train of women followed, with bread, beans, sow-belly, eggs, pies, cheese, coffee. All afflicted with sea-sickness—reversed. Selah. No one was indicted for killing Tally, and his slayer is not known to this day. C. J. Wilson denies this, saying the soldier slayer was well known.

From jocose tradition, one gets the impression that this was a Quixotic campaign. Judge Brown and McJunkin, two of our amateur warriors, for years gibed each other about their prowess, accidents, valor and things. The most salient features of the war were universal cases of summer complaint. It was August, and hot, and the change in water, diet and habits, the excitement, dust and unaccustomed exercise, put most of the troops hors de combat, that is, it was a "horse" on them. For many years the South English war was an active, transitive joke.

Our Col. C. J. Wilson saw Tally shot, throw up his arms and topple out of the wagon. Charley was a lad of thirteen years at the time, visiting relatives up there, and when firing began, he was, boy-like, scared, made a misstep, and as he was falling, got a flashlight of the murder.

One of the funny incidents of the war was this: Several Washingtonians, including J. C. Conger, were hauling a cannon by a rope, as if it were a sulky mule. Perhaps there was a string of cannon. But by a ludicrous mistake, the ammunition train had gone round another way, up north, so that in any event the battery would have been useless in an action. Conger's witticism was this: They say we of the north are not strategists, but this separation of ammunition from ordnance disproves the unjust charge. For suppose the enemy should capture the artillery train, or the ammunition train, it would do them no good. It was a very happy mistake, at least. It was on this campaign that he made his invective against the moon. It was no fun to toil at a rope hitched to a cannon, and haul it thro' the mud in the dark, so he said that the moon has been vastly over-rated—all it is good for is to spoil fish thrown out in its beams, and to write sickish love poetry to, while its practical utility is very small—the confounded thing will never shine in a dark night when we want light. To this very night, fair Luna has hardly recovered from the effect of his gibe at her as an astronomical asset.

On Governor Kirkwood's trip to South English, he spent a night here, and while sitting in J. R. Davis' store on the Klein corner, a citizen whose loyalty was suspected, asked him if the men he was sending would shoot, really. He replied, "my friend, if you have friends among those rebels in Iowa, I advise you to send them word that no blank cartridges will be fired in this war." The man sneaked off, cowed.

The Union element in the county—the bulk of the population—was set on a hair trigger all through the war days, and men were as quick as gunpowder, and got mad and ready to knock at a breath of criticism or sarcasm or scorn. Even a humorist like Dr. Chilcote drew his cane on a man for "remarks made." Col. Palmer's father was as quick to smite a spouting rebel sympathizer as was the impulsive St. Peter. An unnaturalized Irish democrat challenged his vote and just missed the flight of both of Uncle Sammy's "dukes." Everybody was full of tobasco, red and green peppers, lemon extract, ginger and other bitey things.

If news came here, the country was to be signaled by firing a cannon in town, and when farmers heard it, they'd come tearing in on any old plug of a horse that was handy, a lot of Paul Reveres reversed. One morning, Mr. Joe Meek, living out five or six miles, went lickety-split by Mr. Palmer's, and was hailed and stopped and milked of his news. He had heard the gun, and was coming in to feed his ears. Palmer came along, and they got wind of the South English war. Palmer ran back to get his squirrel gun, and off he went in James Galloway's rig. Town teams and country teams were impressed to haul cannon and extempore troopers. Probably, Vint Andrus, home on sick leave, commanded our boys, or it may have been Chris. Jones who had been discharged for sickness. No enemy could be found, and as nothing was doing, Galloway said he'd go home. Palmer was amused and said "you can't leave without a permit." "Why not, pray?" Word was slipped to Andrus, and soon an orderly galloped there to forbid Galloway—"martial law prevails here, sir." But Galloway never saw the joke.

There were plenty of festivities to help the women's aid societies. Chris. Jones was a genius at such things. The first U. P. church (now Music Hall) was ever open for war doings—they would have let it for a pay dance, I guess. Jones once set up a mush and milk party in there, and it was a jam. The first course was a tin cup and a pewter spoon. After a while, they drove up a muley cow and milked her, and her out-put was poured into the cups as far as it would go. Another cow with a bell on was drafted and extracted. When all cups were full, copper and tin boilers of mush were toted in. After the meal dope had been landed, cartoonist Jones exposed a series of pictures of South English soldiers, McJunkin, Brown et al, in ridiculous attitudes. The receipts bought a lot of arnica and court plaster for the boys at the front. Money was poured out like water for them. The board of supervisors at one time appropriated five thousand dollars to care for the families of soldiers that were on short commons, and named Dr. Chilcote, Judge Ross and C. H. Wilson a committee to administer the fund. Learning that flour was soon to advance in price, they bought all the flour in town, and it and other food stuffs were stocked in Chilcote's drug store. Mrs. Pat. King applied for a sack of flour, and that near-sighted man sent one. In a few days she complained to him that she could not make nice white bread. He said, "my wife makes fine bread from that same brand—try again." She did, and the bread was as black as one's hat. She roared. Doctor said, "bring it back and get another." He had given her shorts, by mistake. Folks were merry even at the most pinching crises—had to have fun to relieve the tension. That's why Lincoln told funny stories and read Artemus Ward and Petroleum V. Nasby. That's why Parisians sang, danced, feasted, thronged theaters during the Reign of Terror, as if grimmest, bloodiest tragedy were not a-foot. But probably Washington, and the surrounding country dumped in here, never had two other such days and nights of fun as at the reunion of soldiers here September 30 and October 1, 1879. County companies mustered two hundred and forty-four men, and there were representatives of fifteen Iowa infantry regiments and four of cavalry, and boys from Missouri, Colorado, eleven Ohio regiments, six of Indiana, eight of Illinois, one Wisconsin, two New York, one each from Pennsylvania, Virginia and Michigan, one United States and four United States Colored Infantry, Kirkwood were here, and fifteen thousand to twenty thousand people. I cripple myself, laughing, every time I re-read the Press account of the antics cut.

Floral Hall at the new fair grounds was used, and there were tents galore, and barracks on the north side of the grounds. Lush Teas and Capt. Kellogg were the chief romancers. Lush, son of a preacher, got off a sermon to a mob of yelling bummers, and related the story of the little bald-headed deacon in his father's church, who called folks to meeting with a horn instead of a bell. Some boys on Saturday put a lot of asafoetida, or its equivalent, in the horn, but the deacon could not blow it, and discovering the quality of the strangulated hernia, remarked that, though he was small and had always tried to be a meek and lowly Christian, he'd be —— if he couldn't whip the infernal cuss who stuffed that horn. Two years later, Lush and two unregenerates were at camp-meeting. When the deacon invited them to the mourning circle, Lush was too vile to go. "You have sworn and stolen, I suppose," queried the deacon. "Worse than that," groaned the sinner. "You, perhaps, have committed burglary, or greenbackism, or arson, or fusion, or fiction," said the devout man. "Ah, worse than that." "Can't be possible you have murdered?" "Worse yet," said Lush. The deacon laid his hat on a stump, shucked his coat, and said, "I've found the son of a gun who fixed that horn." Lush came away then.

The first night was as rackety with dare-deviltry as Pandemonium. Commander Cowles was captured in shirt-tail evening dress at a very late hour and given a break-neck sulky ride. The Muscatine Guards were attacked, and prisoners taken. Fellows would sneak in behind the skirmish line, grab a soldier and chuck him over the fence amongst the beggar lice. No one could sleep, the din was so fierce and the graybacks bit so. Kellogg imported a few graybacks, enough to go round, and he said they enjoyed the reunion as much as anybody. There seemed to be regiments of owls, Tom cats, whip-poorwills, and bull frogs. They sang, played cards, danced, screeched on fifes; Sherman's bummers came in with setting hens under their arms; most of the poultry in West Washington was foraged; one fellow towed in a reluctant Wm. Goat to waste its fragrance on the desert air. Along toward dawn, Alf. Chilcote was so tuckered, he sneaked with straw and blanket to the north side fence, to sleep. A soger saw him, jumped outside, stuck his musket under the fence and the straw on which Alf. was already fast asleep, and blazed away. Raise him? You know it raised him. Don't you forget it. He jumped into the air about twelve feet, and lit out half way across the grounds before he discovered he was not massacred. The soldier lay half an hour in spasms and convulsions of tickle. Alf. next tried the lee side of a woodpile, that was tipped over on him; he was not hurt, but fancied he had stepped on one of those infernal torpedoes, and was convinced he bore a charmed life. Capt. Kellogg, when he got all those sterilized and disinfected stories out of his system, lay under an oak tree asleep. An old vet. stole up with a musket that had had a charge in it since the war of 1812, aimed at a zenith star, and exploded the dynamite up the tree, and brought down four bushels of acorns. Kellogg faintly murmured, "Wake me early, mother dear, for I'm to be queen o' the May."

City guerrillas adulterated the tank of drinking water with personal cards.

The spree was getting old toward dawn, when the coming of a circus from Brighton socked in the needed spur. It was halted, wagon by wagon, but none of the sleepy drivers could give the counter-sign, which was "sow-belly," and each was so bedevilled that the procession was an hour and a half passing a given point. Finally, the elephant came swinging along, his trunk checked through to Columbus City, and the boys stampeded him by firing shots, till he was probably the most bughouse 'phant ever seen on this continent. Surgeon Parkinson's sick call was very healthy stuff. The boys were in no shape for a sham battle that day, but Moothart's two hundred and sixty gallons of stout coffee set 'em up, and the arduous day went through as slick as if greased. The late Capt. T. L. Montgomery, a sedate man, and

Col. Welker said that night escapade was the fastest fun they saw in three years of service.

MARCH TO THE SEA AND HOME-COMING.

For our boys in the western armies, the march to the sea, and up to Washington, and the grand review and final discharge, to come home, crowned with glory their martial career. Such mileage as their legs had done! They went out as boys or youths, glad of the adventure, glad of the chance to see the world, glad to have a share in saving the Union, glad even of the danger, and careless of death. A noble pride was in their hearts. They had had a career, had seen much, felt much, learned much, and were broadened by their rare experience. They came back, sure that they would be held in honor and love by the home communities. Probably, it did not occur to them that their records would be passports to preferment, the richest kind of political asset. So it proved. The electorate of the county has been no end kind to the old veterans, but no kindlier than they deserved to be treated. Other things being equal, offices and honors have been freely given by preference to our boys in blue. Most wonderful of all, they cheerfully took up life in shop, on farm, where they had dropped it at the country's call, the soldier lapsing into the citizen. Just so dissolved Cromwell's omnipotent army in England, to the astonishment of all, says Lord Macaulay, relieving all fears. Peace and industry were larger spheres than war. From 1865 to 1898, we basked in peace, as a prairie soaks in sunshine and rain. Over a generation of quiet, then

THE SPANISH WAR.

Again the country sprang to arms, especially the south—she showed a wonderful passion to fight for the old flag, and atone for delinquencies. Martial fraternity proved the strongest bond of union yet.

What a crop of islands the concussion of our naval guns shook down! Cuba, Porto Rico, the Philippines, no one knew how many, or what to do with them. It was embarrassing. The victory proved to be a great bore. It made us play the role of Providence, and it is yet too early to say if we were cut out for Providences.

Washington county raised the bulk of a fine company of young fellows, many of them the sons of soldiers in the Civil war. They had heard their sires brag so much about war, they were crazy to smell gunpowder, too. Their mothers cried, but their fathers did not—they were glad to give the kids their old chance at manly romance. The bearing of the sires was fine to see.

The kids did not put on any airs over the "old man" when they came back. Honors were somewhat even. The contrast in transportation showed the growth of the country in wealth, in thirty-eight years. The old Civil war men went to the front on their feet and hind legs, or at best in box cars and stock cars; the sons in Pullmans, or at least in first-class passenger coaches. Here and there one heard a sneering remark or grouch about this picnic soldiering, as it was called, but why not? It should be a point of national pride that our boys could go and come in that nice way. This was a great country when they went out, thanks to what their fathers did in the '60s.

Our boys did not go further than Jacksonville, Florida. It was not their fault that they were not needed in Cuba. They were eager to cross. They would have been healthier, had they gone, for they would then have been beyond the jurisdiction of fond mothers' delicacies, unwisely sent from home to Florida, and from Floridian pies and other symbols of certain death. Sow-belly and beans are more sanitary. A soldier needs the severe regimen of a pugilist in training. Many fell sick, and three died—Conger, Huff and Crawford. Here is the roster:

FIFTIETH IOWA—COMPANY D.

D. W. Harvey, Capt.; L. Hollingsworth, 1 Lt.; S. W. Brookhart, 2 Lt.; W. M. Shafer, Q. M. S.; E. E. Page, S.; O. B. Stichter, S.; L. R. Morehouse, S.; C. L. Shanefelt, S.; J. L. Neiswanger, S.; O. F. Adams, C.; S. J. Kellogg, C.; J. H. Steck, C.; H. S. Wilson, C.; H. L. Boyer, C.; C. C. Wilson, C.; G. E. Whitacre, C.; C. A. Dewey, C.; Stanley Miller, C.; F. E. Latta, C.; R. L. Manners, Mus.; H. F. Mickey, Mus.; J. F. Durham, Art.; G. F. Howard, Wag.; Peter A. Akey, Marshall Adams, M. D. Aronfelt, J. H. Baird, A. F. Beitle, F. C. Beatty, E. C. Brier, John Bartholomew, Fred Bidwell, C. L. Boone, Howard Burham, Thos. Clancey, R. R. Conger, H. M. Crone, W. J. Crawford, F. N. Crooks, L. R. Diller, W. L. Diehl, F. H. Gray, Wm. A. Hooper, J. L. Hampshire, C. W. Hise, Ed. Humm, F. A. Kilgore, M. D. Kos, W. C. Laughead, G. G. Lemon, G. E. Manatt, H. H. McCleery, C. M. McCoy, J. E. Moore, Maynard Marsh, J. T. McCarty, G. E. McConahey, F. C. Myers, H. J. Nichols, C. R. Nelson, C. B. Olds, L. J. Oldaker, H. O. D. Page, J. E. Peck, P. L. Parker, C. C. Reister, E. C. Rosenbarger, R. H. Riley, Hugh Ruff, Wm. Rhodes, Milan Shields, S. S. Smith, C. L. Stewart, S. J. Schmucker, G. W. Thomas, Jr., C. J. Thorn, E. P. Thompson, Fred Underwood, A. E. Walther, C. P. Warner, R. E. Wheaton, W. A. White, A. G. Wilcox, F. M. Wilkins, Jas. S. Wilson, C. L. Woods, Jack Worthen, W. F. Wilson, H. C. Waddell, G. G. Young,.

COMPANY D, FIFTIETH IOWA

Returning at close of Spanish-American war

Parrott Knouse transferred to hospital corps.

Karl Law transferred to signal corps.

DEATHS.

A. W. Huff, typhoid, Jacksonville, Fla., August 22.

R. R. Conger, typhoid, Jacksonville, August 31.

F. N. Crawford, typhoid, Washington, October 8.

Washington county may properly be proud of her soldiery, of the gallant records they made, of the manly way they carried themselves since discharge, of the civic places they have creditably filled, of the enviable posts they have occupied, honoring themselves in the high services they have rendered. "When can their glory fade?"

CHAPTER XX.

OMNIBUS—SKETCHES, ETC.

A miscellany of things unrelated may crowd into this 'bus. A 'bus can always hold one more.

Pipe organs were put in the M. E. and Presbyterian churches in 1892, and the Baptists installed one in '99. The Second U. P. church put in a piano in 1902, and Fort Sherman began playing a brass horn in its Sunday school in '08. The First U. P. church installed a piano in May, '05, just before the General Assembly met there. In late years the Second U. P. supplied New York city with a minister, Howard Tate, and the First U. P. gave Cedarville, Ohio, a pastor in Mills Taylor.

Our first baseball team was formed in 1866, and played four or five years. Members—C. H. Wilson, Dr. E. F. Clapp, Dr. Emmett Chapman, Dwight J. Norton, J. S. Shearer, Z. T. Lindsey, Mart Whitcomb, Marsh Glenn, G. G. Rodman. The boys held a re-union here in June, '05, and played a spectacle game and sat for another picture, and both groups and a sketch of their history were published in the sporting section of the Sunday Chicago Tribune.

The first bridges in the county were on the Military road, across Goose creek and Whiskey Run. There were no other bridges till 1860. Fords and ferries answered very well. And that Military road was the first road in the county.

The beech tree does not thrive in this county, or, indeed, anywhere in Iowa. So far as known, there are but two beech trees in the county, one on George Fulton's place and one on the old Letts-Brockway farm, both small and slow growers.

We have never tried to produce rain by explosives. It sufficed to call a picnic, a county fair, a Chautauqua, a Memorial Day exercise, or a nominating congressional convention. All those were sure umbrella days.

The first buggy brought here was by one Reed, the date not discoverable. It was a great curiosity, and excited more interest than an aeroplane would now. Any swell fellow, who proposed matrimony, was as sure to bespeak this vehicle for a bridal ride as to engage the county clerk and a minister. On every extra occasion, that buggy was sure to go, like Mary's little lamb.

It is well to record here the successive steps in county population. In 1838 it was 283; in '40, 1,571; '44, 3,120; '46, when state was admitted, 3,483; '47, 3,518; '49, 4,434; '51, 5,079; '53, 7,560; '56, 11,113; '59, 13,366; '60, 14,235; '63, 18,975; '75, 19,269; '80, 20,374; '85, 18,504; '90, 18,468; '95, 18,845; 1900, 20,718; 1905, 20,116.

The stock amusements in the olden times were bee hunts, husking bees, turkey shooting matches, camp-meetings lighted by blazing logs, June bugs and lovers' eye-beams, raisings, dances, kissing parties, spelling and singing schools, picnics, funerals, political meetings, wolf hunts in winter, stray preachers and lecturers on phrenology with good yells in them and furious gestures. The ancient relishes were wild fruits, berries and honey, tho' sorghum was largely used for sweetening.

M. D. Story's claim was on the site of Lexington. He laid it out and called the post-office "Cedarville," though it was nicknamed "Spankem"—a cue to some forgotten history? Lute Martin built the store in '56; the present school house was built in '59 and the parsonage and church in '65.

Three of our citizens have served on governors' staffs—Judge A. R. Dewey on Gear's, and C. J. Wilson and S. W. Brookhart on Gov. Cummins' and Carroll's.

The Washington Guards were organized August 1, '78, A. R. Dewey captain, Robert McGaughey first and W. H. Judson second lieutenants. When mustered in, they became Company D, I. N. G. These veterans have served as officers, Col. Palmer as captain, A. A. Rodman and Col. Cowles as lieutenants. The Washington Independent Battery was formed by Wm. R. McCutcheon, captain, and J. J. Kellogg, lieutenant, in '79. It has two brass six pounders.

Mrs. Rev. E. W. Twining came here in '39 from Virginia where she was born in 1817. In Des Moines she saw five hundred Indians dance on the commons where the court house stands.

In '41 there was a Palace in Washington, called the "Starry House." Jos. and Wm. Terry built it on the west side of the square, just north of the Citizens' Bank, two stories, twenty by forty-two, long way to the street, a grocery below, occupied, in turn, by Smith & Caruthers, Ralph Dewey, Capt. Daugherty and W. A. Stiles. And in one end a restaurant owned, tandem, by Crosby Bros., Carroll, J. W. Morton; and above were flats, Rev. Dr. Vincent using one, Dr. Lee and R. R. Walker the others. A little further north was the "Central House," W. W. Kendall proprietor or landlord. Guests lodged above a grocery and drug store where Stolte and Ralph Smith hold

Charles Hebener

D. S. Cole

J. J. Kellogg

Alex Coffman

J. G. Hise

Mart Whitcomb

MEMBERS OF THE CRACK RIFLE TEAM OF CO. D, 2D REGT., I. N. G.

forth now. The Starry House in the '60s had an infirm, teetery floor and a sky line as sway-backed as Dr. Rice's old black mare. The Central was built in '56. There is some esthetic history connected with it. Mr. Kendall had visited Washington, D. C., and observed the show of things in the dining rooms there, and imported the styles here at his tables. He introduced side dishes and courses, thus putting a gilding on the fine art of feeding. Hitherto, everything had been slung on at once, pell mell, on the table—meats, vegetables, bread, cake, pastry, sauces, fruit, condiments, butter, cheese, eggs, etc., and the order was: "Jest set right up and help yerselves," while girls stood behind the chairs with hands full of bushes and shooed the flies, but now the landlord engaged a corps of girls with white aprons and caps to reel off the names of the dishes—roast beef, corned beef, hamaneggs, beefsteak, liver, bacon, veal, pork chops, lamb cutlets, rooster, calf's brains, mutton, jerked buffalo, etc., and the average patron got all balled up trying to grasp the lingo that was unpunctuated, and would generally say, in desperation, "Oh, bring me some sow-belly and beans," adding a postscript, "Don't fetch none of them calf's brains—a danged fool calf haint got no brains." After awhile the girl came back with a tray full of dishes that she spread out, fan-shape, in front of the patron, with little dabs of prunes, squash, cold slaw, apple sauce, mashed potato, peas, string-beans, turnips in—everything but stewed tomato—the love-apple had not then been discovered as a food. For all this innovation, the old settlers were indebted to Hugh Kendall's father.

The Central lost its identity in 1908, when those three fronts of beauty were put in for Stolte, Ralph Smith and Jas. Work. When the Central was in its prime, Col. Cowles was running the Iowa House on the Crail corner and either Sam Joy or Snodgrass the Washington House on the site of the Colenso.

In '44, the Fourth of July was celebrated in "Yankee Diggins," southwest of Wellman. Geo. Pinkerton was president of the day, and the orator was Mr. Willson, a relative of our Hon. Horace Willson. These men and Bradford, Jackson et al. occupied a row of cabins on the northwest quarter of section 26, range 9.

Is it fancy, or is it fact, that pioneer life develops individuality? Or is it the original men who emigrate, and attest unusual force of character by leaving old associations and challenging fortune in new fields? Or is there a streak of oddity in emigrants, a touch of wander-lust that marks them as original men? At any rate, it was a racy, peculiar, individual lot of men who came here in the earlier years. Take such men as Everson, Keck, Graham, Wm. Wells, Michael Hayes, Whitcomb, J. C. Conger, Cleaves, A. H. Patterson, Henry Parr, Capt. Moreland, the Chilcotes, Iams, Jonathan and Michael

Wilson, Bacon, S. B. Dawson, I. H. Friend, Fleak, the Griffiths, Gideon Bear, the Brintons, Rader, Rev. John O'Loughlin, Peter Sharpe, Van Doren, Carmichael, Father Drake, McGuigan, Wm. McGaughey, Sam Russell, 'Squire B. Verain. Robert Fisher, Rousseau, Teas, Peter Dray,—not one of these men reminded you of any other soul in the universe. The mould and pattern were broken when they were made, and if you sent to the factory for repairs, you could get no duplicates. Each was a new type, but it ended in them—was not transmitted. You would no more mistake any of them for another than take a carnation for a peony or a rose for a skunk cabbage or a phallic fungus. The bore of so-called society is, that folks are either all alike or try to be; they imitate; their flavors are mixed, as in melons grown near pumpkins; they have lost interesting identity, the charm of individuality and the value of personality. They weakly affect the same opinions, if such mushy creatures can be said to have opinions and convictions. But the men named above stood on their own feet, had no reserves or concealments or affectations, talked naturally, acted spontaneously, did things and said things that flowed out of their characters, so that contact and conversation with them were a series of gay surprises; one enjoyed and relished them, and the funny things they said and did, the anecdotes and stories connected with them are still the staple of talk and laughter among groups of survivors, long years after the subjects of these memories had turned to dust. Now and then a squad of men will roar over something recalled of Moreland, or Sam Russell, or Conger, or Dr. Chilcote, Everson et al., and it is as merry as a Celtic wake, a gay post mortem. There is no solemnity about these autopsies. For the subject, this is fame, a sort of immortality; it may last fifty to seventy-five years, or till all his contemporaries are gone. And then tradition may extend the term of tickle. The length of the term seems to depend upon the force of character the man had, the degree of his wit, the quality of his humor and whims. Probably, Sam Russell will last longer than any other man, his drollery was so varied. For over fifty years folks have laughed over Michael Hayes' naive remark while serving on the board of county commissioners or supervisors. He closely scanned bills to protect the public's interests, according to his sworn duty and because he was a scrupulously honest man, and his invariable O. K. was, "as I don't see any way to get out of paying this bill, I move it be allowed." Everson contributed much to the gayety of nations, without intending it, but simply because it was Eversonese. One hot day he was laying stone wall as foundation for a plank walk fronting his north side properties, and was as sweaty, dirty and tired as Henry Clay Dean, when a town teaze squatted to watch him and give advice. Everson paid no attention, and when the job was done he quietly said—"If this work does not suit

Phon Sheets

A. A. Rodman

C. J. Wilson

W. R. McCutcheon

Thomas Teller

MEMBERS OF THE CRACK RIFLE TEAM OF CO. D, 2D REGT., I. N. G.

you, if I were in your place I wouldn't give the workmen a —— cent." His speech to Dr. Parkinson after his fire on the north side was funny, but it would need to be sterilized before it could go into this veracious history.

Morgan's dozen words to Dean have been a classic comedy for forty-nine years, and not less so Iams' slam on a possible president from Dutch Creek.

Dr. Chilcote was walking up town one night with his two brothers, on East Washington street. At Ike Wagner's then a tree stood in the middle of the walk, but he had forgotten it, and being near-sighted, he dashed into the tree, smashed his glasses, barked his nose, cut his brow, lips and chin, but did not kill the tree. Washing his face at his store and improving his beauty with criss-cross strips of court plaster and bandages, he cleverly remarked he was glad it was a soft maple; if it had been a hard maple, it would have spoiled him.

L. B. Fleak, for long the Sage of Brighton, spent a large part of his career in Keokuk, and regarded Heaven as a poor suburb to Keokuk. He was associated with General, afterward Congressman, Curtis, and later exercised his genius as a hotel landlord by keeping "The Box Trap" in that idolized city. An amusing row occurred in it one night. A Gen. Brown had been sent there from Ft. Madison to prevent a division of Lee county. Brown and some merry cronies had an upper room in Fleak's tavern, hitting the bottle between whiles at euchre. At midnight, the gallant general felt like hellooing, and the party said, "Do it." He raised a window, stuck his head out, and yelled several Indian war whoops, waking not only the town, but landlord Fleak, who got hostile at once, yet was polite. Appareled in pajamas, or their equivalent, and a night cap, L. B. F. appeared at the revellers' door as a diplomat, and retired. Brown was equally polite, and regretted the incident—it would not occur again. In a half hour, the General felt the need of getting another college yell or red war whoop out of his system, lifted the window, poked his phrenology out, and made the windows of heaven rattle. Col. Fleak reappeared, somewhat heated, his night cap on askew, in his agitation, but he restrained his passion and was polite and diplomatic, and the colonel and the general played the role of my dear Alphonse and my dear Gaston to the limit. It should not happen again. But it did, the general out-doing a calliope and our Washington water works fire alarm. Then mine host Fleak arose in fury, yanked the corks out of all the vials of his wrath and went on the warpath, but still as a diplomat and polite Lord Chesterfield, merely remarking, "General Brown, your horse will be at the door in five minutes." Brown thanked him politely, and left for Hog Thief Hollow.

Mr. Fleak was a character, full of fun, anecdote and varied information. For many years he was my Press correspondent, and sent in amusing stuff.

He had knocked round the world so much, living so many years in one place, so many years in each of a score or two more places, that in telling of it, he got into a horse's habit of over-reaching with the hind feet, and the local wags amused themselves by counting up these several years of residence, and they made him out several centuries old. Gus Ross played the same trick on a man here—the reader may profitably ask A. H. Wallace or C. J. Wilson to tell about it, in Gus' tone of voice.

Mr. Fleak went to England to live with an uncle, but home-sickness drove him to return ship after three months. He went to Keokuk in '40, and kept the first store, the first tavern, was first justice of the peace and first postmaster there. In the Mormon Nauvoo troubles he and others captured a lot of guns and ammunition, greatly embarrassing the Saints, and they hunted Fleak's party with Joe Smith's orders to kill them. He was a farmer near Fairfield, a landlord and editor of two papers at Brighton, travelled three years as deputy grand master of Masons and lectured, and was private secretary to Gen. Curtis, with the rank and pay of major, to the end of the war.

Two deliciously superstitious old fellows lived apparently in the north part of the county, but really in the Middle Ages. We usually confine the supernatural to our religion, but these men imported it "into their business and homes," as Lord Bacon says. Both were afraid of ghosts, witches and the Evil Eye. One kept a silver Dollar of the Daddies to chuck into the churn to scare off witches and fetch the butter betimes. Witches—did you know that?—"dee-light" to hold butter back. And both hung up horse-shoes everywhere to put out said Evil Eye. A horse shoe flung into the swill barrel and feed-trough shooed off the bad things. That coin was, indeed, the "almighty dollar." It policed the hogs, churn, slop bucket, swill barrel, and was a spy worth its weight in gold. It baffled the imps all the time. If lightning struck in the woods, one would hunt a week for the blasted tree to get splinters to stick up on his doors and windows, an infallible scare-crow and a perfect defense against witches, and a splinter stuck in a hollow tooth instantly cured ache. And as early as June in each year he hunted for the skins snakes sloughed, gliding through bushes; these festooned round the premises were a sovereign guard against the onslaught of the demonic agencies. One of them was an inveterate chewer, but did not want his boys to become slaves to the weed, and when a boy baby was born, this fond sire, who was a sort of protective tariff in the home, treated the kid in a novel way, as Mr. Ol. Brown will explain to those curious in such solemn rites—until he disinfects them, he can't expect me to publish them in this accurate history.

Another queer man was Caleb Cleaves, cobbler, also Congregationalist. His clinical sheep story tried the faith of all who heard it. It has never been

Dr. Joseph McKee

Dr. J. R. Burroughs

Dr. William McClelland

Dr. William H. Rousseau

Dr. W. F. Rodman

Dr. Samuel Marshall

PIONEER DOCTORS

sterilized. He was born in Maine and had been what he called a "seafaring man." When he died, he wanted to go, not to Paris, but to Yarmouth. There was a solitary spot on the ocean's brink, pine-clad, the sea in the offing, and his prayer was "Bury me there, so that I can see the ships coming and going." And at last his prayer was answered. He is dust, but I can still see him sitting on his leather seat, shaking with laughter, and all his fat redundancies, double chin, neck, bow-window quivering with merriment like a bowl of jelly. When fat folk laugh, they also jell.

There is not accessible anything like a complete record of the doctors of the county. Dr. Mallet, of South Bend, Ind., it is said, was the first practitioner in Brighton, but later went to Keokuk. Van Pelt was the first in Clay, an Indianian, long dead. James Waters was the first M. D. in Lime Creek, and moved to Kansas. Dr. Petit, who also practised there, lives in Chicago, aged and rich. John Holland, a Thompsonian doctor, was the first in English River, and he practiced several years, though it is claimed that Simon P. Teeple was the first M. D. on the river called English, but he went to Iowa City in '41. Henry Pringle practiced many years in Clay, a township that turned out nine doctors and veterinaries—Edgar Meacham, Herman Gowry, David Beach, Wm. Brinton, Hattie Whitacre, Ranny Hall, Wm. Nieukirk, Henry Pringle and veterinary R. J. Whitacre. Dr. Geo. H. Stone was the first M. D. in Washington, in '40,—a gruff ex-navy surgeon who moved to Sigourney and named it for the Poetess, and she acknowledged the honor, though knowing he had given her a Stone instead of a loaf of bread or a whole bakery. He was the first doctor to be called into Marion.

In 1839, Dr. Horace Carley was in Brighton, dying that year, and his body was the first seed planted in that cemetery—a sort of poetic justice in that.

Dr. Jos. Hamilton, from Ohio, practiced many years in English River, and was able to resist calls for several years after he ceased practice. He was also an M. E. preacher.

Dr. Wm. H. Rousseau came here from Kentucky in '44. He was a very notable man, eccentric, humorous, full of drive, energy and individuality, and he did an immense business for many years. As late as September 23, '73, he with Drs. W. E. Fraser and J. R. Burroughs organized Washington County Medical Society. A giant in body and powerful in mind, he was a mark for caricature, and Burroughs was exquisitely funny and happy in taking him off, especially in depicting Rousseau's impatience with Dr. Rice, a Homeo. Big Pills had no use for Little Pills, and Burroughs could mimic tones, grimaces and motions to perfection—all kindly done, of course, but with infinite humorous appreciation.

Rousseau and Dr. Wm. McClelland were great friends, though of opposite temperaments, tastes, habits, etc. As quinine in the '40s was four dollars per ounce, these two fixed up a preparation of arsenic that was just as good, and cheap. They tried it on Dr. Abe N. Miller and Richard B. McMillan, with their consent, and as it did not kill them, the compound was used habitually, and medical fees came down fifty per cent. They put cholera patients on hot bricks a la Montezuma on live coals, and it worked like a charm.

McClelland saw the rise of several schools of medicine here, and was tolerant and sweet. M. C. Kilgore introduced the eclectic system, Dr. M. C. Parker, homeopathy, Dr. A. N. Miller, cold water cure, packing, magnetic rubbing, but osteopathy, hypnotism or suggestion, and Christian Science are cults later than his time. Stone, Rousseau and McClelland rode horses over this county before roads, bridges and fences. The latter formed the cavalry man's habit of sleeping on his horse, feet in stirrups, coming home. If the horse stopped suddenly, pitching him on to the pommel, he knew a rattlesnake was coiled in the trail, and, as there was nothing on the prairie to kill it with, and he did not dare get off and prescribe for it, and tell it to run out its tongue—it was doing that anyhow,—and feel of its button as a pulse (for if he had pressed the button, the snake would have done the rest)—and give his snakeship a dose and leave directions to shake the bottle well before using and take every two hours, etc., why, he would either surrender the right of way to the snake, or, if he had matches and it was autumn, he'd fire the grass and thus fight the devil with fire. Rattlesnakes would have taken the country if the dry wild grass fires had not kept them in check.

Often he rode horse eighty miles a day. He had as much confidence in his horse as the deacon has in his pastor, and so both dared sleep in saddle and pew. It was not the up-turn of the virgin soil, that loosed the miasm which shook these prairies with ague like a peat bog in Ireland—it was stagnant water in pools and undrained lands, in which mosquitoes hatched to convey poison germs in their bite. No one knew that fact then.

Dr. J. R. Burroughs filled a large place for many years. No more amusing fellow ever fumbled a wrist or looked at a lolled-out tongue. He was a clever mimic, full of drollery and wit, and his good cheer in a sick room did lots more good than his pills and powders that he rather regarded as innocent fakes and jokes. He practiced allopathy, homeopathy and funopathy. It was killing to see him take off his fellow M. D.'s, in his kindly way, he enjoying the caricature as much as anybody. His sketches of Rousseau, Rice, Miller, Eiskamp et al. were real vaudeville. The fun-makers are the best doctors and health-contrivers, and the men and women who laugh most keep young longest by abolishing the microbe of old age, grouch and cantankerous crankiness.

Dr. O. H. Prizer

Dr. Nelson Van Patten

Dr. A. S. Cowden

Dr. J. D. Miles

Dr. D. Scofield

PIONEER DOCTORS

A laugh is a specific for anything bad. And Burroughs was a very crisp critic. At a concert, he said of a singer, his voice was a bit "lumpy." That was enough—it was a picture, a kodak snapped on the spot.

Dr. Martin was another humorist in the practice of that profession, in spite of nerves and almost chronic invalidism. He managed to get a deal of fun out of the world. The trouble with humorists is, when they get hold of a good thing that tickles the very soul, they have to tell it, and for a man to give away professional secrets is, surely, not according to Hoyle. I could give some illustrations, but they would need to be sterilized, if not disinfected.

In many ways, Dr. G. Eiskamp was a remarkable man. His reading in medicine, in general science, literature and philosophy was wide, deep, thorough, far and away beyond that of any professional man in our whole history. That is no exaggeration at all. His learning was very great, and his memory of it all phenomenal. A St. Louis surgeon had mal-operated on his vocal organs and impaired his speech, but his mastery of English was, as in Carl Schurz' case, a wonder. For years he knew he was doomed, said he should not reach fifty years of age, and beat his prophecy three months; but with that fatal conviction, he took up and carried cheerfully the white man's burden.

Dr. Darius Scofield was also a wide reader of the theoretical side of things, but was not fortunate, in many cases, in applying his theories. He was a useful man, public-spirited, an advocate of such good things as libraries, a public and private sanitation, sewerage, hygiene, and he set the first good example for a very simple funeral and the cremation of his own body.

Speaking of queer men, there was an honest, industrious man, big-boned, of bilious temperament, a giant of strength, who used to get a little off mentally, and under those spells he meditated a new religion that he was going to spring on these parts. He would consult Capt. Kellogg about it, though I can't understand how the Captain could be regarded an expert on such creations as new religions. I do not remember all the tenets, further than this, there were to be five persons in the trinity, and the author quoted Emerson's "Why does Nature love the number five, and the star form repeat?" When Capt. Kellogg asked how soon he would launch the new cult, Hercules answered,

"When the blue birds appear
The time draws near."

This revives one of J. C. Conger's sly jokes. Several years after his removal from York state, Rev. Dr. J. R. Doig came here from Mr. Conger's old home, and at the end of a delightful visit and talk of old times, Conger kept his face straight and gravely asked the divine about the local religious conditions back there, remarking that when he left that region they were just introducing the Bible there. The look that Doig gave Conger!

This picture is unforgetable—our jolly, fat river captain, L. Moreland, was run away with on a Brighton road along Skunk river, and he and the buggy thrown into the river. The reader who recalls the corporosity of the captain can imagine there was a large displacement, as naval architects would say, and if he hit the water slant-wise instead of flat, the concussion would not be great. He was somewhat stunned, but he struggled out under the shelving bank, and was vastly amused by the talk above him, of rescuing parties, who said, "well, I guess Cap is done for. He was probably drowned and the body gone down stream and over the dam," when Cap broke into a laugh and put in a general denial, ending with, "not by a mill-dam site." He was sitting in the sand, as wet as a muskrat, and not hurt a bit.

Cleaves and Conger had a world of fun with Peter Dray, a blacksmith just north of the present Press office. Dray must have been a queer one, for he inspired poetry in Conger.

"Hark to the news of Peter Dray
Who on the Sabbath makes his hay."

Then follows a stanza about a bed tick and prairie grass and Geo. McKay, they cut their wood and mowed their hay all on the holy Sabbath day. Some of the stanzas are repeated by the venerables, but I have to censor the unsterilized things. Peter brought the first steam engine to this town. Conger and Cleaves set a traveling phrenological lecturer, holding forth in the Cowles school house, on Dray, who was very dirty and ragged, just from his shop work, and the speaker, taking him for a tough, gave him a very bad head and character. According to his diagnosis, Dray had the worst "gourd" in the United States and territories, he would steal, lie, murder, etc. Those two wags died several times, laughing. It occurred to them that they could make a nature faker of the lecturer by dressing up Peter for a subsequent meeting, and naming him "Dr. Barker." They coached him as to what to say, dressed him elaborately, armed him with a gold-headed cane, gold watch with long flashy fob, plug hat, etc., and sat him in the back part of the house. When men were called for for examination, gratis, Cleaves and Conger bawled "Dr. Barker!" vociferously, but the doctor demurred, and the lecturer, seeing the style of man, insisted on his coming up, and, like the supreme court, he reversed himself on his estimate. This subject was a compound of St. Paul, Shakespeare, Lord Bacon, Geo. Washington et al. Conger catechised the lecturer, "did you ever see that man before?" "No." "Never felt of his bumps?" "No." "Well, you did, two nights ago, and you gave him a bad roast." The crowd jeered, and the fake left the house and town.

J. C. CONGER

His pastor tried hard to dissuade our first pioneer, Adam Ritchey, from coming here from Illinois, but in vain, and then said, "You may go, but I warn you no good will come of it, and you will receive punishment for it, for you are deliberately leaving your church and communion, going away among heathen, and the Gospel will never cross the Mississippi." That "cloth" was "punk."

The smart things Wm. McGaughey did and the droll things he said will be current talk for many years. He lived into the '90s, and never for a moment forgot his cunning and love of fun. And so of others,—H. D. and Chris. Rogers, Aleck Houck, Mart Kilgore, Michael Schilling, J. G. Webb, and many others, funny things could be said, but there is no room. The next historian may deal with them.

An irascible man on Crooked creek had been annoyed by neighbor cows camping at night in the road in front of his house, and concluded to fix them, but was mean and cruel. One night he sallied out with an ax and cut the tails off from a herd lying down. In the morning he found they were his own cattle, but he did not know they had got out of the corral.

Two men were frolicking on the bank of said creek, one dressed in immaculate white. The other grabbed the dude and with powerful right arm held him out over the creek, by main strength. "Drop me if you dare," said the dandy, not believing he would dare do so, as it was fifteen to twenty feet down to the water, but the challenged did drop him. He came up, soaked, soiled, hopping mad, raging with threats, so deliriously angry he scratched the ground around him like a turkey, said "look over there," pointing to a house where a murder had been committed, and demanded, over and over, "conciliate me," meaning apologize.

However, people are now, probably, as individual and original as were the pioneers, men and women of as distinctive flavor as any in Auld Lang Syne. I could name a score or two, at least, now living, who are as odd, amusing and queer as our forebears, but I shall not do it. They, in turn, will be quoted and laughed over for as long as any of the geniuses I have named.

There is one significant incident that must surely go into this rag-bag chapter: Twenty-five to thirty years ago certain tired house-wives struck on cooking, and an effort was made at co-operative living. Mrs. Malin opened the institution in a big room on the south side over The Fair. Twelve to fifteen families boarded there nearly two years. The cost of provisions was cast up weekly and patrons paid pro rata. Mrs. Malin worked up the raw material. The fare and service were excellent, far above the average the families had known before. But do you know the patrons at last got weary of the promiscuity, and gladly went back to their own flesh-pots in the Egypt of their own kitchens and dining rooms. Privacy was sweet. But the experiment was a sort of protest of housewives against the awful grind and humdrum of cooking three meals a day, washing dishes thrice, their homely work never done. Living as we do is a bore. Civilization has added grievous burdens. Our esthetics cost much more than they come to. There is something wrong in our economy if it is necessary for a man to work twelve hours a day just to live and make both ends meet, and for women to work even more. It doesn't pay. Life is not worth living on such terms. The Indians beat us to a frazzle on dwellings. They do not clean house twice a year, or once a year—they burn it—it is cheaper to build another. We eat too much. Two meals a day, at 9 a. m. and 4 p. m., are a great plenty. Where drink kills one, gobbling slays a hundred. Gluttony beats booze to the goal of homicide. It's disgusting, having a stomach, liver, bowels—if the Creator had only stirred the foods for animals and mankind into the air, as He did for plants, and let us breathe nourishment, what jolly good luck that would have been. O reader, when you make an animal kingdom, make men and animals that way.

We have many more birds than sang for the pioneers. There are infinitely more roosts for them, and food also—our ampler grain fields, orchards, vineyards, gardens, berry lots, and the myriads of insects they attract. We have more forests for them to nest in, and a net-work of wires, telephone and trolley, for their claws to grasp. This county, and all Iowa, and all the prairie states have largely gained in timber over the primitive days. Still, every man, woman and child, in city and county, should be a forester, at least to the extent of planting one tree a year. In a generation, such unity of effort would realize extensive forests. During the war our public square was full of locust trees. Borers killed all but one, that is still alive. Before the soldiers got home there were not as many leaves in that park as there were hairs on either one of Esau's hands. But see now. Prairie fires killed our ancient forests, but man is a cunning little fellow, and can make forests as easily as mud pies. I could wish the writer of the next history of this county, forty to fifty years hence, nothing better than that he could see and say that full one-quarter of our county area's face should then be whiskered with woods. If he shall so see, let him drop a tear on my bier for suggesting it, but for heaven's sake bid him spell that word bier right.

The sole thing this writer is really pleased with is, that he chanced to name it "Sunset" Park, and the name stuck.

Judge E. Ross once built a grist mill on the site of Benz' hotel, and his pottery, kilns, etc., where he made jugs, crocks and the like, stood where his children's home now is.

The year 1857 was a very wet one. A circus, hauled overland, stuck in the mud north of town. It was "broke" but gave daily performances in the hope to recoup its fortunes, and every eve it sent up balloons from the academy lot. All in vain. The manager borrowed money of Everson, giving as security a lion in his cage, placed on his lot now owned by Elmer Mason, back of The Temple. Leo would roar when hungry, and was more effective than the curfew to round up kids at home after dark. Everson did not have to go to Africa to get lions for the Smithsonian, nor lay his hand on the cockatrice's den.

When we were trying to repudiate railroad bonds, as described previously, Dr. Rice, an unbeliever, saw a hole in our armor and took an arrow shot at it, scoring the meeting for their disposition to do an immoral thing, in spite of our tall religious pretensions. He said we were worse than the heathen, and quoted from their philosophers, Confucius, Zoroaster et al. A rusty farmer rose and said, "I don't care a gol-darned what old Con-fu-cus, Zo-roast-er and other old heathens said; they're dead—I'm alive; I am opposed to paying them bonds, b'gosh." Doc just laughed. By the way, he looked exactly like Darwin.

Thirty to forty years ago there was no such functionary as an undertaker, in any such sense as we have them now. A person died, a cabinet maker went to the house and took measurements as for coat or shoes—indeed, a coffin was called an "overcoat"—and an ugly shaped thing was made of black walnut, with a house roof on it, and smelling of varnish, and ever since those who smelled varnish instantly thought of death and the grave, by the law of association. In those days, Wm. Wilson, Jr., a very sympathetic man, used to conduct funerals, and his warm heart always gushed tears from his eyes, to mingle with those of the more personal mourners. He was one of the most useful men we ever had, and at funerals he seemed indeed an angel.

Certainly, Washington never harbored a more unique genius than Gus Ross. He said the most killingly funny things in the fetchiest way. He had been an ocean sailor, I think, and his head was packed full of out-of-the-way information, and his body covered with tattooing. No one took from the library such a superior line of books, that he read in his dirty gun-shop in lulls of work, and he mastered the books, too. Gus goes into my Pantheon, even if I have to cast out other gods and demi-gods. And 'Squire Burkholder stays with Gus in there. If those men had only talked into a phonograph! Charley Wilson and Charley Hebener are not going to live forever.

Probably, the three biggest days in our history, in point of numbers in the turn-out, were: Grangers Day in '73, soldiers' reunion in '79, and Brinton's air-ship day ten or fifteen years later. There might have been more on hangman's day, and railroad day in '58, if the population had been denser. Folk will go further to see some one get hurt or killed than for any other reason. But the murderer was given a new trial, and the aviator did not fly, so could not get "hurted." Actually, hundreds, if not thousands, came expecting to see him fall and smash. Emerson rather ungraciously, but perhaps truthfully, said, "when people hear that any one is sick, all are animated by a faint hope that he may die." Morbid curiosity, you see.

Speaking of railway day, in '58, John W. Morton vividly recalls the evolutions of the Columbus City Guards, in command of the very polite Col. Garner. It was the first company of soldiers Wesley had ever seen, he who was a few years later destined to see thousands of real, not tin, soldiers. Garner would end each command thus: "Shoulder arms, if you please." "Right wheel, march, if you please." It tickled even the mourners.

As this chapter is a sort of clearing house for dead notables, I wish to encyst in amber the queer, delightful man whom all affectionately called "Old Bill" Glover. He was a shoe-maker, a nature-lover, a naturalist, with a rough head packed full of nature lore, and an eye, ear and nostril sensitive to beauty of form, color, sound, odor, fond of music and flowers and children, a heart big and warm, no end kind, sympathetic, helpful; but with all those tender yet steel-strong tendrils reaching out for love he was a bachelor all his many years. Perhaps that detachment was the reason why he was the Commander-in-Chief of all hearts. I muse and pass in slow, searching review the many scores of individual people I have known in Washington city and county, and if I have to select just one who, take him all in all, was The Real Thing, it would be Bill Glover, that rough opal with a constant soul of shifting colored fires.

Or if one asks for samples of men so odd they were unique, just think of Mr. Fitzgerald and his son Gowdy—the limit of individuality. Or think of those men so "con-trai-ry" that it is wittily said if they should drown in a rapid river, their bodies would be found several rods up-stream.

Our railroads used to be more accommodating in the early days, when traffic and travel were less than in this booming time. The old Narrow Gauge would stop at cross-roads to take on an old woman with a basket of eggs. Many years ago on our M. & M., now Rock Island road, when there was one train a day each way, the train crew took all the time there was. One day the fireman dropped his pipe, a few miles from Ainsworth. The train was stopped to recover it, and the conductor would halt anywhere for anybody to alight or to board.

A division roadmaster, long before G. W. Dye, fitted a sail to a railroad tricycle, and one day a gale upset the craft between here and Ainsworth.

THE FAIR GROUNDS ON BRINTON'S AIRSHIP DAY

The Washington post-office has been a wandering Jew. Mrs. Parker, who married Rheinart, was post-mistress in '56, on the present R. T. McCall lot. Dr. M. C. Parker served as P. M. near the Yellow Brick in Buchanan days. Wickersham had the office on an alley that bisected the east side of the square about at Lemmon's jewelry store, and opposite him was public scales, the alley leading to a lumber yard, later run by Boies & Barrett. An alley also bisected the north side, say at Ohngemach's shop, leading to Oz. Phelps' livery barns and to Bryson's lumber yard. Wickersham also had the P. O in the rear of the Democrat office, the Press office above, and stairs leading to the sanctum through a trap-door. Then Cols. Cowles and Bell, in turn, and also Wm. Wilson, Jr., had the P. O. across the street in a room back of Chilcote & Cook's drug store. Col. Bell and G. G. Rodman also served in the first room north of the alley in the rear of Hotel Colenso, and of late years Rodman, Hood, Cunningham and Lytle were P. M.'s in the present quarters. We have wandered long and far enough, from Post-master Everson's capacious hat, all round the square—we must have a federal building—the next historian will describe it, I can't.

To trace the journeys of old buildings is an interesting quest. Mrs. Parker's P. O. is now a dwelling on north Marion avenue, four blocks north of the tracks, opposite Mrs. Hannah Durst's home, north. Dr. Chilcote's drug store is the wood house on Dr. Stewart's home lot, near the M. E. church. The first frame M. E. church stood south of the opera house, and is a residence east of the late Wm. E. Chilcote's old home, opposite Brookhart's home, a four-gabled house. Friday Mason lived in the moved-off old Iowa House, on courthouse street north. Sam Gardner's late home once stood on Michael Schilling's lot on south side of square, where Tondre & Benz' millinery store is now, and in it Mother Axtell took boarders and had such patrons as Everson and Scofield. Hise Bros. snaked the United Brethren and Presbyterian churches to the creamery in N. W. Washington. The Starry House was moved to the lot just west of E. T. Beman's home, and was sold by Hugh Smith to Abe Snider. S. A. White sold the old Axtell house on the site of the present Presbyterian church, and it stands unoccupied and ramshackle the first door north of the button factory. The Iowa House barn and feed lot covered the block now occupied by court house, city hall and jail. It would be interesting if a local antiquarian should identify and chart all these old derelicts. What a map it would be.

The first Methodist service held in this city was in a log cabin between the homes of Harry Shrader and J. W. Morton. It was standing after the war, occupied by the father of John L. and M. C. Kilgore.

The wonderful prosperity of farmers the last dozen years, the enrichment of them by a series of fat crops and high prices, and the marvelous upward appreciation of their land, have resulted in the retirement of many of them to towns to live on the pensions of their fortunes, and the upshot of it is, a guild of tenants or renters. Good judges say over one-third of the active farmers in this county to-day are renters. A considerable per cent of them become farm-owners in due time. Cash rent now averages five dollars per acre, but the prevailing arrangement is a sheer halving of the crops produced. Now and then the owner requires say a dollar an acre cash besides half the grain.

Mrs. B. F. Brown recalls the universal farmer cry, in her girlhood, "Iowa can never be a grass state—what a pity—white clover is impossible." There was blue stem, wild prairie grass almost as coarse-haired as saw-edged slough grass, but farmers wanted mermaid tresses on their lands. The roadsides were then thick-set with dog-fennel. But it was noticed that if farmers cut the fennel before it seeded, white clover, that had been watching for a chance, came in, and all at once there were wide areas as white with this perfect honey-clover as elderberry blossoms and margarites. Infinitely more white clover then, if given a chance, than now. And red clover perpetuated itself when purple-coated, yellow-breeched bumblebees crossed the Mississippi and by their longer injectors fertilized the red-headed blossoms. And little by little, like a deepening dawn, blueglass crept in, perhaps a little before the '70s. It did not come directly from Kentucky, but via Missouri, and started around movers' camps where horses had been fed. Some have surmised that the grass came in with the big white Kentucky Henry Clay cattle that Clemons brought here in the late '50s, but he got them in Illinois. O. E. Brown, a close and generally accurate observer, is satisfied that bluegrass came to us via Missouri, thanks to movers. It was rather slow in spreading, as from one camp to another, ousting other grasses and weeds merely by packing the ground so full of its own rootlets that the other fauna had no chance, and was suffocated. That matter of roots of grasses preoccupying the soil is the entire secret of weed-killing. Bluegrass is the sign manual of a fertile soil, the world over, a soil that will grow clover and all the cereals that feed mankind.

It is strange, what a retinue of seeds, plants, animals follow men in their wanderings. It seems certain, tho' it has been disputed, that 'possums were not indigenous here, but sneaked after the white man. Same as to foxes. Both tag after chickens, as if they watched to see if the emigrant packed in the wagons the coops. They say, though, there was not a 'possum in this county in '54, nor till about '65. But skunks were ever here. Wolves drove back foxes. Woodpeckers, too, were comparatively late comers. Kentucky cardinals have come in within the last ten years. Rats are, notoriously, white men chasers. No sooner was a log cabin built, than rats and mice reported in them for duty. How did they get here? In the packing of furniture, etc.? Anyway, they came, as if the Devil brought them up his sleeves. Men are always losing something, from knives, money, trinkets to their virtue and things. The Mormons in streaking it through Nebraska and the miners who took the Santa Fe trail through Kansas, spilt sunflower seeds all along the way, and Kansas got its pet name from the yellow efflorescence, and in certain seasons both those states are as buff in landscape as the wall tints of churches. Seeds of weeds, good plants, fruits, vegetables, get scattered by birds, cattle, horses, men, and by such agencies bluegrass stole in here to rout out dog fennel and clothe the roadsides and fields with that loveliest of all hair—grass that, like snow, casts a blue shadow.

Here, between two great rivers lie two hundred by three hundred miles of the best soil in the world, and the population is only some two millions, much less than that of New York city and, perhaps, about equal to Chicago's score. It could easily support five or six millions, on the basis of Henry Wallace's estimate that the most profitable cultivation of the soil is about one hundred and fifty-one acres per capita. He thinks it will some near day be one hundred acres, perhaps eighty acres, and that will mean an increase in rural population proportioned to the decrease in the size of farms. The wonder is, that any one ever leaves Iowa, a state so exceptionally rich that it is only the best parts of her adjoining states that abut on her borders—South Dakota, Nebraska, Kansas, Missouri, Minnesota, Wisconsin, Illinois—to keep agreeable company with her, those sister states have to put their best feet foremost, as Wallace says. But thousanads on thousands of restless folk have first and last taken themselves as seed wheat and corn to other states. The Hawkeye club estimates the ex-Iowans in Spokane at three thousand to four thousand. And Los Angeles annually rounds up at the Iowa picnic fifteen thousand to twenty thousand former residents of Iowa. In Oregon our Iowa editorial excursion parties were met at all stations by scores and hundreds of previous citizens of our state. It's so everywhere. If an Iowa tourist of any mark of distinction goes anywhere in this wide western world, he needs to carry himself pretty straight, and cut up no rusties, or he will be spotted, identified, and peached on, very likely, just for fun. Under this subtle espionage, he doesn't have as gay a time as he might, eh? Well, be good, and you'll be lonesome.

Why should no mention be made of a character indeed—Leon Mayer, the pioneer clothier? He, too, had had a world of fun, like Jonathan Wilson and Rheinart. He had a pleasant, cordial habit of promenading round the square every fine morning, smoking, stopping at every store door, and saluting his fellow business men. He had a wonderful capacity for friendship, as, also, had that queen of warm-hearted women, the late Mrs. Simon, mother to Mrs. Sol. Rich.

John Dougherty was an early grocer. When he quit, his accounts were put in a collector's hands. A farmer got notice he owed D. for a bay colt. He came in, wroth, and said, "I never bought no colt of him." "You must, see, here it is down in black and white, 'bay colt.'" The ex-grocer was called. "No, surely not, I never sold him a bay colt—can't you read?—bag salt, colt." That's the way school children spell salt now—colt.

Our greatest hunter was no doubt Jesse Ashby. So said Michael Wilson, who was probably the best shot in our history. He confirms the story told elsewhere, that Ashby would walk right up to a deer grazing. Just before a suspecting deer lifts its head it twitches its tail, as a squirrel jerks its bush. Jesse would halt and stand rigid and look inanimate when the tail twitched, and the deer took him for a stump, and when the head lowered, he strode swiftly forward, a compact, integral body, no lateral movements, just an upright cylinder of a body that would deceive the very elect among deer. Wilson saw him do that many times. Game was so plenty here, it was a paradise to Ashby and Wilson. Even before they went out to seek elk, deer, turkeys, etc., those animals were already tied to the muzzles of their guns, and all the men had to do, was to bag them. Mr. Wilson came in '40. By '44 he wanted to see what Iowa is like. While visiting in Mahaska county, he set out for the headwaters of the Des Moines river, way up in the wilderness Ft. Dodge way, ere Ft. Dodge was. At Des Moines there was only a small fort. He rode a pony, carrying blankets, provisions such a flour, meal, bacon, etc. He fell sick, Indians stole his horse; he was deathly sick, lay on the ground almost too weak to stir; mosquitoes were eating him up; he tried to whittle a screen of boughs to fence his face, but still he could literally scrape them off his face with his palms; he realized he must move or perish there alone, and he staggered to the river, carrying his kit, gun, etc., saw a drift, and summoning the last fibers of his waning strength, he pried loose a few poles and bound them together with grape vines, loaded his stuff, and floated away. At evening he saw a log cabin, tied the raft, and approached the man in front, and begged for lodging, and was gruffly denied. His anger nerved him to say, "but I shall stay, I am sick, it is inhuman to turn me away; you are a cruel man." Drawing his rifle on the brute, "you bring up my things or I'll kill you in your tracks; I'd sooner kill you than a wolf. You're worse than a wolf—start, or I'll shoot you." He obeyed. In the morning his female beast refused breakfast, "we have nothing to eat." "Take my provisions, get me a breakfast or I'll kill you both." Stiff bluff for a man who hadn't an ounce of strength left. But it won. "Take my things down to the raft," drawing a bead on the man who asked, "Aren't you going to pay me?" "Not a cent—I ought to shoot you." He floated to the fort, and was given medical help. Finally, a Mahaska friend, glancing up the river, to a bend, exclaimed, "There comes Mike—he's lost his horse—betcher the Indians stole it." "How do you know it's Mike?" "By the silver plate on his gun shining in the sun."

For five years running, Mr. Wilson took first prize in Ohio squirrel shoots just before corn ripened. They were in such numbers, they destroyed the crop. Often he would kill one hundred and fifty a day. His son Charles J. saw him shoot the head off a turkey at one hundred and twenty-seven paces, when his gun was out of fix as to the trigger, and he had to draw back the hammer with his hand and let fly. No hawk on wing could escape his unerring bullet, so accurate was his judgment as to distance, speed of bird, and calculated aim. He brought down everything he aimed at, except the stars, sun and moon, but really he did not expect to get them. One could make a readable Buffalo Bill book, describing the hunters and their feats in our pioneer period.

As I see my finish, I regret no dates can be fixed for the origins of many things, as, when were finger bowls and napkins introduced into this provincial county? And who first exposed to "showers," with only a lap and no umbrella, girls about to be led to the altar without a halter, as they would not stand without hitching? And when was it? What married couple had the first receptions at the homes of either parents? Who gave the first lap supper, and when? Who first said it was bad form to ask for a second helping of soup, when folks are bored, teazed and bully-ragged to be helped to everything else a dozen times? And who has a picture of the idiot who set the fashion of sipping soup from the side instead of the end of the spoon, without an accompaniment of sound like "sloop" and tilting up the dish to get the very last drop? Who made it a misdemeanor to eat with a knife and compel the awkward Rubes to use a fork? Who forbade, and when, turning hot coffee and tea into a saucer, and swallowing the cooled contents with a sound like many waters? Who exiled a man for eating pie out of his palm? Who gave the first party, and when was it? that people did not want to go to, and stand around and smile and let on that they were having a gay and festive time while bored within an inch of their lives, and eat a lot of unwholesome stuff they did not care for, at an hour that would ruin the digestion of an alligator, and wake next morning with woolly caterpillars walking over their tongues? Who was the first Ananias or Sapphira who, at the door, at last, when the host and hostess were speeding the parting guests, got off the whopper, "We've had a perfectly delightful time?" One would like to fix the dates of all such things.

In the grave-yards, when did the first liar trace something preposterous in carved letters on the stones? We can make a pretty good guess as to the dates marking the progress of sculpture on the headstones. In the earlier catacombs there was engraved a dove, or a lamb whose fore legs were bigger than its body, and growing bigger toward the hooves. At a later time angels superseded bird and lamb—it was hard to give up wings altogether; but finally an interesting youngish widow appeared on the stones, in hoop-skirts, standing under a weeping-willow tree whose foliage resembled carded wool. Her right elbow rested on the top of the stone, and a handkerchief concealed her eyes, except as she lowered it to wipe her also tearful nose. Mortuary art was "progressive," like euchre and reform politics, etc. Sobs shook her cork-screw curls, and sympathetic single men organized expeditions to relieve her grief.

I have spoken of the renaissance in building pretty houses and making charming lawns and flower gardens, inspired by the construction of the court-house. That esthetic influence reached still farther. Ladies began at once to live up to that building by dressing more elegantly. The dress train appeared, and it took as long to cure the men of fright of it as to teach country horses not to shy at automobiles. Men were a long time in drill not to step on that crawling thing, either on a level or in going down stairs. When their awk-ward feet made a rip, they reddened in the face and said "pardon me," and she sweetly replied, "certainly," but really was mad enough to bite off his nose. Gentlemen, too, flowered out in evening suits. The swallow-tail coat came in, and the decollete vest, and broad expanse of shirt bosom so glairy a fly would slip up on it, and cuffs and collars that caused a deal of profanity, and sleeve buttons and white kids, opera hats or silk tiles. Gems flashed, and a sort of shame made men nervous in the unwonted costume, and they fidgeted, and sneaked around, knocking down vases of flowers and bumping into people and saying "Oh, pardon," ill at ease and sweating more copiously than there was need of. The courthouse is responsible for all that. At one time there were some twenty-five young bloods of lawyers, doctors, editors, clerks who split their coat-tails and hair in the middle, and affected a nonchalance and chestiness and self-possession they did not feel. There was never an-other such building as that courthouse for influence. It was spermatic, and shed its fructifying pollen on every breeze.

And, perhaps, the "Central House," that introduced side dishes, made the first stroke at abolishing rude table manners, substituting fork for knife, teaching the gentle art of wiggling the soiled fingers in a bowl without drinking the contents, and wiping them on napkins instead of breeches'-legs, silencing the boisterous tones of deglutition, and regulating the motions of the Adam's apple. It was noticed that men began to cease bathing their mustaches in soup and accumulating frescoes of egg on their goatees.

About 1866 Sam Maloney organized a circus here, and those interested in it were Ben and Clay Welch, Jim Beatty, Henry Sanford, Chris Hartman, Chas. Hebener, John Evans, Ned Knickerbocher, Buck Gardner and Zed Rexrode, who was treasurer. The performance given was creditable, and consisted of tumbling, trapeze and horizontal bar work, vaulting and trick pony stunts. The band of Richmond accompanied the circus, and after about a week or ten days' tour of towns in adjoining counties brought up at Brighton, five hundred dollars in the treasury to the good, when Rexrode absconded without paying performers, hands or incidental expenses. The circus went into liquidation, leaving everyone who had anything to do with it in the hole, except the treasurer, who has never been heard of since.

Jesse Harvey is probably the oldest man born in this county, James Bailey, father to Marsh W. Bailey, is a native of the county, dating from June, '42. Joe Huston was born in Crawford township in the early '40s. James Farrier has, perhaps, lived here longer than any other survivor of the true pioneer period. He is eighty years of age, born in Ohio, September 23, 1828, and came with his parents to Brighton in 1839, the year the county was organized; and after some years they moved into Franklin township, and just lately he moved into this city. His father's was the first family to go north of Skunk river and west of Indian creek, unless Joe Long beat him by just one day. The Longs did not tarry long, pushing into Keokuk county, where in some unexplained way his gentle mooley cow killed his wife while she was milking. His father was George B. Farrier, a shoemaker, making slippers for twenty-five cents, shoes for fifty and boots for six bits. Hides were on the free list. James' wife was Mary Todd, and she is twenty-one days older than he, and is spry and well preserved; they were married in this county. Her father was Abel Todd, and they came about 1845. The late Daniel Anderson's wife was her half-sister. James and Mary had ten children, and seven survive. They belong to The Brethren or Dunkards. His gray hair is thick and long and parted in the middle, and he has not out-grown it, and his whiskers are long, but his teeth are gone. Why are white folks' teeth the first thing to go, while the last with the red people? The patent to his forty acres was signed by President Millard Fillmore, March 10, '52. He says only eight died of cholera in the Brighton epidemic, and Tom Purcell and Dan Powers were two of them. Rank vegetation, rotting, caused the early ague. His playmates in boyhood were red kids, and they never scrapped.

The Indian children were amiable, ever good-natured, and playful as cubs. All the Reds were kind and helpful. The Sacs and Foxes did not tattoo, nor practice polygamy, except that the chiefs were allowed the privileges exacted now by white aristocrats and millionaires. The first thing a get-rich-quick man does is to accumulate a harem. Farrier never knew here but one squaw who had an illegitimate child, and that was by a white man. She did not value that asset, and offered it to Farrier for his "fist."

Here, on the thirteenth of July, 1909, the Chicago publisher cries, "Halt. Advance and give the countersign," which is Finis.

Iowa, Iowa, beautiful land! And Washington county and Washington city right up to the front, with her fair, good women and her brave, canny men. What's the matter with Iowa, and Washington county and city? Indeed, they're all right. So say all of us.

And now, gentle reader, if that fabled creature still exists, we have walked together from the year 1803, and specially from the year 1835 to 1909, our path laid in two goodly centuries. We have studied, and speculated, and gossiped, and laughed together along the way. Here let us part in good will, and go in peace our several ways. Good bye, and God bless you!

ILLUSTRATIONS

ILLUSTRATIONS

INDEX

CPSIA information can be obtained
at www.ICGtesting.com
Printed in the USA
LVHW082144220921
698527LV00002B/39

9 781341 379031